KILLING TRAYVONS

An Anthology of American Violence

KILLING TRAYVONS

An Anthology of American Violence

edited by

Kevin Alexander Gray · Jeffrey St. Clair · JoAnn Wypijewski

Published by CounterPunch Books

CounterPunch
PO Box 228, Petrolia, California, 95558

ISBN 978-0692213995

A catalog record for this book is available from the Library of Congress.

Library of Congress Control Number:
0692213996

Printed and bound in the United States.

Cover: Trayvon Martin mural,
Youth Radio Oakland Building.

Photography: Tennessee Reed

Contents

II. Lay of the Land

III. Diversions

IV. The Trial

V. Aftermath

VI. Coda

Killing Trayvons

Summer 2014: a year since a Florida jury acquitted George Zimmerman for killing Trayvon Martin. Another summer of violence and justification: US shells incinerating Palestinian children, devastating UN refuges in Gaza, pounding Afghan villages, again. Another trial of another white man who says he was scared, who had to defend himself with a blast of ammunition against an unarmed black teenager – a womanchild this time, 19, in Michigan this time, shot through a locked screen door. Another police killing on the front pages of the New York tabloids: a big man, a black father, put in a choke hold, kneed in the back as he gasped for air, as he told cops he couldn't breathe; extinguished for passing a smoke to someone on a street in Staten Island. He may have been selling loose cigarettes, police said, and he refused to submit; they had to bring him down. Then they watched as he expired. "The perpetrator's condition did not seem serious," one stated.

Eric Garner ... Renisha McBride ... so many men, women, children in Gaza that even the most conscientious reporters stopped taking down all the names.

We titled this book *Killing Trayvons* because although Martin's profiling and death received extraordinary attention, they were crushingly ordinary, not only for black and brown youth in the suburbs and city streets of America but in the browner nations of the world, where the US, its clients and proxies stand their ground, claim self-defense, take preventive or pre-emptive action – the verbal sleights-of-hand are many – to deadly effect. As we finalized our work, the title became more grimly apt with each day's news. Those acknowledged here hardly exhaust the body count.

If Trayvon's killing was ordinary, its hold on the national imagination was not. It rang an alarm, banged a drum, a cymbal, a knell for so many more whose names are mostly unknown. We, therefore, offer this book as a commemoration, a warning and an incitement.

The commemoration, first, for Martin himself. Two and a half years since that rainy winter night in Sanford, Florida, we really don't know much about what happened, and the stories, poems, polemics, police documents and court transcripts about the case presented here do not settle the matter beyond what was settled the moment George Zimmerman saw black and presumed Suspect.

We don't know, for instance, if while talking to the police dispatcher Zimmerman used the term "fucking coons" or "fucking punks." Writers here assert both. At trial, "punks" was the word agreed upon by prosecution and defense, though the audio forensic report from the FBI's Digital Evidence Laboratory, included here, plainly states that such certainty is misplaced. We don't know how the fight started, who threw the first punch or why. We don't know who was screaming, wailing, calling for help, or if both were. Zimmerman's attorney Mark O'Mara, whose closing argument is excerpted here, showed the jury an animation that presumed to depict the fight, but that was as imagined as anyone else's conjecture here as to who physically confronted whom in what way. Zimmerman told police at the scene he had been calling for help, a claim police then repeated as fact to some witnesses who believed it had been Martin screaming. At trial O'Mara told the jury that only one person cried out that night, only one could have; naturally, it was his client. But, again, the FBI rejected any notion of official certainty, and the prosecution did not offer other experts whose methods would meet generally accepted scientific standards.

We didn't gather up the voices here to settle what must remain unsettled, unsettling. What dissonance there is among the offerings, what gaps in the story, is the story – of life, of death – and no neat tie-up would bring comfort, or that insipid concept closure, or let Trayvon live again.

Trayvon Martin, as bell hooks says here, was "just being a regular teenager," walking in no particular hurry, chatting on the phone, on his way home during halftime of the NBA All Star Game – "anyone's son," to echo the title of Tara Skurtu's closing poem, and he is dead. That ordinariness is partly what sparked the viral commemorations, the "million hoodie marches," the countless symbolic and material remembrances, of which the artwork in this book is a signal example (see our Note on the Cover, page 419). Mimi Thi Nguyen, who is writing about the hoodie's symbolism for a forthcoming issue of *Signs*, catalogued some of those memorializing acts in a public talk:

> In mourning, militancy and mimicry, posed hoodie photographs – most often consisting of a simple frontal snapshot of a person in a hooded sweatshirt, hood up – proliferated in the aftermath of Martin's murder. Tweeting the widely propagated photograph of the NBA's Miami Heat – hoods raised, heads bowed and hands clasped – LeBron James tagged it: "#WeAreTrayvonMartin... #Stereotyped #WeWantJustice." In addition to photographs of celebrities in hoodies (Common, Jamie Foxx, Sean Combs, Wyclef Jean, the Red Hot Chili

Peppers, New York Knicks' Carmelo Anthony, Arsenio Hall, CNN contributor and journalist Roland Martin, LeVar Burton, US Representative Bobby Rush, the list goes on), others too sought solidarity through the same, seemingly simple act, including Harvard and Howard law students in front of ivy-covered buildings; elementary schoolchildren lined up along a wall holding bags of Skittles; "moms in hoodies"; New York state senators Kevin Parker, Bill Perkins and Eric Adams; New York City Council Speaker Christine Quinn; former Michigan governor Jennifer Granholm; attendants at vigils and marches; black-and-white drawings of a range of humanity published in a special issue of *The New Yorker*; even professional portraiture as protest art. Thousands more appear on Facebook pages like A Million Hoodies for Trayvon Martin and on Tumblrs (often tagged with #MillionHoodies), including I Am Trayvon Martin, featuring photograph after photograph – often snapped with webcams or mobile phones – of persons with their hoodies up. One well-trafficked photograph depicts a pregnant black woman in a hoodie gazing upon her bared stomach, marked with the words "Am I next?"

Ubiquitous and implicating the living with the dead, those photographs, Nguyen observed, "gesture toward a serial murder, the continuing threat that is realizable at any coming moment."

They gesture toward something else as well: a refusal to be next.

There is a reason, in the biting familiarity of memory and experience, that June Jordan's "Poem about Police Violence," written in the 1970s and included here, shot through cyberspace like a fire-arrow in the aftermath of February 26, 2012, and July 13, 2013.

It is not that the first date signaled some newly dangerous season for black youth; or the second, some newly low threshold of impunity for their police or quasi-police killers. Black communities live with these Emmett Till moments every day, and only a desperate hope accounts for anyone's surprise that George Zimmerman got off. Although the Stand Your Ground-style laws of Florida and most other states were much discussed following the killing, and although those laws are vile for essentially issuing a license to kill, Zimmerman didn't invoke a Stand Your Ground defense in court. He didn't need to. Like so many police and white, or white-ish, police stand-ins before him, he already held that license. All he had to do was say he feared for his life.

The anguish and anger that followed the not-guilty verdict, and echo here, were thus not so much responses to the particulars of the trial as they were expressions of pent-up fury over the long list of dead and maimed black men, women and children whose own fear counted for nothing, whose own life was deemed cheap, whose own innocence was never presumed; and over the insecurity and suspicion that dogs the living – black youth especially, for whom there seems to be no safety, no sanctuary, no ground on which to stand.

Other names, other stories, course through these pages, many Trayvons. This book is their commemoration, too. In that sense, it also serves as a warning.

Beware "the trick bag of the perfect victim," Jill Nelson writes. The countless named and unnamed victims were not all minding their own business, not all sober, not all good-looking teenagers with no criminal record. At least part of the mass outpouring of sympathy for Martin and his family relates to his image as a good kid, handsome, armed with nothing but Skittles and sweet tea. The white power faction, the right-wing media, the Zimmerman defense, all strove to vitiate that image, to recast Martin as a dope boy and a thug. That was racist and conniving (also typical, see Alexander Tepperman's close analysis of the drug war's consequences), but the crucial political point is that it shouldn't have mattered if Martin were walking along carrying a bag of reefer or a rap sheet that night. Just as it shouldn't have mattered if he threw the first punch. Such an act might have been wrong, it might have been stupid, but the brawling of boys and men is a hardy staple of the Rugged Individual story America tells its children. It takes a jacked-up disdain for proportionality to conclude that execution is a reasonable response to a fistfight.

And yet ... high or low, power teaches such disdain every day. Lose two towers; destroy two countries. Lose three Israelis; kill a couple thousand Palestinians. Sell some dope; three strikes, you're out. Sell a loosey; choke, you're dead. Reach for your wallet; bang, you're dead. Got a beef; bang, you're dead.

We call this book an anthology of American violence because killing has a social and political, not just individual context. It is as easy to make George Zimmerman a monster as to make Trayvon Martin a saint, but that's a trick bag of another kind. Zimmerman might also be anyone's son, America's son, juiced on ignorance and fear, and dangerous like his country. He, too, is an ordinary man – straight, second-rate at most everything he's tried, a schmuck with a short fuse, dim prospects and a white man's unthinking sense of skin privilege.

In these pages Vijay Prashad likens Zimmerman to "a domestic drone." Dave Marsh, quoting Chester Himes, likens him to "a blind man with a pistol." Thandisizwe Chimurenga compares his action and treatment with that of Johannes Mehserle, the Oakland transit cop who killed Oscar Grant. The Malcolm X Grassroots Movement breaks down statistics indicating that every twenty-eight hours police, security guards or Zimmerman-style vigilantes kill a black person. D. Brian Burghardt combs public records to answer the question "How many people are killed by police every year?" and finds there is no ready answer, no national database (he's creating one from the ground up), no open accounting of what, in the number of dead, might amount to a 9/11 every year. President Obama says, "Trayvon Martin could have been me thirty-five years ago," but a lot has happened in those intervening years. Cornel West calls Obama "a global George Zimmerman"; the president profiles brown people as enemies every Tuesday for an assassin's hit list.

When it comes to Zimmerman, the symbolic associations are thick, and true for that thickness, but symbols aren't put on trial (or shouldn't be); individuals are. That Zimmerman was afforded the presumption of innocence, due process and the benefit of reasonable doubt only seemed strange because so many people – so many who are black and brown, and especially so many who are labeled monsters before any evidence is considered – are not. The writers in this book differ in their assessments of the trial. Beyond particulars, however, as Bruce Jackson writes, "a criminal trial is never about the truth." Except within the narrow limits of the law, it is not really about justice either. On August 7, 2014, Renisha McBride's killer, Theodore Wafer, was convicted of second-degree murder; he faces possible life in prison. "A life for a life," some onlookers cried out afterward in satisfaction, but that isn't justice; it is a legal victory for the state. Justice demands more than an exemplary conviction and another body for the world's largest prison system.

Justice demands restructuring. So, finally, this book is an incitement to justice.

A country that exports violence all over the world and is its biggest jailer, that schools its people in punishment, inequity and racism, that tortures in defense of liberty, that lets presidents get away with war crimes and enables Israel in mass murder – this country will have police who kill at whim; it will have copycats like Zimmerman, and they will get away with it again, unless confronted by a mighty resistance.

The political legacy of the Martin killing is that extraordinary No, of which every contributor to this book is a part.

It is the Dream Defenders in Florida, who occupied the statehouse and whose director, Phillip Agnew, vowed in a speech excerpted here: "We will not be silenced. We will not be stopped. We will not be bought." It is in a national network of youth-led organizations and allies called Freedom Side, convened by the Dream Defenders and others on this year's fiftieth anniversary of Mississippi Freedom Summer to drive a new generation's train toward justice. It is in nationwide organizing against the New

Jim Crow. In people's efforts, sampled here by Dani McClain and Jordan Flaherty, to think and act together on safety, on security and the role of the state. In the ceaseless challenge to "understand our brains on race," as McClain quotes Maya Wiley; to reject the prerogatives, however masked, of a heritage embedded in conquest and slavery; and to embrace our parallel common inheritance of resistance. And it will have to grow wider and go deeper.

As we go to press, police in Ferguson, Missouri, have declared war on the black community. They refuse to release the names of the officers who killed Michael Brown on August 9 and left his body lying in the street for four hours. Brown was black, 18, unarmed and, from witness accounts, shot multiple times while his hands were in the air. Police say they have received death threats. They seem surprised. They made Ferguson a battleground before a single window shattered or fire burned, pathetic acts of indignation next to murder, armored commandos with high-powered weapons and full military gear. Whether this ends in pacification or in blood, in this moment police light up the night with stun grenades and tear gas lobbed at a crowd standing with hands up. Snipers point guns at civilians from rooftops. The FAA has made the St. Louis suburb a no fly zone. "We care about who killed Michael Brown. We don't care about Afghanistan," a youth told reporters soon after the shooting, but those are sides of the same coin. Another black man is dead. There is no peace.

The Editors

Summer 2014

The Killing

cartwheel on the blacktop
(Trayvon Martin 2.0)

Alexis Pauline Gumbs

he has wings in his shoes

Trayvon yawns and stretches in the crook of the tree. Slept til dark again. Shrugs. Stretches out his retractable shoe gliders and hangs a slow swinging backflip out of the branches. Into the world again. Blows a kiss at one leaf. Turns to face home.

a rainbow in his mouth

Notices he is on tilt two-thousand. Off-balance more than the sway of waking up. Sugar low. Annoyed to have to hunt for convenience and its stores of chemical fructose. This is a manicured neighborhood. No fruit in these trees but him himself at twilight.

he has sweet tea time travel in a can

Sweetness reloading he blinks at the mission message in his eyelids. Find the little brother. Teach him about sugar. Teach him that he too can fly as nonchalant as hammock rope. Give him one swift hug and then return to the future to plug in his fingers. Banjo music a much better charge than this watered down fuel. Can't wait to get home. He slept into dark. On this world of all worlds. Right during the time of the nightvision nearsightedness. Sigh. He might be late. His shoes brush the sidewalk.

his hooded sweatshirt forcefield threaded through with angel kevlar

Behind him the loud machine for the heavyfooted hunter slows down. He has been detected. Will his teenage camouflage help him or hurt. He sighs. He is so young. Only four hundred years old. He shakes his head and looks back. Remember how they used guns. Remember how they never felt safe enough to breathe or whole enough to listen. Overslept. Over. He sends one telepathic message to the little brother waiting. Quickly embroiders it with sweetness. Love.

At the moment of the explosion the sweatshirt flickers hieroglyphics. Blue light math. He squeezes the can. Liquid sprays everywhere. Hands to the pavement. He wonders if the little brother will understand what he must do.

REPORT OF INVESTIGATION

CASE NUMBER: 201250001136	Page 2 of 7
INVESTIGATOR: Serino, Christopher F	

DETAILS:

On 02/26/2012 at approximately 1935 hours, I was contacted by Officer T. Smith in reference to responding to Retreat at Twin Lakes to process a homicide scene. I arrived on scene at approximately 1955 hours and met with Officer Ayala and Officer Mead who briefed me on the scene. Currently at this time in the evening, it was dark out and we were experiencing intermittent showers.

The subject noticed a suspicious black male in the complex that did not look like he belonged there, so he called police. The subject began to follow the victim to keep him in eye sight until the police arrived. The subject was following the victim while in his vehicle and then parked it near the club house. He then got out of foot, still on the phone with dispatch. He stated that he lost sight of the victim and got off of the phone with dispatch. The subject then started to walk back towards his vehicle when he was approached by the victim. The victim asked "Do you have a problem". The subject replied "No, I don't have a problem". The victim then stated "You do now" and punched the subject in the face. The two individuals continued to fight in a courtyard between two buildings. The subject was getting beat up by the victim; he grabbed his firearm and shot the victim in the chest.

At that time, I walked through the scene with the officer's and they pointed out items of evidence that were already located, it was still raining at this time. It was dark outside, raining off and on, and there was not much light lighting up in the courtyard. There were a set of keys containing a small flash light that was on, a cell phone, larger flashlight, two plastic bags, first aid kit, medical supplies, the victim's body that was covered by a yellow medical blanket, and an Arizona tea can. According to Officer's on the scene, the Arizona tea can was originally located in the front pocket of the victim's jacket. I then retrieved my camera and started to photograph the scene while I waited for the Volusia County Medical Examiner's Office transport services to arrive. After my photographs of the initial scene were completed, Sgt Ciesla and I measured the items on the scene and then I collected them. The Volusia County Medical Examiner's Office arrived on scene and moved the victim. The victim had $ 40.15 in US currency, a bag of skittles, red lighter, headphones, photo pin in his pockets or on him. I also noticed and documented that there was only a single gun shot wound to the chest. After the victim was transported, Sgt. Ciesla and I looked for a cartridge case while it was still raining. Sgt. Ciesla utilized a metal detector as I searched in the areas the detector would detect. A short time later, a 9mm Luger S&B cartridge case was located, documented, and recovered. All evidence will be transported to the Sanford Police Department and logged into evidence.

I responded to the Sanford Police Department on 01/26/2012 at approximately 2315 hours and met with Office T. Smith. Officer T. Smith assisted me in meeting with the subject in interview room # 2 to photograph his clothing, injuries, hands, collect possible gun shot residue, and to collect his clothing. After I photographed Zimmerman's clothing, hands, and injuries, I asked him if he had any other injuries that were not visible. Zimmerman stated that he did not other than his back hurting but he did not think he had any cuts or bruises. A short time later, his wife arrived at the Sanford Police Department and provided us with a change of clothes for Zimmerman. At that time, Zimmerman changed his clothing and placed them into brown paper bags that I provided for him. When he was done changing, he was escorted back to the interview room. All of this evidence will be logged into evidence.

On 02/27/2012 at approximately 1235 hours, I responded to Retreat at Twin Lakes to take some photographs of the courtyard in the daylight.

On 02/28/2012 at approximately 1030 hours, I responded to the Volusia County Medical Examiner's Office to retrieve the evidence that was documented and collected during the autopsy of the victims. The evidence will be transported to the Sanford Police Department and logged into evidence.

Subject(s):

GEORGE MICHAEL ZIMMERMAN	W/M	10/05/1983
[redacted]		[redacted]

Page 2 of 7

You Really Think the Killer of Trayvon Martin Will Ever Do Time?

Alexander Cockburn

I'd say the chances of George Zimmerman spending time behind bars for killing Trayvon Martin are about zero.

Like most things that happen in America these days, the Trayvon Martin case is turning into yet another hearse trundling the Republican Party to its doom in November.

A brief outline of the facts. It's February 26, 2012. Trayvon Martin is a 17-year-old black kid watching a big basketball game in the home of his father's fiancée in Sanford, a small-town outlier of Orlando, Florida. Sanford has a population of 55,000, about a third black. The fiancée lives in a mixed-race, gated community. At halftime Martin goes to the corner store and buys an iced tea and a bag of Skittles.

It's raining and Martin has his hoodie up over his head and is talking to a friend on his cell phone. On his way back he is spotted by 28-year-old George Zimmerman, a cop wannabe, self-appointed neighborhood crime watcher. Apparently he has pestered the police station for months with reports of "suspicious 12-year-olds" walking through the neighborhood. Zimmerman – white dad, Latina mother – is wearing a red jacket and blue jeans. In his pocket is a Kel-Tec 9mm automatic pistol.

Zimmerman calls the local station and says he's following a suspicious character. He describes Martin as black and says he's acting strangely and could be on drugs. The teenager starts to run, Zimmerman says. A police dispatcher asks Zimmerman whether he's following Martin, and Zimmerman says he is. The dispatcher clearly says that Zimmerman doesn't need to do that.

There's a lull in the transmission, and you can hear Zimmerman mutter to himself, "These assholes ... they always get away." On other calls between Zimmerman and the dispatcher he refers to "fucking coons." CNN says the words are indistinct, which they aren't. CNN also says the case is "complicated," which it isn't.

Later the Martin family lawyer relays Trayvon's friend's account of her last call with him. She says he told her that he was being followed. She says, "Run." He says, "I'm not going to run. I'm just going to walk fast." The girl later heard Martin say, "Why are you following me?" and then another man – Zimmerman – saying, "What are you doing around here?" The girl thinks she heard a scuffle because his voice changes like something interrupted his speech.

Mary Cutcher was in her kitchen making coffee that night with her roommate, Selma Mora Lamilla. The window was open, she said. "We heard a whining. Not like a crying, boohoo, but like a whining, someone in distress, and then the gunshot," she tells Anderson Cooper on CNN's *360*.

They looked out the window but saw nothing. It was dark. They ran out the sliding glass door, and within seconds they saw Zimmerman.

"Zimmerman was standing over the body with – basically straddling the body with his hands on Trayvon's back," Cutcher said. "And it didn't seem to me that he was trying to help him in any way. I didn't hear any struggle prior to the gunshot. And I feel like it was Trayvon Martin that was crying out, because the minute that the gunshot went off, the whining stopped."

The two women said they could not see whether Zimmerman was bruised or hurt. It was too dark.

"Selma asked him three times, 'What's going on over there?'" Cutcher said. "He looks back and doesn't say anything. She asks him again, 'Everything OK? What's going on?' Same thing: looked at us, looked back. Finally, the third time, he said, 'Just call the police.' "

The women, one white and one Latina, tell Anderson Cooper flatly that they don't believe Zimmerman's story of how Martin had suddenly attacked him, punched him in the face, broke his nose – and that when Zimmerman, larger than Martin, felt overpowered he pulled out the gun and shot Martin through the chest. (Later Zimmerman declined medical attention.)

In the immediate aftermath, Zimmerman stakes his defense on Chapter 7776.013 of the Florida criminal statute on home protection and the use of deadly force. Para 3 states:

> A person who is not engaged in an unlawful activity and who is attacked in any other place where he or she has a right to be has no duty to retreat and has the right to stand his or her ground and meet force with force, including deadly force, if he or she reasonably believes it is necessary to do so to prevent death or great bodily harm to himself or herself or another or to prevent the

commission of a forcible felony.

That is what's colloquially known as the Stand Your Ground law. Thirty states, including my own state of California, have versions of this old English legal concept of My Home Is My Castle. Since I live in a remote rural area inhabited by well-armed people, not all of them on the side of the angels, I've read our statute from time to time trying to determine what exactly would be the circumstances under which – if an armed individual was heading for my house, ten yards from the deck and showing no signs of slowing after my challenges – I could justifiably shoot him with my 12-gauge shotgun. It's always struck me as a really hard call. The state may have a Stand Your Ground law, but it really doesn't want people using it as legal shelter.

Not so in Sanford, Florida. Zimmerman, the son of a former magistrate judge, is not charged and walks away free. Although the Sanford cops leak to the press the news that he was once suspended from school as having been in possession of an empty bag that had once contained marijuana, Trayvon Martin had a clean record. On the other hand, Zimmerman was arrested in 2005 for battery on a cop. A former co-worker tells the New York *Daily News* that Zimmerman was fired in 2005 from his job as an under-the-table security guard for "being too aggressive.... Usually he was just a cool guy. He liked to drink and hang with the women like the rest of us. But it was like Jekyll and Hyde. When the dude snapped, he snapped." In 2007 an injunction was issued as a result of a domestic battery complaint by Zimmerman's then girlfriend. He filed a similar injunction against her.

Outrage about the case builds across the first two weeks of March. By the third week the killing is a national scandal. Black columnists describe how they warn their sons not to run in any crisis situation, always be polite to the cops no matter how provoked. The Rev. Al Sharpton covers the case full volume on MSNBC. The usual litter of deadly cop shootings of blacks are exhumed from recent Florida police records. Protest demonstrations are held in Sanford.

There are the obvious questions. If Martin had wrestled the gun away from Zimmerman and shot him, would he have been allowed to walk away free? No, sir. Political pressure forces the appointment of Special Prosecutor Angela Corey to determine whether to charge Zimmerman. If she does so, it will probably be for second-degree murder.

President Obama speaks on March 23 about the killing of Trayvon, saying, "If I had a son, he would look like Trayvon.... I think [Trayvon's parents] are right to expect that all of us as Americans are going to take this with the seriousness it deserves, and we are going to get to the bottom of exactly what happened."

Two Republican candidates for their party's nomination to the presidency promptly bring out the hearse for their electoral prospects – most recently deployed to freight denunciations of women's right to birth control.

Newt Gingrich states that Obama's comments are "disgraceful": "Any young American of any ethnic background should be safe, period. We should all be horrified, no matter what the ethnic background. Is the president suggesting that, if it had been a white who'd been shot, that would be OK, because it wouldn't look like him? That's just nonsense."

Then Rick Santorum chimes in, stating that Obama should "not use these types of horrible and tragic individual cases to try to drive a wedge in America." This unleashes Rush Limbaugh, who says that Obama is using the case as a "political opportunity." Geraldo Rivera suggests Martin brought it on himself by wearing a hoodie. At which point the conservative columnist William Tucker has had enough.

In the hard-right *American Spectator,* under the headline "Count Me Out On Trayvon Martin: Why Gingrich, Santorum, and many conservatives are dead wrong on this one," Tucker writes, "Republicans have no reason to intervene in this fight. Seventy-five percent of the public thinks Zimmerman should be charged with something.... Personally, I can't wait until Newt Gingrich and Rick Santorum get offstage so we can start running a presidential campaign that isn't based on trying to alienate the vast majority of Americans over irrelevant issues."

What is it that prompts Republicans to try so hard to alienate women, blacks, Hispanics, independents and all those millions and millions of Americans to the left of the Tea Party they'll need to beat Obama? Maybe they feel it's their last throw. All the demographics look unfavorable for any future Republican majority. So there is a desperate effort to get everything they can right now. Conning working-class whites with racism, sexism, anti-gay/ anti-immigrant rhetoric, etc. has worked so well since Nixon that it's become an addiction.

NARRATIVE REPORT

SANFORD POLICE DEPT

Agency ORI Number: FL 5 9 0 5 0 0 0

Agency Report Number: 2 0 1 2 5 0 0 0 0 1 1 3 6

Original Date Reported: 0 2 2 6 1 2

Case Name/Info: Shooting

NAME: George Michael Zimmerman

ADDRES[redacted]

D.O.B.: 10/05/1983

SS#: [redacted]

PHO[redacted]

CITY: Sanford

D.L.#:

HGT: 5'8"

WGT.: 194

EYES: Brown

HAIR: Black

In August of 2011 my neighbors house was broken into while she was home with her infant son. The intruders attempted to attack her and her child; however, SPD reported to the scene of the crime and the robbers fled. My wife saw the intruders running from the home and became scared of the rising crime within our neighborhood. I, and my neighbors formed a "Neighborhood Watch Program" We were instructed by SPD to call the non-emergency line if we saw anything suspicious & 911 if we saw a crime in progress. Tonight, I was on my way to the grocery store when I saw a male approximately 5'11" to 6'2" casually walking in the rain looking into homes. I pulled my vehicle over and called SPD non-emergency phone number. I told the dispatcher what I had witnessed, the dispatcher took note of my location & the suspect fled

Signature of person making statement

Sworn to and subscribed before me this 26 day of Feb 2012

Law Enforcement Officer or Notary

Report Contains: Suspect Statement

Officer(s) Reporting: D. Singleton

ID Number: 501

Related Report Number(s) | Unit | Date

Officer Reviewing (if Applicable) | ID Number | Routed To | Referred To | Assigned To | By | Date

Case Status | Clearance Type: 1. Arrest 2. Exceptional 3. Unfounded | 6. Adult 7. Juvenile | Date Cleared | Arrest Number | Number Arrested

Exception Type: 1. Extradition Declined 2. Arrest of Primary Offense Secondary Offense Yields Prosecution 3. Death of Offender 4. V/W Refused to Cooperate 5. Prosecution Declined 6. Juvenile/No Custody | OBTS Number

Page 1 of 17

NARRATIVE REPORT

Agency ORI Number: FL 5 9 0 5 0 0 0 | Agency Name: SANFORD POLICE DEPT | Agency Report Number: 2012 50001136

1. Offense 2. Arrest | Juvenile | 1. Original 2. Supplement

Orig and Date Reported: 02.26.12 | Case Reference: Shooting

NAME: George Zimmerman | D.L.#:

ADDRESS: | HGT:

D.O.B.: | WGT.:

SS#: | EYES:

PHONE: | HAIR:

CITY:

To a darkened area of the sidewalk. as the dispatcher was asking me for an exact location the suspect emerged from the darkness & circled my vehicle. I could not hear if he said anything. The suspect once again disappeared between the back of some houses. The dispatcher once again asked me for my exact location. I could not remember the name of the street so I got out of my car to look for a street sign. The dispatcher asked me for a discription and the direction the suspect went. I told the dispatcher I did not know but I was out of my vehicle looking for a street sign & the direction the suspect was. The dispatcher told me not to follow the suspect & that an officer was in route. As I headed back to my vehicle the suspect emerged from the darkness and said "you got a problem" I said "No" The suspect said "you do now" As I looked

Signature of person making statement

Sworn to and subscribed before me this 26 day of 02 2012

Law Enforcement Officer or Notary

Report Contains: Suspect Statement

Officer(s) Reporting: D Singleton | ID Number(s): 5011

Officer Reviewing (If Applicable) | ID Number | Routed To | Referred To | Assigned To | By | Date

Case Status | Clearance Type 1. Arrest 2. Exceptional 3. Unfounded | A. Adult J. Juvenile | Date Cleared | Arrest Number | Number Arrested

Exception Type 1. Extradition Declined 2. Arrest or Penalty Offense Secondary Offense Without Prosecution 3. Death of Offender 4. V/W Refused to Cooperate 5. Prosecution Declined 6. Juvenile / No Custody | OBTS Number

Page 2 of 4

NARRATIVE REPORT

1. Offense 2. Arrest ☐ Juvenile ☐ 1. Original 2. Supplement ☐

Agency ORI Number: FL0 5 9 0 5 0 0 0

Agency Name: SANFORD POLICE DEPT

Agency Report Number: 2012 50 001136

Original Date Reported: 0 2 2 6 1 2

Case Nickname: Shooting

NAME: George M. Zimmerman | D.L.#:
ADDRESS: | HGT:
D.O.B.: | WGT.:
SS#: | EYES:
PHONE: | HAIR:
CITY:

And tried to find my phone to dial 911 the suspect punched me in the face. I fell backwards onto my back. The suspect got on top of me I yelled "Help!" several times The suspect told me "Shut the Fuck up" as I tried to sit up right, The suspect grabbed my head and slammed it into the concrete sidewalk several times. I continued to yell "Help" each time I attempted to sit up, the suspect slammed my head into the side walk, My head felt like it was going to explode. I tried to slide out from under the suspect and continue to yell "Help". as I slid the suspect covered my mouth and nose and stopped my breathing. At this point I felt the suspect reach for my now exposed firearm and say" "Your gonna die tonight Mother Fucker" I unholstered my firearm in fear for my life as he had assured he was going to kill

Signature of person making statement
Sworn to and subscribed before me this 26 day of 02 2012
Law Enforcement Officer or Notary

Report Contains: Suspect Statement

Officer(s) Reporting: D. Singleton | ID Number: 501

Officer Reviewing (If Applicable) | ID Number | Routed To | Referred To | Assigned To | Related Report Number(s) | Unit | Date | By | Date

Case Status | Clearance Type: 1. Arrest 2. Exceptional 3. Unfounded | A. Adult B. Juvenile | Date Cleared | Arrest Number | Number Arrested

Exception Type: 1. Extradition Declined 2. Arrest of Primary Offense Secondary Offense Without Prosecution 3. Death of Offender 4. V/W Refused to Cooperate 5. Prosecution Declined 6. Juvenile / No Custody | OBTS Number | Page 31 of 17

NARRATIVE REPORT

Agency ORI Number: FL0 5 9 0 5 0 0
Agency Name: SANFORD POLICE DEPT
Agency Report Number: 2012-50001136
Original Date: 02.26.12
Case Reference: Shooting

NAME: George Zimmerman
D.L.#:
ADDRESS:
HGT:
D.O.B.:
WGT.:
SS#:
EYES:
PHONE:
HAIR:
CITY:

me and fired one shot into his torso. The suspect sat back allowing me to sit up and said "You got me". At this point I slid out from underneath him and got ontop of the suspect holding his hands away from his body. An onlooker appeared and asked me if I was ok I said "no" he said "I am calling 911" I said "I don't need you to call 911 I already called them I need you to help me restrain this guy." At this point a SPD officer arrived and asked "who shot him" I said "I did" and I placed my hands ontop of my head and told the officer where on my person my firearm was holstered. The officer handcuffed me and disarmed me. The officer then placed me in the back of his vehicle.

Signature of person making statement
Sworn to and subscribed before me this 26 day of 02 2012
Law Enforcement Officer or Notary

Report Contents: Suspect Statement
Officer(s) Reporting: D. Singleton
ID Number(s): 5011

Page 4 of 4

SANFORD POLICE DEPARTMENT

MIRANDA WAIVER

The Constitution requires that I inform you that:

1. You have the right to remain silent
2. Anything you say will be used in court as evidence against you.
3. You are entitled to talk to an attorney now and have them present now or at any time during questioning.
4. If you cannot afford an attorney, one will be appointed for you without cost.
5. Do you desire to consult with an attorney first or to have one during this interview?
6. If, at any time hereafter, you wish to remain silent or have an attorney present, all questioning will be stopped.
7. Has anyone, at any time, threatened, coerced or promised you anything in order to induce you to make a statement now?
8. Do you understand these rights?
9. Do you wish to talk to us at this time?

I hereby knowingly and voluntary waive my Constitutional Rights as explained to me.

______________ Signature   2/29/12 Date   5:15 pm Time

______________ S04 Witnessed Signature

Singleton

Instructions to Officer: If the person indicates in any manner, prior to or during questioning, that he/she wishes to remain silent, or that he/she wishes to have an attorney, the interrogation must stop, until permission is given by his/her attorney

OFFICE OF THE MEDICAL EXAMINER
FLORIDA, DISTRICTS 7 & 24
VOLUSIA & SEMINOLE COUNTIES
1360 INDIAN LAKE ROAD, DAYTONA BEACH, FL 32124-1001

MEDICAL EXAMINER REPORT

Name	**Martin, Trayvon**	Medical Examiner #	**12-24-043**
Date of Birth	February 5, 1995	Date of Death (Found)	February 26, 2012
Age	17 Years	County	Seminole
Race	Black	Date of Exam	February 27, 2012
Sex	Male	Time of Exam	1030 Hours

FINAL DIAGNOSES AND FINDINGS

I. Penetrating Gunshot Wound of the Chest
   A. Entrance: Left chest, intermediate range
   B. Path of the projectile: Skin, left anterior 5th intercostal space, pericardial sac, right ventricle of heart, and right lower lobe of lung
   C. Direction of projectile: Directly, front to back
   D. Exit: None; fragments of projectile recovered in pericardial sac and right pleural cavity
   E. Associated injuries: Entrance wound; perforations of pericardial sac, right ventricle of heart, right lower lobe of lung with bilateral pleural hemorrhage
   F. Postmortem radiograph: Metallic fragments of projectile identified

Cause of Death: Gunshot Wound of Chest

Manner of Death: Homicide

How incident occurred: Shot by another person

Date: 03/15/12

Shiping Bao, M. D.
Associate Medical Examiner

XC: State Attorney's Office
Sanford Police Department

"*Accredited by the National Association of Medical Examiners*"

OFFICE OF THE MEDICAL EXAMINER
FLORIDA, DISTRICTS 7 & 24

Name Martin, Trayvon ME # 12-24-043

MEDICAL EXAMINER REPORT
REPORT OF AUTOPSY

OFFICIALS PRESENT AT EXAMINATION

None.

EXTERNAL EXAMINATION

The body is secured in a blue body bag with Medical Examiner seal #0000517.

The body is viewed unclothed. The body is that of a normally developed, black male appearing the stated age of 17 years with a body length of 71 inches and body weight of 158 pounds. The body presents a medium build with average nutrition, normal hydration and good preservation. Rigor mortis is complete, and lividity is well developed and fixed on the posterior surfaces of the body. The body is cold to touch post refrigeration. Short black hair covers the scalp. The face is unremarkable. There is average body hair of adult-male-pattern distribution. The eyes are closed and have clear bulbar and palpebral conjunctivae. The irides are brown with white sclerae. There are no cataracts or arcus present. The pupils are equal at 5 millimeters. The orbits appear normal. The nasal cavities are unremarkable with an intact septum. The oral cavity presents natural teeth with fair oral hygiene. The ears are unremarkable with no hemorrhage in the external auditory canals. The neck is rigid due to postmortem changes, and there are no palpable masses. The chest is symmetrical. The abdomen is scaphoid.

The upper and lower extremities are equal and symmetrical and present cyanotic nail beds without clubbing or edema. There are no fractures, deformities or amputations present. The external genitalia present descended testicles and an unremarkable penis. The back reveals dependent lividity with contact pallor. The buttocks are atraumatic, and the anus is intact. The integument is of normal color.

OTHER IDENTIFYING FEATURES

There are identification bands on the ankles.

SCARS

- 1 x ½ inch scar - right shoulder
- 1 x ½ inch scar - right hand

TATTOOS

- Symbol with letters - right arm
- Letters - left wrist

There are no other significant identifying features.

OFFICE OF THE MEDICAL EXAMINER
FLORIDA, DISTRICTS 7 & 24

Name Martin, Trayvon ME # 12-24-043

MEDICAL EXAMINER REPORT
REPORT OF AUTOPSY

EVIDENCE OF INJURY

Penetrating Gunshot Wound of the Chest:

The entrance wound is located on the left chest, 17½ inches below the top of the head, 1 inch to the left of the anterior midline, and ½ inch below the nipple. It consists of a ⅜ inch diameter round entrance defect with soot, ring abrasion, and a 2 x 2 inch area of stippling. This wound is consistent with a wound of entrance of intermediate range.

Further examination demonstrates that the wound track passes directly from front to back and enters the pleural cavity with perforations of the left anterior fifth intercostal space, pericardial sac, right ventricle of the heart, and the right lower lobe of the lung. There is no wound of exit.

Three fragments of projectile are recovered. The lead core is recovered in the pericardial sac behind the right ventricle. Two fragments of the jacket are recovered in the right pleural cavity behind the right lower lobe of the lung.

The injuries associated with the wound: The entrance wound; perforations of left anterior fifth intercostal space, pericardial sac, right ventricle of the heart, right lower lobe of the lung with approximately 1300 milliliters of blood in the right pleural cavity and 1000 in the left pleural cavity; the collapse of both lungs.

Other injuries: There is a ¼ x ⅛ inch small abrasion on the left fourth finger.

EVIDENCE OF RECENT MEDICAL TREATMENT

There is a cardiac monitor pad on the left flank.

EVIDENCE OF ORGAN AND/OR TISSUE DONATION

None.

INTERNAL EXAMINATION: The following excludes any previously described injuries.

BODY CAVITIES

The peritoneum is congested, smooth, glistening and essentially dry; devoid of adhesions or effusion. There is no scoliosis, kyphosis or lordosis present. The left and right diaphragms are in their normal location and appear grossly unremarkable.

OFFICE OF THE MEDICAL EXAMINER
FLORIDA, DISTRICTS 7 & 24

Name Martin, Trayvon ME # 12-24-043

MEDICAL EXAMINER REPORT
REPORT OF AUTOPSY

The subcutaneous fat measures 1.5 centimeters and is normally distributed, moist and bright yellow. The musculature of the chest and abdominal area is of normal color and texture.

NECK AND TONGUE

The neck presents an intact hyoid bone as well as the thyroid and cricoid cartilages. The larynx has unremarkable vocal cords and folds that appear widely patent without foreign material. The epiglottis is a characteristic plate-like structure without edema, trauma or pathological lesions. Both the musculature and the vasculature of the anterior neck are unremarkable. The trachea and spine are in the midline, and present no traumatic injuries or pathological lesions. The tongue is unremarkable.

CARDIOVASCULAR SYSTEM

The heart weighs 200 grams and there is no chamber hypertrophy or dilatation. The left ventricular wall is 1.1 centimeters and the right is 0.2 centimeters. The cardiac valves appear unremarkable. The coronary ostia are in the normal anatomical location leading into widely patent coronary arteries. Right dominant circulation is present. The endocardial surface is smooth without thrombi or inflammation. Sectioning of the myocardium presents no gross evidence of ischemic changes either of recent or remote origin. The aortic arch, along with the great vessels, appears grossly unremarkable.

RESPIRATORY SYSTEM

The lungs are collapsed and together weigh 410 grams. There are no gross pneumonic lesions or abnormal masses identified. The tracheobronchial tree and pulmonary arterial system are intact and grossly unremarkable. The pleural surfaces are pink and smooth with focal mild anthracosis.

HEPATOBILIARY SYSTEM

The liver weighs 1110 grams and presents a brown, smooth, glistening surface. Focal patchy yellow discoloration, due to mild fatty metamorphosis, is present. On sectioning, the hepatic parenchyma is yellow-brown, homogeneous and congested. The unremarkable gallbladder contains approximately 8 milliliters of greenish bile. There is no cholecystitis or lithiasis. The biliary tree is patent. The pancreas presents a lobulated yellow cut surface without acute or chronic pancreatitis.

HEMOLYMPHATIC SYSTEM

The spleen weighs 100 grams and presents a gray-pink intact capsule and a dark red parenchyma. There is no lymphadenopathy. The thymus gland is involuted.

OFFICE OF THE MEDICAL EXAMINER
FLORIDA, DISTRICTS 7 & 24

Name Martin, Trayvon ME # 12-24-043

MEDICAL EXAMINER REPORT
REPORT OF AUTOPSY

GASTROINTESTINAL SYSTEM

The esophagus is intact with normal gastroesophageal junctions and without erosions or varices. The stomach is also normal without gastritis or ulcers, and contains 400 milliliters of gastric fluid with food particles. Loops of small and large bowel appear grossly unremarkable. The appendix is unremarkable.

UROGENITAL SYSTEM

The kidneys weigh 100 grams, and 110 grams, right and left, respectively. On sectioning, the cortex presents a normal thickness above the medulla. The renal columns of Bertin extend between the well-demarcated pyramids and appear unremarkable. The medulla presents normal renal pyramids with unremarkable papillae. The pelvis is of normal size and is lined by gray glistening mucosa. There are no calculi. The renal arteries and veins are normal. The ureters are of normal caliber lying in their course within the retroperitoneum and drain into an unremarkable urinary bladder containing approximately 75 milliliters of urine.

The external genitalia present an unremarkable penis without hypospadia, epispadias or phimosis. There are no infectious lesions or tumors noted. The descended testicles are of normal size encased within an intact and unremarkable scrotal sac. There are no abnormal masses or hernias on palpation. The prostate is of normal size and shape and sectioning presents two normal lateral lobes with a thin median lobe forming the floor of the unremarkable urethra. There are no gross pathological lesions.

ENDOCRINE SYSTEM

The thyroid gland is of normal size and shape and presents two well-defined lobes with a connecting isthmus and a beefy-brown cut surface. There are no goitrous changes or adenomas present. The adrenal glands are of normal size and shape. Sectioning presents no gross pathological lesions.

MUSCULOSKELETAL SYSTEM

The ribs, sternum, clavicles, pelvis and vertebral column have no recent fractures. The muscles are normally formed.

CENTRAL NERVOUS SYSTEM

The scalp is intact without contusions or lacerations. The calvarium is likewise intact without bony abnormalities or fractures. The brain weighs 1400 grams and presents moderate congestion of the leptomeninges. The overlying dura is intact and unremarkable. The cerebral hemispheres reveal a normal gyral pattern with severe global edema. The brainstem and cerebelli are normal in

OFFICE OF THE MEDICAL EXAMINER
FLORIDA, DISTRICTS 7 & 24

Name Martin, Trayvon ME # 12-24-043

MEDICAL EXAMINER REPORT
REPORT OF AUTOPSY

appearance with no evidence of cerebellar tonsillar notching. The circle of Willis is patent and presents no evidence of thrombosis or berry aneurysm. Upon coronal sectioning of the brain, the ventricular system is symmetrical and contains clear cerebrospinal fluid. There are no space-occupying lesions present. The spinal cord is not examined.

MICROSCOPIC EXAMINATION: One slide examined on March 15, 2012.

HEART: No diagnostic abnormality.

LUNGS: The partial collapse of tissues.

LIVER: No diagnostic abnormality.

TOXICOLOGY: See separate report from NMS Laboratories.

SB

End of Report

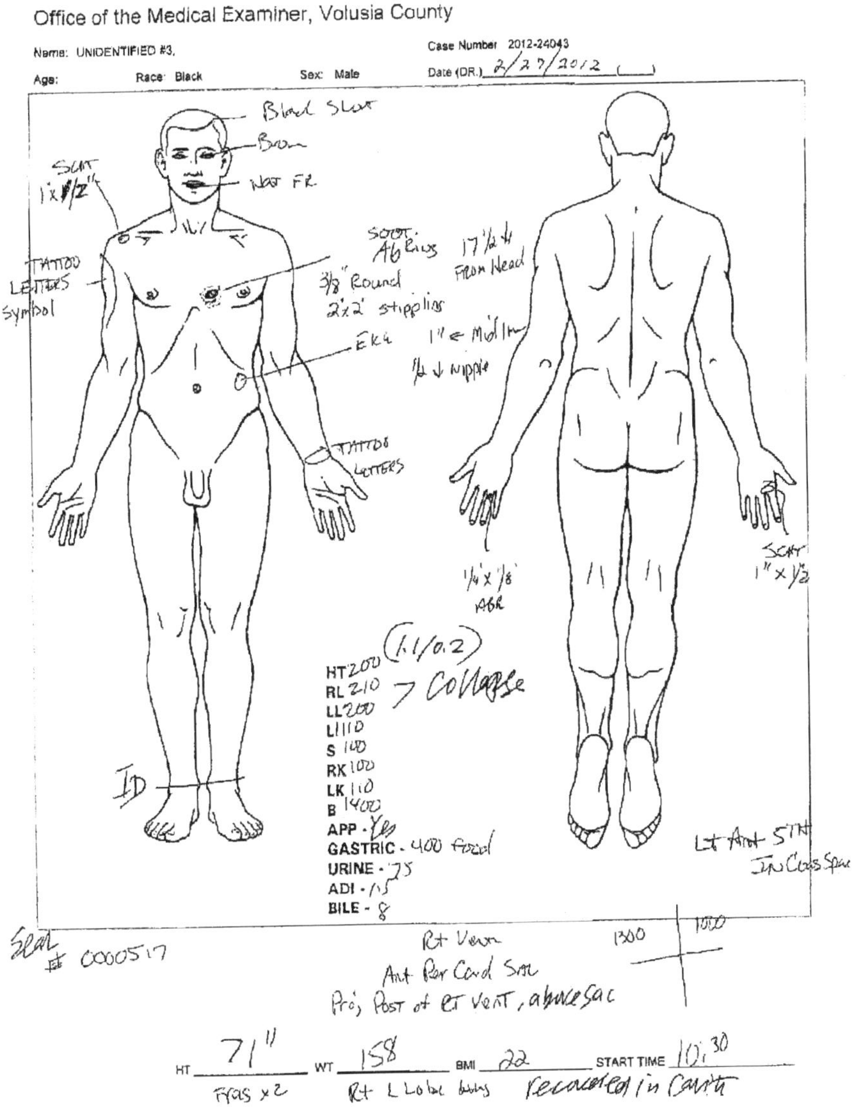
Office of the Medical Examiner, Volusia County
Name: UNIDENTIFIED #3,
Case Number 2012-24043
Age:
Race: Black
Sex: Male
Date (DR.) 2/27/2012
Black Short
Brown
Not FR
Scar 1"x 1/2"
Tattoo Letters Symbol
Soot. A6 Ribs 17 1/2" From Head
3/8" Round
2"x2" stippling
EKG 1" ← Midline
1/4 ↓ nipple
Tattoo Letters
1/4"x 1/8" ABR
Scar 1"x 1/2"
HT 200 (1.1/0.2)
RL 210 > Collapse
LL 200
LI 110
S 100
RK 100
LK 110
B 1400
APP - Yes
GASTRIC - 400 Food
URINE - 75
ADI - 1.5
BILE - 8
ID
Lt Ant 5TH Int Costal Space
Rt Vein
1300
1000
Ant Per Card Sac
Post of Rt Vent, above Sac
Seal # 0000517
HT 71"
WT 158
BMI 22
START TIME 10:30
Fras x2
Rt L Lobe lungs
Recovered in Cavity

SEMINOLE COUNTY
MEDICAL EXAMINER'S
DEATH REPORT

INSTRUCTIONS: *Complete this form for all deaths except Hospice registered patients. Send the form with the deceased to the morgue. If deceased is not sent to the morgue, fax this sheet to the M.E.'s Office — 324-5105 — AS SOON AS POSSIBLE*

NATURAL ☐ HOMICIDE ☒ SUICIDE ☐ ACCIDENTAL ☐

Date: 2/26/2012	Time: 2200	Deputy: SERINO	Case #: 2012-5000 11 JC
Subject's Last Name: DOE		First Name: JOHN	M.I.
DOB: UNK	Age: UNK	Sex: MALE	Race: BLACK

Address: UNDETERMINED Phone: ( )

Next of Kin: UNKNOWN Relationship: Phone: ( )

DOD: 2/26/2012	Approximate TOD: 1930	Pronounced By: SANFORD RESCUE #38

Dead on Arrival ☐ Emergency Room Death ☐ *(Ask ER personnel for this information)*

Place of Death *(Give name and exact address of facility, institute, residence or street)*: WALKWAY BEHIND RETREAT VIEW CIRCLE

Family Physician *(Full name)*: UNK Phone: ( ) Sign Certificate: YES NO

Diagnosis/Medical History: UNK

Funeral Home: N/A Phone: ( )

Last Time Deceased Was Seen Alive: 1915 HRS By Whom: G. ZIMMERMAN

Describe Deceased *(i.e. clothing, rigor/livor mortis, positioning, etc)*: ON BACK, MULTIPLE SWEATSHIRTS/JEANS/SNEAKERS/

COUNTY RESIDENT: YES ☐ NO ☐

Crime Scene Investigator: SMITH Case Investigator: SERINO

CIRCUMSTANCES SURROUNDING DEATH: SHOT IN CHEST BY KNOWN PERSON.

DO NOT COMPLETE IF DEATH WAS BY NATURAL CAUSES

Date of Injury: Time of Injury: Injury at Work: YES ☐ NO ☐

Place of Injury *(Street, Factory, Home, etc.)*:

Location *(Exact address)*:

Describe How Injury Occurred:

(White) M.E.'s Office (Canary) S.P.D. (Pink) Funeral Home

REVISED (12/94)

M.E. Notified Date: 2/26/12	L.E. Case Number: 2012 S001136
M.E. Notified Time: 2032	M.E. Case Number: 12-22-093
M.E. Notified By: EC	ECS CAD Number: 2-0570190
	Investigator to Scene: ☐ Yes ☐ No

Office of the Medical Examiner
County of Volusia
1360 Indian Lake Road
Daytona Beach, Florida

REPORT OF INVESTIGATION BY MEDICAL EXAMINER / INVESTIGATOR

City of Death: Sanford

County of Death: Seminole

Decedent: Trayvon (First Name) ____ (Middle Name) Martin (Last Name) Unit #3 (Suffix (Sr., Jr., III))

Address: ____ (Number and Street) ____ (City, State) ____ (Zip Code)

Age: 17 **DOB:** 02/05/95 **Sex:** ☐ Male ☐ Female ☐ Unknown **Occupation:** ____

Race: ☐ White ☐ Black ☐ Asian ☐ Native American ☐ Hispanic ☐ Other ____

Marital Status: ☐ Single ☐ Married ☐ Divorced **SSN:** ____

2831 Retreat View Circle Sanford

TYPE OF DEATH (Initial Jurisdiction - Check only one)

☐ Accident - Traffic	☐ Possible Drug Overdose	☐ Violent - Other (shot in courtyard)
☐ Accident - Other	☐ Sudden in Apparent Good Health	☐ Non Violent - Suspicious
☐ Homicide	☐ Unattended by Physician	☐ Suspected SIDS / (Or Infant)
☐ Suicide	☐ Homicide/Suicide	☐ Police Custody - Jail/Prison
☐ Natural	☐ Homicide/Suicide (with survivor)	

Notification By: ____ Official Title: ____

Address: ____ Phone: ____

Police Notified: ☐ Yes ☐ No **Investigator Contacted:** Serino Phone: 407-417-1666

Address: ____ Jurisdiction: SPD

	DATE	TIME (24H)	LOCATION	CITY/COUNTY	TYPE OF PREMISES	BY WHOM
LAST SEEN ALIVE	02/26/12	1915		Sanford	Courtyard	resident
INJURY/ ILLNESS		1920				
FOUND						SPD
DEATH/PRONOUNCED		1930				

DESCRIPTION OF PREMISES

INJURY OR ILLNESS ☐ Inside ☐ Outside	☐ House ☐ Apartment ☐ Mobile Home ☐ Workplace ☐ Hotel/Motel ☐ Adult Home ☐ Highway ☐ Retail Establishment ☐ School ☐ Hospital ☐ Jail ☐ Restaurant/Bar ☐ Parking Lot ☐ City Park ☐ Wooded Area ☐ Farm Pasture ☐ Freshwater River ☐ Freshwater Pond ☐ Retention Pond ☐ Ocean ☐ Coastal Waterway ☐ Swimming Pool ☐ Beach ☐ Other Courtyard
DEATH ☐ Inside ☐ Outside	☐ House ☐ Apartment ☐ Mobile Home ☐ Workplace ☐ Hotel/Motel ☐ Adult Home ☐ Highway ☐ Retail Establishment ☐ School ☐ Hospital ☐ Jail ☐ Restaurant/Bar ☐ Parking Lot ☐ City Park ☐ Wooded Area ☐ Farm Pasture ☐ Freshwater River ☐ Freshwater Pond ☐ Retention Pond ☐ Ocean ☐ Coastal Waterway ☐ Swimming Pool ☐ Beach ☐ Other Courtyard

[signature] — Signature of Medical Examiner / Forensic Investigator

F. Mathews — Name (Print or Type)

Office of the Medical Examiner, District 7 & 24

Medical Examiner Case Report

Year: 2012 **Number:** 24043 **Date Reported:** 2/26/2012 8:32:00 PM

Notification By: Emergency Communications Center **ECS CAD #:** 12-0570189

Investigative Agency/Jurisdiction: Sanford Police Dept

Decedent: Martin, Trayvon

Age: 17 **Race:** Black **Sex:** MALE

Date of Birth: 2 /5 /1995 :

Method Of ID:

Permanent Address:

City: Miami **State:** FLORIDA **Zip:** **Country:** USA

Last Seen Alive: 2/26/2012 7:15:00 PM

By Whom: Resident of complex

In Police Custody?: NO

Found?: NO

Date/Time of Death: 2/26/2012 7:30:00 PM

Place of Death: Courtyard behind 2861 Retreat View Circle

City of Death: Sanford

County of Death: Seminole

Date of Injury: 2/26/2012 7:20:00 PM **Injured at Work?:** NO

Place of Injury: Courtyard behind 2861 Retreat View Circle

Next of Kin: Mr. and Mrs. Martin, Parents

Funeral Home:

Investigating Agency: Sanford Police Dept

Law Enforcement Case #: 2012-50001136

Investigator: Serino

M.E. Investigator: Tara Malphurs

Autopsy?: Yes **Examination Date:** 2/27/2012 10:30:00 AM

Mode of Death: Handgun

Cause of Death: Gunshot Wound of Chest

Other Significant Conditions:

Manner of Death: Homicide

Doctor Signing DC: Shiping Bao, M.D.

Page 1 of 2

Year: 2012 **Number 24043** **Decedent: Martin, Trayvon**

Case Summary:

ECC contacted FI Malphurs of an apparent death in Sanford in the courtyard behind 2861 Retreat View Circle. Person of contact (POC) was SPD Inv. Serino. POC advised of an unknown B/M who had been shot by a resident of the complex. POC stated the following:

At approximately 1910 hours on 02/26/2012, 911 dispatchers received a call from a resident of the complex. The resident advised of a B/M who was at the complex between the townhouses. The caller stated that the male should not have been in the area and he observed the male while walking his neighborhood watch. Shortly after the call the resident confronted the male and the two began to physically fight. Witnesses observed the two fighting in the yard and then the resident fired a handgun at the male striking him in the chest. The male fell to the ground. SPD and SFD arrived on scene. The male was pronounced at 1930 hours. The identity of the male was unknown.

FI Malphurs responded to and arrived on scene at approximately 2144 hours. FI Malphurs observed a B/M lying face up on the ground in the courtyard. The male was clothed wearing a sweatshirt, t-shirt, pants and shoes. The male did not have identification in any of his pockets. The contents of the pockets were taken into custody by SPD. One (1) defect was seen on the male's chest with a hole in each of the shirts. SPD did not request to complete a GSR kit. POC advised that the weapon used was a .9mm handgun. Fingerprint identification was attempted; however, the male was not in the database of fingerprints. The male was then named as Unidentified #3. Photographs of the scene were taken. Livery arrived on scene for assistance and placed theB/M in a blue transport pouch. The pouch was sealed with blue tag #VCME0000517. Livery removed the B/M to the MEO. POC was given a 1000 hours examination time for 02/27/2012. FI Malphurs cleared the scene at approximately 2210 hours. TSM

Addendum: On 02/28/2012 at approximately 1230 hours, FI Malphurs received a fax from Sanford Police Department confirming positive identification as: Trayvon Martin, 17yoa B/M, DOB: 02/05/1996. The identification was made by his father from a crime scene photograph. ECC and MEO staff were notified and an identification sheet was completed. TSM

Description	Volume	Specimen
THC	1.5 ng/mL	Chest Blood
THC-COOH (Carboxy)	7.3 ng/mL	Chest Blood
Cannabinoids	Presump Pos	Urine

OFFICE OF THE MEDICAL EXAMINER
Districts 7 and 24
DEATH CERTIFICATE WORKSHEET

TSC
Investigator

Name: martin, Trayvon UNIDENTIFIED #3 ME Case # 2012-24043

Age: 17 Date of Birth: 2-5-1995 Sex: M Race: Black

Residence: , , FLORIDA,

Agency: Sanford Police Dept Case #: 2012-50001136

Place of Death: Courtyard behind 2861 Retreat View Circle

Date of death: 2/26/2012 7:30:00 PM Found?: No

(Check one) [X] Autopsy Performed [X] External Exam Only [X] Records Review Only

Date of Examination 2/27/2012 Time of Examination 10:30 (Hour)

CAUSE OF DEATH: Gunshot Wound of Chest

Due to (b): ______

Due to (c): ______

Other Significant Conditions: ______

Manner of Death: Pending Natural Accident Suicide Homicide Undetermined

How Incident Occurred Shot by another Person

SPECIMENS	Blood	Vitreous	Bile	Urine	Liver	Brain	Gastric	Serum	FTA	Organ Biopsies	Other
Sent	25 ft art	—	—	1 vial	—	—	—	—	—	1 Cass	—
Retained	15 art 25 ft art	1 vial	1 vial	1 vial	1 B	1 B	1 B	1 vial	3 Card	1 Bag	green top

Photos: ✓ Yes __ No X-Rays: ✓ Yes __ No Identification: ✓ Yes __ Pending

Infant Letter Needed __ Yes __ No

PATHOLOGIST: [signature] M.D./ Date: 02/27/12

The Lingering Memory of Dead Boys

Tayari Jones

Like many Americans, I have been glued to the television eager for details about the tragic murder of 17-year-old Trayvon Martin. I am not sure what I hoped to discover, as each new piece of evidence is more disturbing than the last.

I listened to the recently released 911 tapes on my office computer and cried in public. I was up until after midnight scanning my Twitter feed for news and comfort, a twenty-first century vigil of sorts.

I am the latest in a long line of black women speaking the names of our murdered boys. This is my role as woman in the African-American community. But my ties to his case stretch back to when I was a little girl growing up in Atlanta. When I was in the fifth and sixth grade, dozens of African-American children were murdered. Almost all of them were black boys. Even though Wayne Williams is believed to be the murderer, questions and scars persist.

Learning about death and dying is part of growing up. If we are lucky, we come to understand that death is natural through the passing of a grandparent or some other elder. If we are lucky, we will be taught something about a life well lived.

But for too many of us, we are made aware of our own mortality seeing our peers – the boys we want to go to the movies with, the boys who used to pull our hair – we learned that they could be killed for the crime being themselves. Young. Black. And Male.

When the Atlanta child murders occurred, I was just at the age when we were noticing the differences between the sexes. As the body count increased, I realized that in my community the difference was that if you were a boy, someone might try to kill you.

Recent reports have surfaced that Trayvon was on the phone with a girl as he walked from the store where he had bought candy. The girl on the phone was the last person to speak to Trayvon Martin.

I am filled with sorrow for her.

When I was young, girls were not mere bystanders as we watched our mothers groom our brothers to live in a world that feared them. Boys were taught not to look police, security guards, or anyone with authority directly in the eye. They should say only "yes, sir" or "no, sir." We, too, were in training, learning to protect the men we loved. We became our mothers' surrogates, reminding the guys to "keep cool," to "keep quiet." We knew they wanted to impress us, but we begged them not to talk back, as boys always do.

Today, at 41 years old, my girlhood is behind me, but the memories of dead boys linger. Most childhood fears are terrors that you grow out of. As you age, you realize that there is no monster under the bed.

But the worry that someone will look at a black man and deem him to be "suspicious," and feel justified in killing him, is a threat that only deepens as he grows older. If he is lucky enough to get older.

A Short, Racist History of Sanford, Florida

Sean Yoes

When I heard the murder of Trayvon Martin took place in Sanford, Florida, the first person I thought about was the late, legendary sports editor of the *AFRO*, Sam Lacy, a member of the journalists' wing of the Baseball Hall of Fame.

When I became a reporter for the *AFRO* in 1989, I was blessed to share the same office with Mr. Lacy; I couldn't put a price on the education in journalism and history he gave me that first year.

The series of stories he told me about his involvement in Jackie Robinson's breaking of the color barrier in Major League Baseball were the most mesmerizing of them all, and the story he relayed that was most harrowing originated in Sanford, Florida.

Lacy and his contemporary Wendell Smith of the *Pittsburg Courier* – another pioneering sports writer – traveled around the country for two years lobbying Major League Baseball and Brooklyn Dodgers owner Branch Rickey for Robinson's admission to the Majors.

But, on March 4, 1946, it was Lacy who accompanied Robinson to the small ballpark in Sanford, Florida. Robinson had been signed by the Dodgers a month earlier, and he was traveling for spring training with the Dodgers minor league team, the Montreal Royals, during a tour of the Deep South.

Of course, Robinson's presence on the team as they traveled through the South was wrought with great peril for him.

When Robinson and Lacy approached the stadium by car that first evening, a large crowd of Sanford's white citizens had gathered – some of them members of the Ku Klux Klan, which was very active in that region of the state – and they were determined to keep Robinson out of "their" ballpark.

Further, they were determined to run Robinson out of Sanford. Some of those white citizens met with the mayor of Sanford and demanded Robinson be forced out of town. As a result, Sanford city officials informed the Royals that black and white ballplayers would not be allowed on the same playing field together.

According to Mr. Lacy, Robinson, the future Hall-of-Famer, was undeterred by the hostile throng gathered at the stadium. The two drove to the back of the ballpark and entered the field through a plank in the outfield fence.

It's unclear whether Robinson actually played in that game, but what was abundantly clear is that racial oppression was as heavy in the air of Sanford as the infamous humidity; Robinson exited Sanford that night by order of Dodgers owner Branch Rickey.

In 2012, more than seventy years later, Sanford still proves to be a racial powder keg.

As the world focuses on Sanford in the wake of Trayvon Martin's murder, it has been alleged that the Klan is still active there. The police department has been accused of corruption and blatant discrimination against Sanford's citizens of color, including dubious investigations by the department in the murder of at least three other black men in recent years.

But the murder of another black man and his wife in Sanford – five years after Jackie Robinson was run out of town, and decades before the Trayvon Martin tragedy – shook the black community of Central Florida to its core.

Harry Tyson Moore was the founder of the first branch of the NAACP in Seminole County, the county in which Sanford is located. Moore, a teacher, worked tirelessly for equal pay for black teachers in public schools, filed lawsuits against voter registration barriers for blacks, investigated lynchings and eventually became the state secretary for the Florida chapter of the NAACP.

From 1944 to 1950 Moore's work led to an increase in black voter registration in Florida, to 31 percent of those eligible to vote, higher than in any other Southern state.

Moore was a bold "race man," and because of his relentless methods he was dangerous in the eyes of many in the white community. So much so that on Christmas night of 1951, the home of Moore and his wife, Harriette Vyda Simms Moore, was firebombed.

It was the couple's twenty-fifth wedding anniversary. Moore died on his way to a Sanford hospital, and his wife died nine days later. After their deaths, firebombing became a popular method of white racist intimidation in the South.

No one was ever indicted for their murders. However, in 2006 the State of Florida concluded that the Moores were murdered as a result of a conspiracy by the Central Florida Ku Klux Klan.

Decades after Robinson and Lacy's precarious racial encounter and the assassination of Harry Moore and his wife, Sanford's legacy of racial animus lives.

A Senseless Shooting in a Soulless Place

Alan Farago

It is called The Retreat at Twin Lakes: the platted subdivision where Trayvon Martin was shot to death by George Zimmerman. The *Tampa Bay Times* has described it this way:

> The building of the Retreat at Twin Lakes is a classic Florida story. Developers saw potential in the sandy acres east of Orlando and determined to turn them into an oasis. They planned a gated subdivision just 10 minutes from downtown – a cloistered community near the interstate, close to good schools, outlet malls and the magic of Disney World.

What kind of an oasis is a gated community, really? There are no lakes at The Retreat at Twin Lakes, and it is a retreat only in the sense of withdrawal. Subdivisions across the American landscape are places where getting lost is crystallized. "The idea, as always, was that people could live peacefully in a paradise where nobody could park a car on the street or paint the house an odd color."

The houses are all the same here, and not because that is what the market wants. Subdivisions like The Retreat at Twin Lakes fed the Wall Street derivatives machine. Mortgage-backed securities were fabricated on the flimsiest of foundations; the notion that investor and shareholder risk could be dispersed and rewarded, using subdivisions to conform demographics to scalable investment models.

George Zimmerman was virtually a self-appointed law enforcer in a soulless place dragged down by the real estate crash. He had the law on his side in a place that wasn't much of a place at all the night Trayvon Martin died.

According to the *Tampa Bay Times*: "In 2004, Engle Homes began construction on 263 two-story townhouses, with upstairs porches and covered back patios and plenty of green space. Inside, the townhomes boasted granite countertops, hardwood floors, master suites and walk-in closets. Outside, there was a pond, a clubhouse and a community pool. Everything was walled in, to keep out the unknown."

As the only person to volunteer when the Homeowners Association wanted to organize a community watch, Zimmerman was appointed coordinator by his neighbors, according to Wendy Dorival, Neighborhood Watch organizer for the Sanford Police Department. I bet you couldn't find two "neighbors" who vetted George Zimmerman.

Yes, there is a "community pool" at The Retreat, like any one of the million half-hearted attempts at builder-created civic life in gated subdivisions in Florida. The chief feature of communal value: a soda machine.

The same way that it is difficult to be healthy living on an unhealthy planet, how can anything last in platted subdivisions where nothing is built to last beyond the lifetime of particle board and sheetrock?

The *St. Pete Times* notes that the average price of The Retreat's homes has dropped from $250,000 in 2004 to less than $100,000 today: "The developers had envisioned a stable neighborhood with homeowners planting long-term roots, but now townhouses were turning over all the time. Insiders moved out. Outsiders moved in." Police had been called to The Retreat at Twin Lakes 402 times from January 1, 2011, to February 26, 2012.

The place where Trayvon Martin lost his life is not on trial. But as surely as the places we build reflect us, we are reflections of our surroundings. In a real estate market driven off the rails by oversupply, mortgage fraud and greed, why would builders be held to account? They build only what the market wants, right? Their legal rights to build sprawl are as solid as George Zimmerman's right to carry a weapon and to stand his ground. Right?

The police department's Wendy Dorival told the *Miami Herald* that she met Zimmerman in September 2011 at a community Neighborhood Watch presentation. "I said, 'If it's someone you don't recognize, call us. We'll figure it out." Places don't shoot people, people do.

In the land of the blind, the one-eyed man is king.

Sanford Police Department
Truth Verification Release Form

I, George M. Zimmerman do hereby voluntarily, without duress, coercion, threat or promise made to me, submit to a Computer Voice Stress Analysis examination. I hereby release, absolve and forever hold harmless the Sanford Police Department, its servants, agents, and anyone acting in its behalf, from any and all claims, demands, or other damages from any matter or act, arising out of a foresaid examination. I understand that is examination will be video and/or audio taped recorded. To the best of my knowledge, I have not physical or mental condition that would prevent me from taking this examination.

Signature of person being examined

2/27/2012
Date

8014
Signature of examiner ID #

2/27/12
Date

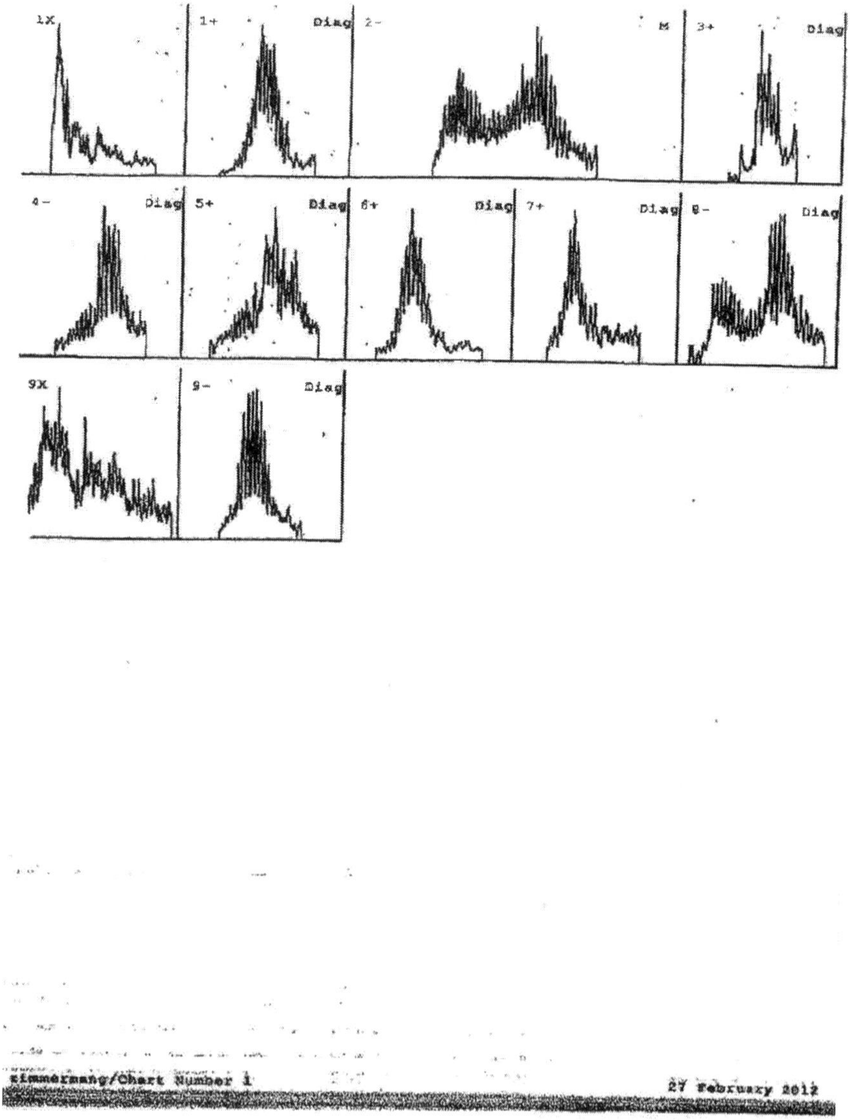
1X
1+
Diag
2-
M
3+
Diag
4-
Diag
5+
Diag
6+
Diag
7+
Diag
8-
Diag
9X
9-
Diag
zimmermang/Chart Number 1
27 February 2012

Date: 27 February 2012
Test Format: ZOC
est Medium: Manual
.ime Began: 07:09:29 PM
Requested: Inv. C. Serino
Case Number: 201280001136
Verification:
Confession:
Time Ended: 07:09:29 PM

Examiner: Inv. W. Erwin
Type of Test: Suspect
Offense: Crime Against Person
Subject: George Zimmerman
Outside Agency:
CVSA Unit Number: 1
Cold Call:
Deception: Not Indicated

1. (IR) Is your name George? YES
2. (C) Is the color of the wall green? NO
3. (IR) Is today Monday? YES
4. (R) Did you confront the guy you shot? NO
5. (IR) Is this the month of February? YES
6. (R) Were you in fear for your life, when you shot the guy? YES
7. (IR) Are we in the city of Sanford? YES
8. (C) Have you ever driven over the posted speed limit? NO
9. (IR) Am I wearing a watch? NO

zimmermang/Chart Number 2 27 February 20

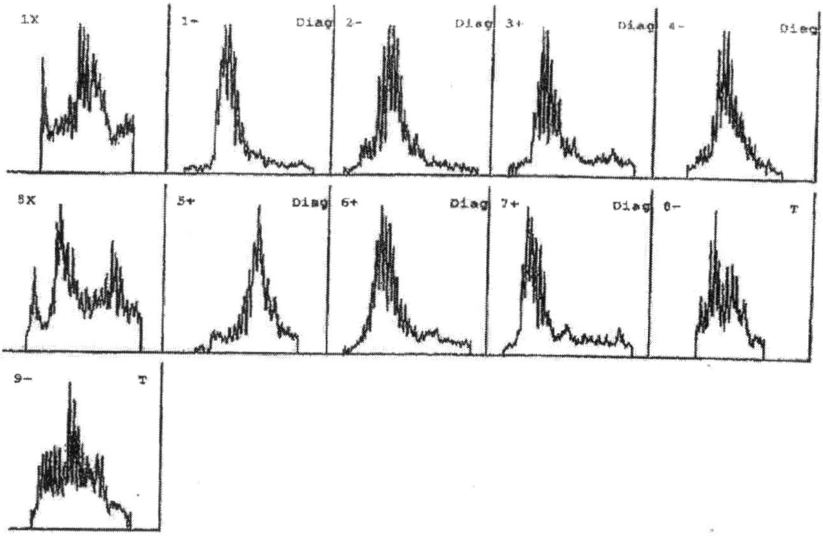

[illegible]/Chart Number 2 27 February 2012

Date: 27 February 2012
Test Format: ZOC
Test Medium: Manual
Time Began: 07:09:29 PM
Requested: Inv. C. Serino
Case Number: 201250001136
Verification:
Confession:
Time Ended: 07:09:29 PM

Examiner: Inv. W. Erwin
Type of Test: Suspect
Offense: Crime Against Person
Subject: George Zimmerman
Outside Agency:
CVSA Unit Number: 1
Cold Call:
Deception: Not Indicated

1. (IR) Is your name George? YES
2. (C) Is the color of the wall green? NO
3. (IR) Is today Monday? YES
4. (R) Did you confront the guy you shot? NO
5. (IR) Is this the month of February? YES
6. (R) Were you in fear for your life, when you shot the guy? YES
7. (IR) Are we in the city of Sanford? YES
8. (C) Have you ever driven over the posted speed limit? NO
9. (IR) Am I wearing a watch? NO

Zimmerman/CHART Number 1 27 February 2012

CONFIDENTIAL REPORT

Arrangement:

At your request George Zimmerman was administered a CVSA Truth Verification to determine his/her truthfulness pertaining to:

- [ ] Pre-employment interview
- [x] A criminal investigation

Procedure:

The following marked standard CVSA Truth Verification format was employed during the entire examination:

- [x] ZOC
- [ ] MZOC
- [ ] MZOC / SKY
- [ ] OS
- [ ] Structured / POT

Conclusion:

After analysis of the examinee's CVSA stress pattern charts, it is the opinion of this examiner that:

- [x] The examinee has told substantially the complete truth in regards to this examination.
- [ ] The examinee has told substantially the complete truth, but did make admissions.
- [ ] The examinee has not told the complete truth, but declined to make any admissions.
- [ ] The examinee did not tell the complete truth, but did make admissions.

Comments:

The Client was classified as No Deception Indicated (NDI). The client made admissions to collaborate the case prior to the exams.

Trayvon, Redux

Rita Dove

It is difficult/to get the news from poems /yet men die miserably every day/for lack/of what is found there./Hear me out/for I too am concerned/and every man/who wants to die at peace in his bed/besides.

– William Carlos Williams, "Asphodel, that Greeny Flower"

Move along, you don't belong here.
This is what you're thinking. Thinking
drives you nuts these days, all that
talk about rights and law abidance when
you can't even walk your own neighborhood
in peace and quiet, *get your black ass gone.*
You're thinking again. Then what?
Matlock's on TV and here you are,
vigilant, weary, exposed to the elements
on a wet winter's evening in Florida
when all's not right but no one sees it.
Where are they – the law, the enforcers
blind as a bunch of lazy bats can be,
holsters dangling from coat hooks above their desks
as they jaw the news between donuts?
Hey! It tastes good, shoving your voice
down a throat thinking only of sweetness.
Go on, choke on that. Did you say something?

Are you thinking again? Stop! – and
get your ass gone, your blackness,
that casual little red riding hood
I'm just on my way home attitude
as if this street was his to walk on.
Do you do hear me talking to you? Boy.
How dare he smile, jiggling his goodies
in that tiny shiny bag, his black paw crinkling it,
how dare he tinkle their laughter at you.

Here's a fine basket of riddles:
If a mouth shoots off and no one's around
to hear it, who can say which came first –
push or shove, bang or whimper?
Which is news fit to write home about?

Extract: 'If I Had a Son...'

President Barack Obama

March 23, 2012. Obviously this is a tragedy. I can only imagine what these parents are going through. When I think about this boy I think about my own kids, and I think every parent in America should be able to understand why it is absolutely imperative that we investigate every aspect of this and that everybody pulls together, federal, state and local to figure out exactly how this tragedy happened.

I'm glad that not only the Justice Department is looking into it. I understand now that the governor of the State of Florida has formed a task force to investigate what is taking place.

I think all of us have to do some soul searching to figure out how something like this happened. That means that we examine the laws and the context for what happened as well as the specifics of the incident.

But my main message is to the parents of Trayvon. If I had a son, he would look like Trayvon. I think they are right to expect that all of us as Americans are going to take this with the seriousness it deserves, and we will get to the bottom of exactly what happened.

What I Have to Teach My Son

Etan Thomas

What do I tell my son/He's 5 years old and he's still thinking cops are cool/ How do I break the news that when he gets some size/ He'll be perceived as a threat and see the fear in their eyes

– Talib Kweli

My son Malcolm is 6 years old. He is a fun-loving kid, loves sports, Avatar: The Last Airbender and swimming. Everyone thinks he is adorable. They look at his long dreadlocks, his big smile, his kind and playful heart; they comment on how respectfully he speaks to adults. He is a big kid. I am 6 foot 10 and my wife is 6 foot, so he's head and shoulders above everyone in his class. But soon I have to explain to him that he will not always be viewed as a cute little kid; that as he gets older, that tall-for-his-age, charming little kid with long dreadlocks will be looked at as a threat. He has an innocence that I am going to have to ruin for him very shortly. He is still under the impression that everyone will be treated fairly.

The case of Trayvon Martin is disturbing on so many levels I don't know where to begin.

According to published reports, on February 26, Trayvon had gone to a 7-Eleven during halftime of the NBA All Star Game. George Zimmerman, who is not a member of any police force but rather a Neighborhood Watch captain, called police to report a "suspicious" person in the neighborhood.

Zimmerman: "Hey, we've had some break-ins in my neighborhood, and there's a real suspicious guy at [address redacted]. This guy looks like he's up to no good, or he's on drugs or something..."

He later informed the dispatcher that that the guy looks black.

He then says, "He's staring at me."

While on the phone with the dispatcher Zimmerman is heard saying that Martin is "running." When asked where he replies "entrance to the neighborhood." You can hear deep breathing as the dispatcher asks Zimmerman, "Are you following him?" Zimmerman replies, "Yeah," and the dispatcher clearly says, "We don't need you to do that."

From this tape, it sounds as if Trayvon was the one who was scared, which would be understandable if anyone turned around and saw a man looking at him or her in an SUV in the dark for no apparent reason. I would have been a little uneasy myself.

When police arrived, 17-year-old Trayvon Martin, who had a squeaky clean record, no priors and only a bag of Skittles, an iced tea, his cell phone and his headphones, was dead from a gunshot wound admittedly inflicted by Neighborhood Watch captain George Zimmerman.

Zimmerman wasn't arrested, because the police claimed to have no probable cause and Zimmerman claimed self-defense.

My question is What exactly constitutes self-defense?

An unfortunate reality is that in Zimmerman's mind, he didn't have to see a gun, or actually see Trayvon doing something wrong. All he saw was that he was black, as he repeated two times in the short call to police. Is the unfortunate reality that young black male equals threat? Or does a young black male at night equal even more of a threat?

I'm not going to stress the fact that the National Crime Prevention Council, which sets guidelines for how you run a Neighborhood Watch, has a primary rule of thumb that you are not supposed to be armed.

Nor am I going to focus on the fact that since January of 2011, Zimmermann has called police forty-six times, or that in 2005 he was charged with resisting arrest and battery of a police officer and that alone should make him questionable as a Neighborhood Watch captain.

Nor am I going to argue that the Florida Stand Your Ground law couldn't be applicable in this case, for the simple fact that as heard from the released tapes, Zimmerman left his vehicle and went after Trayvon.

"A person who is not engaged in an unlawful activity and who is attacked in any other place where he or she has a right to be has no duty to retreat and has the right to stand his or her ground and meet force with force, including deadly force, if he or she reasonably believes it is necessary to do so to prevent death or great bodily harm to himself or herself or another or to prevent the commission of a forcible felony."

Nor am I going to make the race of Zimmerman an issue.

To quote the Rev. Al Sharpton: "The race/ethnicity of Zimmerman or any citizen in this type of scenario doesn't matter, because at the end of the day, it is the race of the victim – Trayvon – that does matter. It is his race and his demographic that is consistently depicted as the threat, and negatively portrayed in popular culture."

It is this perception that I have to teach my son very soon: that the unfortunate reality is that in Zimmerman's mind, he was justified and understandably afraid as soon as he laid eyes on young Trayvon. He didn't see a cute kid who was drinking an iced tea. He saw a threat, a criminal, someone who could be on drugs or "up to no good."

Very soon I have to ruin my son's rose-colored-glasses view of the world we live in.

I have to teach him that:

1) There are going to be people who view you as the enemy when you have done nothing wrong;

2) You are going to be feared, cause suspicion, harassed, accused, and some people will be terrified of you;

3) If the police stop you, make sure you stop in a well-lit area and don't make any sudden moves;

4) Keep your hands visible. Avoid putting them in your pockets;

5) Verbally broadcast your actions (i.e., "Officer, I am now reaching into my pocket for my license");

6) Always get the receipt after making a purchase, no matter how small, so no one can falsely accuse you of theft, later;

7) Many times actually being guilty has nothing to do with being viewed as guilty.

I have to teach him about Emmett Till, James Byrd, Amadou Diallo, Sean Bell, Oscar Grant and Rodney King.

I have to teach him these things for his own safety. I wish I didn't have to take away his innocence, but for his own well-being, soon, I will have to.

Extract: In Memory of Trayvon Martin and Bo Morrison

Matthew Rothschild

From a speech delivered at the Capitol in Madison, Wisconsin, on April 7, 2012, to a rally in memory of Trayvon Martin and Bo Morrison, a 20-year-old African-American who was killed on March 3 after being mistaken for an intruder following the break-up of an underage drinking party in the town of Slinger, Wisconsin. Under the state's Castle Doctrine, the shooter was not charged.

There is something terribly wrong in America today.

And there is something terribly wrong in Wisconsin today, when two young black men can be gunned down, unarmed, and the shooter goes free.

A lot of people are comparing the Trayvon Martin case to that of Emmett Till back in 1955, who was savagely beaten to death by whites in Mississippi for allegedly whistling at a white woman.

And what was Trayvon Martin doing? He'd gone out to buy a bag of Skittles!

And what was Bo Morrison doing? He was hiding from the cops on a nearby porch. Hell, my own sons have done the same thing. Did that give someone the right to shoot them dead?

So let's name what's terribly wrong in America, and in Wisconsin, today.

One obvious thing is racism.

It has not gone away. We are not living in the mythical post-racial society. It's with us like a virus that we just can't kick, and it flares up in lethal forms.

But it's not just racism we're dealing with here. There's another virus afflicting this country. It's a virus that hasn't been here as long as racism, but almost half as long.

It's called oligarchy. It's called plutocracy. It's rule by the rich and by the corporations and by the special interests.

Because let's look how the Castle Doctrine and Stand Your Ground laws got passed. These are the laws that legalize and immunize vigilantism.

There was no groundswell for these laws. Tens of millions of people weren't clamoring for them.

No, these laws were pushed by the National Rifle Association, and by a shadowy group called ALEC, which the NRA funds, as do a lot of corporations.

ALEC stands for the American Legislative Exchange Council. It's a coalition of corporations and right-wing state legislators whereby the corporations actually vote on "model" legislation that they then pass on to state legislators to ram through.

That's right. The citizens don't vote. The corporations vote, and then their water boys in statehouses like this one pass the legislation.

That's what happened in Florida.

And that's what's happened here.

Scott Suder, the State Assembly majority leader, last year was chair of the Public Safety and Elections Task Force of ALEC, and the NRA was the corporate co-chair. Scott Suder and Governor Scott Walker, an ALEC alum, pushed through the Castle Doctrine.

It says that homeowners have the right to shoot to kill someone who is unlawfully on their premises. And in Wisconsin that means not only in their house but on their porch, as Bo Morrison was. And it also means in their driveway, on their lawn or even in their swimming pool.

How many people own swimming pools in Wisconsin? This law is meant for them.

And just think for a minute: it's a hot summer night, and the neighborhood kids want to sneak a dip in the rich man's pool. It's now OK for that man to blow those kids away.

That's where we've come to here in America.

The gun owner and the property owner now have a license to kill, and they're using that license to kill young black men.

This racism has got to stop. And this rule by shadowy corporate groups like ALEC has got to stop.

We must eradicate racism.

We must beat back oligarchy and plutocracy so we can at last have a chance at a real democracy in this country.

And so we can say, as Langston Hughes once said:

> O, let America be America again—
>
> This land that never has been yet.
>
> And yet must be.
>
> The land where every man is free.

Sighs of Fire

Zimmerman as a Domestic Drone

Vijay Prashad

Blood stained the street a few days before we moved into our home in Hartford, Connecticut, in 1997. Our welcome block party was to be a vigil. It smelled of something rancid, perfumed in eulogies of self-righteousness.

The corner down the street had become a transit point for the drug trade, already in its decline. One of the residents, Jay Boland, had taken on the role of vigilante for the street, defending it against the predations of the gang members. He carried a .38 caliber Smith and Wesson, once made down the road in Springfield, Massachusetts. Boland, the gangsters later said, used to sit in his car on the street with his gun in his lap. If any of them walked around, he'd threaten them. They claimed that on at least one occasion, Boland had used racist language against them. One hot August night, Boland returned home at 1 a.m., confronted Samuel Davis near his home and – as Maxine Bernstein of the *Hartford Courant* wrote the story – "at least one neighbor heard an exchange of words, followed by one gunshot, a pause, and then a burst of gunfire." The police accused Davis of shooting Boland first, and then Boland returned fire with his gun. Boland died in a neighbor's arms, while Davis, bleeding, made a getaway, only to be later arrested.

In court, Davis flailed about, calling the judge a Nazi and suggesting that the police had given the actual killer a deal while stringing him up. The press at that time characterized Davis as someone out of touch with reality. Another way to see it is that Davis well knew what was coming; he got a 100-year sentence. "You did postgraduate work in street crime," said the judge. It was open and shut.

No candle at the vigil was shaped like a .38, nor was one burning out the obscenities that might have polluted the languid air. It was clear to my neighbors that Boland was the hero, and Davis the criminal. Even if

Davis was a "postgraduate" in street crime, what made Boland a hero? The West End of Hartford had become a bastion of liberalism – lots of college professors and social workers, liberal preachers and massage therapists. The red meat of conservatism was not to be found here. "We moved *to* Hartford," a man told me proudly. It was enough of a badge to live here, even with this anxiousness, to prove post-racism. It is the urban way of saying "We have black friends," which is now politically expressed as "We have a black president." Because these things happen, where you live, who your friends are, who your president is, seem sufficient to inoculate one from the structures of racism that encage not only our homes but our imagination. What was a Connecticut Yankee doing sitting in his car, not far from Mark Twain's home, with a police special in his lap, threatening drug dealers as they strayed from the corner?

What was George Zimmerman doing in his Honda Ridgeline, driving around Sanford, Florida, looking for trouble? If Trayvon Martin had been wearing a suit and driving a BMW, Zimmerman would have resented him – envy refracted through an enduring sense of racial hierarchy. That is why so many wealthy African-Americans in fancy cars find themselves being unduly pulled over by white police officers – just checking, I suppose, if the car has been stolen. But Martin, age 17, had on a hoodie, which does not evoke resentment for the racist consciousness, only a strange mixture of fear and anger. If it were fear alone that struck Zimmerman, he would have turned off and driven home, left a lot of distance between himself and the person whom he would have seen as a predator. But the racist consciousness does not experience fear without anger; it is the latter that forces him to go on the hunt. He had to get the target.

Zimmerman forced the confrontation, held out the gun and pulled the trigger. That is beyond question. What he did had been legally sanctified by the State of Florida. Zimmerman was Florida's domestic drone, hovering around in his Ridgeline, looking for the "bad guys," asking the home base – in this case the local police station – for permission to engage and then going in for the kill. Nothing he had done from the minute he began to stalk Martin was illegal, just as nothing is illegal to the drone operators as they set their Reapers into flight and let loose their Hellfire missiles on some unsuspecting "bad guys" who are en route to a wedding or just going out to get some kebabs on the ridge. Black youth on American streets or "military-age males" in the badlands of Af-Pak and Yemen are in the strike zone – combatants, as the White House put it of the latter, "unless there is explicit intelligence posthumously proving them innocent." If there is such intelligence (over the killing of 16-year-old Abdulrahman al-Awlaki, for example, vaporized by a Hellfire missile while sitting in a café with friends in 2011) the US does not apologize for it, though in private the president says he is "surprised" and "upset." No one was charged with Abdulrahman's murder, and if they were, they'd say that they stood their ground in killing all in the strike zone. Zimmerman and the drone operators fire the shot, but the ideology comes from above their pay grade.

Long before the financial crisis of 2007, it was plain that the US economy was in disarray. Jobless growth and credit-funded consumerism fueled the growth rate. But beneath that lurked a growing social divide. During the Clinton years (1993-2000) society was laid on the rack, as the new economic policies ratcheted widening social inequality. The elites knew what they were doing: in a landscape of joblessness, they cast off the indigent (Welfare Reform) and sent them to prison (Crime Bill). The future was left to the resilience of families and communities and to the underground economies (legal and illegal). Chronic joblessness, with a collapse of state institutions to expand the social wage, is met by an increase in the means of repression (police and jails) and the ideology of consumerism. It is a dangerous social soup. In Springfield, Massachusetts, Michaelann Bewsee of Arise for Social Justice calls these neighborhoods "an economic dustbowl."

Parallel to the defeat of the US working class in the 1990s, thrown into chronic unemployment and debt, was the rise of multiculturalism. To settle the aged question of racism, the state and society would have to uncover and unravel the ligaments of power. But this was not possible short of a major social transformation. Instead, the state and society encouraged a mild social policy – multiculturalism – which allowed the most talented and fortunate of the oppressed populations to become shining emblems of racism's end. Look, these darker bodies suggest, *we* have arrived. But what is always in question is what this *we* refers to – to those few who have arrived or those many whose Sisyphean journey to the American Dream is to be short-circuited by someone else's arrival. Obama is the president, ergo racism is over. What had succeeded over the course of the 1990s and into the 2000s was not anti-racism but multiculturalism, whose success did not undermine racism. In fact, multiculturalism's success sharpened racism. Obama's ascent sharpened resentment, as does the sight of a black family in a fancy car. What we live in now is what Martin Luther King, Jr. called "the stagnant equality of sameness." Integration with resentment, King suggested, is not a community. It is stagnant because there is little hope of transcending the resentment. It is sameness because there is no understanding that ancient inequalities that have now hardened cannot be simply wished away. They have to be confronted and overcome.

Trayvon Martin and Abdulrahman al-Awlaki were teenagers, children eager to make something of themselves in this world. To the eyes of the racist consciousness neither was human; they were threats to be liquidated. The awful immediacy of vigilante justice is back, with bearers of this terrifying reality being its executioners – a Zimmerman here, a drone operator there. In a society that seems to doff its cap only to the military and the police, it is no wonder that ordinary civilians want to be associated with that kind of heroism. They believe that heroism is to be found on the trigger end of a gun or a missile.

Real heroism might be found elsewhere – in the byways of US society where ordinary people are working hard to transform this ghastly jobless growth engine into something meaningful. The real heroes are the ones who will organize the Justice for Trayvon rallies, raising awareness amongst their neighbors of the social costs of the policies plotted by the elites. If people like Zimmerman dreamed a little less about being a hero in the conventional sense, he'd have lived a more generous life. As someone put it on Twitter, wouldn't it have been nice if on February 26, 2012, a man in a Honda Ridgeline pulled up beside a teenager out to get some snacks in the pouring rain and asked him if he wanted a ride home?

Lay of the Land

A Memory: On Queens Boulevard, the Night Sean Bell's Killers Got Off

JoAnn Wypijewski

Dusk in Queens, April 25, 2008, the first march after the verdict in the police killing of Sean Bell started among the cherry blossoms; in front of the cool stone courthouse, where that morning Judge Arthur Cooperman announced that essentially his decision had pivoted on believing that police feared for their life or taking the word of a bunch of thugs with rap sheets and an interest in milking the city for cash. He had decided the victims brought it on themselves.

Fifty shots!

That's murder!

The protesters flowed from the little park in front of the courthouse across the street crying "Murder!" The judge had not thought so. He didn't entertain manslaughter, or felony assault, or reckless endangerment either. Maybe carelessness, but that would be for the Police Department to decide. Sean Bell was dead at 23, too bad. He and a friend had had heated words with another man outside Club Kalua, an exotic dance club, after his bachelor party there. Did anyone really say he had a gun, or say he was going for a gun? The testimony was inconsistent, but the judge wasn't bothered by that inconsistency. Police "perceived" that Bell and his crew might have had a gun in their car, he stated. They no more had a gun than Saddam Hussein had weapons of mass destruction. But they were Angry Black Men, the defense had argued. They were drunk. And when they saw yet another dark-skinned man in plain clothes pointing a gun at them, they didn't wave a white flag and sit still. It was just past 4 in the morning. They were drunk, and they tried to get away. The man pointing the gun at their car may or may not have said, "Police." He and the two other shooters on trial said they had identified themselves, but their own lieutenant on the scene testified that he had not heard it. The judge was not bothered by that inconsistency. The cops may or may not have shown their badges, another inconsistency that did not concern him.

One, we are the people!

Two, a little bit louder

Three, we want justice for all people ...

The protest massed down Queens Boulevard and onto Jamaica Avenue, past the nail shops and the beauty shops, past fast food parking lots where tattooed young men and sedate-looking older couples joined in the chants, past intersections where people stuck waiting in their cars didn't seem to mind, past tenements where pretty girls hung out the windows smiling and waving, past idling buses whose black passengers nodded or gave a thumbs up. The emotion of plain, unarmed people in the early hours of November 25, 2006 – confusion, disorientation, fear in the night – did not matter to the judge in deciding the facts of the case. They might have mattered to a jury, but once a court refused to allow a change of venue out of the city, the cops put their fate in the judge's hands.

"That was good," I overheard a couple of white guys at a Manhattan diner say later. The papers quoted legal experts saying the case was so complicated plain people never could have decided it. Judge Cooperman took eleven days before rendering his decision, but in delivering it he expressed only steely purpose. The baby son of one of the victims started crying while Cooperman was reading his verdict. "I'm not going to continue unless the child is removed," the judge snapped, and the boy's mother hurried him out of the courtroom. What the victims felt or thought at the time of the shooting was irrelevant, the judge lectured; it's what they did that mattered. They had tried to get away; Sean Bell's Nissan Altima hit the man who was pointing a gun at him and hit an unmarked police van. Then it hit the van again. That was enough for a pre-emptive execution. What the cops thought and felt, not what they did, is what concerned the judge, and they thought Bell and his friends were going to kill them.

Fifty shots.

Within seconds Liverpool Street was a scene of carnage. Two years later the survivors took the witness stand, and their inconsistencies counted for everything. Their anger under cross-examination, their background with the law, their shifting memory of what happened in a few horror-filled seconds after a long night of drinking that ended with their friend drenched in blood and themselves ripped with bullets, counted for everything, as did the background of other prosecution witnesses, some of them strippers and drug dealers. "These factors played a significant part in ... eviscerating the credibility of those prosecution witnesses," Judge Cooperman declared.

1 - 2 - 3 - 4 - 5 ... 48 - 49 - 50.

Fifty shots!

That's murder!

We have done these countdowns before. Up to forty-one after Amadou Diallo was killed by four plain clothes cops in the Bronx in 1999. Those cops got off, too, after a jury in Albany, New York, decided they feared for their life. They were all big men with guns, and the little immigrant had only a wallet. It looked like a gun, they said. Who knew?

Fifty shots is a new high, but among the placards in the march there were relics of many an earlier outing, creased and dog-eared and listing the names of the dead at police hands. There were pictures of some of the better-known victims: Anthony Baez, Timothy Stansbury, Diallo, Abner Louima, who wasn't killed, merely sodomized with a broomstick in a police station... Most of us don't know the other names unless we look them up or they died down the street from where we live. Most were killed by only a few shots or, like Baez, by a chokehold or a beating. A crazed old woman with a steak knife – what was her name, again? She was pumped full of lead by a SWAT team in her kitchen. Some were killed in custody; some have been killed since Bell but without the enticing detail: the bikini clad pole dancers, the wedding day in ruins, the unfulfilled redemption of a man about to "turn his life around." It doesn't matter; the story is always the same. The police are always scared. Their training is always irrelevant. "What would you do in their shoes?" someone, some many ones, in the newspapers always demand. As if we can know. We, the untrained, are just scared. Bell and his friends were just scared. It doesn't matter. If police training could go out the window, the victims' conjured training could not. As thugs, they should have been ready. The trial was theirs, really, and the judge found them guilty.

No justice!

No peace!

And fuck the police!

The police are trained not to mind such abuse and to behave accordingly. The evening of the protest they were out in windbreakers and baseball caps rather than riot gear. "Oink, oink, oink!" people shouted. They didn't flinch. No protester said, "Off the pigs!" but it probably wouldn't have mattered this night, the first night, where everyone from the mayor on down had decided that a little repressive tolerance couldn't hurt. And there were children in strollers in the march. A nice black dog in the march. Some old people and a lot of teenagers. Not many of the protesters were white. Not one of the cheering spectators was white, at least not that I noticed. Along the route three buxom Latinas in the doorway of their nail shop swayed their hips and arms as if welcoming a parade of heroes.

The killing of Bell and wounding of his friends were an advertisement for multicultural law and order in action. Of the three defendants, Marc Cooper is black; Gescard Isnora is black Hispanic; Michael Oliver is Arab-American. The defense team was a rainbow coalition, black, Latino and white, with the most dogged cross-examiner in the bunch a black man. After the verdict he made a point of telling the press that his client, Isnora, the man who pointed his gun at Bell first, was a dark-skinned man who decided not to sell drugs, not to get involved in the life of the streets. As offensive as the broader implications of that assertion was, the opposite is true.

Isnora and his partners have made careers juicing the life of the streets. They were in Club Kalua that night trying to trap someone into buying drugs or agreeing to sex for hire. They had been forced to drink a couple of beers so as to fit in. (The NYPD will eventually decide if that was going overboard.) Four hours in that seedy joint, and they couldn't snag a soul. After the place closed and just before the shooting, one of the cops tried one last time to lure one of the dancers into prostitution. No luck. The night had been one fat zero for the cops until they imagined the crime-about-to-happen and killed Bell. In a play-out of the grim cliche that these killings have become, the only thing separating the cops from gangsters is the badge, the blue and the benefit of the doubt.

After the judge delivered his verdict, Trent Benefield, who was injured in the shooting and excoriated by the judge as a liar, wept among his friends and said, "If I did it, I'd be doing twenty-five to life." This verdict had been preceded, a few weeks before, by another one, the sentencing verdict of John White, a 54-year-old black homeowner in Long Island, who shot and killed an unarmed drunken white teenager, who had come to his house shouting "Nigger!" and, White thought, threatening his family. White wept, too, on the witness stand, telling the jury of his fear, the whirl of historical memories, of real and imagined terrors that combined in some mad vortex that ended in a killing that day. He called it an accident. The essential facts of White's case were as clear as those of the three cops. He was armed; his victim was not. He was afraid a gun or guns might appear from somewhere in the dark, some lynch mob on the way; they did not, but he killed a 16-year-old. A jury convicted White of manslaughter. His fear, like the drunken, repulsive behavior of the victim, did not figure in the conviction; they were matters for mitigation, and at sentencing White was given two to four years.

Supporters of Bell's killers have taken to railing against protesters for having no respect for presumption of innocence, reasonable doubt and other noble features of the trial system that seem almost quaint until they're written in bright capital letters when cops kill someone. Like the three cops only with more justification – he had not gone out looking for a confrontation with his victim – John White said he had feared for his life. No doubt that fear was real, but killing an unarmed teenager was not an act of self-defense, and it didn't look like an accident. A jury was able to make the distinctions that Judge Cooperman and his champions in the legal profession suggested were beyond anyone's capability in the killing of Sean Bell.

We are all Sean Bell!

We are all Sean Bell!

Our words bounced off the walls and the underside of the bridge at the Jamaica station of the Long Island Railroad, amplified, thunderous. We all meant them. But there were no pictures of white women on that whiskered sign of police victims, and no white men either. Leftists who have worried that an electoral victory for Barack Obama will somehow remove the oppression of blacks as a subject in American politics need not fret. Whatever Obama's fortunes, it's a good bet that another black family's loved one will be shot dead in the streets by police somewhere in America, and another court will decide that the trained killers had every reason to be afraid. Again they'll walk, and protesters will march, and editorialists will say we must honor the rule of law and take steps so it never happens again. "Unfortunately, sometimes people die," Michael Oliver, who got off thirty-one shots, said after acquittal. "I have to live with that for the rest of my life." If the pattern follows, he'll get a desk job, and the police union will say how unfair it all is.

(2008)

Extract: 1 Black Person Killed Every 28 Hours

Adam Hudson

Police officers, security guards or self-appointed vigilantes extra-judicially killed at least 313 African-Americans in 2012, according to a study by the Malcolm X Grassroots Movement (http://mxgm.org/wp-content/uploads/2013/04/Operation-Ghetto-Storm.pdf). This means a security officer, or those operating under the color of law, killed a black person every twenty-eight hours. The report notes that it is possible that the real number could be much higher.

MXGM, a national anti-racist grassroots activist organization, collected the data for the report, titled "Operation Ghetto Storm," from police and media reports, along with other publicly available sources. The 2012 study is a follow-up to a similar study in 2011, showing that law enforcement authorities and individuals operating under the color of law kill a black person every thirty-six hours. From this data, extrajudicial killings are on the rise.

Of those 313 persons killed, the age breakdown is as follows:

124 (40 percent) were 22 to 31 years old;

57 (18 percent) were 18 to 21 years old;

54 (17 percent) were 32 to 41 years old;

32 (10 percent) were 42 to 51 years old;

25 (8 percent) were youths under 18;

18 (6 percent) were older than 52;

3 (1 percent) were of unknown ages.

Twenty-three of these people, or 7 percent, were women: eleven were killed accidentally or in crashes; three were mentally ill or self-medicated or both; two were accused "car thieves"; two were "innocent bystanders";

four were fleeing police; one had slashed her sister's tires; and one was allegedly involved in criminal activity, a kidnapping.

Close to a quarter of those killed, sixty-eight people, or 22 percent, suffered from mental illness and/or were self-medicated. The study says that "[m]any of them might be alive today if community members trained and committed to humane crisis intervention and mental health treatment had been called, rather than the police." In 19 percent of the cases, someone was killed after a 911 call reporting an "emotionally disturbed loved one."

The percentage of people killed in the course of a criminal investigation was only a tad higher than the rate for the mentally compromised: 24 percent. Otherwise, 43 percent of the shootings occurred following an incident of racial profiling; 7 percent following a 911 call reporting domestic violence; another 7 percent for no stated reason.

Most of the people killed were not armed. According to the report, 136 people, or 44 percent, had no weapon at all at the time they were killed by security forces. In 27 percent of the cases police claimed the individual had a gun, but there was no proof of that. Six people (2 percent) were alleged to have possessed knives or similar tools. Of those persons who were demonstrably armed, sixty-two (20 percent) had guns, and twenty-three (7 percent) had knives.

Most police officers, security guards or vigilantes who extrajudicially killed black people claimed they "felt threatened," "feared for their life" or "were forced to shoot to protect themselves or others." Those were the explanations given in about 47 percent of the cases (involving 146 of the 313 dead). Other allegations made to justify the use of deadly force:

the person killed was a suspect fleeing (14 percent);

the person killed drove a car toward officers (5 percent);

the person killed reached for a waistband (3 percent);

the person killed lunged at an officer (3 percent).

Forty-two people, or 13 percent of those killed, had fired a weapon "before or during the officer's arrival."

Of the 313 killings, the report found that 275 of them – that's 88 percent – were instances of excessive force. Only 8 percent were not considered excessive, as they involved suspects who shot at, wounded or killed a police officer or others. In 4 percent of the cases the facts surrounding the killing were "unclear or sparsely reported."

The vast majority of the time, police officers, security guards or armed vigilantes who extrajudicially kill black people escape accountability.

Face to Face With the NYPD

What They Look Like to a Guinean-American

Ibrahim Diallo

It is far more important to hold accountable the enforcers of the law than the perpetrators because if you don't, you will have a nation of warlords.

– Mahmood Mamdani

New York's Finest (also known as the NYPD) came under a lot of scrutiny once activists from Occupy Wall Street took to the streets of New York City on September 17, 2011. From the videos of pepper spraying on YouTube to the mass arrests, the brutality of the NYPD shocked many. However, it came as a shock only to those who never before had to deal with a police force inspired by a culture of brutality, which encourages officers to instill fear and contempt in those whom they are supposed to serve and protect. From the yellow-cab driver to the street vendor, and from the high school students in working-class neighborhoods to young men in Harlem, Brooklyn and the Bronx, people encounter this culture of unprofessionalism and brutality on a daily basis. What former Mayor Michael Bloomberg and his Police Commissioner, Ray Kelly, called the "best police force in the world" has in fact been the greatest fear factor in many communities, despite its mission to "preserve the peace, reduce fear and provide for a safe environment."

Under Commissioner Kelly, the policy of "stop, question and frisk" was expanded, giving NYPD officers the authority to stop civilians, question and search them. Officers then proceed to enter the names of those searched into a database, which they claim is "valuable in helping solve future crimes." The reason for the stops, you might ask? "Because you fit a description," I was told following a search in which the officers did not ask me a single question.[1]

1 In 2013, Bill de Blasio made opposition to stop-and-frisk a major part of his successful campaign for mayor. He and his Police Commissioner, Bill Bratton, have not, however, eliminated the practice. In the first quarter of the de Blasio administration, from Jauuary 1, 2014, to March 31, NYPD officers made 14,261 stops, according to an

The stop-and-frisk policy has systematically terrorized and humiliated people – especially young men of color in working-class neighborhoods from Harlem to Brownsville, Brooklyn – under the false presumption of "crime prevention." In 2011 the NYPD made 685,000 stops, mostly of black and Hispanic men. It recovered guns and contraband in 0.1 percent and 1.8 percent of the stops, respectively. One of the many successes of Occupy Wall Street was its exposure of this debased police culture to the general public. Indeed, over a few months, the world saw what had long been the reality of many young men in New York City: police officers acting with impunity, knowing that they'll be protected as they assault peaceful civilians.

In response to media attention to instances of police violence, the NYPD has typically offered mere fabrications. When Brooklyn City Councilman Jumaane Williams and his aide were thrown to the ground and handcuffed during the West Indian Day Parade in 2011, the NYPD immediately stated that "a crowd formed and an unknown individual punched a police captain on the scene," suggesting that somehow the councilman had been part of that crowd. We witnessed the same level of denial on behalf of the police when Deputy Inspector Anthony Bologna, a repeat offender, indiscriminately pepper-sprayed a group of peaceful mostly white female protesters. The Police Department immediately rose to the officer's defense, claiming rather forcefully that he did nothing wrong and that the use of pepper spray was "appropriate." The Deputy Inspector (the "white shirt") was punished: a loss of ten vacation days. But the video of defenseless young women being attacked by police ripped off the veneer of New York's Finest, and systemic police abuses, particularly stop-and-frisk, became an unavoidable public issue.

In New York City, there are endless examples of police brutality. Commissioner Kelly said that he wanted to instill fear in young blacks and Hispanics. In a private meeting, the commissioner told lawmakers, "The reason we stop and frisk and target the groups that we do is because we want all people who fit that group to feel that anytime they leave their house they can be searched by the police." Walking down the street in my neighborhood, I know that this is what I can expect. The feeling of nakedness and anxiety that one has knowing that at any moment police officers, whether in uniform or in plain clothes, can approach you, take your identification and pat you down, is overwhelming.

I first experienced that reality in 2007. I was walking to the subway

---

analysis by The Wall Street Journal. Although an 86 percent decline from the 99,788 stops in the same period of 2013, the 2014 numbers represent a small spike from the final three months of the Bloomberg administration, when there were 12,495 stops. Under de Blasio, the racial demographics of stop-and-frisk are essentially unchanged: 54 percent of those stopped in the first quarter of his administration were black, and 29 percent were Latino. (Ed.)

from my apartment in Brooklyn when I was approached by two undercover police officers. "Spread your legs and place your hands behind your head," they shouted, running out of an unmarked police car. I was with my cousin, who simply responded to the command as if it were second nature. This was not his first time. I, on the other hand, was home on winter break from my first semester in college, and after having just completed a seminar titled Debating Human Rights, I naively thought I should demand the reason for my search and debate with the officers. Before I could utter a word, the officers went ahead and patted both of us down and asked for our IDs.

"Can I ask why we are being searched?" I asked. My request went ignored, as we were never given a reason for the search. Before we could even ask for their badge numbers, one of the officers handed me my ID and wished me a "happy birthday." The experience left me distraught. After consulting with a friend, I decided the next day to call my local precinct to notify it of the incident and file a complaint. I was surprised when the operator informed me that the officers had reported the search, stating that the reason was because my cousin and I "fit a description."

In August of 2013, US District Court Judge Shira Scheindlin ruled that the NYPD's policy of collective suspicion was unconstitutional. The judge did not end stop-and-frisk; she ordered that police comply with a longstanding principle of civil liberties – that police stops must be based on a reasonable suspicion of criminal behavior – and ruled that they be monitored by an independent agent. A few months later, in November, a Federal Appeals Court panel blocked the ruling from going into effect and removed Judge Scheindlin from the case, questioning her impartiality and chastising her for speaking to the press (once to counter attacks from City Hall that she was unfair to police). Meanwhile, human rights organizations, activists, lawmakers and concerned citizens continue to work tirelessly to stop the NYPD's fear tactics. They are demanding an end to stop-and-frisk, the institution of checks and balances to reel in the power of the police, and increased transparency.

To be fair, my criticism of the NYPD is not directed at the poorly trained police officers caught up in a corrupt, arrogant and unethical system of criminal injustice. There are indeed hardworking officers struggling just to get by. Those officers do not set the culture of the NYPD; their actions simply reproduce an offensive culture that is shaped from upstairs: a culture that supports, defends and encourages abusive police practices. There is something fundamentally wrong with a system that allows officers to stop and search civilians simply because they fit a "description," meaning that they are black or Latino. There is more to it than the individual actions of any one police officer raping a woman at gunpoint[2] or lodging dozens of bullets in the bodies of innocent New Yorkers, such as Sean Bell and my fellow countryman Amadou Diallo. There are systemic abuses in the NYPD, and it is no surprise to those who live it.

2 On August 19, 2011 (just months after two NYPD officers were acquitted of rape despite considerable evidence they'd assaulted a young woman who was too drunk to get home on her own), Officer Michael Pena accosted a 25-year-old woman who was waiting for a ride to her first day on the job as a teacher in a Bronx school, then threatened to pump a bullet in her face and brutalized her in an alley. Pena was convicted of sodomy and other charges in 2012, but got a hung jury on the rape charges; three months later he pleaded guilty to two counts of rape rather than face retrial. (Ed.)

A Very Short History of Driving While Black

Scenes From the Highway Profiling Patrol

Jeffrey St. Clair

The issue of racial profiling by police briefly grabbed the attention of the press in June of 1999 when New Jersey Governor Christine Todd Whitman fired the head of the state police after he accused blacks and Hispanics of being more likely to be drug dealers and therefore deserving of heightened police scrutiny. Whitman earned glowing coverage for her swift action.

In fact, Whitman had sedulously ignored the problem for most of her term, insisting that racial profiling was not a practice of the state police. Even after two New Jersey state troopers fired eleven shots into a van carrying four black men on their way to a basketball clinic in 1998, Whitman clung to her contention that the action was not racially motivated. In 1995 a New Jersey state judge threw out charges against fifteen black drivers who, the judge concluded, had been pulled over without cause. During the trial it emerged that on a twenty-six mile stretch on the southern part of the New Jersey Turnpike minorities accounted for 46 percent of the drivers stopped, even though they accounted for only 15 percent of suspected speeders.

Whitman also kept her mouth shut when Emblez Longoria, a New Jersey state trooper, filed suit against his department claiming that he was being pressured to make illegal stops of black and Hispanic drivers in order to fulfill his arrest quotas. Longoria, who is Hispanic, alleges that he was denied promotions and harassed by his superiors when he refused to pull over drivers using racial profiling. Ultimately, the governor's hand was forced by the racist remarks of Col. Carl Williams, the head of the New Jersey State Police. Responding to a report showing that 75 percent of all motorists arrested on the New Jersey Turnpike in the first two months of 1997 were minorities, Williams told the *Newark Star-Ledger* that cocaine and marijuana traffickers were most likely to be either black or Hispanic.

Williams was canned, but that was it. The investigation of his department was put into the hands of Attorney General Peter Verniero, who has fiercely denied that New Jersey cops use profiling. Black leaders in New Jersey demanded that Verniero's investigation be taken up by an independent panel. Whitman refused and instead nominated Verniero (who obediently buried the troublesome issue) for a spot on the New Jersey Supreme Court.

Racial profiling is neither new nor isolated to the Garden State. Criminology has had these genetic typing obsessions as far back as the days of eugenicists such as Cesare Lombroso, who attempted to define criminal types through head shapes and other physical characteristics. Particularly influential in the US was Earnest Albert Hooten, a Harvard professor of anthropology and an appalling racist, who published *The American Criminal* in 1939. Now these racist theories have pervaded the policing system of the United States from coast to coast. To be a black driver in America is to invite police scrutiny, as thousands are daily singled out for groundless pullovers, "pretext" stops, and subjected to intrusive, warrantless searches and abusive treatment by police.

The problem is not merely one of racist cops but of a policing system that encourages and promotes racial typing. In Amherst, Massachusetts, the police department held seminars for its officers on "perpetrator profiles." The officers were told that "interracial couples" were more likely to be engaged in drug dealing than white couples.

In San Diego the police are ever vigilant to pull over black people driving expensive cars. In October of 1997 a black man named Shawn Lee and his girlfriend were stopped by the California Highway Patrol on Interstate 15. Lee, a member of the San Diego Chargers football team, and his girlfriend were handcuffed and held by police for more than an hour. The patrolman said that they were detained because Lee was driving a car that fit a description of one that had been reported stolen that night. That story was false. Lee was driving a new Jeep Grand Cherokee; the stolen vehicle was a Honda.

A similar kind of racial typing is evident up the coast in supposedly liberal Santa Monica. In the fall of 1996 a pair of police cars tailed Darryl Hicks and George Washington, two black men, as they pulled into the parking garage of their hotel. The police cruisers turned on their lights and at gunpoint ordered the men out of their car. The men were handcuffed and placed in separate police cars. Washington and Hicks's car was searched. The police claimed the men were being detained because they fit the description of suspects wanted in a string of nineteen armed robberies. The officers also said one of the men appeared to be "nervous." Washington and Hicks later sued the police officers for false arrest and civil rights violations. In ruling for the two men, the court determined that the armed robberies had not occurred in Santa Monica and that neither of the men fit the descriptions of the robbers.

In Carmel, Indiana, an affluent suburb of Indianapolis, a state trooper pulled over a black man named David Smith. The trooper was unaware that Smith was a sergeant in the Carmel Police Department and the sedan he was driving was actually an unmarked police car. Smith was ordered out of his car and, according to Smith, the trooper appeared to be "shocked and surprised" when he saw that Smith was wearing his police uniform. The trooper said he had pulled Smith over because he had three antennas on the back of his car.

A similar incident occurred in Orange County, Florida. In April of 1997, Aaron Campbell was pulled over by sheriff's deputies on the Florida Turnpike. The deputies ordered Campbell from the car, forced him to the pavement, drenched his face with pepper spray and arrested him. Campbell was a major in the Metro-Dade County Police Department and had identified himself as a policeman when he was pulled over. The Orange County deputies later said Campbell had been stopped for having an "obscured license tag" and for making an illegal lane change.

As is so often the case, the pretext for the profiling is the drug war, itself an ill-disguised form of state-sponsored racism. Nowhere has this kind of racial typing in the name of drug interdiction been used as aggressively as in Maryland, where since at least 1988 it has been the policy of the state troopers to pull over, detain and search drivers for drugs and guns, using a race-based "drug courier profile." According to the testimony of one Maryland state trooper, those race profiles explicitly targeted: "1) young, black males wearing expensive jewelry; 2) driving expensive cars, usually sports cars; 3) carrying beepers; and 4) in possession of telephone numbers."

In 1990 the state police set up a drug task force called Special Traffic Interdiction Force, or STIF. STIF targeted drivers along Interstate 95 in northeastern Maryland. The unit was composed of six white troopers. Over the course of six years, the STIF unit, using the drug courier profile, pulled over and searched black drivers four times as often as they did whites. One of the troopers, Bernard M. Donovan, searched only black drivers.

In 1992 the Maryland State Police's Criminal Intelligence Division developed a "Confidential Criminal Intelligence Report," which troopers used to make stops and searches based on race. The report encouraged troopers in Allegheny County to increase searches of black male drivers by saying that "the county is currently experiencing a serious problem with the incoming flow of crack cocaine." The "Intelligence Report" professed that "the dealers and couriers [traffickers] are predominantly black males and females."

"The Criminal Intelligence Report" came to light through a lawsuit filed in 1993 by Robert Wilkins. Wilkins, a Harvard Law School graduate, was a public defender in Washington, DC. In May of 1992 he was returning to DC from a family funeral in Ohio in a rented Cadillac. He was accompanied by his aunt, uncle and a 29-year-old cousin. Wilkins was pulled over by a trooper in western Maryland for speeding. He and his family were ordered out of the car and forced to stand in driving rain for more than an hour as the state trooper brought in drug-sniffing dogs to search the car. No drugs were found. Wilkins and the American Civil Liberties Union filed suit and, in 1995, won a substantial settlement from the Maryland State Police. As part of the Wilkins settlement, the state police agreed to compile a database of all stops of drivers on Maryland highways in which police ask to perform searches or in which a search is done by a drug-sniffing dog.

White motorists make up 78 percent of Maryland highway traffic, while black drivers account for about 17 percent and other minorities about 5 percent in the state. When the Wilkins data were submitted to the court in late 1998, they showed that between January 1, 1995, and December 15, 1997, more than 70 percent of the people who were stopped and searched on Interstate 95 were black and about 77 percent were minorities. Only about 23 percent were white. The data also revealed that the vast majority of drivers who were stopped and searched and not found to be carrying any drugs were also black, more than 67 percent. The ACLU used such data to bring a class action suit against the Maryland State Police.

Clearly, the Wilkins litigation did nothing to alter the racist practices of the Maryland troopers, as evidenced by the testimony of State Trooper Michael Lewis in a recent criminal case. Lewis told a court that he pulled over Robert Ware in large measure because he was a young black man. Lewis admitted that he factored in the race of drivers on a daily basis as part of his drug interdiction work. In late 1998, the Maryland State Police assigned Lewis to a post as an instructor, training other troopers in how to identify potential drug couriers on the state's highways.

One of the plaintiffs in the ACLU suit was Nelson Walker, a native of Liberia and a student at the University of North Carolina. In April of 1995, Walker was stopped on Interstate 95, purportedly for failure to have his seatbelt buckled. The trooper who pulled him over insinuated that his 1990 Infiniti was too nice a car for Walker to be driving and ordered Walker and his passenger out of the car. Drug-detecting dogs were summoned, and the car was searched. Walker and his friend, Mecca Agunabo I, were made to stand in the rain for nearly two hours while the car was searched.

When Agunabo said he needed to get out of the rain because he had recently recovered from a bout with pneumonia, the trooper threatened to arrest him. In a search for drugs, the troopers rummaged through the men's luggage and other personal belongings. Then the troopers largely dismantled Walker's car, tearing out a door panel, the back seat and part of the sunroof. No drugs were found. One of the troopers went to his cruiser and returned with a screwdriver, which he handed to Walker saying, "Here, you're going to need this."

Oscar Grant, Trayvon Martin and the Protection of Police Murder

Thandisizwe Chimurenga

Seconds before Oscar Grant was shot in the back on January 1, 2009, by Bay Area Rapid Transit (BART) Officer Johannes Mehserle, the words "bitch ass nigger" were yelled to Grant's face – twice – by Mehserle's mentor and "big brother," BART Officer Tony Pirone. Mehserle and Pirone brutally restrained an already compliant Grant by kneeling on his head and neck and lower legs, before Mehserle stood over Grant and fired a bullet into his back from a Sig Sauer 9mm pistol.

George Zimmerman, initially identified as a Neighborhood Watch captain who called police on February 26, 2012, to report Trayvon Martin as a "suspicious person," can be heard on the tape saying under his breath "fucking coons." Ignoring the police operator's directive not to pursue Martin, Zimmerman all but chased the teen down, confronted Martin and then shot the youth with his Kel Tek 9mm PF9 pistol once in the chest.

Once again a young black man was killed under highly questionable circumstances, and once again the perpetrator benefited from the "blue line" of protection and support that the brotherhood of law enforcement extends to its own automatically, regardless of facts, racial hostility or, ultimately, outcomes. The blue line of protection is in effect an extension of protection from a white supremacist state: anti-black violence is state-sanctioned violence.

Although Zimmerman is not a sworn representative of law enforcement, he assumed the role of and received treatment befitting the white vigilante, who historically has maintained close, fraternal and comradely ties with actual police agencies, and has been given the privileges of law enforcement by those same entitics. Zimmerman's actual status in The Retreat at Twin Lakes subdivision is less important than the perception of it. Literature distributed in the subdivision identifying safety tips carried Zimmerman's name and number. When police arrived on the scene of the shooting they treated him with the respect they would extend to a colleague. Several times in the police report of the first interview with him, Zimmerman is referred to simply as "George."

And, so, African-American fear that justice would not be served on the perpetrator in the murder of Trayvon Martin was neither imagined nor an overreaction; it was grounded in the concrete reality of the ways in which the blue line works. The following "glimpses" illuminate how that line works to shield law enforcement personnel and their allies from responsibility for heinous crimes.

1. *Slow response to arrest the perpetrator*

Johannes Mehserle was arrested almost two weeks after Grant's murder, following protests in Oakland that saw 100 people arrested and millions of dollars in damage, garnering national and international coverage. George Zimmerman was not formally charged with murder in the death of Martin until six weeks later, amid extensive nationwide protests that involved thousands of people. (Mehserle was convicted of involuntary manslaughter in Grant's death, sentenced to two years in state prison and released after spending one year in county jail. Zimmerman was found not guilty in the death of Martin and is now a free man.)

2. *The perpetrator is not deemed a threat to the (black) public's safety*

George Zimmerman was known to authorities to be fixated on crime and black males. He carried a pistol on his person, yet he had a violent past that included an arrest for assault on a police officer and several incidents of domestic violence. Since his acquittal, Zimmerman has had at least two more complaints lodged against him for assault/domestic violence. Approximately six weeks before shooting the unarmed Oscar Grant, Johannes Mehserle violently assaulted Kenneth Carruthers, an African-American man, for the latter's criticism of the BART police force after his car was broken into at a BART station parking lot. Carruthers alleged that Mehserle and other officers "punched, kicked and eventually hogtied" him and that while on the way to a hospital to treat his injuries Mehserle asked him, "Well, have you learned not to mess with police officers?"

3. *Legal statute shields the perpetrator before he is ever charged with a crime*

Immediately after shooting Trayvon Martin, George Zimmerman told police who responded to the scene that he shot Martin in self-defense. It was instantly assumed that he asserted his right under the state's Stand Your Ground law, which justifies deadly force if a person is gravely threatened in his or her home or in any public place. That was suitable to halt the police department from pursuing a thorough investigation of Zimmerman and the case.

In California, the Peace Officers' Bill of Rights Act, in conjunction with different parts of the state's penal code – "the law of the land" – keeps citizens from gaining access to the personnel files of police officers. Citing the officer's right to privacy, police departments keep us from learning whether an officer has a history of shootings (warranted or not) and brutality complaints.

4. *Legal requirements are either loosened, flaunted or thrown out altogether for the perpetrator*

The "Offenses Section" of an undated Sanford police report states that the shooting of Martin was "an unnecessary killing to prevent an unlawful act." It and another report, dated the night of the shooting, also references "HOMICIDE-NEGLIG MANSL" under "Charges," yet Zimmerman was not arrested. The form used by the BART authority for shootings involving its officers, which Johannes Mehserle signed, has a space marked for "accidental shootings." Mehserle's then-attorney requested a box be written on the form to indicate that his client's shooting of Oscar Grant was "intentional," and Mehserle initialed the box. This form was not allowed into court as evidence during Mehserle's criminal trial in Los Angeles. Zimmerman was not tested for drugs or alcohol immediately after the shooting; Mehserle was tested, but those results were also not allowed in court.

In spite of the Zimmerman police report listing the incident as a "needless killing," Zimmerman was not arrested because his explanation was automatically accepted. BART officers involved in on-duty shootings are required to give an in-person interview to the authority's internal investigators even though the content of the interview cannot be used against the BART officer. Mehserle resigned from the agency on the day of his scheduled interview with investigators.

5. *The victim may have had an unsavory background*

Oscar Grant was on parole from state prison at the time of his arrest, and in the past he had run from the police and had been shocked with a Taser. That information, spread wildly by police supporters and conservative groups, was also officially entered into evidence in court, partly to show that Grant was "prone" to resisting arrest. Conservative groups and law enforcement supporters began to insinuate that Trayvon Martin, who was under a school suspension at the time he was killed for possession of a pipe and a baggie with trace amounts of marijuana, may have committed more serious infractions.

6. *The victim was not a victim but an aggressor*

The group that Oscar Grant was traveling with on the BART train on New Year's Day 2009 was involved in some type of altercation. One witness states that Grant had been held in a headlock with a man, David Horowitch. Other witnesses could not identify who the person was who had been in the altercation with Horowitch. Police supporters also stated that Grant had attempted to assault Officer Pirone by kneeing him in the groin. Trayvon Martin was said to have been on top of George Zimmerman, punching him, which is why Zimmerman was observed with wet, grass-stained clothing and a bloody nose after chasing and confronting Martin. One commentator on a conservative website proclaimed that the now-ubiquitous photo of a sweatshirt-hooded Martin looking into a computer camera is "menacing."

7. *Because the victim was an aggressor, it was his own fault*

Law enforcement supporters have stated, and continue to state, that had Oscar Grant not been "fighting," "causing trouble" or "resisting arrest," he would be alive today. Trayvon Martin has been criticized for not answering Zimmerman's questions demanding to know his identity etc. once Zimmerman exited his vehicle and confronted Martin, and that had Martin simply chosen to go home, he might still be alive today.

8. *'Questionable conduct' as 'fellow officer sympathy and support'*

A woman who came forward as a witness to some of what occurred in the Trayvon Martin killing says that when she told an investigating officer that she heard Martin calling for help, she was corrected by the officer and told it was Zimmerman who had been calling for help. Officer Tony Pirone stated that he clearly remembered Mehserle say that he was going to tase Oscar Grant but did not clearly remember that Oscar Grant was allegedly trying to knee him in the groin. Additionally, Pirone and other officers testified that the scene of the incident was very unruly and that they feared for their lives to justify the shooting, when video evidence and witness testimony clearly showed that such was not the case.

9. *'Benefit of the doubt' gets taken to an entirely new level*

A regular person who used a firearm to shoot and kill someone would have been automatically detained, arrested and the case turned over to a district attorney, who would then make the final decision on whether to file charges or drop the case against the perpetrator. George Zimmerman's claim of self-defense was sufficient to send him home for the night after questioning by police. Johannes Mehserle refused to speak with BART investigators about what led to his shooting of Oscar Grant; he fled the state of California and went to Nevada. His bail was set by the court at $3 million, which was paid for by a nonprofit association of law enforcement officers, as were the fees of his legal defense team.

10. *The 'triers of fact' also toe the line*

Johannes Mehserle's trial for the murder of Oscar Grant was moved to Los Angeles County, where it was assigned to Judge Robert Perry, a former federal prosecutor. After the jury found Mehserle guilty of involuntary manslaughter and of intentionally using a gun, Perry dismissed the gun finding, saying he had erred in giving the jury proper instructions on the gun allegation, which would have automatically added ten years to Mehserle's sentence. Perry said the evidence in the trial did not show that Mehserle had intended to shoot Grant. He sentenced him to the lowest term possible – two years in state prison – and ordered Mehserle released from county jail (where he had been spending his sentence) after one year.

Judge Perry is known in Los Angeles as being a "friend of cops" due to his sentencing of Rafael Perez, the former LAPD officer at the center of the notorious late-1990s Rampart Scandal, to five years in state prison for his role in the beatings and shootings of several citizens and the planting of evidence on their persons. He ordered Perez's release from a local detention facility (not a state prison) after three years and allowed him to serve his parole out of state.

In Florida, Judge Debra Nelson made a number of rulings that allowed George Zimmerman's defense team essentially to put Trayvon Martin on trial, and the prosecutors seemingly threw the case, allowing Zimmerman to walk free.

To date, there is no concrete evidence that Zimmerman received any leniency from the courts or benefitted in any way due to the fact that his father, Robert, is a retired magistrate judge and his mother, Gladys, was a court interpreter; however, his familial connection to the criminal justice system is still worth noting.

11. *Support remains regardless of the level of callousness and inhumanity*

George Zimmerman used foul language and a racial slur in reference to Trayvon Martin. Some 911 callers reported the 17-year-old Martin may have been wailing for help before being shot to death. Oscar Grant, who had also been cursed at and called a racial slur, can be seen on the videos taken by BART train riders as being on his knees, seemingly pleading with Officer Tony Pirone not to harm him. His head and neck would soon be pinned under the knee of the 200-plus-pound officer, and a witness said Grant told the officer "he could not breathe."

George Zimmerman was initially identified in the media as being white. His father later wrote to the press that his son was "a Spanish-speaking minority" ... "more like the boy he killed than people thought." Being a person of color in the United States does not make one immune to white supremacist ideology or behavior on its behalf. When it comes to white supremacist violence against black people, the blue line has often overlooked color and/or ethnicity as long as the violence is anti-black.

As it turns out, Zimmerman was not part of any official Neighborhood Watch, and had designated himself as "captain." In settling a wrongful death claim brought by the family of Trayvon Martin, The Retreat at Twin Lakes Homeowners Association admitted on April 5, 2013, that it had never set any parameters or guidelines for a Neighborhood Watch, or ensured that neighborhood personnel were properly trained and supervised. In a nutshell, it was negligent, allowing Zimmerman to represent himself as acting in an official capacity, to operate freely – in spite of complaints by his neighbors that he took his job "too zealously."

Obviously, he wanted to be "one of the boys," and members of the Sanford, Florida, Police Department treated him like one.

And both history and current reality show that "boys will be boys."

Terrorist

David 'Judah 1' Oliver

They use my tax money for WAR
It makes me wanna
Match a match
With a tank of gasoline
Somewhere within my bloodline
Lies a terrorist in between
bar Kochba with a dagger
Nat Turner with a burner
No, call me Hannibal with a pen.
When all your enemies' skin
Is darker than yours,
Indeed you breed your own Terrorists
Turn purity into bitterness
Label us "Heathen"
Still you wanna assimilate this:
Our minds,
Our civilization,
Our religion,
Our resources.
And don't cry when you find
Your daughter fiend for this
Eight to ten inch....

You threatened by my mind
So you pack your erectile dysfunction
With a nuclear tip
You got:
Bigger bombs,
Bigger planes,
Bigger tanks,
Bigger house,
Bigger car,
Smaller wife.
What more do you need?!?
You go to other lands
And import the best seeds
So you can have bigger trees.
But in 2008
You still can't hide your bigotry

And we see you from
N.Y.
to
L.A.
P.D.
Jena 6
Gave the nation a better sense
Of Judicial Injustice

I remember in elementary
Getting jumped by the same three white kids on a weekly
Yet I was the one to be suspended.
Laws are not equal,
Economics are segregated
In 2007
They said a shoe was a deadly weapon.
But bombs are still justified?!?

I damn near cried,
Sean Bell was unarmed when he was murdered by the Police
He was shot 50 times.

I damn near cried,
He was shot 50 times.

Sean Bell was murdered by the Police
Yet, somehow they was found "not guilty"
Bet if I burn some buildings down
They gonna find a "Terrorist" in me
And if I blow up a gas station,
Will they feel my indignation?!?

This Roman Babylonian Government
Makes me wanna
Match a match
With a tank of gasoline
Somewhere within my bloodline
Lies a Terrorist in between
Judah Maccabee with an army
Marcus Garvey with a BlackStar
No, call me Sun Tzu with a pen.

(2008)

The Cancer of Police Violence

Mike King

Police brutality and murder are arguably the plainest expressions of racialized state power in the United States. To say they are epidemic, however, as many have, is a simplification. An epidemic is an indiscriminate force of nature, seemingly emerging from nowhere, affecting people at random, often with a cure that is elusive. Epidemics grab hold of the public's attention, demand strategies for containment and prompt a universal concern that a cure must be sought. Police violence, specifically police murder, is not new, seemingly random or mysterious as to cause and cure. It is well understood in urban communities of color, yet hardly captures the national imagination. Counterpose national responses to "invasions" of killer bees, West Nile virus or Avian flu (themsleves fueld by a manic Orientalism) and attention to findings that a black person is killed by police or others acting "under the color of law" every twenty-eight hours.

The continued gap between what America says it is and what it actually is finds no clearer illumination than through racialized state violence. It is a gap that consistently finds its starkest expression through the end of a police officer's gun, with periodic and spontaneous reciprocal violence taking the form of broken windows, looted stores and burnt buildings. From Watts in 1965 and Detroit and dozens more cities in the late '60s, to Miami in 1980, Los Angeles in 1992, Cincinnati in 2001, Oakland in 2009 – with other uprisings in between – resistance and demands for change have accompanied persistent police violence. But the cycle persists. Riots have been "the rhyme of the unheard," the ringtone from an alarm clock on which America has consistently hit the snooze button. Riots have also left burnt factories, warehouses and storefronts that have helped solidify capital flight and deindustrialization in neighborhoods within cities like Los Angeles and Detroit. The charred former shells of industrial production stand as broken monuments to rebellions long past, their use as good places to get high an index of pain unresolved, as structural violence persists and deepens.

White America: from active participation to duplicitous blind eye

Under Jim Crow, there was an average of one lynching a week for almost a century. A key difference between yesterday's weekly lynching and today's six killings a week lies in the visibility and the conscious complicity of white America. While the white terrorism that was lynching drew out many in their Sunday best to actively participate and revel in, the sanitized modern equivalent is something that white America prefers to ignore, something it doesn't publicly celebrate but shows little sign of wanting to change, either. Today, racist violence is a practice white people would rather not have to think about, not see and not feel morally complicity in.

In whatever era, the extrajudicial killing of black people is rooted in white supremacy and the dehumanization of dark bodies necessary to maintain the existing order. A combination of psychological projection and self-exoneration arises to rationalize the persistent horror that white supremacy has itself uncoiled – from the fear of slave revolts, to the fear that a white woman may have been whistled at, to the fear that a black family is moving next door or black kids are getting bussed to white-flight schools, to the fear that every hoodie hides a weapon, or every cell phone is a gun.

To keep with the medical metaphor, institutionalized racial violence is more like metastatic cancer, a deadly mutation of cells already present in this political order, cells built into the very nature of "American democracy" – the primary condition that has kept it forever fragmented, hypocritical and lying to itself with one eye closed so as not to see its own behavior.

The police do not call their persistent violence an epidemic or a cancer. They call it a war – a war on drugs, a war on gangs, a war on crime. They train with US and foreign military units as if it were a war; they have the same body armor and the same weapons as foreign troops; they have been known to call *themselves* an occupying force. They criminalize whole communities, which many police-soldiers patrol with an irrational fear, with predictable results of unwarranted violence. "Collateral damage" is expected. The language, the practice and the popular understanding of urban policing as a form of warfare does not just rationalize police violence. It allows the American public as a whole to disconnect from it morally, the same way people distance themselves from responsibility for this country's foreign neocolonial wars. This "war" is seen to take place "someplace else," and due to persistent segregation, it does – the same way that prison is seen to be outside of society and is often physically remote as well. And yet, if this is a war being fought against communities in cities and towns all over the country, it needs to be a war with two sides, a war where there are no sidelines, no space for the glib normalization of violence or false positions of moral unculpability.

Making America face the diagnosis, toward a politics of cure

"Power cedes nothing without a demand," Frederick Douglass said. Change comes most often from the coupling of organized and networked grassroots agitation from below with the translation of festering problems long ignored into political issues that demand resolution or immanent reckoning. Discussions are starting to emerge in Oakland, in California more broadly, and nationally to forge a coordinated effort to address this cancer of police violence.

In November of 2012 a march in Oakland brought together the families of Alan Blueford, Derrick Gaines, Idriss Stelley, Jared Huey and Oscar Grant, all lost to Bay Area police violence. More than 500 people marched, demanding the firing of Oakland Police Officer Miguel Masso, who shot Alan Blueford that May under questionable circumstances, and for justice for all of those killed by police. The Bluefords had just got back from New York, where they gave speeches and attended meetings with the family of Ramarley Graham – killed that January by an NYPD officer while trying to flush marijuana down his grandmother's toilet – and from Pennsylvania, where they met with Mumia Abu-Jamal.

The families who marched alongside the Bluefords don't just share a lost loved one, or questions unanswered, or justice denied. They share a missing piece of themselves. Those missing pieces are all the result of deadly force used not as a last resort but as "normal" practice. Common to all these families' stories is a combination of police unaccountability, fear, violence and intimidation as the primary means of communication. This makes racial profiling and police unaccountability – the before and after that create and re-create the cycle of police violence – a logical point of coherence, solidarity and mutual struggle. Diagnosing this condition means challenging the benefit of the doubt that police get, compelling the public at large to deal with the dehumanizing suspicion and fear of occupied populations and making policing a political issue.

The Justice for Alan Blueford Coalition is seeking more than immediate justice for Alan. The Bluefords are demanding that Masso be made to account for his actions, while simultaneously they are building a wider Bay Area struggle to take on racial profiling and the California Police Officers' Bill of Rights, a key legal foundation that enables police misconduct by helping to shield cops like Masso.

The building of non-sectarian campaigns, networks and organizations to address root causes and issues like racial profiling on a regional and national scale is long overdue. It is a process being forged by a number of like-minded groups that are outside of the formal constraint of those clamoring for funds and legitimacy from city officials and foundations. The Oscar Grant movement tried to make this transition from the original core goal of justice for Oscar toward addressing police violence more broadly but failed due to a combination of sectarianism, repression and organizer burn-out, among other factors. Nevertheless, around the country there are movements in numerous cities trying to make that transition. And whether we call it an epidemic, or a cancer, or an occupation, or terrorism, there is widespread sentiment that policing along with mass incarceration are the major civil rights issues of our time. There is some cause for hope that this activity we are seeing will cohere into a civil/human rights struggle.

Although the specifics of the case do not involve uniformed police but rather vigilantism, the killing of Trayvon Martin has brought national attention to racial profiling and violence. By making policing a political issue, whether vigilante citizen policing or vigilante uniformed policing, structural change around racial violence, and the broader racial inequalities it upholds, can be more squarely put on the table.

The struggle to make police violence a political issue involves more than raising awareness to the everyday realities that so many people face in poor communities – particularly poor black and Latino communities – but realities so few see, and even fewer see for what they are. The causes are deeper than rogue cops or rogue individuals, "bad apples"; and real solutions are broader than reforming the police. Change will involve bringing all who get their understanding of the inner city from the 11 o'clock news, or all who are comfortable with their ability to rationalize brutality, to recognize their position. It would be naïve (to say the least) to base a strategy for racial justice on the good will of the American people. But by placing moral responsibility in their lap, alongside the police and political structures, the choice between humanity and violence can be made unavoidable and clear. By demanding substantial structural changes to the nature of policing, a radical project of our own making, we can begin to materialize the power necessary not only to identify the roots of the problem but also to rip them out and burn them once and for all.

For a National Alliance for Racial Justice and Human Rights

Ajamu Baraka

The irrelevant, disconnected, abstract chatter that we see on the "mainstream" human rights listserves as it relates to issues that concern black and oppressed communities – and concomitant complete lack of substantive discussion about the Trayvon Martin case – demonstrates once again the need for a formation that centers the perspectives, interests and political objectives of human rights defenders from oppressed communities who are grounded in a radical understanding of human rights.

Mainstream formations dominated by middle-class lawyers seem to be unable to see or understand the major impact that Trayvon Martin's case is having in the black community, and the progressive social change movement in general. Limited by their race and class perspectives (including "people of color" who have not dealt with their internalized white supremacist influences), and lacking any connection to grassroots organizations or popular social change networks, alliances or coalitions, they are unable to grasp when conditions are created that could allow for the advancement of a human rights understanding and framing that could influence the national discourse.

Hamstrung by a stale, mechanistic approach to human rights work dictated and controlled by the narrow and confused priorities of liberal funders who only pay lip service to supporting social change efforts not tied to the interests of the Democratic Party, the elites of the mainstream human rights movement in the US will either opportunistically co-opt an issue (especially if there are funding opportunities to be had – think national security and human rights, racial profiling and so-called immigrant rights) or, as in this case, largely ignore it.

Yet, within the mainstream human rights circles there are decent and dedicated people who understand the limitations of a domestic movement that is dominated by middle-class lawyer advocates and 501(c) NGOs. They understand that the only way that the human rights movement in the US can escape the class-based fragmentation and opportunism that characterize so much of the approach to human rights work is to ground the movement in the interests, perspectives, objectives and leadership of the black, Latino, indigenous and oppressed communities that are dedicated to anti-colonialism, anti-imperialism, anti-oppression (in all its forms) and self-determination. This should not be paternalistic "empowerment" but a renouncing of class privilege and gatekeeping – a getting out of the way so that authentic democratic leadership and processes can emerge out of a social change movement that is embracing a radical people-centered approach to human rights.

We know that the displacement of opportunism will not come about as a result of appeals to morality and conscience alone. We are not that naïve. There are powerful material incentives (including the ability to secure and waste literally hundreds of thousands of dollars) and non-material advantages that ensure that the various cabals of gatekeepers won't give up easily. It is only through self-organization and independence that we will be able to develop and advance a people's agenda for human rights, democracy and social justice. That is why a National Alliance for Racial Justice and Human Rights is needed.

This would be an alliance of human rights defenders who understand an analytical framework informed by human rights principles that elucidate and give life to the connection between the political demands for self-determination for all oppressed nations and peoples, and the peoples' insistence on dignity – expressed through the demands for the right to education, housing, health and health care, a clean environment, water, individual and collective development, real social security throughout life and an end to all forms of racial, gender (patriarchal), sexual, national, ethnic and religious oppression.

Those who take such an approach to human rights advancement understand that these demands will be realized only when there is a shift in power away from the capitalist state and the white supremacist Republican and Democratic parties (the advancement of the interests of the white supremacist 1 percent is not dependent on the color of its agents!) to the organized people. This shift will require struggle and organization. An alliance of human rights defenders who recognize the historic tasks that this period demands will greatly facilitate the creation of an "alternative bloc" of the 99 percent.

As horrific as the killing of Martin was, the cold objective fact is that every few years a case emerges, whether it is Oscar Grant or Sean Bell, just to mention a couple of contemporary cases, that reminds us of the disparate value that is placed on black life by the agents of white authority. As human rights defenders who have an internationalist understanding and perspective, we would be morally remiss and politically irresponsible if we did not link the devaluation of Trayvon's life to the general devaluation of non-white life that is a permanent feature of European and US imperialism worldwide. The initial non-indictment of Trayvon's killer should not have surprised anyone with just a cursory understanding of what this country stands for and its real interests – from the "collateral damage" of predatory drone strikes in Yemen, Pakistan, Afghanistan and Somalia to the killings of seventeen women and children by a US occupation soldier in Afghanistan to the killings, torture and assaults perpetrated by the US and its NATO criminal gang allies against people of color. All exemplify a lack of respect for non-white life. Sanford, Florida, is not very different from southern Afghanistan in that respect.

So while we mourn the death of Martin we must also remember the countless victims whose names we will never know and who have lost their lives at the hands of racist police, 500-pound bombs made in the US or vicious mercenaries and economic sanctions. Those who understand that we must struggle against precisely those enemies in our fight for our human rights must work together to build a powerful alliance for racial justice and human rights.

Gun Laws and Race in America

Robert Chase and Yohuru Williams

"The simple fact is we are not safe. Not in our homes, not anywhere... People now cannot walk on their streets without fear of crime!" Interestingly, those are not the words of people around the nation protesting over the slaying of Florida teen Trayvon Martin. Rather, they were the words of admonition and fear used by Jeb Bush to kick off his 1998 campaign for governor of Florida. Once in office, Bush burnished his law-and-order credentials by pushing through two laws that now stand at the heart of the Trayvon Martin and George Zimmerman controversy.

The first, Stand Your Ground (SYG), extends the concept of no "duty to retreat" beyond the home and into public space. The second, which has received less media attention, is the 10-20-Life mandatory minimum gun laws that mock any notion of equal justice in their disproportionate application against people of color. Although scores of pundits have taken to the airwaves to profess to us all that the law is color blind, the implementation of both of these cornerstone Bush-era statutes demonstrates disturbing racial disparities and deep, historically rooted mythologies concerning public fears over guns and race.

With the catchy legislative slogan of "Use a Gun and You're Done," the 10-20-Life law, implemented in 1999, set mandatory minimum sentences in Florida for any convicted felon who carried, displayed or used a gun during a crime. Rather than act as a separate charge, these mandatory minimums were to serve as "sentence enhancements," denying even a judge's ability to lessen the sentence. Under the law, penalties escalate depending on the use of the firearm. In cases of simple possession, those convicted receive a mandatory minimum sentence of three years; those who use a gun receive ten years; those that fire a gun receive twenty years; and if a victim was injured or killed by a gun during a crime, the state imposes a mandatory minimum sentence of twenty-five years to life in prison.

Since Governor Bush signed off on the 10-20-Life law, African-Americans have made up the largest percentage (64 percent, or 2,482 individuals) convicted under the law. Whites, by contrast, account for only 33 percent (1,284) of the convictions, and Hispanics only 2.6 percent, according to Florida Department of Corrections statistics from 1999 to 2006. The racial disparity is even more glaring when reviewing the length of the sentences imposed by race. Perhaps, not surprisingly, African-Americans receive much longer sentences (a mean of over eight years). In addition, fifty-nine of the life sentences imposed have been on African-Americans, compared with nineteen for whites.

In addition to the political capital garnered from these laws with certain constituencies, the Florida legislature recognized another benefit. Prior to enacting 10-20-Life, lawmakers considered how this statute might affect the state prison system. The legislators discovered that a booming prison construction business in the 1990s left the state with a surplus of 4,000 to 5,000 prison beds. With "zero tolerance" for those that carried or used a firearm during the commission of a crime, this proposed legislation promised to "make our streets safer," as supporters' rhetoric put it, by adding to the prison system 3,887 new inmates, who had longer stays because they carried or used a gun.

Although the Zimmerman defense team chose not to evoke a Stand Your Ground hearing – in which George Zimmerman would have had to testify and answer for his contradictory public statements – we should place Trayvon Martin's shooting within the context of a national trend that shows that states with Stand Your Ground laws have experienced more homicides.

According to a 2012 study by two researchers at Texas A&M University, economics professors Cheng Cheng and Mark Hoekstra, the rates of murder and non-negligent manslaughter increased by 8 percent in states with a Stand Your Ground law. That has meant an additional 600 homicides annually in states that have enacted such laws.

In Florida alone, a recent study by the *Tampa Bay Times* found a racial disparity of immunity from prosecution under the law. In a case sample of 200 Stand Your Ground hearings, the newspaper found that 73 percent of individuals who killed a black person avoided prosecution, while 59 percent of those who killed a white person were given immunity.

Moreover, in a study of "justified homicides," which are defined by the FBI as those incidents in which a private citizen kills someone who is committing a felony, John Roman of the Urban Institute's Justice Policy Center found that in Stand Your Ground states whites were more likely to be found justified when killing an African-American than when killing another white person. In an analysis of the Supplemental Homicide Reports (SHR) submitted by local law enforcement to the FBI between 2005 and 2010, Roman found that when the shooter in these states is white and the victim is white, the percentage of shootings ruled justifiable is 11 percent. When the shooter is black and the victim also black, the rate of justifiable homicides is 8 percent. However, when the shooter is white and the victim is black, the justifiable rate jumps to 34 percent. While clothed in the language of legal color blindness, the real-life implementation of Stand Your Ground has simultaneously increased the number of homicides while also threatening to provide legal justification for the killing of black people by white people.

The story of Jacksonville, Florida, resident Marissa Alexander speaks to the disturbing double-sided racial nature of these two supposed color-blind gun laws. In 2010, Alexander fired a warning shot in the air when her husband, who had a history of domestic violence, threatened her. In 2012, however, a Florida judge rejected her plea for immunity under the Stand Your Ground law. In a subsequent trial she was found guilty, and received a twenty-year sentence under the mandatory minimum prescribed by the 10-20-Life law.

Her story and Trayvon Martin's killing provide the starkly ironic reminder that the "we" Jeb Bush spoke of in 1999 was far from inclusive. The fate of two shooters, one "white-Hispanic" and one black, speaks to the highly problematic racial nature of such laws in a state where guns and gun violence are sanctioned as self-protection for whites, on the one hand, and imbued with a deep fear of armed African-Americans, on the other. As the nation grapples with the injustice that Trayvon Martin and Marissa Alexander experienced, we should recall that Bush-era crime and justice policies have simultaneously criminalized African-Americans and endangered the lives of black people. Indeed, these cases remind the nation that African-Americans in Florida and in other Stand Your Ground states are "not safe, not in our homes, not anywhere."

The New Vigilantes

Chris Kromm

In 2007, 61-year-old Joe Horn looked out the window of his Pasadena, Texas, home and saw a pair of black men in his neighbors' yard, apparently involved in a burglary. Horn called 911, and, as journalist Liliana Segura would later report, became agitated, deciding he needed to stop the crime himself. "I've got a shotgun," Horn told the 911 dispatcher. "You want me to stop him?"

The dispatcher tried to talk him down. "Nope, don't do that," he told Horn. "Ain't no property worth shooting somebody over, OK?" It was not OK with Horn. With the dispatcher still on the phone, he grabbed his gun, went outside, yelled, "Move, you're dead!" – and shot the two men in the back.

Both men, Colombian immigrants Diego Ortiz and Miguel de Jesus, were declared dead on the scene.

The details of the case differ somewhat from the shooting of Trayvon Martin in Florida that's generated a national uproar. There is no evidence, for example, that 17-year-old Martin was engaged in any criminal act. But the two fatal shootings also share eerie similarities: both involved black "suspects" being gunned down by armed, non-black residents taking the law into their own hands. In both cases, the emergency dispatchers tried to prevent a vigilante shooting.

And both cases ignited debate about state laws – pushed aggressively over the past decade by the nation's gun lobby – that allow people who aren't law enforcement officials to use deadly force on the mere suspicion that someone else is putting their life or property at risk, a decision easily infused with racial stereotypes.

In 2005, Florida passed the first Stand Your Ground law in the country. It was an expansion on the Castle Doctrine, a legal concept now codified by more than twenty states that declares individuals have the right to defend their person or homes with force

Stand Your Ground, which was signed by Governor Jeb Bush, took the concept one step further. Even away from the home, the statute says, a person can "meet force with force." The law further "provides that a person is justified in using deadly force under certain circumstances," and "provides immunity from criminal prosecution or civil action for using deadly force."

As many predicted, the vague measure opened the door for a rise in vigilante shootings. As the *Tampa Bay Times* reported in October 2010, "justifiable homicides" tripled after the law went into effect. By 2009, two deadly shootings a week were being excused as warranted under the new law.

Florida's rise in extralegal deadly shootings reflects a national trend: as more states have enacted laws embracing the Castle Doctrine or variations of Stand Your Ground, the number of justifiable homicides has also grown.

According to FBI crime statistics, in 2005 there were 196 cases nationally where a killing was deemed justifiable. By 2010, that number had grown to 278, leading critics to warn about a rising "shoot-first mentality" that was taking hold in states with the new laws.

Only twenty lawmakers voted against Florida's Stand Your Ground bill in 2005, which is largely a testament to the power of the state's gun lobby.

The shoot-first lobby

The lead figure pushing the bill was infamous National Rifle Association lobbyist Marion Hammer. Hammer earned notoriety in the 1980s when she called those supporting a tweak to the state's conceal/carry law a "modern-day Gestapo" tactic.

Republicans quickly distanced themselves from Hammer then, saying she had "lost any effectiveness or credibility she might have" with such inflammatory rhetoric. One said she had the "lowest standard of integrity I have ever seen for a lobbyist" in Florida.

Hammer wasn't deterred. In 1996 she told *The New York Times* that the solution to the nation's gun debate was to "get rid of all liberals."

That was tame compared with the demagoguery Hammer used to push SB 436, the Stand Your Ground bill. She labeled all opponents – among them, police chiefs from cities including Miami and St. Petersburg, the National District Attorneys Association and the Florida Prosecuting Attorneys Association – as "bleeding heart criminal coddlers" who wanted Florida residents to "turn around and run" instead of protect their family and property.

Even though they couldn't point to a single case where a law-abiding gun owner had been prosecuted for legitimate self-defense, Hammer and the gun lobby even stoked fears that without their proposed law residents would be left "on their own" in the supposed fight for survival after hurricanes.

Concerns that the law might lead to a tragedy like Trayvon Martin's shooting? "Emotional hysterics," they said.

Florida Republicans not only passed Stand Your Ground; they later successfully lobbied to install Hammer in the Florida Women's Hall of Fame.

The victory in Florida emboldened the NRA to push for more state laws to allow the use of deadly force. As of January 2012, thirty states had some version of the Castle Doctrine; seventeen states, clustered in the South and West, have versions of the more aggressive Stand Your Ground law. The NRA has pledged to bring a version of the law to all fifty states.

Legal killing?

Now in the wake of the shooting of Trayvon Martin, the authors of Stand Your Ground in Florida are saying the law shouldn't apply to George Zimmerman.

Because the police dispatch tape clearly indicates Zimmerman decided to pursue Martin, they say, that rules out the "justifiable" use of force. As McClatchy News Service reported: "'They got the goods on him. They need to prosecute whoever shot the kid,' said [former Senator Durell] Peaden, a Republican who sponsored the deadly force law in 2005. 'He has no protection under my law.'"

But what if Martin's shooting hadn't caught national attention, thanks to an explosion of celebrity tweets and other social media? As of this writing, local police have yet to charge Zimmerman in the shooting, which they have claimed falls under the self-defense statute – a decision they made based on Zimmerman's increasingly untenable assertion that he was being attacked.

In Texas in 2007, Joe Horn also claimed that he "was afraid for his life" in justifying his fatal shooting of Ortiz and de Jesus. As in the Martin case, the 911 tapes are damning as evidence that Horn's life was clearly never at risk; that he, like Zimmerman, *pursued* the supposed burglars, even though they weren't even on his own property.

In the summer of 2008, Joe Horn was cleared of any wrongdoing. A grand jury failed to indict him, due largely to the Castle Doctrine law that came into effect in 2007.

Indeed, the 911 tapes demonstrate that Horn knew about the law, and guessed that it would give him immunity to shoot, even though his claim to self-defense was shaky at best. As Horn told the dispatcher, who was vainly trying to dissuade him from shooting: "I have a right to protect myself, too, sir.... And the laws have been changed in this country since September the first, and you know it and I know it."

As Stephanie Storey, the fiancee of one of the men killed by Horn, would later say: "This man took the law into his own hands. He shot two individuals in the back after having been told over and over to stay inside. It was his choice to go outside, and his choice to take two lives.

And, thanks to the laws of vigilante justice in Texas and beyond, it was all perfectly legal.

Fatal Encounters

D. Brian Burghart

May 18, 2012: I was on my way home from work when I noticed a bunch of cop cars down by the Truckee River in Reno. As the editor of a newspaper, the *Reno News & Review*, I was curious. We're a weekly, so we don't much cover the police beat – not the day-to-day stuff anyway – but it's my nature to satisfy my curiosity. So when I got home, I launched the police scanner app on my cell phone, fired up my laptop and poured a glass of red wine.

It turned out the police had pulled over a stolen car, and they'd shot and killed the driver. (Jace Herndon, 41, we found out later.) Honestly – and not because I'm one of those hard-boiled, cynical types – I wasn't particularly surprised or offended. Criminals often come to a bad end.

But I'm an editor, so I noticed when a gaping hole appeared in every single news story I read about the incident. There was no context. I kept looking for a sentence that said something like "This was the *x* person killed by police in Washoe County this year."

It was never there. I searched the web for a few minutes, came up short and started doing something more productive. I simply considered the missing information a failing of the local news media, and I moved on. Still, the lack of context bugged me. I felt as though I'd accidentally left my wallet on my nightstand; while I knew I could retrieve it if I needed to, not having it was bothersome.

Herndon, as the local media portrayed him, was a hard guy to feel sorry for. He was a tweeker, a meth addict, a junkie. He was also a thief, a violent four-time felon who'd spent time in prison. He was, in addition though unreported, a father, a husband, a guy who laid tile for a living, the lead singer of a local Christian band named Risen and member of a church called A Voice in the Wilderness, which ministers to people who crave redemption from drugs and alcohol. The pastor, Danny Rost, said Herndon was struggling with his addiction. Before his fatal encounter with Reno police a "friend" of Herndon's told a detective he was on his way to trade a stolen Pontiac Grand Am for $100 and an ounce of meth. When cornered by police and ordered to show his hands, Herndon is said to have yelled, "Fuck you, you're going to have to shoot me." Dr. Ellen Clark of the Washoe County Medical Examiner's Office found fifteen bullet wounds in his body. In the car, two knives and a baseball bat-shaped club were found. One of the knives was designed to look like a revolver with brown wooden grips, a trigger guard and a hammer and a flip-out blade. He'd brought knives to a gunfight.

A few months later, on December 6, 2012, an 18-year-old naked and unarmed college student, Gil Collar, was shot to death by a University of South Alabama policeman. Early reports said the kid never got within five feet of the officer, and no less-lethal methods to subdue him were tried.

It was a national news story. But, again, a complete lack of context. And this wasn't some mid-sized city's overburdened media workforce not reporting; these were the nation's biggest news sources – the Associated Press, *The New York Times*. I began to search in earnest, but nowhere could I find out how many people died during interactions with police in the United States. There are all kinds of articles that point out the lack of data, the best being the Las Vegas *Review-Journal*'s series "Deadly Force," which stated on November 28, 2011: "The nation's leading law enforcement agency [FBI] collects vast amounts of information on crime nationwide, but missing from this clearinghouse are statistics on where, how often, and under what circumstances police use deadly force. In fact, no one anywhere comprehensively tracks the most significant act police can do in the line of duty: take a life."

Try as I might, I just can't wrap my head around that idea. In the twenty-first century, the only reason this information would not be tracked, databased and available to the public is because somebody somewhere decided Americans shouldn't know how many people are killed by police and under what circumstances.

No Big Brother conspiracy theory is necessary. The information is out there. It's not censored or hidden, even if it is underreported. Certainly, though, it's uncollected by the logical entity to assemble it, the US Department of Justice.

But it is out there.

Somebody just has to collect it. And so I began fatalencounters.org. The goal: a comprehensive, searchable database of people who die for any reason through encounters with police.

Why no database?

The first thing reporters say to me when I say there is no national database of people killed by law enforcement is "Bullshit." Almost to a person, they believe I missed something somewhere, and the database exists. Almost no one questions whether it should exist; after all, agencies with nothing to hide would have nothing to fear from transparency.

So, despite my certainty, I started looking systematically for it, keeping track as I did of other databases that might assist in making the information publicly available once I figured out how to collect it. I also talked to various colleagues at the Donald W. Reynolds School of Journalism at the University of Nevada, Reno, where I teach beginning reporting.

While I found many different, helpful types of lists and databases online that I have used to devise a strategy for collection and publication of this project, only a few provided more than inspiration.

Homicide Watch D.C. (http://homicidewatch.org) – which says of itself, "Using original reporting, court documents, social media, and the help of victims' and suspects' friends, family, neighbors and others, we cover every homicide from crime to conviction" – is an incredible site, allowing users to drill down by name, death date, age, gender, race, cause of death, incorporating location and public documents.

There's also an awesome series called "Deadly Force: Police & the mentally ill," which was published by the *Portland Press Herald/Maine Sunday Telegram* in December 2012 (http://www.pressherald.com/special/Maine_police_deadly_force_series_final.html).

The most comprehensive list of people killed by police that I found was on Wikipedia (http://en.wikipedia.org/wiki/List_of_killings_by_law_enforcement_officers_in_the_United_States). It's a surprisingly good effort, far wider than it is deep, but it links to more than 1,000 possible instances, and it will, with caveats, be included in the first version of my database. Other than its "dirty" data and lack of credentialed authority, its biggest drawback is that it is just a list, allowing for no comparisons the way a proper database does. Many entries seem sketchy to me, like one instance in which "law enforcement" was a Wal-Mart security guard, or those in which the person killed is unnamed. Still, there is enough information present to follow up, to verify and fill in facts, so I made a spreadsheet that I and others are filling in with the missing parts: http://tinyurl.com/cz3rafa.

A couple of "gun death" databases I find very interesting, both from crowdsourcing and straight journalism points of view. The first is *Mother Jones*'s "Guide to Mass Shootings in America" (http://www.motherjones.

com/politics/2012/07/mass-shootings-map). Its publicly accessible spreadsheet on Google Docs is instructive (https://docs.google.com/spreadsheet/ccc?key=0AswaDV9q95oZdG5fVGJTS25GQXhSTDFpZXE0RHhUdkE#gid=0), and the Twitter feed submissions @GunDeaths are intriguing means of crowdsourcing.

I also found Slate's database "How Many People Have Been Killed by Guns Since Newtown?" provocative, although it doesn't allow me to drill down as far as I'd like. A few words about circumstances would be handy, because I notice some of the deaths listed were a result of police interactions. Slate has passed the data onto Michael Klein's Gun Violence Archive project (www.gunviolencearchive.org).

In my researches I found more Internet sources than I could enumerate; what follows are some good ones:

Seattle Post-Intelligencer: http://www.seattlepi.com/local/article/List-of-2012-homicides-in-Seattle-4230418.php

Los Angeles Times Data Desk: http://datadesk.latimes.com/

Wichita Eagle: http://www.kansas.com/news/databases/#navlink=navdrop

Propublica: www.propublica.org/tools/

Center for Investigative Reporting: http://cironline.org

Guidestar: www.guidestar.org/

Open secrets: www.opensecrets.org/

Center for Public Integrity: www.publicintegrity.org/

GlobalPost: www.globalpost.com/special-reports

International Consortium of Investigative Journalists: www.icij.org

Documenting innocent victims of police violence: http://www.innocentdown.org

The Las Vegas *Review-Journal* "Deadly Force" series: www.lvrj.com/deadlyforce. This database is especially handy, and any national model could be based upon it.

Investigative Reporters & Editors, which through the National Institute for Computer-Assisted Reporting has a treasure trove of databases: http://ire.org/nicar

The more you know

Weirdly, the occasional person asks what can be learned by knowing about deaths that occur when people encounter law enforcement, and they assume the pursuit of facts requires bias.

I don't feel that way at all. I can think of many ways this information could be used by law enforcement agencies to enhance their interactions with individuals that result in fewer people dying. I mean, most of us can agree that it's not good for police officers to kill people, even when it's entirely justified, can't we?

But how does one agency learn from the best policy practices of another if this information is not collected in a way that makes comparisons easy and accurate? Simply put, one agency should know which other to talk to if it decides its own policies are flawed. How does any agency know whether its own use of deadly force is greater or lesser than any other if there is no way to compare? Are there predictable situations that could keep officers out of harm's way that could be learned from incident comparisons? And why do different jurisdictions whose officers train at the same police academy have different outcomes to similar situations?

Law enforcement has a vested interest in figuring out best practices when dealing with deadly force incidents. The National Sheriffs' Association and the Treatment Advocacy Center in Arlington, Virginia, has formally requested that the Justice Department do a more complete job of collecting data on police use of deadly force (http://tacreports.org/storage/documents/2013-justifiable-homicides.pdf).

Moreover, modern police forces have new technology, like Tasers and beanbag guns, that are designed to avoid lethal use of force but that have created a whole new category of deaths. How often do people die when the officer has made a conscious and conscientious decision that the situation does not call for a death?

I have no difficulty imagining a hundred story ideas. How about a story set in the city where an individual is most likely to die from police bullets (or maybe Taser or vehicle or nightstick)? I'd like to make comparisons to see if some ages or groups are more likely to die at the hands of law enforcement. We know that a high percentage of these killings are considered justified – but with this database, we'd be able to see anomalies, like cities with a higher or lower than average level of justified killings, and a higher or lower than average number of killings per capita. Where might that lead? A story about the most average person to be killed by police would be insightful. Who was he/she? It's easy to visualize a portrait: a black male in his 20s. But is it accurate?

And in the end, when the database exists, I hope to get my wish that journalists would add context to every story that includes someone who had a fatal encounter with police.

I began with a simple three-year, three-step plan: 2013, collection; 2014, compilation; 2015, publication.

Step 1: Request information of every agency necessary to create a comprehensive database. Simultaneously, do regional Internet research to compare/contrast the information provided government agencies.

Step 2: Compile the data into an Internet-based searchable database.

Step 3: Analyze the data and publish periodic free-with-attribution stories for a year.

Add to that a Step 4 and Step 5: Figure out how to sustain the project after this first three-year phase is complete, and lobby Congress to require the Department of Justice to maintain a database of this information.

Transparency and the Freedom of Information Act

The first thing I had to figure out was exactly what information would be useful. The second was what information I could ask for that wouldn't be dismissed out of hand. My instinct was to use the Freedom of Information Act – a law that requires government agencies to provide public information to the public – to get the data I wanted.

There are nine exceptions to the Freedom of Information Act, but different offices phrase the exceptions differently. Here's a short version gleaned from the Security & Exchange Commission and other sources.

1. National defense or foreign policy information properly classified pursuant to an Executive Order. 2. Documents "related solely to the internal personnel rules and practices of an agency." 3. Documents "specifically exempted from disclosure by statute" other than FOIA, but only if the other statute's disclosure prohibition is absolute. 4. Documents that would reveal "[t]rade secrets and commercial or financial information obtained from a person and privileged or confidential." 5. Documents that are "inter-agency or intra-agency memorandum or letters" that would be privileged in civil litigation. 6. Documents that are "personnel and medical and similar files the disclosure of which would constitute a clearly unwarranted invasion of personal privacy." 7. Documents that are "records or information compiled for law enforcement purposes," but only if one or more of six specified types of harm would result: (a) could reasonably be expected to interfere with

law enforcement proceedings; (b) would deprive a person of a right to a fair trial or an impartial adjudication; (c) could reasonably be expected to constitute an unwarranted invasion of personal privacy; (d) could reasonably be expected to disclose the identity of a confidential source; (e) would disclose techniques, procedures or guidelines for investigations or prosecutions; (f) could reasonably be expected to endanger an individual's life or physical safety. 8. Documents that are related to specified reports prepared by, on behalf of or for the use of agencies that regulate financial institutions. 9. Documents that would reveal oil well data.

And, by the way, FOIA is a federal law that constrains only federal agencies. My experience has shown, however, other jurisdictions will honor a FOIA request if that agency feels inclined to be helpful. If agency personnel don't want to be helpful, they'll ignore the request and require it be made under state statutes. In Nevada, for example, the statute is NRS Chapter 239 (www.leg.state.nv.us/nrs/nrs-239.html).

This is a long way of saying that the Freedom of Information Act is pretty toothless, and it would behoove individuals not to ask for information that could be loosely interpreted as falling under one of those exceptions, because the agency will turn down the entire request.

I drew up a list of fifteen data fields that would be most useful and not fall into the FOIA exception list: subject's name, age, gender, race, date of death, location of death (address, city, state, zip code), agency responsible for death, cause of death, brief description of the circumstances, and the official disposition of death (justified or other). I added mental state to this, knowing that in most cases, this would be subjective on the part of the person reporting the incident, and the only truly clear indication is if police were called because the individual was suicidal or having an obvious emotional crisis.

Another piece of information I think would be handy is the name of the officer or officers involved, but that would fall directly under agencies' interpretation of the "personnel" exception, which would get the whole request denied. Still, there are officers who have lost their jobs under a shadow of police brutality, and since this information is kept nowhere publicly, it's worth trying to find out, since it seems possible they can forget to mention it on future job applications in other areas of the country.

The logical place to start trying to acquire all of this information is the FBI's Uniform Crime Report, the single largest collection of crime data in the United States. Participation is voluntary, but some 17,000 police jurisdictions report finely detailed information on all kinds of crime.

The UCR is also the most sensible place to assemble information about incidents of fatal encounters with police in the United States. It is the national clearinghouse for information about law enforcement officers killed or assaulted in the line of duty. To include data on the individuals they kill, all it would take is a line from Congress on the appropriations bill that funds the report.

The first step seemed simple enough. Just FOIA – that is, "formally request public information from a federal government agency" – the mailing list of all the agencies that contribute to the FBI's Uniform Crime Report, and then FOIA the agencies. I know a mailing list exists; it has to. Here's the guts of the request I sent:

> This is a request under the Freedom of Information Act. Date range of request: January 1, 2011-December 31, 2011. Description of request: I would like a searchable database of all agencies that participated/reported in the Federal Bureau of Investigation's Uniform Crime Report for 2011. I would like it to include the name of the agency, contact information including contact personnel with title, telephone number, mailing address, and email. I would like to receive the database on a CD or DVD at this address: D. Brian Burghart, c/o Reno News & Review, 708 N. Center St., Reno, NV 89501. Please search the FBI's indices to the Central Records System for the information responsive to this request related to the Federal Bureau of Investigation's Uniform Crime Report. I am willing to pay up to $100 for the processing of this request. Please inform me if the estimated fees will exceed this limit before processing my request. I am seeking information for personal use and not for commercial use. Please note that I've cc'd several parties/email addresses in this request, but only one copy of the database is necessary.
>
> Thank you for your help,
>
> D. Brian Burghart, Editor/Publisher, Reno News & Review.

Here's the response I got:

> This is in response to your Freedom of Information Act request regarding a "searchable database of all agencies that participated/reported in the Federal Bureau of Investigation's Uniform Crime Report for 2011." The FOIA does not require federal agencies to answer inquiries, create records, conduct research, or draw conclusions concerning queried data. Rather the FOIA requires agencies to provide access to reasonably described, nonexempt records. The questions posed in the referenced letter are not FOIA requests because they do not comply with the FOIA and its regulations.

I've uploaded an image of the letter and its attachment with the idea that the agency's lack of assistive direction will be instructive to others who file a FOIA request. See them here: https://docs.google.com/file/d/0B-l9Ys3cd80faHhjUE9Gd016VUk/edit?usp=sharing and https://docs.google.com/file/d/0B-l9Ys3cd80fN2JtMnpkdHFQN1k/edit?usp=sharing.

I called David P. Sobonya, the FBI's public information officer/legal administrative specialist, and he suggested I simply call the contact person for the Uniform Crime Report, Stephen G. Fischer, Jr., and ask for the information. I called, and the secretary refused either to connect me to him or to let me leave a voicemail message. "He only responds to email," she said in so many words. I sent an email to which he responded:

> Mr. Burghart – I am not authorized to receive/process FOIA requests. For information on how to do so, please see the link below: http://www.fbi.gov/foia/

So, I sent another FOIA to the FBI's Record/Information Dissemination Section, the place I sent the first one. Here's the guts of it:

> This is a request under the Freedom of Information Act. Date range of request: January 1, 2012-December 31, 2012. Description of request: I would like to request copies of any records, electronic or hard copy, that include the contact information for local, county, state and federal agencies that participated/reported in the Federal Bureau of Investigation's Uniform Crime Report for 2012. I am specifically requesting information that includes the name of the agency, telephone number, mailing address, and email. It is acceptable if this is made available in electronic or paper format.

Through the first runaround I suspected that my request was too specific, and the agency could claim that I was asking for something to be created. But, frankly, it's a game. It's a game that our government plays with legitimate news reporters on a daily basis. The strategy is to put things off because most editors – *not* reporters – will lose patience long before a request is satisfied and move the reporter onto something else. Forget the idea that a small newspaper or private citizen would sue for information that is plainly both public information and of public interest; few can afford to take on the federal government.

My second request was much broader and would require much more work on the part of government researchers, but I thought it was more likely to get a response. But there's the rub: the government can charge for the time required to answer a request, possibly tens of thousands of dollars, which I could never afford.

I received a response to my second request about five months after making it, and almost a year after I began seeking information that I know the FBI has, and to which every American is legally entitled.

The government's response can only be described as Orwellian. The very database I asked for, which may have been denied on the basis that it had to be created, was smooshed from an 11" x 17" spreadsheet onto 8.5" x 11" pages, printed and then scanned into PDFs that couldn't be placed back into a spreadsheet or database. Useless. Here they are: https://drive.google.

com/folderview?id=0B-l9Ys3cd80fSl9ELTNnMXRjclU&usp=sharing.

Fortunately, there were other places to query for public information, like local agencies including law enforcement or coroner offices. There was also an agency called the Bureau of Justice Statistics' Census of State and Local Law Enforcement Agencies, from which I ultimately got the mailing addresses for all 17,985 state and local law enforcement agencies. It was from this spreadsheet that I made the public records tool by which people can determine all the police agencies within any county, http://www.fatalencounters.org/for-public-record-requests, for purposes of requesting records.

Still, as a result of the FBI's stonewalling, I was forced to modify my strategy. I decided I would collect information by any means at my disposal to make the most comprehensive database within my power. That meant simultaneously working along four parallel lines: continue FOIA efforts; scrape what information currently exists from databases on the web; collect new information through daily media accounts; and create a system by which "the crowd" could find and report data.

Fatalencounters.org launched on February 27, 2014, and it has features to allow and assist people to submit incidents of fatal police violence, to make public records requests of every state and local law enforcement agency in the United States, and to make comparisons based on name, location, year, age, race or signs of mental illness.

This is the democratic hope: that people will help build the public record that public officials have disdained. The Tools bar on the site offers a drop-down menu that includes "Submit fatal encounters." One click, and there are instructions for doing the rest.

Guesses and statistics

Early in the process, I estimated that about 1,000 individuals were killed by police every year since 2000. Fourteen thousand deaths in fourteen years seems like a lot, and I'll be honest, my original estimate is barely an educated guess. I arrived at it based on the numbers that came out of the Las Vegas *Review-Journal*'s series "Deadly Force." By some rankings, Las Vegas is the thirtieth-largest city in the United States. I simply assumed that Las Vegas's average of seven deaths per year was the average for the top sixty cities in the country, and that police were more likely to use deadly force in those sixty biggest cities than in smaller towns, where police are more likely to know the people they interact with. It's conjecture. To take the guesswork a step further, I assumed that the top sixty cities' body counts would be about 40 percent of the US total (even though they only make up about 16 percent of the total population). There are some 19,000 cities in the United States, according to the 2010 US Census. The number that emerged from all this speculation is about 1,000 deaths resulting from interaction with law enforcement in the United States every year. That would be two or three deaths a day.

But, as part of the modified plan of data collection, I started creating automated methods by which I could get a constant stream of reported deaths. One of the Google Alerts that I get every day is the search string "police shot killed." Now instead of seeing two or three deaths related to law enforcement a day, it appears there are closer to five or six deaths reported in the nation every day. That could mean close to 2,000 deaths a year. But I don't want to speculate; I want real data, which is the whole purpose of this project.

What's my goal? Ultimately to create a database so large and so comprehensive that members of the public and Congress will be able to see the benefit of systematically and accurately collecting this information through the FBI's Uniform Crime Report. In the end, when I drive by a scene of police use of deadly force, I want to be able to answer that one simple question: How often does that happen?

The Ground We Stand On

On Inaugurations, Anniversaries and the Deaths of Trayvon Martin

Pier Gabrielle Foreman

February 2013. At triumphal moments, the past and its presents can fade like ships at a distance.[1] With a president's hand on King's bible, the inconceivable in two eras converge in place and time.[2] A martyr once violently derided – beaten, bloodied, spat and spied upon – celebrated as "we" witness a second inaugural day, announce a second quatrain, that seemed to change the rhythm, rhyme and face of power, a new verse to pierce the veil of what we – and they – could once imagine.

With such triumphal cymbals' promise of drum majoring for justice, who among us doesn't want to join as marching feet parade, bridging the hard-fought past with the hard-won present?[3] Last year's injuries' bleeding stops; its wounds seem cauterized; its bruises no longer tender to the touch. Complaining's droning on drops down on deafened ears; sounds, to some, tinny, whining, small.

Still, for me, as King's day delivers, this year, things we never dared to dream at this century's inauguration, rolling with incessant and insistent power are the echoes of the still fresh anniversaries of our dead and wounded: Trayvon Martin, Kenneth Chamberlain, Albert Florence, Anna Brown. They, too, sanctify the ground we stand on.

1 When this piece first appeared in print, as a guest blog on Rae Paris's Black Space: Crafting a Place for Black Women Writers, on February 27, 2013, it was accompanied by images and a video, "A Day Late and a Dollar Short." http://blackspaceblog.com/2013/02/27/the-ground-we-stand-on-on-inaugurations-anniversaries-and-the-deaths-of-trayvon-martin/. This language comes directly from the opening of Zora Neale Hurston's *Their Eyes Were Watching God*. "Ships at a distance have every man's wish on board."
2 Raushenbush, Paul. "Obama To Use MLK, Lincoln Bibles During Oath At Presidential Inauguration." www.huffingtonpost.com/2013/01/10/obama-using-mlk-lincoln-b_n_2447174.html (accessed January 16, 2014). Obama's second inauguration took place on Martin Luther King Day.
3 The original blog post features the iconic photograph of Hosea Williams (SCLC) and John Lewis (SNCC), followed by Albert Turner (SCLC) and Bob Mants (SNCC) as they lead the march down from the Edmund Pettus Bridge towards the waiting troopers and posse men. "Veterans of the Civil Rights Movement - Images of a Peoples' Movement." www.crmvet.org/images/imgselma.htm (accessed January 16, 2014).

This piece, then, is a zig-zag switch-back path meant to help us continue to climb the racial mountain without having its pitch, its incline steeped in history's insults, steep in current injury, steer us too easily toward imagined upward stepping stones of historical progress. "It's a very high mountain indeed for the would-be black" progressive to continue at these heights where the peaks of progress and achievement, looking closer than they are, beckon like temptation, to borrow from, some of you may have heard and will hear in my phrasing, Langston Hughes and June Jordan.[4]

Anniversaries of senseless, unsettling, unsettled, black death still catch my breath, snaring the seemingly smooth historical surface historic moments offer, disrupting in its muted continuation Obama's cymbalic win. As black loss goes on, goes unwhipped of justice, I need "to take a walk and clear my head" about our prospects, about why, on the streets of Chicago and Detroit and White Plains, New York, and on every regular day on the nation's Mall, we can't go out unmolested, often by those sworn to serve and protect, "without changing our clothes, our shoes, our body posture."[5] And, as we celebrated King's life and Obama's inauguration, I wanted to be thinking about wins, thinking about love's equalizing power, thinking about what choice means to me, and my students, and untold women who need to control their bodies and destinies, and not thinking about, not still reeling from, endless anniversaries of violence, death and disregard——"Long Live Zimmerman" painted on the walls of Ohio State's Black Culture Center, while the cultural kin of eras past hope that those who cut black boys' lives so short might do just that – live long and free – as they have, as, history whispers, they will continue to do.[6]

I am a nineteenth-century literary historian who regularly wonders if she's walked through a portal and landed in an updated version of her least favorite Octavia Butler novel, triumphal moments quickly fading as we're snatched back again to the 1850s, fugitive slave law past, Dred Scott decision coming.[7] No voting rights, anymore, in any Northern states save five, no rights to witness, to say your piece in court, no public schools meant to prepare your children for citizenship or jobs. How is today not yesterday, when last year's days and nights passed with us demanding not justice, just an arrest, when Trayvon was gunned down, on his way home, during half-time, during Black History Month?

---

4 Hughes, Langston. "The Negro Artist and the Racial Mountain" (1926). www.english.illinois.edu/maps/poets/g_l/hughes/mountain.htm (accessed January 15, 2014).

5 Jordan, June. "Poem about My Rights." The Poetry Foundation. www.poetryfoundation.org/poem/178526 (accessed January 16, 2014).

6 Foreman, P. Gabrielle. "Palin's Extra Chromosome (Choice) - And Mine." *The Huffington Post*, September 10, 2008. www.huffingtonpost.com/p-gabrielle-foreman/palins-extra-chromosome-c_b_125286.html. http://thegrio.com/2012/04/06/long-live-zimmerman-graffiti-appears-on-ohio-state-campus/ (accessed January 16, 2014).

7 I'm referencing Octavia Butler's novel *Kindred* here.

It's hard not to hear, pitched high above cases of individual and exceptional success, the loud and resonant message that black life and rights don't matter. After the murder, after the burial, how many parents' open-casket courage, how many children's feet marching like prayers so today's self-appointed overseers of gated communities, two centuries past self-designated patroller of expanding territories, can't stalk and kill and walk away, the law still on, the gun still by, his side?[8]

In March 1857, Justice Taney wrote for the seven justices in the majority: "The words 'people of the United States' and 'citizens' are synonymous terms.... They both describe the political body who ... hold the power and conduct the Government through their representatives. . . . The question before us is whether the class of persons described in the plea [people of African ancestry] compose a portion of this people, and are constituent members of this sovereignty.[9] We think they are not . . . and were not intended to be included, under the word 'citizens' in the Constitution, and can therefore claim none of the rights and privileges which that instrument provides for and secures to citizens of the United States. On the contrary, they were at that time considered as a subordinate and inferior class of beings, who had been subjugated by the dominant race, and ... yet remained subject to their authority, and had no rights or privileges but such as those who held the power and the Government might choose to grant them."

In the today that is also yesterday, a Supreme Court majority held that guards have the right to strip search those arrested (as, at least some are, easily, consistently) for the most minor of infractions, not crimes; arrests, not convictions – for walking dogs without leashes, for overdue traffic tickets that had, in this case, been paid – the evidence presented as it was also erased, effaced, ignored.[10] We all know, or should, that blacks smoke pot, drive fast, run red lights at the same rates as whites do, and that the rich, behind their wheels and white-collared suits, tend to commit infractions with more rudeness and regularity than do the poor, a new study shows.[11]

Yet over-surveillance leads to highly, shall we say, disproportionate impact – more patrollers, we're finding out, riding, demanding passes, asserting their dominion to "hold the power and conduct the government through their representatives," making sure we don't forget, despite our fancy wheels, degrees and titles, despite our first black president, that we

8 Brooks, Gwendolyn. "The Last Quatrain Of The Ballad Of Emmett Till." See at http://allpoetry.com/poem/8530221-The-Last-Quatrain-Of-The-Ballad-Of-Emmett-Till-by-Gwendolyn-Elizabeth Brooks (accessed January 16, 2014). First published in 1960 in Brooks' *The Bean Eaters*.

9 *Dred Scott v. Sandford* 60 U.S. 393 (1857). www.law.cornell.edu/supremecourt/text/60/393.

10 *Florence v. Board of Chosen Freeholders*. www.supremecourt.gov/opinions/11pdf/10-945.pdf (accessed January 16, 2014).

11 Research Areas. www.nsf.gov/news/news_summ.jsp?cntn_id=123301&WT.mc_id=USNSF_51&WT.mc_ev=click (accessed January 16, 2014).

"yet remain subject to their authority."[12]

In the today that is yesterday, Albert and April Florence, their 4-year-old son and baby coming were stopped by the New Jersey police while April was driving their spanky BMW to nearby family, intent on celebrating an All American day, their closing on a home. Cops looked for and found a warrant for 6'3" strapping, black and handsome Albert (who was not behind the wheel that day), based on a fine he had paid – the notarized receipt he carried with him, shown, to no avail, to police who, stripping him from family, from body politic, jailed then showered then sprayed then squatted strapping Albert, commanded that he "hold up my genitals and cough," Florence testified.[13] In two different places where he was held, he spread his cheeks while, for six days full of his absence, April tried to find her fine-paid-up, carrying-the-notarized-receipt husband. When he took his case to the Supreme Court, like any done-no-wrong, humiliated citizen executive who thought he had rights in the twenty-first century would, he was told, to my mind, to my ears, that he had no "rights or privileges" the state was bound to respect.

In another anniversary, in another today that is yesterday in pairs, 29-year-old Anna Brown, a mother of two who lost her home in the 2010 tornados that Missouri's New Year brought, then lost her job, then lost her children, then lost, it seems, her natural mind, thinking she did not have to leave a hospital when she was told to get out, thinking that she could hold on tight to what she knew, what doctors more than once denied, as if three months of pains in ankles, shins and thighs had lied.[14] Police took the woman – about whom they would write on intake forms, "suspected drug use" – from the emergency room where she sat insisting on the care she needed, lugged her by her hand-cuffed arms, as she declared, quite loudly, that she could not stand, dragged her, quite literally, to jail. Dumped on her back, beetle-like, writhing, dying on cell-cement floor where hospital bed should be, Anna Brown joined the many thousands gone before half an hour passed away.[15] *A Year ago? Two Hundred Years ago?*

And when this black mother, like Trayvon Martin, was tested in death for drugs and alcohol, there were no traces of transgressions. She passed, the autopsy reported, from the blood clots that had prompted her to go to,

12 *Dred Scott v. Sandford* 60 U.S. 393 (1857).
13 Totenberg, Nina. "Supreme Court OKs Strip Searches For Minor Offenses." NPR. www.npr.org/2012/04/02/149866209/high-court-supports-strip-searches-for-minor-offenders (accessed January 16, 2014).
14 Dickinson, Emily. "The First Day's Night Had Come." www.americanpoems.com/poets/emilydickinson/10362 (accessed January 16, 2014).
15 "The OP-NAT EYE." http://opnateye.com/?p=400 (accessed January 17, 2014).

to declare her intention to stay at, the hospital someone decided she had no right to visit, from which she had no right to expect care.

Just a year and some months, some centuries ago, a retired, twenty-year veteran corrections officer, former marine, Kenneth Chamberlain, Sr., somehow set off his medical pendant while sleeping.[16] His service dialed the police – stressing it was not a criminal call. When they arrived, Chamberlain, groggy and in boxers, assured them, through the door, that he was fine and told them they could go. For an hour as the police insisted they weren't going anywhere except inside his apartment, they managed to call him a "nigger," to tell him they didn't give a "f*ck" that he had served his country, that he was 68 or that he had, as he was telling them through the door he didn't want to open, the heart condition that was the reason for the medical pendant system the police did not know was recording all of this. Alarmed, the service called to cancel its request, requested that those cops banging on the door at 5:30 a.m. call Nathan Chamberlain, Jr., an idea the police pushed away, as they pushed away Chamberlain's 51-year-old pajama-clad niece, her uncle's upstairs neighbor, pushed away the door from its hinges, tasering the heart sick man they were called to help before they shot him dead. Images contest the police report: a threatening knife-wielding crazy man, "hatchet" in hand some papers report, this elder, as big, as brute, as suspicious as the teenaged Trayvon, who had just turned 17 when he was shot down, his killer not arrested after saying it was he, the stalker with the gun, who cried for help, when it wasn't, experts agree; saying it was he who was attacked, who feared for his own life.

Months later, no tasering, shooting officers had been *named* even; none had been suspended, charged or arrested for Chamberlain's death. Grand jury convenings lag and tarry, tardy before acquittals of killers of minding-their-own-business black boys, men, marines, all questionable "constituent members of this sovereignty," "with no rights or privileges but such as those who held the power and the government might choose to grant them."[17]

Talk to me about triumph and ascendance this Black History Month, and I'll ask about the continued devaluing of black life and time and pride, about purged voters lists and endless lines, about the black hole of time, the cost of opportunity, the endless energy spent to get so very little other citizens expect so poignantly, painfully, late. Last year, it crossed my mind, that 2012 was 1857, a year in which, no matter if you play by rules, no

16 "NY Grand Jury Probes Killing of Kenneth Chamberlain Sr. Amidst Broad Allegations of Police Misconduct." *Democracy Now!* www.democracynow.org/2012/4/11/grand_jury_probes_killing_of_kenneth (accessed January 16, 2014).

17 *Dred Scott V. Sandford* 60 U.S. 393 (1857).

matter if your president has children who look like yours, no matter your degrees, your service, your respectability, you have no rights, no rights still, that others are bound to respect.

Despite the balls and speeches, feting time has not arrived. Feeling out of space, feeling out of time, spirits haunt me as anniversaries pass, this year, this 1857. I'm hoping we can help each other hear, through cymbalic success that sometimes covers the din of death and disrespect, exactly what they're saying, before too many more anniversaries, before too many more losses, go bye.

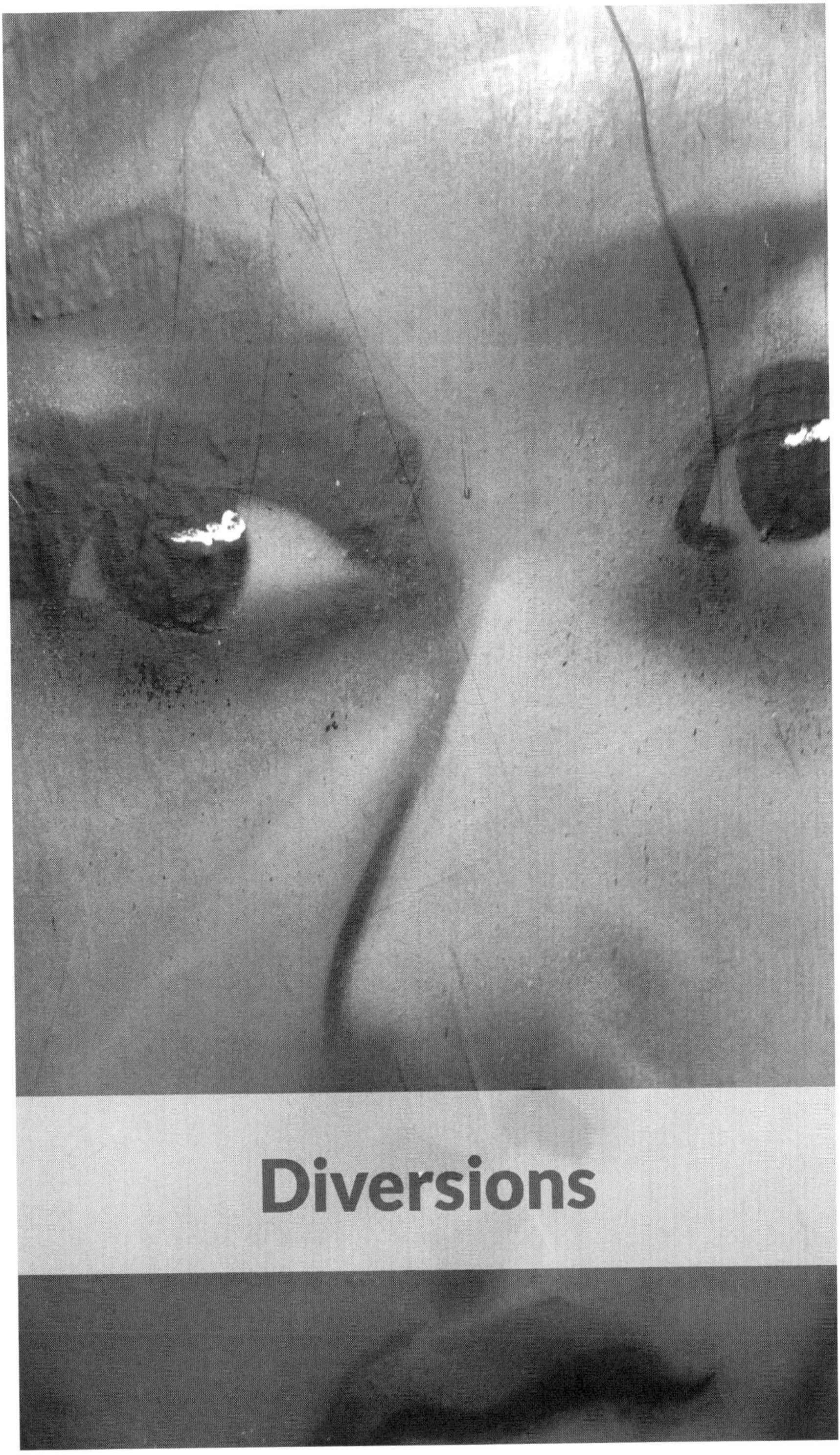

Diversions

Marijuana's 'Dark Side'

Drugs, Race and the Criminalization of Trayvon Martin

Alexander Tepperman

They've killed my son and now they're trying to kill his reputation.

– Sybrina Fulton, mother of Trayvon Martin, March 25, 2012

It seems at first blush that, when she called out those vocal media members who questioned her son's character, Sybrina Fulton was merely engaging in the sort of hyperbolic catharsis one might expect from a grieving parent. Her contention, however, was hardly an exaggeration. In the weeks following Martin's shooting death at the hands of George Zimmerman in Sanford, Florida, a multitude of traditional and online media outlets levied a counteroffensive against the public hostility facing Zimmerman,[1] renewed discussions of racial profiling in American life and, most important, the gun culture and racial profiling that many commentators claimed facilitated Martin's shooting.

Some of Martin's defenders would later claim that the aspersions cast upon the 17-year-old's character were simply a transparent and self-conscious form of racism, though this claim is a half-truth at best. Such explanations ignore the possibility that the criticisms emanating from Martin's critics were also cynical tools of necessity, employed toward wholly utilitarian ends. The most vigorous defenders of Florida's now-infamous Stand Your Ground laws, one could reasonably argue, were simply countering critiques of the policy the most effective way possible, beginning by discrediting Martin's reputation and, in turn, his status as

1 One could point to any number of articles that subtly suggest Martin was responsible for his own death, but two of the more notorious examples of this tendency include the March 26, 2012, *Miami Herald* article "Multiple Suspensions Paint a Complicated Portrait of Trayvon Martin," and the March 24 *Daily Mail* piece "Trayvon suspended THREE times for 'drugs, truancy, graffiti and carrying burglary tool' and did he attack bus driver too? New picture emerges of victim as parents claim it's all a smear."

a victim. This allowed Stand Your Ground's defenders to deflect public discussion away from the embattled policy, keeping it safe from state and federal interference.

Regardless of what Martin's critics' true motivations were – and granting that their motives may not be rational or clearly articulated in the first place – one still confronts a pair of plainly obvious points about the nature of Martin's media vilification. First and foremost, the omnipresence of the "Trayvon Martin was a drug dealer" rumor has its roots in five decades of popular political rhetoric, being most dynamically shaped by the ongoing federal wars on drugs and crime, as well by the accompanying rise of the prison industrial complex. Secondly, debates about Trayvon Martin's morality should be understood as part of a common present-day political language that binds together a variety of social, cultural and racial biases. In reviewing the popular discourse on drugs one finds that members of the American public tend to harbor strikingly divergent perceptions of marijuana use and abuse in the black and white communities, respectively. This fact is highlighted by the rapid metamorphosis of the Martin-Zimmerman affair from a story merely *involving* drugs into being a story that, in some important ways, was *about* drugs.[2]

To understand how and why the popular press turned the Martin case into a story about marijuana use, drug dealing and black male deviance, one must look back to a historical lineage of racialized public discourse on law and order, drugs and race. When brought together, careful readings of Barry Goldwater's 1964 campaigning, the 1968 Safe Streets Act, the Republican Party's successful Southern Strategy, President Reagan's War on Drugs and the rise of warehouse imprisonment policies show not only why, in 2012, George Zimmerman's defenders had, through employing the racialized language of national drug debates, some success in branding Trayvon Martin a "gangsta" but also why historians might not find the success of this particular form of demonization surprising in the least. It is, as Michelle Alexander explains in her influential monograph *The New Jim Crow,* simply another example of the employment of the "criminal justice system to label people of color 'criminals,'" a practice used to validate "all the practices we supposedly left behind" with the formal outlawing of racial segregation. The willful mischaracterization of Trayvon Martin as a drug dealer is a direct legacy of that continued racist anachronism, Jim Crow.

2 The extent to which "drugs" served as a master theme for the Martin case can be seen in the sheer mass of reporting on the case through that lens. A simple Google News search for the leading stories on "marijuana" between the beginning of 2008 and the end of 2012 shows that the Martin case was the second most widely reported "marijuana" story of that five year span, outpacing the Michael Phelps bong-use "scandal" and following only the revelation that, prior to his death, Osama Bin Laden had grown marijuana on his private compound in Abbottabad, Pakistan.

Moral panic strikes

Within a fortnight of his death, a pair of revelations regarding Trayvon Martin's exposure to, and involvement with, drugs gave way to Zimmerman's defenders' open questioning of Martin's morality and innocence. The first revelation was that on the night of his death Martin was serving a school suspension for possession of a bag that contained trace amounts of marijuana.[3] The second revelation, which turned out to provide even greater fodder for Zimmerman's defenders, was that an autopsy revealed trace levels of tetrahydro-cannabinol (THC), the primary medicinal agent found in marijuana, in Martin's blood. The latter finding led legions of journalists and pundits to cast suspicion upon Martin's character, supposing that Zimmerman's lethal actions were, perhaps, just defense against an abusive "druggie." These were intellectually dishonest and fatuous claims, as the 1.5 nanograms of THC and 7.3 nanograms of THC-COOH present in Martin's system may have been weeks old and were of such low levels that they would not even have affected Martin's character in the first place.[4] There is every reason, in fact, to believe Martin had not been "toking" the night of his death.

That there is little or no reason to believe the THC in Martin's system would have affected his behavior – or that marijuana would tend to make anyone *violent* for that matter – is beside the point. The argument that Trayvon Martin was a drug user was merely the *entrée* to a more general and baldly cynical attempt at character assassination, part of a larger argument about Martin's deviant identity. Following the drug-related "revelations," attacks expanded into other fronts, frequently concerning Martin's looks, the presumed character of his friends and a number of other unrelated behavioral transgressions, such as the *Daily Mail*'s concern that Martin had been said to have once possessed "burglary tools" (a flat-head screwdriver). A pointed example of this sort of discourse comes from Wagist.com, which published the widely circulated anti-Martin conspiracy piece "Was Trayvon Martin a Drug Dealer?" The article's author, Dan Linehan, speculates that yes, in fact, Martin was likely a dealer, as evidenced by the fact the 17-year-old seemed like a troublemaker. At 17, Linehan explains, "he was already sporting gold teeth, and several large tattoos." Linehan stops there, however, neglecting to explain how tattoos and gold "grills" indicate anything about Martin's culpability in his own death. Meanwhile, according to Linehan, "Zimmerman was very good at this job" and "this is a textbook self-defense case."

---

3 This suspension was not due to any reasonable suspicion that Martin was using or trafficking drugs on school property; rather, it was merely because he was in possession of a detectable quantity of marijuana, thus exposing him to the school's "zero tolerance" policy.

4 M. Szalavitz, "Traces of Marijuana Found in Trayvon Martin's Body: Does it Matter?" *Time.com*, May 18, 2012.

While the presumption of Martin's guilt being related to his appearance has clear and troubling racialist elements, Linehan's piece does not provide satisfactory evidence that the many pundits who echoed the views found on Wagist knowingly practiced racial profiling. Presumably, many of Zimmerman's defenders were merely describing a conception of Trayvon Martin that, while undoubtedly chauvinistic and racist in practice, legitimately jibed with their understanding of what "sort of person" constituted America's "criminal class."[5] For many Americans, Martin must have "seemed" like a criminal, with his race playing one (albeit critical) role, along with his age and appearance, in creating such a feeling.[6]

The nadir of the drug-based Trayvon Martin vilification came at the end of March when a white supremacist, going by the handle 'Klanklannon,' hacked into Martin's personal e-mail, Facebook, MySpace and Twitter accounts and repackaged Martin's private information and messages in such a way as to present him as a drug dealer with many criminal acquaintances. Posting on a 4chan message board,[7] Klanklannon posted a series of slides featuring titles like "Trayvon Martin Used Marijuana Habitually" and "Trayvon Martin was a Drug Dealer." The neo-Nazi website Stormfront was quick to pick up these pieces and republish them as "news."[8] Lastly, Klanklannon changed Martin's account passwords to a series of racial epithets. While Klanklannon's actions were egregiously racist, however, it must be noted that the hacker's neo-Nazi affiliations are not necessary to understanding, in a macro sense, the racial underpinnings of the Martin-as-deviant-and-criminal rumors. By the time George Zimmerman shot and killed Trayvon Martin, the racist language of drugs, crime and deviance had been embedded into the fabric of mainstream American politics for quite some time, and it was popularly elected American politicians, not radical hate-mongers, who had made it so.

---

5 The most famous example of this came on the morning of March 23, 2012, when Geraldo Rivera, appearing on the *Fox and Friends* morning show on Fox News, proclaimed that Martin was as responsible as Zimmerman for his death, having worn a hooded sweatshirt, a garment that Rivera claimed constituted "thug wear" and thus invited vigilante violence.

6 There was, of course, no shortage of outwardly racist rhetoric online. A Yahoo! Answers discussion board titled "Trayvon Martin, drug dealer or just user?", for instance, saw 'robzuc97' opine "'Skittles' must be Ebonics for drugs.... I suppose then the "Arizona Ice Tea" is some sort of malt liquor?"

7 4chan is an imageboard website that allows users to post anonymously. While it is most popular as a site for planning pranks and memes, it has also recently been a popular online meeting space for political activists of the extreme right and left.

8 Tellingly, Stormfront editors presented these slides along with a picture of a menacing-looking black youth who was *not*, in fact, Trayvon Martin. Michelle Malkin's arch-conservative website, Twitchy.com, then picked up the Stormfront photos, only to sheepishly retract the story, downplaying the seemingly racist instincts of the site's coverage of the case.

A new alliance: drugs, politics and the law, 1946 to the present

Historical commentary on America's mid- and late twentieth century attitudes toward drug crime is broad in scope and rich in insight, as decades of research has uncovered reams of telling, and often troubling, patterns in law and corrections. The extensive documentation of the post-New Deal political order, including the nation's adoption of hyperpunitive correctional policies, has shown not only that the fierce anti-drug legislation and enforcement of the past three decades is unprecedented in American history but that it was undertaken by power elites who understood full well its racist and classist implications.

As Michael Tonry explains in the introduction to his recent monograph on the prison industrial complex, *Punishing Race: A Continuing American Dilemma,* "long before open appeals to racism disappeared from American politics, conservative Republicans fashioned the Southern Strategy," a deliberate attempt to "focus on issues – initially states' rights and later crime, welfare fraud, busing, and affirmative action" – that the public generally understood as "coded appeals to whites' antiblack animus, anxiety, and resentment." Tonry acknowledges that the coded racist language of "law and order" policy did not originate in Republican Party spin rooms, as segregationist Democrats had considered joining like-minded Republican conservatives in a concerted effort to criminalize the disobedience borne of the civil rights movement as early as the 1940s. It was, however, the dramatic rightward political shift undertaken by the Republican Party under the leaderships of Barry Goldwater and Richard Nixon that ultimately allowed politicians and state and federal judiciaries to institutionalize a new language of racialized legal discourse.

As the civil rights movement made significant legal and social gains throughout the mid-1950s, white supremacists felt (understandably, when seen from their perspective) an increasing frustration and anxiety about the country's future. Southern segregationists fought the rising tide of black civil rights not only by characterizing equal rights legislation as "rewarding lawbreakers" but by pointing to high crime rates in Northern industrialized cities as evidence that segregation was a necessary crime prevention measure.[9] The discourse of civil rights as a criminal threat to white freedom found such sympathy with conservative whites throughout the nation that, by the time Barry Goldwater ran against Lyndon Johnson for president, the Republican Party was openly discussing the evils of racial equality on the national stage. Attending the 1964 Republican National Convention,

9 Alexander, *The New Jim Crow: Mass Incarceration in the Age of Colorblindness*, The New Press, 2010, p. 40-1.

lifelong conservative and civil rights icon Jackie Robinson, the man who famously "broke the Major League Baseball color barrier," remarked, "That convention was one of the most unforgettable and frightening experiences of my life. The hatred I saw...embodied a revulsion for all [Lyndon Johnson] stood for, including his enlightened attitude towards black people. A new breed of Republicans had taken over the GOP. As I watched this steamroller operation in San Francisco, I had a better understanding of how it must have felt to be a Jew in Hitler's Germany."[10]

Although Goldwater lost the general election, his racially regressive message seemed ever more attractive to the white American electorate throughout the second half of the decade. By the late 1960s, federal crime rates were skyrocketing, with particularly high rates of robbery and stranger murder, the sort of offenses the public finds most terrifying. The combination of exceptionally high violent crime rates and the perceived social and political instability of the era led an embattled President Johnson to push through the Omnibus Crime Control and Safe Streets Act of 1968, a measure creating sweeping new federal-level provisions regarding arrest and punishment.[11] Ironically, it was this measure that, though passed by perhaps the most civil rights-minded president in American history, enabled and entrenched the political language of the racially discriminatory War on Drugs.

The Safe Streets Act made law breaking a unifying national concern, providing a national, bipartisan vocabulary for crime prevention that, while not consciously discriminatory, left ample room for regressive racial philosophies in its execution. Among many other policies, it gave birth to prosecutorial policies and police practices that, through their selective targeting and draconian scope, devastated urban inner-city neighborhoods. In an effort to create a post-New Deal language of political unity, it also encouraged politicians to engage in a full-on assault on the supposedly non-partisan, non-racialized issue of drugs. The antecedents of the federal War on Drugs can be traced back to the Nixon Administration, though the policy began in its current form under the leadership of President Ronald Reagan, who, in 1982, declared a determined national assault on drug traffickers, traders and users. By 1985, Reagan's administration would identify the emergence of crack – a low-grade form of cocaine commonly found in black inner-city neighborhoods – as yet another threat to America's moral fabric and justification for a further expansion for the drug war.

The Reagan Administration paired the domestic war, which saw

10 Jackie Robinson, *I Never Had It Made: An Autobiography of Jackie Robinson*, HarperCollins, 1995, p. 169.
11 Jonathan Simon. *Governing Through Crime: How the War on Crime Transformed American Democracy and Created a Culture of Fear*. New York: Oxford University Press, 2009, p. 26.

police and judges doggedly incarcerate drug users and sellers, with an extraordinarily effective mid-decade media offensive that, for the majority of Americans, validated the federal government's new crusade.[12] Certainly, one can understand why many Americans may have felt that the War on Drugs was working, as violent crime shrank steadily and dramatically throughout the 1980s and 1990s. The problem with such reasoning is that Reagan's policies – which were too recently passed to have a significant effect on national crime rates in the first place – did not even target violent offenders, but rather sent legions of young, disproportionately black men to prison for drug trafficking and possession. Drug warriors' enthusiasm led police to focus their attentions on "high risk" populations, mainly those located in high-density urban neighborhoods, where they had the best chance to catch crack, cocaine and heroin users. This created and perpetuated a cycle of racial profiling that ultimately bloated US prisons with record numbers of African-Americans. As Ruth Gilmore points out, "drug commitments to federal and state prison systems surged 975 percent between 1982 and 1999."[13] By the early 1990s, 50 percent of state and federal prisoners were black, an all-time high.

In the 1990s not only did the Clinton administration continue the racially regressive War on Drugs but the White House expanded the campaign, making public schools a major battleground for new, often merciless, public safety initiatives. Jonathan Simon draws out this development in depth in *Governing Through Crime: How the War on Crime Transformed American Democracy and Created a Culture of Fear*. Simon documents the period's growing conservative movement against public school systems, noting the eagerness of right-wing anti-union groups to frame public schools as "rife with crime" and generally unfit to educate. That message, repeated ad nauseum in conservative political circles, led both Presidents George H.W. Bush and Bill Clinton to pass "safe schools" initiatives that focused far more on keeping institutions of education drug-free than on providing students and teachers with sufficient *anomie-fighting* academic and extracurricular resources.

Befitting the general ethos of the War on Drugs, mid- and late-decade discussions of drugs in school became increasingly hyperbolic, and punishments grew ever more extreme, leading to policies like the one that saw Trayvon Martin suspended from school for holding an amount of marijuana that was all but invisible to the naked eye. Martin was one of the hundreds of thousands of African-American youths targeted and marginalized by the

12 The implementation and subsequent ubiquity of Nancy Reagan's *Dare to Resist Drugs and Violence* (D.A.R.E.) campaign showed the power of the Reagan administration to control the terms of the War on Drugs debate.
13 Ruth Wilson Gilmore. *Golden Gulag: Prisons, Surplus, Crisis, and Opposition in Globalizing California*. University of California Press, 2007, p. 18.

War on Drugs, being handed an unsuitably harsh penalty for an ultimately insignificant transgression. The severity of drug-related "zero tolerance" policies, combined with well-established inequities in the levying of school suspensions,[14] have only exacerbated class and race divides, as Simon puts it, transforming school safety "from a set of expectations for administrators to a zero-sum game between aggressors who are criminals or criminals in the making, and their victims – a shifting group consisting of everyone not stigmatized already as criminal." The politics surrounding the holding of a baggie with trace amounts of marijuana both led to Martin's suspension from school and gave George Zimmerman's supporters a means of framing Martin not as a victim of senseless violence but as a member of America's criminal element.

Policy proposals and the future of 'black dealer' archetype

One of the unfortunate realities of racial profiling in popular political culture is that many ideas that derive from stereotyping gain an ethereal-yet-believable quality. Perceptions of the nature of black (and white) culture, deviance and criminality tend to gain general acceptance over time as being axiomatic, no longer needing to be "proved." If American culture on the whole – from the popular press to network television to internet memes – stresses the idea, even implicitly, that blacks are more likely to commit drug crimes, one can understand why the general population would have trouble shaking that feeling, regardless of how problematic or factually inaccurate such a simplistic view may be. Heavy social conditioning is monumentally hard to undo, as recent historical scholarship has explored just how deeply (and chemically) anxieties about black criminality run, showing that most Americans, including most African-Americans, are more likely to feel suspicion and distress upon encountering blacks than whites.[15] For that reason, the wisest course of action may be to raise awareness of these pervasive racial double standards in society in the hopes that both the media and the public will actively and thoughtfully rebel against regressive learned behaviors.

---

14 According to the US Department of Education's study "Revealing New Truths About Our Nation's Schools" (http://www2.ed.gov/about/offices/list/ocr/docs/crdc-2012-data-summary.pdf), black public school students are 3.5 times more likely to face suspension than their white counterparts.

15 The greater fear of blacks than whites among blacks is, in part, a product of the intraracial nature of most violent crime. As recent research on cognitive functioning suggests, however, race bias may be so ingrained in American culture that it can even subsume rational thought and stimulate immediate, unthinking emotional anxiety through stimulation of the amygdale. For an overview of this research, see Jeffrey Adler's "Cognitive Bias: Interracial Homicide in New Orleans, 1921-1945" *Journal of Interdisciplinary History* v. 43 no 1 (Summer 2012).

The most important action legislators could take on a federal or state level is the immediate de-escalation of, and then unequivocal end to the War on Drugs. The vilification of Trayvon Martin is facilitated by two stances: (1) the continued racial profiling of black marijuana users and dealers; and (2) the justification and entrenchment of such attitudes in policy and enforcement. Like a snake swallowing its own tail, popular and political culture justify each other, with images of black drug crime giving continued justification to drug warriors who target the most likely areas in which to find drug crime, all at the expense of hundreds of thousands of imprisoned, and subsequently disenfranchised, American citizens. By declaring an end to the War on Drugs and, in essence, freeing a legion of black men from the "felon" stigma that makes them second-class citizens in all but name, the popular media would lose much of the impetus for promoting the "black drug dealer" stereotype.[16]

Furthermore, such measures could reintroduce a generation of ex-cons back into society. As Alexander notes, "once you're labeled a felon, the old forms of discrimination – employment discrimination, housing discrimination, denial of the right to vote, denial of educational opportunity, denial of food stamps and other public benefits, and exclusion from jury service – are suddenly legal." Perhaps ending the drug war might result in a measure of economic equality, as a generation of felons could be made eligible for welfare, social insurance and student loans, and might even find themselves less hampered by the exceptional limitations on earning power placed upon black ex-convicts.[17] If nothing else, the restoration of suffrage rights for this group would give former inmates the chance to live out the penal system's rehabilitative ideal.

Granted, "changing popular culture" and "ending the War on Drugs" are broad solutions that provide few directives for immediate action. This is because the problem of racial profiling and stereotyping is so broad and runs so deep that it seems overly ambitious to begin the search for solutions with anything more than general progressive-minded goals for the future. Academics, politicians and the public are best served by deciding, on an

16 The claim that the systemic racism of the War on Drugs can be addressed through institutional reform is a compelling point. I sincerely doubt, however, that the state would have any more success in ending the racist elements of the War on Drugs than it has had when dealing with similar issues involving capital punishment (which is to say, very little). Moreover, both the conception and enforcement of drug laws are bound to have highly classist implications, as that has been the case with most status offense-related public policies throughout US history. Aside from being morally and legally unjust, the class dimensions of drug law enforcement would undoubtedly affect black Americans disproportionately, creating an unavoidable form of *de facto* racism.

17 In her tremendously powerful work *Marked: Race, Crime, and Finding Work in the Era of Mass Incarceration* (Chicago: University of Chicago Press, 2007), Devah Pager quantitatively measures the trouble black convicted felons face in finding work. Her studies – all of which are statistically significant – show that 38.2% of polled employers were not likely to hire a convicted drug offender who had been sentenced to prison (p. 124) and that black males not convicted of a felony have approximately the same prospects (14%) as white men convicted of a felony (17%) of receiving a job call-back (p. 92).

individual level, how they can contribute their talents to these macro goals.

Discussions of the Martin-Zimmerman incident are emblematic of twenty-first century American race politics. Within the superstructure of Barack Obama's supposedly post-racial America, animosities not only remain but thrive, stoked by the continued power of the coded language of crime and punishment. There is, therefore, no better way to understand the culture that gave rise to the vilification of Martin as a drug dealer than as a product of deeply entrenched, and often subliminal, racism. As Alexander notes, racialist discourse has led the United States to imprison "a larger percentage of its black population than South Africa did at the height of apartheid," an unsurprising fact given that "no other country in the world imprisons so many of its racial or ethnic minorities." This suggest that the debate left to have on the issue of race and corrections is not whether this issue is plagued by racist impulses but whether the time has come for the American people to end the War on Drugs and choke the life out of the industrialized West's last functioning gulag.

The Trick Bag of the Perfect Victim

Jill Nelson

The collective, sustained outrage and organizing in response to the killing of Trayvon Martin by George Zimmerman has been both effective and inspiring. Trayvon's parents, Sybrina Fulton and Tracy Martin, refused to accept that their son's murder was justified or that, despite Florida's insane Stand Your Ground law, the man who shot him should not be held accountable. In the midst of unfathomable grief, they relentlessly used the media to get the word out about what had happened and to demand that the legal system take action.

Without their work, joined by black online journalists and bloggers who drove the story – particularly the Huffington Post's Trymaine Lee – it's doubtful that most of us would ever have heard of the shooting of the 17-year-old killed on his way home from a 7-Eleven.

The national response – including demonstrations, media coverage, scrutiny of police operations, spontaneous local demonstrations by young people and a million hoodie march – forced a re-examination of the circumstances of Trayvon's death and the eventual arrest and indictment of Zimmerman for second-degree murder.

Trayvon Martin is not alone in being the victim of an unacceptable tragedy. While the mass protest has been effective (we'll see what the legal system does in the months ahead), it raises the question of why we fail to respond similarly to other victims of such violence meted out by the police or their enthusiasts. Have we fallen into the trick bag of being able to perceive state criminality and demand justice only for those we perceive as innocents? Have we bought into a 'perfect victim' mentality?

In a piece in *The New Republic*, "What a Florida Teenager's Death Tells Us About Being Black in America," John McWhorter describes one of the tragedies of the confrontation between Trayvon and Zimmerman as "the senseless death of a bright, good-natured boy." I'd argue that the central horror of Trayvon's death is that it wasn't senseless but was actually par for the course. Much as we might like to convince ourselves otherwise, too often the function of formal and informal policing in America is to repress, intimidate and at times execute when the policing is of black males (and, less frequently, black women).

As historian Robin D.G. Kelley writes (in an essay in an anthology I edited, *Police Brutality*), "Even before formal police forces were established in cities at the end of the nineteenth century, people in power relied on 'legal' and extralegal violence and terrorism to pacify, discipline, and exploit communities of color." Kelley is no naif concerning the real need for police in communities of color, but he is clear that existing systems do not work. "The colonial mentality, rooted in slavery and imperialism, that has structured the entire history of policing in urban America needs to be overturned," he writes.

The case of 25-year-old Manuel Diaz, killed by police in Anaheim, California, on July 24, 2012, as he allegedly fled, is an instance of unchecked police brutality. Eyewitness accounts say that Diaz was shot in the leg, fell and was then shot in the head. When outraged citizens, many of them women and children, demonstrated, police responded by shooting bean bags and pepper spray at them and unleashing a police dog.

No one was killed, though in a separate incident the following night, Anaheim police shot and killed Joel Acevedo, who allegedly fired on them from a stolen vehicle as they pursued him. According to the Anaheim police, Acevedo was a "documented gang member."

McWhorter is not alone in indulging in the idealization of Trayvon Martin. Descriptions of Trayvon by those who did not know him often include words like 'normal,' 'promising,' 'outgoing,' 'average,' 'brave,' 'smart,' 'college-bound.'

Perhaps he was all of those things. But do these characteristics make his murder more heinous? Is our outrage in response to acts of murderous aggression by officials, or to the affect of the victim? Do we require innocence, a spotless record and a cheery – or at least not scary – countenance to determine the value of a life? If you are angry, have a criminal record, were formerly incarcerated, smoke marijuana or aren't photogenic, would your murder go without public cries for justice?

As Michelle Alexander writes in *The New Jim Crow*, "More African Americans are under correctional control today – in prison or jail, on probation or parole – than were enslaved in 1850, a decade before the Civil War began." Given the staggering numbers of black and Latino men who are or will at some point be under the control of the criminal justice system, it's crucial that we relinquish our notion that some victims of police or vigilante violence are less deserving of our sympathy than others.

Too many young black men are effectively demonized in life. We can choose not to allow or participate in this dehumanization, in life or death, of those who could be our sons, brothers, nephews or friends. On February 2, 2012, three weeks before Trayvon Martin was killed, police in the Bronx followed 18-year-old Ramarley Graham home. After Graham, unarmed, went inside, the police broke down the door, rushed in and shot him to death in the bathroom as his 58-year-old grandmother and 6-year-old brother watched in horror. Graham's grandmother was thrown to the ground, held at gunpoint, taken into police custody and held incommunicado for seven hours.

There was no collective fury over the killing of Graham. Why? Because Graham had allegedly been arrested a number of times? Because in photographs, Graham did not look suitably angelic? Because the police initially alleged that he was flushing marijuana down the toilet? Because Graham's two half-brothers were awaiting trial on unrelated charges?

Graham's parents, Franclot Graham and Constance Malcolm, like Trayvon's parents, refused to let the circumstances surrounding his killing be ignored. They held a public funeral, a weekly vigil and a march demanding justice. On June 13, 2012, Officer Richard Haste was indicted for manslaughter, the first time a member of the New York Police Department has been charged in the death of a citizen since Sean Bell was killed in a hail of fifty bullets in 2006. Haste pleaded not guilty.

Those accused of the murders of Trayvon and Graham have been indicted and will stand trial.[1] But what accountability is there in the case of others killed in states that have Stand Your Ground laws? What about the three other people shot and killed by police in Anaheim in 2012? What about the two other black men shot by police in New York City the same week as Ramarley Graham? What of the many others whose names we do not know and whose deaths will remain unrecognized and unresolved unless communities organize to challenge excessive and deadly violence whatever the personal history of the deceased?

We must not succumb to the notion of good and bad victims. The organizing slogan "I am Trayvon Martin" should apply to all who are victims of murder – whether by police, vigilantes or those who reside in our communities. Our outrage and demands for justice cannot be confined only to those victims perceived as innocents.

1 In May of 2013 a Bronx judge, Steven L. Barrett, threw out the indictment, saying the Bronx DA had erred in telling the grand jury to disregard testimony that Haste had been told by other officers that Graham was armed. A second grand jury, impaneled in August of 2013, voted not to indict. In January of 2014 US District Court Judge P. Kevin Castel cleared the way for two federal civil suits to proceed against Officer Haste, former New York Police Commissioner Raymond Kelly and the NYPD. (Ed.)

Who's Afraid of Black Men's Eyes?

John Eskow

On Memorial Day, in Miami, a 14-year-old black kid named Tremaine McMillan was walking down the beach with his mother – and bottle-feeding his puppy – when cops blocked his path in ATVs. A few minutes before, the kid had been rough-housing in the surf with a friend, and the cops wanted to question him about it.

Moments later, the cops body-slammed the boy – still holding his puppy – onto the beach, got him in a chokehold, and arrested him for resisting arrest.

So far, so sickeningly normal.

But in this case, the police's cover story for the body slam, the chokehold, and the kid's subsequent arrest – that he was "clenching," or, in other accounts, "flaring" his fists – was hard to sell, due to one small but troublesome fact: cell phone video showed that *the kid never stopped cradling his puppy.* So the police spokesman invoked a truly terrifying specter: the teenager, he said, was giving the cops "dehumanizing stares."

Well, of course you can't blame battle-toughened Miami cops for starting to panic when a 14-year-old black male – armed with a puppy, mind you – starts to look at them funny.

But the truth is that these so-called "dehumanizing stares" are really "humanizing" stares, stares that forced the cops to realize that they were not successful in terrorizing this kid, and that he was committing that ancient Southern offense of looking a white man in the eye.

One can't help remembering the statutes against "reckless eyeballing," under which, in 1951, Matt Ingram, a black tenant farmer in Yanceyville, North Carolina, was charged with assault with intent to rape a white girl, although he was seventy-five feet away from her at the time.

And in good conscience we will never forget Emmett Till, slaughtered in Mississippi for looking at – and, supposedly, whistling at – another white girl, Carolyn Bryant. Till's torture and murder were once heartily defended by feminist Susan Brownmiller, who said that the glance and (alleged) wolf-whistle constituted "a deliberate insult just short of physical assault, a last reminder to Carolyn Bryant that this black boy, Till, had in mind to possess her."

Nice touch, eh, that "black boy"?

And to the ranks of Miami cops, wealthy New York gender theorists and rural racists, we can add the name of George Zimmerman, the morbidly obese Chaz Bono-lookalike who killed Trayvon Martin because – according to transcripts of the Mommy-I'm-scared call he made to police – "He was just staring...looking at the houses...now he's staring at me!"

Readers with more stomach than me for literary theory will no doubt be familiar with the academic racket centered on the concept of "the male gaze." Once I struggled in good faith to understand it, but then my ADD kicked in and I went outside to play catch with my daughter instead. So I don't have any intellectual framework for this rage I feel today, sensing that for all the distance we've supposedly traveled, we remain stuck on Square One in America – a ragged patch of ground defended by certain cops, certain feminists and vigilantes of all stripes against That Crime That Goes By Many Names ... a powerless black man looking at white folks.

Federal Bureau of Investigation
Digital Evidence Laboratory

Operational Technology
ERF Building 27958A
Quantico, Virginia 22135

REPORT OF EXAMINATION

To: Tampa
Squad ORA-2
Attention: SA James Majeski

Date: April 2, 2012

Case ID No.: 44A-TP-74471 – 9

Lab No.: 120323250 KR GA

Reference: Communication dated March 22, 2012

Ref. No.: Serial 3

Title: TRAYVON MARTIN-VICTIM;
GEORGE ZIMMERMAN-SUBJECT;
RACIAL DISCRIMINATION- FORCE AND OR VIOLENCE

Date specimen received: March 23, 2012

Specimens:

Q1 One Memorex CD-R marked in part "911 Calls" and "Case# 201250001136"

Request:

Special Agent James Majeski of the Tampa Division requests, per the above referenced communication, that the Forensic Audio, Video and Image Analysis Unit (FAVIAU) conduct an audio enhancement examination on specimen Q1. Also, analysis of the word following "fucking" at approximately 2 minutes and 20 seconds of file 20120571656-S13PIR.wav was requested to be identified.

On March, 24th, 2012, Special Agent Majeski requested via telephone that FAVIAU conduct a voice comparison examination of the designated area of specimen Q1 (screams in the background of the 911 call of file SPD TWIN TREES S35 EVT

Page 1 of 3

An ASCLD/LAB-*International* Accredited Laboratory Since January 16, 2007

For Official Use Only

20120571669.wav) and the caller's voice of file 20120571656_S13PIR.wav of specimen Q1. In addition, a signal analysis examination of specimen Q1 recordings was requested, including a chronology of the specimen Q1 audio events.

Opinions and Conclusions:

This report contains the opinions and conclusions resulting from the voice comparison and signal analyses.

Summary of Examination:

The audio on all eight files of specimen Q1 was enhanced and three FBI CD-R discs were made each containing direct and enhanced copies from specimen Q1.

The specific request to identify the word following "fucking" at approximately 2 minutes and 20 seconds of file 20120571656-S13PIR.wav could not be done due to weak signal level and poor recording quality.

Voice comparison is not possible for the designated voices due to extreme stress and unsuitable audio quality.

Details of Examination:

Specimen Q1 was electronically enhanced to optimize the intelligibility of the voices and attenuate interfering or distracting features in the recordings.

The specific request to identify the word following "fucking" at approximately 2 minutes and 20 seconds of file 20120571656-S13PIR.wav could not be done due to weak signal level and poor recording quality.

Critical listening and digital signal analyses were conducted on the first approximately 45 seconds of the 911 call on file SPD TWIN TREES S35 EVT 20120571669.wav of specimen Q1. During this 45 second segment, the designated screaming voice is audible for approximately 18.82 seconds in the background while a neighbor talks to the 911 dispatcher. Of the 18.82 seconds, the screaming voice is superimposed for approximately16.29 seconds by a simultaneous exchange between the calling female neighbor and the 911 female dispatcher. The total duration of the screaming voice without another voice overlapping is approximately 2.53 seconds long.

Critical listening and digital signal analyses further revealed that the screaming voice of the 911 call is of insufficient voice quality and duration to conduct a meaningful voice comparison with any other voice samples primarily due to the screaming voice being: (1) produced under an extreme emotional state, (2) limited in the number of

44A-TP-74471
120323250KR
Page 2 of 3

For Official Use Only

words and phrases uttered, (3) superimposed by other voices most of the time, and (4) distant, reverberant and very low signal level.

Three FBI CD-R copies were made containing direct and enhanced audio from specimen Q1. One of the discs was designated as Derivative Evidence "DE1" and the other two are labeled "Copy".

It is recommended that a high quality set of headphones be used when listening to the direct and enhanced audio files to obtain the optimum intelligibility.

Special Agent Majeski advised telephonically on April 2, 2012, to discontinue the request for preparation of an audio event chronology of specimen Q1.

The audio enhancement and signal analyses were conducted by Kenneth Marr. The voice comparison analysis was conducted by Dr. Hirotaka Nakasone.

Disposition of Evidence:

Specimens Q1, DE1 and the two additional copies were forwarded to your office via FedEx on March 24, 2012.

Examiner: Kenneth W. Marr

Operational Technology Division
Forensic Audio, Video and Image Analysis Unit

Examiner: Hirotaka Nakasone

Operational Technology Division
Forensic Audio, Video and Image Analysis Unit

44A-TP-74471
120323250KR
Page 3 of 3

For Official Use Only

The Deadly Legacy of Vigilantism

Jamilah King

For many observers, George Zimmerman's vigilantism exists in a long and deadly history for black Americans in the United States, one that dates at least as far back as the country's lynching epidemic of the early twentieth century. More than 4,700 lynchings occurred in the United States between 1887 and 1968, and the vast majority of the victims – an estimated 3,446 – were black.[1] Many of the victims were black men accused of raping white women and were often burned and maimed in front of large mobs of white onlookers.

Koritha Mitchell, an English professor at Ohio State University, takes an unusual approach to tackling this history in her new book, *Living With Lynching: African American Plays, Performance, and Citizenship, 1890-1930.* Her goal was to recount the ways in which black folks told their own stories of heartbreak and survival after these brutalities. She focuses on early twentieth-century black playwrights including Alice Dunbar-Nelson, Angelina Weld Grimke, Mary Burrill and Georgia Douglas Johnson.

Mitchell spoke with me about the significance of the plays, the dangers of black success and the moments throughout history – like this one – where collective dialogue becomes a crucial point for communities of color.

The history of lynching in the US is really horrific and painful for a lot of black Americans. Why was it important for you to tell this story, in particular?

Mitchell: As painful as it is, we have not necessarily shied away from it – which I think is a good thing. One of the ways we haven't shied away from it is through our support of (and our facing it through) the "Without Sanctuary" exhibition – those gruesome lynching photographs which were on display at the Martin Luther King, Jr. Center in Atlanta. People remarked upon how much black families were coming to the exhibit and using it as a way to grieve losses through generations.

1 See the Charles Chesnutt Digital Archive, http://www.chesnuttarchive.org/classroom/lynchingstat.html

What I found is that by using those photographs as our way of trying to grapple with what lynching meant in our nation's history, we really did ourselves a disservice. We weren't able to engage with what black people who survived this violence had left us in terms of understanding what the violence meant.

The "Without Sanctuary" photographs are a big reason why it was important for me to tell the story through the lynching plays: the lynching plays tell us exactly what the photographs *cannot* tell us, because the photographs are from a white perspective. You needed to be somewhat safe at a lynching to take those photographs. You've got this isolated black victim surrounded by a mob of righteous-looking whites, and that is all that we knew about lynching. But the construction of those photographs is very specific: it's to make sure that you think this was an isolated man who didn't have any connection to community. The plays give us a sense of just how connected to community and family those victims were.

One thing that stood out for me was that many of the playwrights that you talk about were black women. It underscores the profound impact that lynching had on black women even though the majority of documented victims were men. Can you talk a little bit more about that?

Mitchell: I think that women take a front seat with these plays for a couple of reasons. One is that they didn't necessarily have access to formal political activism through organizations like the NAACP and the Urban League. They were more likely to not have actual leadership positions in those organizations. I feel like the lynching plays are part of how they used non-traditional political activism.

The other reason is that writing was a way of telling the truth about how this person's death is really the beginning of a long struggle. It's the beginning of a long engagement with pain. 'How do we figure out how to continue to live in this country that allows our brother, our father, our husband, to be lynched?' I think that women taking the lead on the plays gives us a real sense of the lasting impact that lynching had on black communities.

The other thing that strikes me is that a lot of the playwrights were living in Washington, DC, when they wrote these plays. It's a real commentary on, number one, the fact that Washington is below the Mason-Dixon line. As our nation's capitol, I think we need to remember that, and all of the things that has meant. But, also, these playwrights had front row seats to the nation's hypocrisy, as anti-lynching bills were rejected time and time again by the legislature right there in Washington. I think that gave them a real perspective on the hypocrisy of the nation.

And to get a little bit more into the historical legacy of that hypocrisy, what immediate connections can you draw between the legacy of these plays and contemporary black media? I know that's a huge question.

Mitchell: We need to know just how much black success has been a part of our history. We need to know that success has not been something that was separate from experiencing attacks and violence from the mainstream. In other words, you don't get to be the largest prison population just because you're doing something wrong. That's not what's going on. It's also in the midst of a culture that's very much against your success. If we know more about how success – even in the face of the worst odds – has been made a part of our legacy, I think that gives us a certain kind of strength that we need right now.

It also seems to me that the plays, because they appealed to black audiences in the midst of this violence against blacks, remind us of the importance of community conversation. The importance of speaking to each other about who we are and what we face. That seems really crucial to me, because you always need people who are going to address the mainstream and try to get them to understand the nature of the injustice that's circulating around us. The Trayvon Martin situation is an excellent example of that. We need people who are willing to articulate why this is a grave injustice, to articulate why 'post-racial' claims are not helping anything. We need people who will do that.

But just as much, we need people who are focused on black communities and affirming black communities and making sure that we don't believe the hype, because that is what can be so telling, it seems to me. When we don't focus on affirming ourselves and each other because we're so busy addressing whites.

In the process of your research for this book, did you come across anything that was surprising?

Mitchell: Absolutely. The most surprising thing was that Ida B. Wells, who became the foremost anti-lynching crusader in our nation's history, had, in 1892, written in her diary that until her close friends were lynched, she thought that lynching might be justified. She has this moment of realizing that she had accepted the mainstream discourse that lynching – maybe it's horrible – but it is a response to rape against white women. And maybe these men who fell prey to the mob really did something to deserve it. But once her close friends were lynched, she realized that that was a lie that she had accepted. And, feeling that she had been duped, that is what made her so committed to exposing the truth about what actually caused lynchings. And, very often, she found that it was success. So when her friends were lynched, it was because they had a successful grocery store that was competition for the white-owned grocery store.

So I would say that was the most surprising thing – to see her admit that. For me, it's so important because what it means is that you're not immune to mainstream messages just because you're black. You're just as likely to believe the hype as anybody else. Because you're bombarded with messages constantly about how bad the race is, and how they brought most of what they're suffering on themselves, and if they'd just make better decisions things would be better. Who is immune to that message? None of us are. The only way that we can become immune to it – or at least resist it – is through community conversation: telling the truth to ourselves and one another about what is really making our realities and our situation.

I think that knowing the truth about these types of things is empowering. It doesn't have to be depressing. What's depressing is going through the society thinking that you're being treated fairly and not really being able to figure out what exactly is wrong with this picture.

Russell Simmons Tells Black People Not to Start a Race War Over Trayvon Martin

Yvette Carnell

There are certain black people you can count on to step up whenever there is any slight, perceived or real, to the black community. Al Sharpton will march no matter what. Whether anything changes after the march is another thing altogether, but you can certainly count on him to lock arms and dust off the old spiritual "We Shall Overcome." It's the activist's version of comedian Chris Rock's cure-all, Robitussin. No matter what ails the black community, a march will fix it.

Just as you can always depend on Sharpton to go out front with a march, you can always depend on Russell Simmons to chime in with some pseudo-black yogi wisdom. During the Occupy Wall Street protests, Simmons showed up at Zuccotti Park a few times, at least once with a dazed and befuddled-looking Kanye West.

Don't get me wrong, I'm fine with Simmons financially supporting a movement, as long as he remains in the background. But Simmons, like so many other so-called leaders, never met a camera he didn't like, and never had a thought he didn't want to share with the world. And since Simmons is not self-aware, which is odd for a meditation enthusiast, he has no clue that his Rush Card and his blood diamond make him far too compromised a person to stand at the center of any principled movement.

Nevertheless, I fully expected to hear from Simmons after Trayvon Martin's murder, and I wasn't disappointed. Simmons took to Twitter to add this tidbit to the conversation black people are having about the slaying:

> Trayvon Martin didn't die so we can create a race war; he died so we can promote better understanding. We must start honest dialogue.

Actually, no. Trayvon Martin didn't die so we could start a dialogue. Trayvon Martin died because he was shot in the chest. He died because a vigilante Neighborhood Watch captain, who'd called police forty-six times previously to report a "suspicious person," stalked him and murdered him in cold blood.

And who said anything about a race war? Does Simmons believe that black people are poised to take to the streets and start chucking spears at white people over Trayvon Martin's murder? I've heard a lot of discussion in black circles about getting the Justice Department involved, filing civil suits and the like, but remarkably nothing of a pending race war.

I imagine that not everyone can successfully navigate two worlds. Not everyone can muster the effort of being a bona fide star in white society and a principled activist within their own community. Russell Simmons is no Harry Belafonte.

But what bothers me most about Simmons's comment is that it vilifies the victims instead of the perpetrators. Yes, black people are angry. But black people aren't the ones in need of a lesson on how to behave. Black men aren't going around targeting white youth. It's the other way around, and if Simmons is honest with himself, he knows it. So why is Simmons equating justifiable black anger with the violence of a race war?

Right now, as black men all over America are discussing how to modulate their blackness so as not to be viewed as a threat in white society, Russell Simmons is reinforcing the myth of the angry black man by intervening to calm the savage black beast.

The White Right to Riot

Chuck Modiano

Oh, here we go again. The end of March Madness brought us another sports-fueled violent white riot after Kentucky won the 2012 NCAA Basketball Championship. The riot, which many predicted, came just sixty fires and two days after the first one, in which Kentucky fans burned cars to celebrate the team's win over Louisville.

The Final Four riots came just months after Penn State fans took to the streets, crashed down lampposts and flipped over trucks after football coach Joe Paterno was fired for not using his power to prevent the rape of young people.

The Penn State riots came a year after the Vancouver Canuck riots, which came a year after San Francisco Giants fans cheered their World Series win by looting, setting fires and attacking cars – or, as *The San Francisco Chronicle* put it, "joyful mayhem."

And when the games are over, there are the other crowds, reacting to real-life problems such as the shooting of Trayvon Martin and the larger criminal justice system his death symbolizes. Led by, but not limited to, right-wing media, many have wondered: "Is the Media Inciting Violence?" and "Is Spike Lee's Tweet the Same Kind of Violence that Killed Emmett Till?"[1] while "Sanford Frets About Prospects of Riots Over Trayvon Martin Killing."

While thousands of mostly white Kentucky fans were tearing up their campus, more than 1,400 mostly white people were gathered in Albuquerque, New Mexico, for the thirteenth annual White Privilege Conference to understand better what white privilege is, what it is not, what's inside the

1 Following the February 26, 2012, killing of Martin, director Spike Lee retweeted to his quarter-million Twitter followers what he thought was the home address of George Zimmerman. It turned out to be the address of a white Florida couple whose son is called William George Zimmerman. The couple, David and Elaine McClain, said threats forced them to decamp from their home and take to a hotel. Lee subsequently made apologies, tweeted "Justice in Court," said of his action, "It was stupid" and made a $10,000 settlement with the McClains. In November 2013, the McClains filed a personal injury suit seeking an estimated $1.2 million in damages from Lee. (Ed.)

"invisible knapsack" of privileges, and to use this knowledge to facilitate positive social change.

Law professor Kimberle Crenshaw gave the keynote address, titled "Intersectionality in the Age of Post-Racialism." Besides being a pioneering scholar, Dr. Crenshaw also happens to be a big sports fan, with childhood heroes named Jim Brown and Muhammad Ali. I had the privilege of sitting down with Dr. Crenshaw to get her thoughts on today's sports landscape. The first part of our conversation took place just a couple of hours before the first Kentucky riot. She had this to say in response to the Penn State riot:

> Fundamentally, we see how outrage, hurt and pain are framed sympathetically when they're about white pain, white institutions, white patriarchs, white heroes; and how just the fear of that kind of acting out [by blacks] will create such different reactions.
>
> So nothing bad has happened around all of the protests around Trayvon Martin, but everybody is saying: "just so it's nonviolent" ... "just so it doesn't get out of control" ... "let's not desecrate his memory."
>
> Well, nothing has happened.
>
> So that very disparity represents precisely the disciplinary fear of black people that led to Trayvon's death in the first place.

The sort of mindset, or "gutset," that produces greater concern over imagined black violence than over actual white violence is what continually produces so many variations of Trayvon Martin.

Dr. Crenshaw's comments were in line with the goals of the conference, which served as an introspective and productive gut-check for white people (and others) to help eradicate harmful biases by first recognizing their existence. As Dr. Eddie Moore Jr., founder and program director of the White Privilege Conference, put it, "It is important to look at white privilege in comprehensive ways, so when you look at Trayvon, you don't say 'I am Trayvon Martin,' but instead you explore the various ways in which you could identify and say, 'I am George Zimmerman.'"

Dr. Moore's statement signifies an honest recognition of everyday skin privilege, even if – especially if – that involves getting away with less than murder. It means identifying with George's stereotyping of Trayvon, even if his gunshots are replaced with disapproving stares. While identifying with Zimmerman may not be quite as comforting for white participants (including this author) as throwing on a hoodie in symbolic support of Trayvon, it's definitely necessary if we are going to get real about racism.

In this broader context, recognizing white privilege includes questioning "the white right to riot," for which the larger white community never has to pay a racial price. Those guys who set all the fires in Kentucky? "It wasn't me, not my problem." Being white means never having to suffer group punishment.

In the aftermath of the O.J. Simpson trial, for instance, as Dr. Crenshaw noted, despite legitimate reasons for doubt about the prosecution's case (and a racist lead cop), African-Americans were viewed, discussed and punished *as a group* – both socially and politically – for the celebratory response to the verdict. Conversely, the violent response to Joe Paterno's firing drew no group punishment or even group analysis of "white culture" or a "culture of white male privilege," but instead focused on every conceivable subculture besides race. According to one poll, even after months of reflection almost half the Pennsylvanians surveyed favored changing the current stadium name to Joe Paterno Stadium.

Honest national conversations by white people about white people as a group just don't happen. At least not in too many circles outside of the White Privilege Conference, where I learned at least three things:

(1) I have largely taken my hoodie-wearing for granted like I'm Bill Belichick;

(2) "Erupt Big Blue" means the right to riot twice in forty-eight hours without racial group repercussion; and

(3) "I Am Not Trayvon Martin."

A Post-Verdict Note From the Author

This article was written more than a year before the Zimmerman verdict, after which the phrase "I AM NOT TRAYVON MARTIN" took on a life of its own across websites, testimonials and Youtube videos. Symbolically, the meme was valuable in directly confronting the widespread belief among whites, and Zimmerman jurors, that "race had nothing to do with it." This point is not meant to detract from genuine acts of solidarity, such as that of white teen Alex Bearup, who proudly joined his African-American teammates at an AAU Basketball tournament while tweeting: "We will be rocking the 'I AM TRAYVON T-SHIRTS' in tonight's showcase game! #JusticeForTrayvon." Bearup's commendable call for justice, the spirit of his shirt, should trump the letters on it, and any shirt wrinkles can be ironed along the way "#JusticeForTrayvon."

'So, I Ask You, What if Trayvon Martin Were Asian?'

Scot Nakagawa

In 2012, I asked the question, What if Trayvon Martin were Asian? The question remains timely – at this particular moment, in light of warnings against rioting in reaction to the verdict in the George Zimmerman case. The sentiment seems to be that when African-Americans don't get their way, violence is likely to follow.

The reality is that the most damaging race riots in US history have been led by whites against people of color. In 1923, in Levy County, Florida, a white woman accused a black man of sexually assaulting her. More than 200 whites descended upon the city of Rosewood, the town in which the alleged assailant resided, and rioted, resulting in the deaths of at least six blacks and two whites and completely destroying the town, which was later abandoned.

In Bellingham, Washington, in 1907, hundreds of whites marched against Sikh immigrant workers, demanding they be fired immediately. When their demands weren't met, a mob of 150 whites rioted, assaulting Sikh workers and corralling them into the basement of Bellingham City Hall. Police officers cooperated, under the same rationale that would be used forty years later to imprison Japanese-Americans in concentration camps, claiming that holding the Sikhs hostage would reduce violence. No rioters were brought to trial, and their actions were widely supported by white people in Bellingham, some of whom claimed Sikh men had insulted white women.

In 1951, 4,000 whites rioted in protest against a black family moving into the all-white Cicero neighborhood of Chicago. Police did next to nothing to stop the rioters, who also stoned firemen called to put out fires they started. It took the Illinois National Guard to finally stop the riot.

And those are just a few incidents in which angry whites have rioted and taken the lives of both white people and people of color. And they don't begin to address the long history of white-led organized terrorism against people of color waged through organizations like the Ku Klux Klan. Yet, in spite of all the evidence of real and potential violence by whites, the speculation concerning riots in the wake of a verdict in the Zimmerman trial all revolve around the fear that black people will riot.

But what if Trayvon Martin were Asian? Here's what I had to say about that after the killing but before the trial:

In a Daily Kos article, Laurence Lewis asks the provocative question, "What if Trayvon Martin had been white and George Zimmerman were black?" I'm guessing you get the point. Clearly, if the races were reversed, things would be very, very different.

This got me to thinking, what if Trayvon Martin had been Asian, say Japanese-American? Would he have been profiled as a potential menace? Would he have provoked George Zimmerman to say, "These a**holes always get away"?

I'm guessing, no. Moreover, a Japanese-American Trayvon would be exempt from the kind of character assassination being attempted by right-wingers. No one would be combing his school records for evidence that he was a troublemaker. And if it turned out he was once caught with a little pot, it's not likely he'd be labeled a drug dealer.

And would white conservatives be defending the adult Zimmerman by presenting evidence that an Asian minor, described by his teacher as a cheerful A and B student, was suspended from school? I doubt it.

Nor would Bill O'Reilly speculate that an innocent verdict for Zimmerman "could very well lead to violence as we saw in the Rodney King case." The Japanese-American community up in arms rioting is not exactly the nightmare vision keeping conservative white folks up at night.

In fact, imagining the victim of this tragedy as Asian-American makes our society's negative stereotyping of African-Americans especially apparent. Why? Because Asian-Americans are subject to a different kind of stereotype, which was created as a foil to the racist, victim-blaming narrative about African-Americans that continues to serve as a justification for attacking the welfare state.

That stereotype casts Asian-Americans as the model minority: a group of mathletic (though not athletic) superachievers, overcoming prejudice and economic disadvantage not by protest but through hard work and uncritical patriotism.

The model minority myth popped up in the media during the civil rights era in a 1966 *New York Times Magazine* article titled, "Success Story: Japanese American Style." Until then, Asian-Americans were mostly labeled as evil outsiders in order to justify immigration limits and internment during World War II. But in the midst of black uprisings and protests, the article recast Japanese-Americans as a group that had quietly and politely pulled itself up by its bootstraps in spite of terrible obstacles (like being put in a concentration camp because, well, you're making white people nervous 'cuz you're Japanese-American).

The article made the claim that Japanese-Americans have a strong culture that values work, family and education, which prevents J.A.s from becoming a "problem minority." *Problem* minority? W.T.F! But the idea caught on, and over time, the myth expanded to Asians in general.

By the 1980s, Ronald Reagan twice publicly congratulated Asian-Americans for their success, while smacking down African-Americans for supposed dependency on welfare. In a "some of my best friends are black" move, Reagan used black conservative Alan Keyes as a wing man in this strategy. Reagan's crazy false logic says that if Asian-Americans can succeed in spite of terrible obstacles, then persistent poverty among African-Americans must be a product of a defect in black culture or black people.

And while Reagan was praising Asian-Americans, the architects of the Reagan revolution were confounding attempts on the part of black people to achieve success by ginning up anti-black racism in order to attack welfare. I'd call Reagan a genius, except that would be a compliment, and I just can't go there.

Nowadays, the model minority myth is just accepted as truth, even by lots of Asians. In fact, many Asian-Americans commit what they presume to be a victimless crime by taking cover behind the myth of the model minority. But there are victims, and they aren't only non-Asians. The victims include 54 percent of Asian-American kids who say they are bullied in school, at least in part as a result of stereotyping. And it includes the members of Asian ethnic groups that haven't been as successful, such as Bangladeshis, Laotians, Cambodians and the Hmong, all of whom have lower per capita incomes than African-Americans. The model minority myth marginalizes, even makes invisible, their suffering.

But the greatest danger of anti-Asian stereotyping, whether it is "positive" or not, is that it continues to hold Asian-Americans separate from other people. This makes us vulnerable to the flip side of the myth of Asian exceptionalism: the idea of Asian-Americans as a threat to "American" jobs. It was this kind of stereotyping that led to the murder of Vincent Chin, a

Chinese-American who was beaten to death by two displaced auto workers in 1982 during the US vs. Japan auto wars. Neither assailant ever did any jail time.

Today, as China's rise as an economic superpower inspires anxiety, even hatred, of the Chinese, the specter of more Vincent Chins ought to get us wondering, Is it ever a good thing to be used, no matter what the pay-off?

The stereotypes that afflict African-Americans and Asian-Americans may be very different, but they are really flip sides of one card, a race card. And that card is played against us all the time.

'Do You Care When Blacks Kill Other Blacks?'

Thandisizwe Chimurenga

This is for those who ask the question "Why don't you all care about black folks who kill other black folks?"

It is a legitimate question, kind of-sort of. I say that because it is a false equivalency, most often used to throw us off topic when we vent righteous indignation at state violence, meaning violence carried out by those forces that represent the government (local/municipal, state or federal) or those forces that act without penalty or censure by government – in effect, with the approval of government – specifically white vigilantes.

State-sponsored violence is a violation of human rights.

All police agencies are the armed forces of government, and it is the government that has created the situation, the conditions, that enable blacks to kill blacks. "Responsible" policing and crime control take place in white communities, while crime has been relocated to black communities *historically*. Government has shown indifference to the conditions of unemployment, poor housing, inequitable education and other ills it has created (or refused to alleviate) in black communities, while at the same time responding affirmatively to those same needs in white communities. The government has *openly* engaged in criminal activity in black communities (for instance, flooding black communities with guns and drugs during the Iran/*contra* period), and its police agents have actively encouraged and watched blacks kill blacks over drug money and gold chains. To top it all off, when the government commits state violence against us, when they kill us, there is no due process; there is rarely if ever a trial; no jury reflecting the community from whence the victim came; and there is no sentencing as punishment.

Police officers have an automatic "get out of jail free" card that consists of less than ten words: "I thought he had a gun," or, "I was in fear for my life."

It is black folks who should be in fear for their lives from the government. The government has a track record like no other.

While it is true that black folks do kill each other every day, the difference is that in the overwhelming majority of those cases an arrest is made and a perpetrator held; those cases go to court and the perpetrators are punished. "Lateral violence" – the violence of oppressed peoples striking out at one another, those closest to us instead of those who have caused our oppression – is a tragedy not only because of the lives lost by a historically persecuted (and prosecuted) people but because of the real-life contradiction it exposes. Lateral violence is absolutely encouraged by a white supremacist state, and yet it is still treated as illegal!

Black people are just as hurt and concerned and angry when black men die from gang violence, drive-by shootings and "being caught up" every single day as we are when the armed representatives of a white supremacist state (that says it exists to protect and serve) and "ordinary" white racist citizens murder us in cold blood.

Black people are just as hurt and concerned and angry when black women die from domestic violence (murdered by those who say they love us), *and* from gang violence *and* drive-by shootings *and* "being caught up," as we are when the armed representatives of a white supremacist state (that says it exists to protect and serve) or "ordinary" white racist citizens murder us in cold blood – as they did Tyisha Miller, Mitrice Richardson, Aleasia Thomas and Rekia Boyd.

BUT:

1. If you are dependent on the mainstream media to tell you that, you will not see it; they have no stake in that.

2. If you are dependent on black media, you may not see it there either; they may not have the resources to do it consistently.

3. If you are not in close proximity to black institutions or black people – in other words, if you don't know the folks that know – you are OOL, Out Of Luck.

In answer to your question "Why don't you all care about black folks who kill other black folks?", I must answer with this question: How come *you* don't care? *You* bring this up only when we rightly condemn and vent our anger at unjustified, racist murders.

If *you* really cared, then you would know that numerous organizations exist to stop the senseless, everyday murders of black people by black people.

1. You would know the names of these organizations;

2. You would know when their meetings are;

3. You would know where their meetings are held;

4. You would know the people who are a part of these organizations by name;

5. You would know the people who are a part of these organizations by sight;

6. You would go to their meetings;

7. You would ask them, "What can I do to help you all?";

8. You would ask your black and mainstream media, "Why don't you all write/broadcast anything about these organizations on a *regular* basis?";

9. You would give them much-needed money;

10. You would not have to ask the question.

I live in Los Angeles. These are the names I know: Cease Fire, 2nd Call, Unity One, Unity Two, the Professional Community Intervention Training Institute, Project Cry No More, Mothers of the Community, Unity in the Community, Peace in the Streets, Stop the Violence.

What city do you live in? Do you know the names of those who have taken it upon themselves to stop the *internal* bloodshed? Why not?

That's what I thought.

And that is as much of a shame as you claim black-on-black violence to be.

The Race-Baiting of America

Patricia Williams

As the nation takes stock of the 50th Anniversary of the March on Washington, I'm listening to a news program playing a recording of Dr. Martin Luther King, Jr. speaking of peace and reconciliation and mountaintops to be crested. I'm also online, watching my screen blink with discussions about current events like the dismissal of a racial harassment suit against Paula Deen and the debate over New York's stop-and-frisk policies. The decades-long span of unsolved issues and endless crises fills me with sadness and unease.

According to a recent Pew poll, "Blacks were nearly three times as likely as whites to be living in poverty. And the median net worth of white households was 14 times the median net worth of black households." But this disparate reality is felt very differently: nearly twice as many blacks as whites feel that blacks are treated less fairly by police and the courts; blacks are three times more likely than whites to feel that blacks are treated less fairly in employment, education, hospitals and stores. These findings are consistent with a trend documented by a 2011 article in the journal *Perspectives on Psychological Science*: whites now see anti-white bias as a bigger problem than bias against blacks – or, as the study's title puts it, "Whites See Racism as a Zero-Sum Game That They Are Now Losing."

It is one problem to have immense disparities. It is quite another when those inequalities are rendered invisible by those who stoke the fears and resentments that apparently feed the non-empirical perceptions of many Americans. Take the media treatment of the searingly tragic murder of Christopher Lane, a white Australian student attending a university in Oklahoma on a baseball scholarship. Three teens have been arrested for shooting him in the back while he was jogging, apparently because they were "bored." But while that so-called boredom is being mined for all its shock value, it is far too cavalier a way to describe the well of such inhuman callousness. Indeed, together the three suspects had histories of assault, little to no schooling, imprisoned parents and untreated trauma from gun deaths in their own families.

Initial reports were that all three suspects were black. In fact, one of them is white, though one right-wing outlet blithely and wrongly substituted the image of an uninvolved, angry-looking black man in his place. Before this mistake was revealed, the pre-existing liturgy was pushing the rapture that only demagoguery can create. Lines were drawn so that "gun culture" referred to those white people ostensibly exercising their Second Amendment rights to stockpile weaponry for the apocalypse, while "gang culture" referred to those black people (rarely accorded the imagined grace of Second Amendment rights) who also stockpile weaponry for the apocalypse. In either case, some of these arms end up in the hands of the unstable or mentally ill, or children, or the outlandishly aggrieved, or the intentionally criminal. America is not only where Christopher Lane was killed but also where – if we want to play the "reversals" game – the very next week, a black woman named Antoinette Tuff talked a disturbed young white man into putting down his AK-47 after he walked into an elementary school full of minority kids threatening a massacre. She did so by speaking to him in human, not bestial, terms. "I tried to commit suicide last year," she said. "We all go through something in life." America is also where there are more mass murders like those in Newtown and Aurora than anyplace on the planet other than war zones – and where, every day, more than 100 people of every stripe kill themselves, half by gunfire.

This violence is a national disgrace, a problem that knows no racial boundaries. We are a shoot-'em-up nation. How, then, does the small fraction of interracial killings end up as the dominant narrative, cast in terms that play out fantasies of a race war?

Trayvon Martin is not the same person as the troubled teenagers who allegedly shot Christopher Lane, yet he is endlessly figured as though he were. Questions like "Why doesn't Obama admit that these guys look like his son?" and "Where's the outcry from the NAACP now?" ricochet around the media.[1] But, seriously, who would protest the arrest and prosecution of the young men who committed this crime? What exactly is being imagined here? That members of the civil rights movement would actually defend murder? Or write it off when committed by black people?

---

1 Glenn Beck's co-host, Pat Gray, said "Did he [Obama] come and say, 'If I had an illegitimate love child with a white woman, he would look like Lane?" In a blog post, right-wing pundit Bernard Goldberg wrote, "If Barack Obama had a son he might look like the alleged shooter, Chancey Luna," or his lighter-skinned alleged accomplice. He didn't mention the other alleged accomplice, who is white. Rush Limbaugh fumed, "No matter where you look in the media,.... they're not focusing on the racial component of any of the people involved in this. We have not heard from the Reverend Sharpton, the Reverend Jackson, the NAACP.... This is worse than a double standard. This is a purposeful, willful ignoring of the exact racial components (but in reverse) that happened in the Trayvon Martin shooting." David Webb of Fox News had Robert Zimmerman, brother of George, as a guest on his show to discuss the "glaring double standard." (Ed.)

We can argue all day about what causes people to take potshots in Oklahoma or gang-rape women in India or slash schoolchildren in China or traffic sex slaves in Belgium. Yes, yes, personal responsibility – but not *racialized* responsibility. Perhaps it helps to put the question of violent crime in a global context, for then it becomes clearer that across humanity, the greater or lesser incidence of such crime is linked to factors like social upheaval and dislocation, poverty, population density, availability of weapons, untreated mental illness and lack of education.

In Australia, where homicides by gunfire have diminished dramatically since strict gun control laws were enacted in 1996, Lane's death has prompted calls for tourists to stop coming to the United States. "This is the bitter harvest and legacy of the policies of the NRA that even blocked background checks for people buying guns at gun shows," one politician observed. The Australian media have not only foregrounded the scandalous availability of firearms here; they have also discussed the broken humanity of the young suspects. It might be interesting if, after spending too much of the past fifty years talking in circles, we in America could see ourselves as reluctant tourists in the land of our own psyches. It might be helpful to begin shifting our discussion to the way in which all our souls are broken when we dehumanize by general habit.

The Trial

A Trial Is Never About the Truth

Bruce Jackson

Every criminal jury trial I've ever attended began with the prosecutor, the defense attorney, the judge or all three of them telling the jury that what is about to unfold is a search for the truth, and it is the jury's job to decide whether the prosecutor or the defense is telling the true story.

That is, of course, not the least bit true, and everyone in the courtroom knows it. A criminal trial is about winning and losing. Getting at the truth is at most an occasional lucky consequence. No one in the room, save the defendant and the victim (or the victim's survivors) has any real investment in the truth. Some judges may; all attorneys, whether for the defense or the state, represent their clients. What happened before – those events in the world outside the courthouse that set in motion the legal process resulting in the moment the bailiff has everyone rise for the entrance of the judge – is only the occasion for the battle within the courtroom.

The trial proper begins with opening and closing statements: the prosecutor makes an opening statement saying "what the evidence will show." The defense attorney tells a totally contradictory story (some trial lawyers save their opening statement for the defense part of the trial). Then there is the presentation of evidence, again followed by two stories. The second stories, this time limited to narratives based on what actually was seen and heard during the evidence phase, are told first by the prosecutor, then by the defense attorney. Sometimes the prosecutor gets to rebut. Then the judge tells the jury the law, instructs them that conviction requires them to accept the charges are true "beyond a reasonable doubt," and often reminds them that "beyond a reasonable doubt" is a very high bar. Then they go off to deliberate.

Sometimes the jury buys the story offered in summation by prosecutor or defense attorneys; sometimes they come up with their own theory of what happened. If they can't agree, there is another trial. If they do agree, that's it. They come out, the foreperson reads the verdict. If it is "not guilty," everybody goes home; if it is "guilty," the judge sets a date for sentencing. The acts of the drama are the same in every felony jury trial.

William Kunstler, the great civil rights attorney who died in 1995, once told me he believed in the jury system absolutely. "If I didn't," he said, "I'd quit this tomorrow and get a gun instead." "Even in the South?" I asked him. "Even in the South."

It was his experience, Bill said, that even in bigoted communities, juries would, with rare exceptions, make their decisions on what transpired within the courtroom.

And there is the rub: juries hear not what happened in the place the purported felony occurred but what is admitted into evidence. Before the first juror is seated there are heated arguments about what can and what cannot be admitted into evidence. Sometimes the judge excludes things because he or she thinks they are peripheral, or because the chain of possession from the time of the crime is not clear, or because they might be inflammatory (i.e., the jury might be so outraged at seeing a mutilated body it would convict a piece of wood). There are all sorts of reasons things that we "know" from reading the newspapers or watching CNN do not ever appear before the jury.

Sometimes things are said by a witness or one of the lawyers, and the lawyer on the other side objects, whereupon the judge may say, "The jury will disregard what was just said." Nobody believes for a moment that such statements from a judge erase things from jurors' memories; but they do reduce their weight, and they do keep them from being used in arguments in the jury room, where someone may mention them, but someone else will likely say, "But we were told to pay no attention to that."

All of these things – evidence or apparent evidence excluded before start of the arguments, the judge telling the jury to ignore this or that, and evidence (Trayvon Martin's sweatshirt) improperly handled (because of police screw ups, which compromised DNA evidence) – happened during George Zimmerman's trial. What that jury heard in the courtroom about what occurred that night in Sanford, Florida, and what we've heard about that night only occasionally overlapped. The jurors were sequestered from June 24 until July 13, when they entered their verdict.

The trial was about what Zimmerman had in mind when the killing occurred: did he encounter and then shoot Martin because he was a black person in a hoodie, or was Zimmerman doing ordinary Neighborhood Watch work that wound up in a scuffle and a shooting? "We truly believe the mindset of George Zimmerman, and the reason he was doing what he did fit the bill for second-degree murder," said Angela Corey, the state attorney who brought the charges, in a press conference after the trial ended.

Issues of race, which were central to the perception most of us had about what happened in Sanford, Florida, were totally excluded from the trial. Discussion of Florida's Stand Your Ground law, which permits people to shoot other people they feel threatened by rather than doing everything they can to get out of the situation first, were also excluded. Many people – correctly, I think – consider Stand Your Ground a racial hunting license. (According to *The New York Times*, Texas Governor Rick Perry said, "I think our justice system is color blind." Ho, ho, ho.)

The basic question, which the prosecutors could never put before the jury, is this: had Trayvon Martin been a blond white boy on the way home with a bag of goodies, would Zimmerman have thought him worth tracking in the first place?

A criminal trial is the drama occurring in that courtroom, one in which the only props and voices are those admitted by the judge. There is one further key factor: the competence and judgment of the attorneys on either side, the two sets of script-writers, in effect. Think, for example, of the O.J. Simpson trial twenty years ago and the prosecution's fiasco around the glove that did not fit. Prosecutors got Simpson to perform in front of the jury, and gave defense lawyer Johnnie Cochran one of the key lines of his brilliant summation: "If it doesn't fit, you must acquit." Which the jury proceeded to do. (The other masterly thing Cochran did was to spend much of his summation indicting the Los Angeles Police Department for racism. Instead of just arguing over the prosecution's narrative, he put before the jury an entirely different narrative.)

In the Zimmerman case, the prosecution's failure to get over that "beyond a reasonable doubt" bar did them in. "Even after three weeks of testimony," Lizette Alvarez and Cara Buckley wrote in *The New York Times* on July 14, the fight between Mr. Martin and Mr. Zimmerman on that rainy night was a muddle, fodder for reasonable doubt. It remained unclear who had started it, who screamed for help, who threw the first punch and at what point Mr. Zimmerman drew his gun. There were no witnesses to the shooting."

"Not guilty" is not the same as "He's innocent." All "not guilty" means is, "The prosecutor made a claim and then didn't convince us, beyond a reasonable doubt, that it was true." There is talk now of asking the Justice Department to take this on as a civil rights crime. Unless some startling new evidence surfaces, that is unlikely to go anywhere: it was a dark and lonely night on that street in Sanford, Florida, and only one living person knows what really happened there, and, by this point, he might not be too sure of anything either.

CAPIAS REQUEST

Sanford Police Department

S.P.D.

SUSPECT

Region S
CSA 13 GRID
Agency ORI # FL0590500 OBTS #

23/62 For The Statute No
Juvenile Yes
Agency Report # 201250001136

CAPIAS REQUEST

Name ZIMMERMAN, GEORGE MICHAEL Race W Sex M DOB 10/5/1983 Or Age
Height 507 Weight 200 Eyes BRO Hair BRO Alcohol Related N Drug Related N
Local [redacted] Residence City
NOK Phone Religion
Business Name Business Address
Job Business Phone
DL # [redacted] DL State FL SSN [redacted] Marital M Place of Birth Citizenship US
Weapon Type 01 HANDGUN Local # FDLE #

Alias Name(s) | Person Identifier(s):

Co-Defendant(s):

Name	Race	Sex	DOB	Or Age

CHARGE(S)

OFF #	Description	Statute #		UCR	Ordinance	Attempt/ Commit	Warrant #	DVR	Drug Activity
1	HOMICIDE-NEGLIG MANSL-	782.07	1	090C	No	C		No	
									0.00

PROBABLE CAUSE

Investigative findings show that on 2/26/2012 at approximately 1912 hrs George Michael Zimmerman initiated a nonemergency call to Sanford Police dispatch to report a suspicious person. Zimmerman reported a suspicious person, Trayvon Martin, whom he observed entering the gated community of The Reserve at Twin Lakes on foot, walking between residences from the northwest. Zimmerman initiated his call by stating there had been "some break ins" to his neighborhood in the recent past, and that Martin was a "real suspicious guy". Zimmerman went on to state that Martin was "up to no good", "on drugs or something", and stated that it was raining and that Martin was "walking around looking about". Zimmerman went on to tell the call taker that Martin was "here, now, just looking at houses" and then stated "now he's staring at me", "now he's coming toward me", "he has his hand in his waist band". Zimmerman described Martin as a Black male in his late teens. Zimmerman further stated that there is "Something wrong with this guy. He's coming to check me out. I don't know what his deal is". Zimmerman then says "These assholes. They always get away. Yep".

Zimmerman maintained contact with the call taker, and stated about Martin, "Shit, he's running". The call taker asked of Zimmerman, "Are you following him?", to which Zimmerman stated "yes", and the call taker replied, "we don't need you to do that". Zimmerman referred to Martin as a "fucking punk" under his breath. Investigation reveals that Martin was in fact running generally in the direction of where he was staying as a guest in the neighborhood.

Investigation reveals that on August 3, August 4, and October 6, 2011, and February 2, 2012, George Zimmerman reported suspicious persons, all young Black males, in the Retreat neighborhood to the Sanford Police Department. According to records checks, all of Zimmerman's suspicious persons calls while residing in the Retreat neighborhood have identified Black males as the subjects.

Investigative findings show that Zimmerman admitted to avoiding a confrontation with Martin while Zimmerman was observing Martin from his vehicle, because, as he told investigators, was afraid of Martin. Later in the encounter, Zimmerman exited his vehicle, in spite of his earlier admission to investigators that he was afraid of Martin, and followed Martin in an effort to maintain surveillance of him while Zimmerman awaited the arrival of law enforcement officers. His actions are inconsistent with those of a person who has stated he was in fear of another subject.

Investigative findings show that George Michael Zimmerman had at least two opportunities to speak with Trayvon Benjamin Martin in order to defuse the circumstances surrounding their encounter. On at least two occasions, George Michael Zimmerman failed to identify himself as a concerned resident or a neighborhood watch member to Trayvon Benjamin Martin. Investigative findings show the physical dimensions of Trayvon Benjamin Martin, and that of George Michael Zimmerman, coupled with the absence of any specialized training in hand to hand combat between either combatant, did not place George Michael Zimmerman in an extraordinary or exceptional disadvantage of apparent physical ability or defensive capacity. Investigative findings show the physical injuries displayed by George Michael Zimmerman are marginally consistent with a life-threatening violent episode as described by him, during which neither a deadly weapon nor deadly force was deployed by Trayvon Martin.

The following sequence of events were obtained by admissions made by Zimmerman and cannot be corroborated by independent witnesses, nor can be refuted by independent witnesses: While Zimmerman was returning to his vehicle, he states he was attacked by Martin, but only after Martin inquires to Zimmerman "What's your problem?" Zimmerman, instead of attempting to inform Martin of the reason he was following him, stated to Martin "I don't have a problem". As Zimmerman responds to Martin, by his own admission, Zimmerman reaches into his pocket attempting to

201250001136 Printed On: 3/13/2012 14:50 Page 1 of 3

CAPIAS REQUEST

Sanford Police Department

Region: S
C.S.A.: 13 GRID:
Agency ORI #: FL0590500 OBTS #:

For The Public: No
Juvenile: Yes
Agency Report #: 201250001136

locate his cell phone. As Zimmerman reaches for his cell phone, he stated Martin replies "You have one now", and Martin punches Zimmerman in the face, knocking him to the ground. Zimmerman stated that he was battered by Martin to the point of almost losing consciousness. He stated he ultimately had no choice but to shoot Martin in self-defense.

At 1916 hours, a 911 call, placed by [redacted] was received where Zimmerman can be heard in the background frantically yelling for help. At 1917 hours a gunshot was heard in the background of the [redacted] 911 call, and moments later Officer Tim Smith arrived on scene.

The encounter between George Zimmerman and Trayvon Martin was ultimately avoidable by Zimmerman, if Zimmerman had remained in his vehicle and awaited the arrival of law enforcement, or conversely if he had identified himself to Martin as a concerned citizen and initiated dialog in an effort to dispel each party's concern. There is no indication that Trayvon Martin was involved in any criminal activity at the time of the encounter. Zimmerman, by his statements made to the call taker and recorded for review, and his statements made to investigators following the shooting death of Martin, make it clear that he had already reached a faulty conclusion as to Martin's purpose for being in the neighborhood.

Attempts to locate additional witnesses have consisted of multiple canvasses of the neighborhood on the evenings of 2/26/2012, 2/27/2012, and 3/1/2012. The distribution of informational flyers throughout the gated community was completed on 2/29/212 and a community meeting, which was held on March 1, 2012.

All digitally recorded interviews were submitted as evidence, and all forensic laboratory requests are being submitted to the Florida Department of Law Enforcement for analysis.

Based upon the facts and circumstances outlined in this narrative, I believe there exists probable cause for issuance of a capias charging George Michael Zimmerman with Manslaughter, in violation of Ch. 782.07 FS.

This case is being forwarded to the Office of the State's Attorney as a request for capias.

ADMINISTRATIVE SECTION

I swear/affirm the above and entered and attached statements are true and correct. Officer's/Complainant's Signature	Verified By: Sworn to and subscribed before me, the undersigned authority, this ___ day of ___, in the year 2012. Name/Title of Person Authorized to Administer Oath

201250001136 Printed On 3/13/2012 14:50 Page: 2 of 2

REPORT OF INVESTIGATION

CASE NUMBER: 201250001136	Page 2 of 13
INVESTIGATOR: Serino, Christopher F	

DETAILS:

Case Synopisis:

On 2/26/2012, at the Retreat at Twin Lakes community, located on Oregon Avenue in Sanford, Seminole County, Florida, a twenty-eight year old white male, identified as George Michael Zimmerman and seventeen year old black male, identified as Trayvon Benjamin Martin, engaged in a physical confrontation in a common area behind two rows of townhomes. The incident was witnessed by several people, all of whom called 911 however the initial harmful event has no known eyewitnesses.

Preliminary investigation showed that Zimmerman, a member of his community's Neighborhood Watch Program, observed Martin walking in the community, and perceived Martin as being "suspicious". Zimmerman acted on his suspicion of Martin, and called the Sanford Police non-emergency line. Zimmerman reported he was following Martin, and requested police assistance by the dispatching of a patrol officer. Zimmerman, who was in his motor vehicle, initially followed Martin, who was on foot. During his surveillance of Martin, Zimmerman was on a recorded telephone line with the Seminole County Communications call taker. As Zimmerman followed Martin, Martin apparently became aware of Zimmerman, and allegedly attempted to confront Zimmerman by walking towards Zimmerman's vehicle. Zimmerman, instead of informing Martin as to the reason he was following him, raised the window to his vehicle and did not acknowledge Martin or engage him in any conversation.

As Martin continued on his way, in a direction which would have led him to the residence of [redacted] where he was an authorized guest, Zimmerman continued to follow him in his vehicle. When Martin arrived at a pedestrian cut-through, consisting of a walkway between the 1200 block of Twin Trees Lane, and the 2800 block of Retreat View Circle, Zimmerman told the dispatcher that Martin started to run.

Upon viewing Martin taking flight, Zimmerman exited his vehicle in an attempt to see where Martin was going, in order to relay that information to the dispatcher. According to Zimmerman's audio recorded version of events, after he exited his vehicle which he parked on Twin Trees Circle, he walked toward Retreat View Circle. Zimmerman stated he looked generally southward, down the walkway, and did not see Martin. During the course of this activity, Zimmerman was still speaking to the call taker, who asked if Zimmerman was following Martin. Zimmerman replied that he was, and the Police call taker told Zimmerman "we don't need you to do that". Zimmerman stated he terminated his phone call with the dispatcher when he was at the end of the cut through at Retreat View Circle, and started walking back to his vehicle.

Zimmerman stated that as he was walking back to his vehicle, "out of nowhere" appeared Martin who approached him from his left rear. Zimmerman stated that Martin approached him and asked Zimmerman what his problem was, then with a closed fist, struck Zimmerman in the face, causing Zimmerman to fall to the ground. Once on the ground, Zimmerman stated that Martin struck him multiple times in his facial area, and at one point, smashed the back of his head onto the cement walkway to the point that Zimmerman almost lost consciousness.

Zimmerman stated that while being battered by Martin, Zimmerman felt Martin reaching for his firearm, which he had on his person in an inside the waistband nylon holster, with no safety features. Zimmerman is licensed in the State of Florida to carry concealed firearms . Zimmerman stated that he believed Martin was attempting to remove his firearm, at which time Zimmerman was able to free himself to the point of being able to clear the firearm from its holster, and fire one round at point blank range, which struck Martin in the chest. Zimmerman stated that after he discharged the firearm, Martin ceased battering him, and fell over, which enabled Zimmerman to get back on his feet. Immediately after the incident, Officer T. Smith arrived on scene, and placed Zimmerman into custody. Zimmerman claimed a self-defense explanation of the encounter, which he maintained throughout subsequent investigation.

Victimology:
The decedent, positively identified by means of a postmortem photograph by his biological father as Trayvon Benjamin Martin, was a 17 year old resident of Miami Gardens, Florida, and a high school student with no criminal background. When asked as to his propensity towards violence, his father, Mr. Tracy Martin, states his son was a well- mannered, non-violent child. A local Miami Gardens Police Department background check revealed one field contact conducted in November of 2011. Martin was a guest of [redacted] who

Page 2 of 13

resides on [redacted] and he had been sent there by his father due to having been suspended for ten days from his high school in Miami Gardens for possession of cannabis. He had been in Sanford for seven days prior to this event.

On 2/26/2012 at approximately 1926 hours, I was notified of a shooting with injuries event by the Seminole County Communications Center, and I was instructed to contact the duty Watch Commander, Lieutenant M. Taylor
At approximately 1930 hours I contacted Lieutenant M. Taylor, via NexTel, and I was informed of the location of the incident, and that one person (unidentified black male) was pronounced dead on scene, and that the individual who shot the decedent, identified as George Michael Zimmerman, had remained on scene, was cooperative, was in police custody. I was told that Zimmerman had been transported to the Sanford Police Department for interviewing purpose. I was also advised that the weapon used was also in police custody.

On arrival at the scene, at approximately 2000 hours, I met with SPD Officer Ricardo Ayala, who produced the preliminary report. Officer Ayala briefed me as to the known circumstances. I was informed by Officer Ayala that an apparent confrontation occurred between the then unidentified black male, later positively identified as Trayvon Benjamin Martin, age 17, and George Michael Zimmerman. Officer Ayala further informed me that during the confrontation, Zimmerman stated that he produced a 9mm semiautomatic pistol (for which he had a valid Florida concealed firearm carry permit), and fired a single round, striking Martin in the chest. Officer Ayala informed me that lifesaving efforts performed by Sgt. R. Raimondo, and Officer T. Smith, and Sanford Fire Rescue proved unsuccessful, and that Martin was pronounced dead on scene by Sanford Fire Rescue 38.

I then interviewed Officer T. Smith, who was the first officer on scene. Officer Smith informed me that upon his arrival he came in contact with George Zimmerman, apparently moments after Zimmerman had shot Trayvon Martin. Officer Smith informed me that Zimmerman offered no resistance while he was placed into custody at gunpoint. He stated that Zimmerman's facial area was bloodied, and the posterior of his clothing was soiled with wet grass, indicative of having recently been on his back on the grass. Officer Smith stated Zimmerman freely admitted to having shot the decedent, and stated he had shot the decedent after the decedent attacked him. While Officer Smith was in contact with Zimmerman at the scene, Officer Smith overheard Zimmerman state "I was yelling for someone to help me, but no one would help me", as he was being treated for his injuries by Sanford Fire Rescue personnel.

I was also informed that statements made by Zimmerman on scene to Officer T. Smith were corroborated by several witnesses, and led to the possibility of this shooting having been in self-defense. Written statements were obtained from [redacted] Audio recorded statements from these witnesses were conducted at a later date (referred to later in this narrative).

After I learned from Lieutenant Taylor that George Zimmerman had been transported to the Sanford Police Department, I requested Inv. Doris Singleton respond to the police station in order to interview Zimmerman. I contacted Inv. Singleton, informed her of the apparent nature of this matter, and advised her to remove Zimmerman's restraint devices prior to conducting her interview.

I remained on scene and coordinated crime scene processing efforts with Sgt. L. Celsia and Crime Scene Technician D. Smith. The scene was an outdoor crime scene, in a predominately grassy area with a paved walkway between two rows of townhomes, bordered by Retreat View Circle, and Twin Tree Lane. The time of the evening when the shooting occurred was approximately 1916 hours, after sunset, on an overcast evening with sporadic rain showers. The only ambient lighting was produced by the porch lights of several residences, and overall the location can be best described as dark. The decedent lay supine directly behind [redacted] covered by a yellow police issued emergency blanket. He was wearing a dark gray hooded pullover sweatshirt, tan pants, and tennis shoes. I observed no blunt force trauma to his head or facial area.
At approximately 2020 hours I spoke with Volusia County Medical Examiner's Office Investigator T. Clark, and requested her response.
At approximately 2030 hours I interviewed [redacted], who resides at [redacted] stated that while inside of his residence he heard a commotion and two "pops" coming from the area behind his residence. Upon exiting his residence to investigate, he encountered a white male, established to be George Zimmerman. Zimmerman asked [redacted] if he had blood on his face. Zimmerman then stated "the guy he was beating up on me and I had to shoot him". [redacted] stated he did not witness the sequence of events which led up to the confrontation between Martin and Zimmerman. [redacted] provided a written statement, and his interview was audio recorded and submitted into evidence.

On 2/26/2012 at approximately 2055 hours I interviewed [redacted], who was in her bedroom, stated she heard "loud voices" coming from the area behind her

Page 3 of 13

residence. She stated she heard a commotion, which sounded to her like arguing. She then stated that she, from her bedroom window, observed two men on the ground, and she then heard someone yell "help, help". She then heard a 'pop" noise and then saw the decedent laying on the ground, motionless, and the other male, who she described as "larger" and "Hispanic looking", standing over the decedent. Upon inquiry, [redacted] stated she did not witness how the confrontation between the decedent and the shooter occurred. [redacted] provided a written statement, and her interview was audio recorded and submitted into evidence.

On 2/26/2012 at approximately 2105 hours I interviewed [redacted] stated that while inside of his residence he heard a commotion coming from the walk way behind his residence. When he investigated, he witnessed a black male, wearing a dark colored "hoodie" on top of a white or Hispanic male who was yelling for help. He elaborated by stating the black male was mounted on the white or Hispanic male and throwing punches "MMA (mixed martial arts) style". He stated he yelled out to the two individuals that he was going to call the police. He then heard a "pop". He stated that after hearing the "pop", he observed the person he had previously observed on top of the other person (the black male wearing the "hoodie") laid out on the grass. Upon inquiry, [redacted] stated he did not witness how the confrontation started between the two individuals, and that he could not positively identify either one due to the lighting conditions. [redacted] stated he was in his living room at the onset of the commotion, and looked out of his sliding glass door, which placed him approximately 30 feet directly in front from where the physical altercation between Martin and Zimmerman was taking place. [redacted] provided a written statement, and his interview was audio recorded and submitted into evidence. [redacted] written statement reads as follows:

"I heard yelling out back in grass area of home but not sure at first but after second "help" yell I opened blinds, and saw clothing but everything dark outside. I opened door and saw a guy on the ground getting hit by another man on top of him in a strattle [sic] position hitting a guy in red sweatshirt or on the bottom getting hit was yelling help (guy getting hit on ground was wearing red calling out help). I said I was calling the cops and ran upstairs then heard a gunshot. When I got upstairs I saw the guy on top who was hitting the guy in the red laid out on the grass as if he had been shot. I also saw the guy in red standing near end of sidewalk where a guy with flashlight probably neighbor was talking to him asking what happened."

On 2/26/2012 at approximately 2130 hours, VCME Office Investigator Tara Clark arrived on scene and assumed jurisdiction over the decedent. Initial inspection on the decedent showed no significant trauma, other than a solitary gunshot wound to the chest, just left of midline. The decedent was found to not be in possession of any form of identification, and was transported to the Volusia County Medical Examiner's Office as "John Doe #3". On his person was a can of Arizona brand iced tea, a bag of Skittles candy, and $40.15 in US currency.

On 2/26/2012, while at the Sanford Police Department, 815 West 13th Street, Sanford, Investigator Doris Singleton conducted an interview of George Zimmerman after he waived his rights as indicated by his signature on a prepared Miranda Warning card. In his interview, Zimmerman maintained he shot Martin in self-defense, and only after being placed in fear for his life by Martin. Detailed information pertaining to statements made by George Zimmerman is provided by Investigator Singleton in her Report of Investigation. Zimmerman provided a four (4) page written statement which reads as follows:

"In August of 2011 my neighbor's house was broken into while she was home with her infant son. The intruders attempted to attack her and her child; however, SPD reported to the scene of the crime and the robbers fled. My wife saw the intruders running from the home and became scared of the rising crime within our neighborhood. I and my neighbor formed a "Neighborhood Watch Program". We were instructed by SPD to call the non-emergency line if we saw anything suspicious & 911 if we saw a crime in progress. Tonight, I was on my way to the grocery store when I saw a male approximately 5'11" to 6'2" casually walking in the rain looking into homes. I pulled my vehicle over and called SPD non-emergency phone number. I told the dispatcher what I had witnessed, the dispatcher took note of my location & the suspect fled to a darkened area of the sidewalk, as the dispatcher was asking me for an exact location the suspect emerged from the darkness & circled my vehicle. I could not hear if he said anything. The suspect once again disappeared between the back of some houses. The dispatcher once again asked me for my exact location. I could not remember the name of the street so I got out of my car to look for a street sign. The dispatcher asked me for a description and the direction the suspect went. I told the dispatcher I did not know but I was out of my vehicle looking for a street sign & the direction the suspect went. The dispatcher told me not to follow the suspect and that an officer was in route. As I headed back to my vehicle the suspect emerged from the darkness and said "you got a problem". I said "no". The suspect said "you do now". As I looked and tried to find my phone to dial 911 the suspect punched me in the face. I fell backwards onto my back. The suspect got on top of me. I yelled "help" several times. The suspect told me "shut the fuck up" as I tried to sit up right, the suspect grabbed my head and slammed it into the concrete sidewalk several times. I continued to yell "help". As I slid the suspect covered my mouth and nose and stopped my breathing. At this point I un holstered my firearm in fear for my life as he had assured he was going to kill me and fired one shot into his torso. The suspect sat back allowing me to sit up and said "you got me"! At this point I slid out from underneath him and got on top of the suspect holding his hands away from his body. An onlooker appeared and asked if I was ok, I said "no", he said "I am calling 911". I said "I don't need you to call 911 I already called them I need you to help me restrain this guy". At this point a SPD Officer arrived and asked "who shot him"? I said "I did" and I placed my hands on top of my head and told the officer where on my person my firearm was holstered. The officer handcuffed me and disarmed me. The officer then placed my in the back of his vehicle."

On 02/26/2012 at approximately 2345 hours I spoke with Assistant State Attorney Kelly Jo Hines and apprised her of the circumstances surrounding this case.

On 2/27/2012 at 0005 hours, I met with George Zimmerman at the Sanford Police Department. At that time I showed him with a photograph of the decedent. Zimmerman stated he did not recognize him. Zimmerman informed me that on the evening of 2/26, he had called the Sanford Police Department non-emergency line to report the decedent as a suspicious person. Zimmerman stated the decedent approached him in the walkway between Retreat View Circle and Twin Trees Lane and stated to him "What's your problem?" Zimmerman stated he replied "I don't have a problem" at which time the decedent stated "You have one now", at which time the decedent attacked him without provocation, battered him to the point that Zimmerman almost lost consciousness.

Zimmerman stated that Martin attempted to manually suffocate him and attempted to assume possession of Zimmerman's firearm. Zimmerman stated that Martin said to him "You're gonna die motherfucker". Zimmerman stated he would cooperate fully with the investigation and asserted he discharged his firearm out of fear for his life.

Zimmerman displayed injuries to his facial area and to the back of his head, which were treated by Sanford Fire Rescue at the time he was detained by Officer T. Smith. He also stated he was going to follow up with his primary care physician to have his injuries further evaluated. No visible physical injuries were noted or documented to his body/torso area, nor were any defense wounds noted on his arms or hands. Zimmerman had been treated on scene while in Officer Smith's custody, and he declined transport for emergency medical treatment. While in my presence, on 2/27/2012, Zimmerman complained of a headache, and stated he intended to follow up with his primary care physician.

Based on all of the information available at the time of this contact with Zimmerman, coupled with the consistency between Zimmerman's account of events and those provided by witnesses, and injuries sustained by Zimmerman which appeared generally consistent with the facts and circumstances known at the time, Zimmerman was released from police custody, pending further investigation of this matter pursuant to Chapter 776.032 (2) F.S.

On 2/27/2012, at approximately 0920 hours, after learning of a missing persons' complaint in progress at [redacted], I responded along with CSO Ed Manning, and SPD Officer B. McIntosh. On arrival I met with Tracy Martin who stated his 17 year old son, Trayvon Martin, had not returned from going to the store sometime on the evening of 2/26. Mr. Martin informed me his son was not from this area, and that his son is visiting from Miami Gardens, and that his son did not have a State of Florida Identification Card or Driver's License. While conversing with Mr. Martin, I noted several physical characteristics he had in common with the decedent, thereby establishing a reasonable factual basis to believe that the decedent was the son of Mr. Martin. Upon presenting Mr. Martin with a photograph of the facial image of the decedent, taken at the scene, positive identification was made in conjunction with Next of Kin notification. I explained the circumstances surrounding the passing of his son, and summoned for a victim's advocate to assist. Victim's Advocate Debra Wagner responded and assisted Mr. Martin and his family.

On 2/27/2012 at 1030 hours, Trayvon Martin underwent a forensic autopsy at the Volusia County Medical Examiner's Office. Preliminary autopsy findings ruled cause of death was injury stemming from a gunshot wound to the chest which perforated the heart organ, manner of death established as homicide. A single projectile was recovered from the chest cavity of the decedent, and submitted into evidence by CST D. Smith.

On 2/27/2012 I was provided with the audio recordings of six (6) 911 calls stemming from this incident, along with a recording of George Zimmerman's non-emergency call.

I reviewed Zimmerman's nonemergency call to SPD dispatch. Zimmerman described Martin as "real suspicious", and that he "was up to no good". Zimmerman also relayed to the call taker that Martin was "on drugs or something", and that "something's wrong with him". Zimmerman commented "these assholes always get away", and later referred to Martin as a "fucking punk".

I reviewed the 911 calls, specifically 20120571669, placed by [redacted]. In the background I could clearly hear a male's voice yelling either "Help" or "Help Me", fourteen (14) times in an approximately 38 second time span. This voice was determined to be that of George Zimmerman, who was apparently yelling for help as he was being battered by Trayvon Martin.
Investigator D. Singleton, using information obtained from the Seminole County Sheriff's Office Computer

Page 5 of 13

Aided Dispatch (CAD), established the following timeline:

Event 2012571656
1911:12 Call received from George Zimmerman reporting suspicious person
1913:19 Zimmerman relays suspicious person is running from him
1913:36 Dispatcher asks Zimmerman if he is following suspicious person
1913:36 Dispatcher advises Zimmerman "Okay; we don't need you to do that"
1915:53 Approximate time call with Zimmerman ends
Event 2012571669
1916:43 911 call placed by [redacted] where Zimmerman is heard screaming for help
1917:20 Shot fired; screams from Zimmerman cease
Event 20120571671
1917:40 Officer T. Smith arrives on scene
1919:43 Officer T. Smith locates and places Zimmerman in custody

On 2/27/2012 at approximately 1730 hours, Sergeant R. Smith, Investigator D. Singleton, Crime Scene Technician D. Ripley, and I met with George Zimmerman at his residence for the purpose of retracing his steps on 2/26 on video. Zimmerman's route was videotaped by CST Ripley and the DVD was submitted as evidence.

On 2/28/2012 at 1030 hours I met with Tracy Martin, and [redacted] at the Sanford Police Department. The purpose for this meeting was to brief the decedent's next of kin as to the progress of this investigation. Mr. Martin, concerned over there being no arrest made in the shooting death of his son, was advised of the nature of this case, and ultimately assured that a proper investigation would be conducted. Mr. Martin acknowledged the complexity of this case prior to departing.

On 02/28/2012, Investigator Trekell Perkins received a telephone call from an unidentified female. This female, who refused to provide her name, call back number, or any other type of contact information, disclosed to Inv. Perkins that George Zimmerman has racist ideologies, and that he is fully capable of instigating a confrontation that could have escalated to the point of Zimmerman having to use deadly force. Inv. Perkins was able to record a portion of his conversation with this anonymous female and said recording was placed on a compact disc and submitted as evidence. No other information has been obtained to corroborate this anonymous female's information and her identity has not been established.

On 2/29/2012 at approximately 1720 hours, George Zimmerman was re-interviewed at the Sanford Police Department. This interview was digitally recorded. After being advised of his rights under Miranda, Zimmerman agreed to be interviewed. Upon inquiry, Zimmerman stated he was suffering from Post-Traumatic Stress Disorder (PTSD). He further informed me that he has been diagnosed with Attention Deficit Disorder, and is currently on medication for that condition. Upon inquiry, Zimmerman stated Trayvon Martin aroused his suspicion due to a recent break in his neighborhood, because Zimmerman observed Trayvon stop in front of a house that had recently been burglarized. Zimmerman further stated he found Trayvon's pace while walking was out of the ordinary due to the fact that it was raining, and Trayvon did not appear to be making any attempt to get out of the rain. Upon my inquiry as to what may have incited Trayvon Martin to attack him so violently, Zimmerman could not provide any reason.
During the interview, Zimmerman stated at one point, Trayvon approached his vehicle, apparently after Trayvon noticed he was being followed by Zimmerman. I asked Zimmerman why he had not engaged Trayvon in conversation at this point. Zimmerman replied that he did not engage Trayvon due to being afraid for his safety. Upon inquiry, Zimmerman denied chasing Martin at any time, and stated he was simply following him prior to losing sight of him.

Research on the prior incident referred to by Zimmerman revealed that Zimmerman, on 2/2/2012, called in a suspicious person a[redacted] Subsequent police response showed the person described by Zimmerman as staking out this residence, identified by Zimmerman as a black male, in a black leather jacket, and printed pants, had departed the area prior to police arrival, and criminal offense report was made (SPD Event 20120332595).

On 3/1/2012, at approximately 1900 hours, while conducting a re-canvass of the neighborhood, I located [redacted] stated she was home on the evening of 2/26/2012 at approximately 1915 hours when she heard a commotion coming from the walkway behind her residence. [redacted] states she looked out her sliding glass door and observed two men chasing each other, a fistfight between the two men, and then she heard a gunshot. When asked to clarify her observations, she stated she could not identify either of the two men, but she did state the person in pursuit of the person being pursued was approximately 10' -12' behind. On 3/8/2012 I called and left a message for [redacted] in order to coordinate a second interview. On 3/9/2012 at 1826 hours I re-interviewed [redacted] at the Sanford Police Department. [redacted] stated that what she witnessed was only a "glance" at the happenings outside of her residence, and only after she had removed her contact lenses. Her

Page 6 of 13

vantage point was from the upstairs bedroom of her residence, and she stated the chasing she saw was in the direction towards the "T" where the walkway leads to either Retreat View Circle or Twin Trees Lane. [redacted] could not distinguish who was chasing whom, and cannot identify either of the persons she witnessed on the evening of 2/26/2012. This interview was digitally recorded and submitted as evidence.

On 3/1/2012, at approximately 2100 hours, I conducted a telephonic interview with [redacted] and was at home at the time of the incident. She states she was in her kitchen when she heard what she interpreted as someone crying, or moaning in desperation, before hearing a gunshot. Upon investigating, she observed a male standing over another individual who was lying on the ground. She states the individual standing over the other individual appeared to be holding the person on the ground by pressing on his back. She stated it was too dark to distinguish who was standing or who was on the ground. [redacted] could not provide any other information, however her friend, [redacted] who was assisting with translation, was adamant that there was no physical fighting at the time when the gunshot rang out. Based on these statements, I requested both [redacted] and [redacted] appear at the police department for more thorough interviewing in a controlled setting. Both [redacted] and [redacted] agreed to interviewing, which was scheduled for 3/2 at 1830 hours.

On 3/02/2012 at 1856 hours, I re-interviewed [redacted] at the Sanford Police Department. [redacted] stated she was home at the time of this incident. She stated that while inside of her kitchen, she heard someone crying, just prior to hearing a gunshot ring out. She stated that upon investigating, she observed one individual standing over another individual who was lying on the ground. She called out "what's going on out there?" She stated the person standing over the other person did not respond to her. After repeating "What's going on out there?" the person standing over the other person stated "just call the police". [redacted] states she noticed the person on the ground was face down only after police arrived on scene. [redacted] could not provide any information pertaining to how the confrontation between the Zimmerman and Martin originated, and she could not articulate anything reference words spoken between the two. When asked to best describe the crying or sobbing she heard, she stated it was if coming from a young person, and the tone was that of fear, and/or complaining. [redacted] stated she could not positively identify Zimmerman or Martin due to the poor lighting conditions. [redacted] interview was digitally recorded, placed on a compact disc, and submitted into evidence.

On 3/2/2012 at 1120 hours I interviewed [redacted] at the Sanford Police Department. [redacted] stated she and [redacted] were inside of their residence at [redacted] on 2/26/2012 at the time of this incident. When asked what she witnessed, she corrected me by stating she did not see anything, but she had heard what she perceived to be arguing coming from the walkway behind her residence. She stated she could not decipher what words were being spoken between the arguing parties, but stated there appeared to be three (3) exchanges of words to the argument. When asked if she was acquainted with George Zimmerman, she replied in the affirmative, and she knows him to be an even-tempered "laid back" type of person. She stated she perceived him as being passionate about the neighborhood watch program, and stated she "could see him" confronting someone he perceived as a threat to the neighborhood. [redacted] could not provide any information pertaining to how the violent episode between George Zimmerman and the decedent occurred and stated she was not familiar with the decedent. [redacted] interview was digitally recorded, placed on a compact disc, and submitted into evidence.

On 3/2/2012 at 1132 hours, I interviewed [redacted] who resides at [redacted] stated he was at home on 2/26/2012 at approximately 1910 - 1915 hours. He stated he was with [redacted] watching television in the living room of their residence. He stated that the sliding glass door to his residence was wide open. He states he and [redacted] heard a "scuffle" or "rustling of bushes" coming from behind his residence, and upon first impression, he thought it might have been some rowdy teenagers. [redacted] stated that the tone of voices became more "serious" and then thought it was several people possibly attacking one person. [redacted] articulated the sounds he heard as "ah, ah, ah", and then he heard the same voice yelling "help!, help!", approximately twenty (20) times. He then heard a "pop", ran upstairs, and then heard someone saying "I've got a gun, I've got a gun", "take my gun from me". Upon inquiry, he stated he did not see anyone due to the fact that in order to see what was going on outside of his residence he would have had to move the blinds over his windows in such a way that the person(s) outside would see [redacted] which is something he wanted to avoid out of concern for their personal safety. [redacted] could not provide any information pertaining to the origin of the confrontation between Zimmerman and Martin. His interview was digitally recorded and it was placed on a compact disc and submitted into evidence.

On 3/2/2012 at 1914 hours, [redacted] arrived at the Sanford Police Department. She resides at [redacted] and was home on 2/26/2012 when this incident occurred. She stated that while in the kitchen of the residence with the window open, she heard a "whining" sound, and she didn't hear any words spoken, but she deduced it was a sound of distress. She stated she and her roommate went to the sliding glass door when they heard a gunshot. She stated she observed a male standing over another male who was lying on the ground. She stated she retrieved a telephone and called 911. She stated she does not know why

Page 7 of 13

the incident occurred, and could not provide any other information pertaining to the occurrences prior to her hearing the "whining" sounds she heard. [redacted] interview was digitally recorded, placed on a compact disc, and placed into evidence.

On 3/5/2012 at 1700 hours at [redacted], I met with [redacted] [redacted] I interviewed [redacted] due to the possibility of him being a witness, after learning his sister, [redacted] had placed a 911 call on 2/26, and she had stated [redacted] had told her about "someone being shot". Also present during this interview was [redacted] and Investigator D. Singleton. [redacted] stated he observed "someone laying on the ground that looked like they couldn't get up and was yelling for help". Upon inquiry, he could not say the race of the person lying on the ground, he looked like he had a red shirt, he didn't hear any arguing, and he didn't see anyone else other than the person on the ground. [redacted] impression was that someone had perhaps fallen down due to the wetness of the ground and had possibly broken their leg. [redacted] interview was digitally recorded, placed on a compact disc, and submitted into evidence.

On 3/8/2012, this case was presented to ASA James Carter in a meeting conducted at the Sanford Police Department.

On 3/9/2012 I received a fax from Altamonte Family Practice, which contained the medical records identifying the injuries sustained by Zimmerman on the evening of 2/26/2012. Said medical records list Zimmerman's injuries as:

1. Open wound of scalp, without mention of complication
2. Nasal bones, closed fracture
3. Assault by other specified means

On 03/10/2012 at approximately 1330 hours, I interviewed [redacted] at her residence, [redacted] whose identity was made known due to her having called 911 on 2/26/2012 at 1918 hours, agreed to being interviewed (digitally recorded) at her residence. Upon inquiry, [redacted] states she had just arrived home when she was about to let her dog go outside her back porch area when she heard a voice crying for help. She stated she looked through her back sliding glass door and observed an individual lying on the ground, apparently calling for help. She stated she observed a neighbor, whom she could not identify, asking the person on the ground if he was "okay" and if the person on the ground wanted him to call 911. [redacted] states that upon hearing the term '911", she chose to secure her sliding glass door, and retreated to the bathroom of the second floor of her townhome. She stated that as she raised the window of the bath room, in order see what was happening with the person laying on the ground, she heard a "pop" noise that she construed to be a gunshot. She stated that upon reacquiring a view of the occurrences, she observed a female and male giving CPR to the person on the ground. Upon inquiry, [redacted] states she did not witness anyone fighting with anyone, and she reiterated she did not witness the event in its entirety.

On 3/10/2012, at approximately 1310 hours, I attempted to contact [redacted] in order to re-interview her pertaining to her 911 call placed on 2/26. I left a business card on her front door and have left two messages on her cell phone voice mail.

Investigative findings show that on 2/26/2012 at approximately 1912 hrs George Michael Zimmerman initiated a nonemergency call to Sanford Police dispatch to report a suspicious person. Zimmerman reported a suspicious person, Trayvon Martin, whom he observed entering the gated community of The Reserve at Twin Lakes on foot, walking between residences from the northwest. Zimmerman initiated his call by stating there had been "some break ins" to his neighborhood in the recent past, and that Martin was a "real suspicious guy". Zimmerman went on to state that Martin was "up to no good", "on drugs or something", and stated that it was raining and that Martin was "walking around looking about". Zimmerman went on to tell the call taker that Martin was "here, now, just looking at houses" and then stated "now he's staring at me", "now he's coming toward me", "he has his hand in his waist band". Zimmerman described Martin as a Black male in his late teens. Zimmerman further stated that there is "Something wrong with this guy. He's coming to check me out. I don't know what his deal is". Zimmerman then says "These assholes. They always get away. Yep".

Zimmerman maintained contact with the call taker, and stated about Martin, "Shit, he's running". The call taker asked of Zimmerman, "Are you following him?", to which Zimmerman stated "yes", and the call taker replied, "we don't need you to do that". Zimmerman referred to Martin as a "fucking punk" under his breath. Investigation reveals that Martin was in fact running generally in the direction of where he was staying as a guest in the neighborhood.

Investigation reveals that on August 3, August 4, and October 6, 2011, and February 2, 2012, George Zimmerman reported suspicious persons, all young Black males, in the Retreat neighborhood to the Sanford Police Department. According to records checks, all of Zimmerman's suspicious persons calls while residing in the Retreat neighborhood have identified Black males as the subjects.

Page 8 of 13

Investigative findings show that Zimmerman admitted to avoiding a confrontation with Martin while Zimmerman was observing Martin from his vehicle, because, as he told investigators, was afraid of Martin. Later in the encounter, Zimmerman exited his vehicle, in spite of his earlier admission to investigators that he was afraid of Martin, and followed Martin in an effort to maintain surveillance of him while Zimmerman awaited the arrival of law enforcement officers. His actions are inconsistent with those of a person who has stated he was in fear of another subject.

!

nvestigative findings show that George Michael Zimmerman had at least two opportunities to speak with Trayvon Benjamin Martin in order to defuse the circumstances surrounding their encounter. On at least two occasions, George Michael Zimmerman failed to identify himself as a concerned resident or a neighborhood watch member to Trayvon Benjamin Martin. Investigative findings show the physical dimensions of Trayvon Benjamin Martin, and that of George Michael Zimmerman, coupled with the absence of any specialized training in hand to hand combat between either combatant, did not place George Michael Zimmerman in an extraordinary or exceptional disadvantage of apparent physical ability or defensive capacity. Investigative findings show the physical injuries displayed by George Michael Zimmerman are marginally consistent with a life-threatening violent episode as described by him, during which neither a deadly weapon nor deadly force was deployed by Trayvon Martin.

The following sequence of events were obtained by admissions made by Zimmerman and cannot be corroborated by independent witnesses, nor can be refuted by independent witnesses: While Zimmerman was returning to his vehicle, he states he was attacked by Martin, but only after Martin inquires to Zimmerman "What's your problem?" Zimmerman, instead of attempting to inform Martin of the reason he was following him, stated to Martin "I don't have a problem". As Zimmerman responds to Martin, by his own admission, Zimmerman reaches into his pocket attempting to locate his cell phone. As Zimmerman reaches for his cell phone, he stated Martin replies "You have one now", and Martin punches Zimmerman in the face, knocking him to the ground. Zimmerman stated that he was battered by Martin to the point of almost losing consciousness. He stated he ultimately had no choice but to shoot Martin in self-defense.

At 1916 hours, a 911 call, placed by [redacted], was received where Zimmerman can be heard in the background frantically yelling for help. At 1917 hours a gunshot was heard in the background of the [redacted] 911 call, and moments later Officer Tim Smith arrived on scene.

The encounter between George Zimmerman and Trayvon Martin was ultimately avoidable by Zimmerman, if Zimmerman had remained in his vehicle and awaited the arrival of law enforcement, or conversely if he had identified himself to Martin as a concerned citizen and initiated dialog in an effort to dispel each party's concern. There is no indication that Trayvon Martin was involved in any criminal activity at the time of the encounter. Zimmerman, by his statements made to the call taker and recorded for review, and his statements made to investigators following the shooting death of Martin, make it clear that he had already reached a faulty conclusion as to Martin's purpose for being in the neighborhood.
Attempts to locate additional witnesses have consisted of multiple canvasses of the neighborhood on the evenings of 2/26/2012, 2/27/2012, and 3/1/2012. The distribution of informational flyers throughout the gated community was completed on 2/29/212 and a community meeting, which was held on March 1, 2012.

All digitally recorded interviews were submitted as evidence, and all forensic laboratory requests are being submitted to the Florida Department of Law Enforcement for analysis.

Based upon the facts and circumstances outlined in this narrative, I believe there exists probable cause for issuance of a capias charging George Michael Zimmerman with Manslaughter, in violation of Ch. 782.07 FS. This case is being forwarded to the Office of the State's Attorney as a request for capias.

CONCLUSION:

Case forwarded to the Office of the State's Attorney

SPECIAL CONSIDERATIONS

Page 9 of 13

Extract: Trial Testimony

Sybrina Fulton

Bernie de la Rionda (prosecutor): Ma'am, can you state your name for the record, please?

Sybrina Fulton: Sybrina Fulton.

de la Rionda: And could you spell your first name and last name?

Fulton: My first name is S-Y-B-R-I-N-A. The last name is Fulton, F-U-L-T-O-N.

de la Rionda: Are you married, ma'am?

Fulton: I'm divorced.

de la Rionda: And do you have any children?

Fulton: Yes, I do.

de la Rionda: And could you tell us who they are and their names?

Fulton: My youngest son is Trayvon Benjamin Martin. He's in heaven. And my older son is Jahvaris Lamont Fulton.

de la Rionda: Do you live in Miami, ma'am?

Fulton: Yes, I do.

de la Rionda: And have you lived in Miami your entire life?

Fulton: Yes, I have.

de la Rionda: And who do you live in Miami with?

Fulton: My son Jahvaris Fulton and my brother Ronald Fulton.

de la Rionda: OK. Was Trayvon Benjamin Martin your son?

Fulton: Yes, he was.

de la Rionda: And was his date of birth February the 5th of 1995?

Fulton: Yes, it is.

de la Rionda: Are you working at this time, ma'am?

Fulton: I am employed. I'm on leave right now.

de la Rionda: OK. Where are you currently employed, or who are you currently employed with while you're currently on leave?

Fulton: I actually work for Miami Dade County Public Housing and Community Development.

de la Rionda: OK. How long have you been working there, ma'am?

Fulton: I've been with the county for twenty-four years. I've been with the housing agency for about ten years.

de la Rionda: And prior to going to the housing agency, what did you do?

Fulton: I did code enforcement for eleven years.

de la Rionda: And can you briefly tell us about your education background, ma'am?

Fulton: I have a bachelor's degree with a minor in communications, from Grambling State University was half of my course, and I graduated from Florida Memorial University in Miami.

de la Rionda: What was your major, I'm sorry?

Fulton: My major was in English with a minor in communications.

de la Rionda: Was Trayvon right or left handed?

Fulton: Trayvon was right handed.

de la Rionda: Trayvon Martin had two tattoos on his body. Do you know where they were on his body?

Fulton: He had praying hands on his right upper shoulder, with his grandmother's and great grandmother's name. That's the first tattoo. They were praying hands, and they had pearls going through them.

de la Rionda: Do you know where the other tattoo was?

Fulton: The other tattoo was on his left wrist. He had my name there.

de la Rionda: OK. Prior to your son's death ... had you ever heard while he was growing up, and while you were raising him, had you ever heard him crying or yelling?

Fulton: Yes.

de la Rionda: OK. I want to play a recording for you m'am.

[*plays a tape*]

911 operator: 911, do you need police, fire or medical?

[*indistinct screaming, crying in the background throughout*]

Unidentified female: Um, maybe both. I'm not sure. There's just someone screaming outside.

911 operator: OK, what's the address that they're near?

Unidentified female: 1211 Twin Trees Lane.

911 operator: Twin Trees Lane? Is this in the [*inaudible*] town homes in Sanford?

Unidentified female: Yes.

911 operator: OK. And is it a male or female?

Unidentified female: It sounds like a male.

911 operator: And you don't know why?

Unidentified female: I don't know why. I think they're yelling "Help," but I don't know. Just send someone quick, please.

911 operator: Does he look hurt to you?

Unidentified female: I can't see him. I don't want to go out there. I don't know what's going on.

...

Unidentified female: They're sending them.

911 operator: So you think he's yelling "Help"?

Unidentified female: Yes.

911 operator: All right, what is your— [*inaudible*]

Unidentified female: There's gunshots. [*screaming in background stops*]

911 operator: You just heard gunshots?

Unidentified female: Yes.

[*tape ends*]

de la Rionda: Ma'am, that screaming or yelling, do you recognize that?

Fulton: Yes.

de la Rionda: And who do you recognize that to be, ma'am?

Fulton: Trayvon Benjamin Martin.

...

Mark O'Mara (defense attorney): Good Morning, ma'am. Firstly, I truly apologize for your loss—

de la Rionda: Objection. Improper. Not a question....

Judge Nelson: You need to ask a question.

O'Mara: You— will you tell us the first time that you listened to that tape? When you listened to it, where were you?

Fulton: I was here in Sanford. I believe it was the mayor's office.

O'Mara: And that was pursuant to a request made by your lawyers to have that tape released, correct?

Fulton: That's correct.

O'Mara: And my understanding is that it happened actually in the mayor's office, correct?

Fulton: Yes.

O'Mara: And there were no law enforcement officers present?

Fulton: They were there, but they wasn't actually in the room.

O'Mara: They were actually not allowed in the room, correct?

Fulton: I don't know about that.

O'Mara: Were you present there when Chief Lee was talking to the mayor and to city manager Bonaparte about the concern with having the tape released?

de la Rionda: Objection, as to hearsay....

Nelson: Sustained as to hearsay.

O'Mara: Were you there during the time that Chief of Police Lee was having a conversation with the mayor and City Manager Bonaparte?

Fulton: No.

O'Mara: When the tape was played for you, who played it for you?

Fulton: I'm not absolutely sure. I'm just trying to remember back. I think it was the mayor.

O'Mara: It was not a law enforcement officer, correct?

Fulton: It was not.

O'Mara: And who was in the room when that tape was played?

Fulton: Trayvon's dad, Tracy Martin; Jahvaris Fulton, Stephanie Sands, Darian Sands, Benjamin Crump, attorney Natalie Jackson. I believe Mayor Triplett was there, and there may have been one other person. I'm not absolutely sure, but I think Bonaparte was there.

...

O'Mara: The first time you heard that tape was it played at one time for everybody who was in the room?

Fulton: Yes.

O'Mara: Did any one of those witnesses listen to the tape individually, or was it all at one time?

Fulton: I don't know if they listened individually, but that was my first time hearing it.

O'Mara: Well, had anybody indicated to you in that group that they had listened to the tape before?

Fulton: No.

O'Mara: Did Tracy Martin tell you that he had listened to the tape before?

Fulton: No.

O'Mara: Had you had any conversations with him about listening to the tape before that event?

Fulton: No.

O'Mara: I imagine that it was probably one of the worst things that you went through to listen to that tape, correct?

Fulton: Absolutely.

O'Mara: And that if it was your son in fact screaming, as you've testified, that would suggest that it was Mr. Zimmerman's fault that led to his death, correct?

Fulton: Correct.

O'Mara: And if it was not your son screaming, if it was in fact George Zimmerman, then you would have to accept the probability that it was Trayvon Martin who caused his own death, correct?

Fulton: I don't understand your question.

O'Mara: OK. If you were to listen to that tape and not hear your son's voice, that would mean that it would have been George Zimmerman's voice, correct?

Fulton: And not hear my son screaming? Is that what you're asking?

O'Mara: Yes, ma'am.

Fulton: I heard my son screaming.

O'Mara: I understand. The alternative, the only alternative – would you agree? – would be that if it was not your son screaming that it would be George Zimmerman, correct?

de la Rionda: Objection as to speculation.

Nelson: Sustained.

O'Mara: You certainly had to hope that was your son screaming even before you heard it, correct?

Fulton: I didn't hope for anything. I just simply listened to the tape.

O'Mara: Mhm. And in your mind, as his mother, there is no doubt whatsoever that it was him screaming, correct?

Fulton: Absolutely.

O'Mara: Did you have any thought in mind how you would react if you believed, or didn't hear your son's voice?

Fulton: I really didn't know what the tape was all about.

O'Mara: And everybody else in the room, when they listened to the tape, who was the first one to react?

Fulton: I was.

O'Mara: And everybody else then reacted similarly to you, correct?

Fulton: Well, they also heard the tape themselves.

O'Mara: Correct. And every one of them then told you that they agreed with your opinion that it was Trayvon Martin's voice, correct?

Fulton: They didn't tell me anything.

O'Mara: When you mentioned a moment ago that you didn't know what the tape was about, nobody spoke to you to tell you that you would soon be listening to screams from the event that led to your son's death?

Fulton: No.

O'Mara: Mayor Triplett never said anything like that to you?

Fulton: No.

O'Mara: Nor did any of your other family members?

Fulton: They hadn't heard the tape at that time.

O'Mara: But the question is whether or not anyone told you to prepare yourself for the event, for the trauma, of having to listen to somebody scream moments before your son was shot?

Fulton: No.

O'Mara: Nobody mentioned that to you?

Fulton: No.

O'Mara: Tracy Martin never told you about that?

Fulton: No.

O'Mara: And you just needed to listen to it one time, correct?

Fulton: That's it.

O'Mara: [*to the judge*] May I have a moment, your honor? [*sidebar with co-counsel*] Thank you, your honor.

...

de la Rionda: You were asked about hope. Did you hope your son wouldn't be dead, Trayvon Martin? You were asked by defense counsel about hope. Were you still hoping that he would still be alive?

Fulton: I hoped he was still alive.

de la Rionda: And, I don't know how else to ask this, but I'm going to ask it. Did you enjoy listening to that recording?

Fulton: Absolutely not.

de la Rionda: Thank you. No further questions.

...

O'Mara: I don't mean to put you through this anymore than what's necessary or than we need to. But you certainly would hope that your son Trayvon Martin did nothing that could have led to his own death, correct?

Fulton: What was your question again?

O'Mara: You certainly hope— as a mom, you certainly hope that your son, Trayvon Martin, would not have done anything that would have led to his own death, correct?

Fulton: What I hope for is that this would not have ever happened, and he would still be here. That's what I— that's my hope.

O'Mara: Absolutely. And now, dealing with the reality that he's no longer here, it is certainly your hope, as a mom, hold out hope as long as you can, that Trayvon Martin was in no way responsible for his own death, correct?

Fulton: I don't believe he was.

O'Mara: I know. And that's the hope that you continue, correct?

Fulton: I don't understand what you're trying to ask me.

O'Mara: Again, I don't mean to put you through more than you need to. No other questions, your honor.

'Thank You, Rachel Jeantel'

Mychal Denzel Smith

Rachel Jeantel was the last person to speak to Trayvon Martin before George Zimmerman killed him on the night of February 26, 2012. On the third day of Zimmerman's murder trial, after opening statements that featured the words 'fucking punks' and a knock-knock joke, and testimony from a number of witnesses, Rachel took the stand.

Visibly shaken, Rachel recounted the details of her phone conversation with Trayvon the night he was killed. She says he told her that a "creepy-ass cracker" was watching him. He attempted to lose him, but the man kept following, at which point Rachel suggested that Trayvon run. The phone was disconnected shortly after, and when the two were reconnected, Trayvon told Rachel, "The nigga is behind me." Rachel then heard a bump, the sounds of "wet grass," and what she thought to be Trayvon saying, "Get off."

The court took a recess after the state was finished questioning Rachel, as she was too broken up to continue at that moment. When they returned, Don West, a lawyer on Zimmerman's defense team, resumed the questioning. Rachel's demeanor noticeably shifted. She became agitated, answering West's questions with a quick "yes," an exasperated "no." The more tedious the questions, the more frustrated she became. She was looking at a man trying to get someone off for killing her friend. West was doing what a defense lawyer does, of course: trying to catch Rachel in a lie, poke holes in her story and cast doubt on her credibility. From the way she responded, she knew exactly what was going on, and she was determined not to let him rattle her. She may have frustrated him just as much as he did her.

Rachel's testimony is an emotional reminder of just what happened. A teenage boy was killed. His family and friends were left to mourn. For some of them, the pain is still fresh. The man responsible walked free for more than a month. There's a possibility he could be found not guilty.

Several times West brought up the fact that Rachel had lied about her reasons for not attending Trayvon's wake. "You. Got. To. Un-Der-Stand," she told West, emphasizing her frustration. "I'm the last person – you don't know how I felt. You think I really want to go see the body after I just talked to him?"

Rachel Jeantel isn't a Hollywood actress. She's not a trained professional. She doesn't testify in court regularly. She's a young black woman missing her friend. She showed up to court to give all the information she had as to what happened the night he died.

"Are you listening?" she asked West at a highly contentious point in her testimony when it seemed he had either lost interest or chosen to ignore what she was saying. How many young black women could ask that question to the world daily? We should be listening more. We should hear what the Rachels of the world have to say. It's unclear how Rachel's testimony will affect the jury and the ultimate outcome, whether they'll read her as hostile and uncooperative. No matter what, though, Rachel stood and defended herself and Trayvon (and, frankly, many other black youth) against the condescension, against silencing and against the character attacks. For that, she should be commended.

Thank you, Rachel Jeantel.

Extract: Defense Closing Argument

Florida v. George Zimmerman, July 12, 2013

Mark O'Mara

The whole system only works when it works with you.

Strange in a way, as it happens, that we have a system that has been ongoing for a couple hundred years, and we intentionally bring in people who know as little as possible about the system, and tell them to make the most important decisions within it. And that's what we've asked you to do. And I have some fears I want to talk to you about in that regard, because when we talked in jury selection, we talked about sort of what this process is and how you have to come to us; I used words like 'unique', 'strange' even, as far as the system that you're now involved in. We're used to it. We do it every day. Sort of like doctors with blood, you know, you just, you get used to it; it's just part of what you do. We deal with things like autopsy photographs and jury instructions and evidence and witnesses who may or may not remember things, or maybe not tell the truth, witnesses who come with biases, and we come into my office and I look at that I know exactly how to focus my inquiry because I'm a lawyer. I couldn't do it if I was in a hospital, but I can do it in a law office. And yet we ask you to come in and to take on all of our rules and all of our regulations and to apply them as though you've done it all your life.

And my fear is that that's a very difficult task that we're asking you to do – cause the reason why it's difficult is you're completely unused to it. You don't know how to apply a standard of beyond a reasonable doubt. You just don't. You don't know how to wait until you go back in that room to have any thought or any impression about how this case has gone so far; it's impossible.

We're not really asking you to do that, but we sort of are – cause what we've said to you is, *Come from your homes, come from your jobs. Sit with us for a month. Get rid of, I guess, almost everything as to how you decide things in your life, except bring your common sense* – we've talked about that a lot.... *Take on somewhat artificial* – and by 'artificial' I certainly don't mean inappropriate or improper, and don't want to diminish it at all – *but this sort of unusual standard that we're asking you to take on.* And my fear is that you will default to what you're used to. You will default to the idea that you make decisions in a split second, like all of us do; that you can't help but have a first impression.

If I were to walk in today, let's say, and I just, as an example, walked in like this [*puts on dark glasses, loosens tie and transfers ring to his pinky*] – just walked in the courtroom as a lawyer, you would have an impression. *What in God's name is he doing with the sunglasses on, and who does he think he is? What's with the pinky ring?* I put that on because obviously this case has got some publicity, and I became known as some pinky-ring-wearing attorney. It's actually my dad's high school ring; it's never been on my pinky, but that's all it takes is an impression. And we look at people and we keep that with us. So you might have an impression of George Zimmerman....

You might have an impression of him because he's sitting at the defense table, and that maybe, as we've talked about, he's not just a citizen accused, but maybe he is a de-fend-ant, meaning he has something he has to defend. Maybe, in fact, that because the state attorney's office has decided to charge him, he has to have done something wrong. Maybe that's the impression that you have. Fortunately, we're not going to ask you not to have impressions; that's absurd.

My fear, as I was telling you about, is that if that allows you to sort of diminish or minimize your task that you've taken on here, that it works against my client. Because even when we talk about things like common sense – we want you to use your common sense – but be, be careful with your common sense. I know it's a dangerous thing to say. Be careful with your common sense, because common sense is the way we run our everyday lives, the way we make those snap decisions that we have to make every day, in order to work, in order to live, in order to deal with our children and our parents.... My concern is that it may in fact work against my client, because if you start using those same processes that we're used to every day, to just look at things, make a decision and move on, that subtly and unintentionally you're going to minimize or diminish the standard that has to be applied in this case.

And I'm afraid of that for this reason: if you do that, not only is it going to go against my client, and I don't want that, but any verdict you come up with is going to be sort of a compromise verdict – a verdict that's not based upon the standards that you agreed to ... and that is the only way that this system really works.

We talked about the difference in civil cases and criminal cases in jury selection. We talked about the fact that if this was a civil case you would go back in the jury room and say, *Well, you know the state wants money, and we just got to decide, maybe more than half, you know 51 percent or whatever it might be.* And then that's the standard, and we talked that I think that's probably the standard we use in our everyday lives: everything but those most important decisions. Even when the decision is made to move out of state, to come down to Florida, to move your life here ... you weigh the consequences, you weigh the possibilities, but you never are certain. You never look at a situation like that and say I've addressed and resolved all variables, and all variables are resolved in favor of this. What you basically do is look at it: it's an opportunity or an alternative or a necessity; you figure it out, you weigh what you can weigh, you accept what you have to accept, and then you make the decision.

I would argue to you, I would submit to you, that that's not what you can do here today. I think that what you have to do is be absolutely vigilant, diligent, in looking at this case and deciding it with a standard foreign to you but one that you have to take on.

... [F]ailing to do that, you will do some of what the state has asked you to do. They asked you to do it in voir dire, when they talked about assumptions. Voir dire is jury selection. They asked you to do it in opening, when they yelled those words that you know weren't yelled. They asked you to do it throughout the entirety of their case. So far, they even asked you to do it in closing.

...

Assumptions presume a lack of evidence, because if you have to presume something you don't know it. And if you don't know it, it hasn't been proven. And if it hasn't been proven, as the [judge's] instruction tells you, it's just not there. And you can't consider it. You can't fill in the gaps. You can't connect the dots for the state attorney's office in this case. You're not allowed to.

So, I'll give you a couple of examples. They're not utterly significant, but I'll give you a couple of examples.

What do you know about George Zimmerman?

Well, use your memory, but you know he went to college. You know he's in Neighborhood Watch, and he lived there [Retreat at Twin Lakes] for a couple of years. I think you know he's married, because we mentioned his wife's name, I believe. You know that his mom and dad are still around, because they testified. You don't know a lot more about him than that.

There are a few more things. You'll remember them, and I'm not going to have a complete review of all of the evidence, but you don't know a lot about him. To the extent that there are questions or issues that you don't know about George Zimmerman, we're done with the evidence. You're not getting any more information from the state attorney's office to prove their case against George Zimmerman.

Don't assume it. Don't presume it. Don't connect dots. Don't fill in the blanks with anything.

I'm not saying that you'll be sinister in doing that; I'm just saying that no matter what it is, you can't do it. That's why when we say to you that this case has to be decided on the evidence presented in court, it sounds sort of grandiose almost. *Well, of course we're going to decide on the evidence in the case. There is nothing else.* Well, the problem with it is that if you're not careful, as we do in our everyday lives, you *will* connect the dots when you're not supposed to. You'll fill in the gaps when you're not supposed to. You will make those assumptions, some of which the state actually asked you to do in their closing. You will do that, because – you know what? – it's natural. It is very natural. But not in a criminal courtroom.

It is not only unnatural; it is inappropriate.

What do you know about Trayvon Martin?

Not much either. But, but, you're not supposed to. What happened that day is what happened that day. What I don't think you should do is fill in *any* gaps, at all. Connect any dots for him, either. For any fact but, honestly, for any witness. If the decision was made by the state not to present additional evidence to you, do not presume. Do not assume. And do not give anybody the benefit of any doubt, except for George Zimmerman. Because, one, you said you would; and, two, that's the only way whatever verdict you come up with is going to be just, and it's going to be fair.

So, one filter: be careful. Address my fear, if you would, by just being careful. Just making sure that when you're back there talking and somebody says, *Well, you know, he's sort of this*, or *I really think that...* That one other of you just says, *I hear ya, sort of thinkin it too; can't do it.* Let's just take that thought, that very natural extrapolation, and put it to the side. And you might say to yourself, since it's the state who carries the burden alone, *You know something, that's what the state didn't give us. That's what they didn't show to us.*

So, let's look at the jury instructions and see if it matters.... [I]f it is a significant issue, if it's something that you need to consider and decide in a case of whether or not George Zimmerman committed second-degree murder, then sit back and say, *I have to look at the instructions*. And the instructions say that reasonable doubt can come from a *lack* of evidence, as well as it can come from a conflict of the evidence.

The reason why we tell you, and you're instructed by the court, that George Zimmerman need not prove anything is precisely that reason. Again, a strange system; those, anyone with children know[s] that you want to get them separated, and you want to get the story from both sides. That's the only way you figure it out. And then you know who stole the cookies, who gave the cookie to the other one to cover up the crime or whatever it might be. You get an idea, because you get 'em both. So why does he have that benefit? Why does he come before you and say, *You know what? Decided not to testify*. And then you get to sit back and go, *Wait a minute, my assumption is, I want to hear from him.*

Now, this case obviously is different than others because you've heard from him. Time and time and time again, you've heard from him telling you what happened that night. But, you know what? Even if we didn't put on his statement, you still would have to go back there and say, *I'm not considering that.*

Why?

Why do we take away that common sense presumption of finding out all the information that we can about a case? Cause we've already talked about it. If you want to take away somebody's liberty, they gotta prove the case. The burden is on the state.

And it goes back a long, long way. I've got a quote to talk to you about.... John Adams, 1770, when we sort of started this experiment, a couple of hundred years ago – God, I guess it's 250 now.

"It is more important that innocence be protected than it is that guilt be punished."

Now, if I stop there it sort of sounds like I'm asking you to let my guilty client go. I'm not. He's not guilty of anything but protecting his own life. But the quote continues:

> for guilt and crimes are so frequent in this world that they cannot all be punished. But if innocence itself is brought to the bar and condemned, perhaps to die, then the citizen will say, "Whether I do good, or whether I do evil is immaterial, for innocence itself is no protection." And if such an idea as that were to take hold in the mind of the citizen that would be the end of security whatsoever.

...

So, that's why we have a system that puts so much of a burden properly on the state attorney's office in this case: to make sure that we don't cut any corners, and we don't make any assumptions. And this is a compliment to you, because Thomas Jefferson talked about you guys about 200 years ago as well when he said, "I consider trial by jury as the only anchor ever yet imagined by man by which government can be held to the principles of its Constitution."

That's you guys. I think he was talking about jurors in general, but it applies to you as well. Because we talked about living the Constitution; well, planned or not, you guys are it. You are living the Constitution.

... This is a solemn matter. We don't take this lightly, whether it's through jokes, or kidding around, or you see us smiling on each other, or whatever, this is a serious, serious matter for Mr. Zimmerman. And it's an utterly serious matter for you. And I don't say that to scold you into acting a certain way, but just to make sure that we don't do what the state has asked you to do on a couple of occasions now. *Now, you know what, you guys figure it out. Use an assumption. What about this?*

It's interesting in a case like this, because— I call this case the bizarro case in my practice, because it sometimes seems like it's turned upside down, to me. I'm not saying that you should agree with that but just a perspective that I've had in this case.

How many coulda beens have you heard from the state in this case? How many what ifs have you heard from the state in this case? Well, they don't – I don't think, anyway – they don't get to ask you that. I don't think they get to say to you, *What do you think?* No, no, no. No, no, no. *What have I proven to you? What have I convinced you beyond a reasonable doubt occurred in this case so much so that you don't have any reasonable doubt as to those issues that I presented to you?* They are supposed to use words like 'certainty' and 'definite' and 'without question' – 'beyond a reasonable doubt.' No other explanation.

These are the words and phrases of good prosecutors. I used to be one; I know. I've used them. What aren't good words of good prosecutors are 'maybe,' 'what if,' 'I hope so,' 'you figure it out,' 'coulda been.' Because those are the assumptions that, please, do not make. Do not cheapen *your* role in this case by doing anything less than holding them to the burden that they said at the beginning of the case that they would gladly accept and prove to you.

You know, the upside down nature of it is that's what defense attorneys do, if you really think about it. You want to know some of the underbelly of criminal defense work. We're the ones who live in coulda beens and what ifs.

Well, you know what, here's some reasonable doubt: what if blablablablabla? Or, you know, *It coulda been! It coulda been that it happened this way.* And that coulda been, ... that's where defense attorneys learn to practice, and words that they learn to bring to a jury.

I'm not going to do any of that with you today. I want you to know exactly what happened that night. I don't want you to presume anything. I would like you to presume whatever you can for my client's benefit, because, after all, that's what good defense attorneys do.

But in this type of a case we're going to do something that will probably upset or enrage defense attorneys anywhere who are listening to this case. Because at the risk of confusing you, I'm going to take a side trip for just a few minutes. And that side trip is I'm going to take on the obligation to prove to you that my client is innocent, something I absolutely do not have to do. It is the opposite.

...

[T]hat presumption of innocence that we talked about never dissipates, ever. The presumption of innocence never dissipates – until the state proves their case beyond a reasonable doubt. Which really makes sense. It took us from the king's days, where he decided if you were guilty or not, to your days, where you get to.

...

George Zimmerman is not guilty if you have *just a reasonable doubt* that he acted in self-defense.... We're going to spend about ten minutes with me bringing you all the way up to here [*pointing to a chart labeled "Self-Defense Burden of Proof"*], proving to you beyond a reasonable doubt that he acted in self-defense. But I don't need to. The state needs to convince you all the way down here [*points to bottom of chart*]:

- Self-defense likely, is there reasonable doubt as to self-defense?
- Is self-defense suspected? Well, if you have a reasonable doubt as to self-defense: not guilty.
- May not be self-defense; you're not quite sure: not guilty.
- Unlikely self-defense, but it might be; you have a doubt as to whether or not it's self-defense: not guilty.
- You know, it's less than likely that it's self-defense; if this was a 50-50, I wouldn't vote self-defense if this was a civil trial.
- Highly unlikely that it's self-defense, but I have a reasonable doubt as to whether or not it's self-defense: not guilty.
- ... I have no doubt, no reasonable doubt, that the state has convinced me

he *didn't* act in self-defense the way he should have, then he's guilty, and only then is he guilty.

So let's talk about my burden to prove to you beyond a reasonable doubt of his innocence. At the risk of confusing you, I'm going to request that you not allow me to confuse you as to the standards. But I want to show you what the evidence has shown concerning my client's absolute, beyond question, beyond a reasonable doubt, innocence.

Where shall we start? Well, let's start, let's start before the beginning. Let's start with what the state wants you to focus on: that he was a cop wannabe. And, he did want to be a cop. He also wanted to be a prosecutor. And he wanted to be a lawyer. And he wanted to continue his education. And he wanted to help out his community. And he wanted to help out people like Miss Bertalon by giving her a lock. And he wanted to be involved. You even heard that he mentored some kids from Officer Serino. Yeah, he wanted to be involved. And, yes, he wanted to be a cop; he even applied for it. I think what you also heard, I would argue to you, is you heard from the other officers, who actually wanted to be cops and then became cops, that it's a fairly noble profession. It is a profession that its moniker is "Protect and Serve." I think it's apparent that George is going to serve. I think it is; all the evidence that you do have supports that, and actually it doesn't support any other contention. It also supports the contention that he's going to protect. I think that's readily apparent from all of the evidence.

Keep in mind the state had the opportunity – no, I take that back – they had the *obligation* to show you any piece of evidence that they thought was appropriate that they could to show you that his actions were inappropriate.

And what did they decide to bring to you? Two professors.... Two professors, who said, *Yeah, I taught him. I taught him. I don't know if he read that book. But I definitely, it was in the class, it was an online class, and we spoke about it. And he told me he wanted to be a prosecutor....* And then the other professor they brought in to say to you, *Oh yeah, I taught him this, and we talked about self-defense. And, yeah, we talked about it, and he knew about it.*

So, yeah, that's what they want you to focus on, cause this cop wannabe knew what self-defense is. So they have that.

What else did they decide to bring you about his background? That he didn't make it as a cop one time. I think you know that he works as a fraud guy at a mortgage company. And what else did they show you to buttress their position that George Zimmerman is before you acting with ill will, spite, hatred, and just didn't— just hated, hated Trayvon Martin that night?

What is their evidence? I'm not being sarcastic. I might be forgetting some as far as his background. The five phone calls to non-emergency. You heard them. You have them in. You know something, you also have the sixth one, because I put that in.

Because for whatever reason the state didn't present to you call number six. It doesn't support their case, I guess, because it's just him calling, being concerned about the fact that a bunch of kids are playing outside and cars are swinging by them. He just— *I'm not complaining; I just want to make sure, there are some 4-year-olds out there, there are some 6-year-olds out there.* Listen to that, cause you haven't heard it; I didn't play it to you, but it's in evidence. I think it just sort of rounds out a little bit. Instead of having five of six, you have six of six. And then you sort of know what the state didn't show you. They don't *have* to show you good stuff about George Zimmerman, but they did say they were going to seek justice. Let's not forget that. They told you in the beginning of this case that they were going to seek justice. So, you have the five phone calls and now a sixth one.

I also put into evidence but didn't shove in front of you yet, but it's here: it's this whole pile of reports, police reports, of what other things happened in the past year at Retreat View area. They're there.... And they will show you a lot of alarm calls, a lot of burglaries, the home invasion that Miss Bertalon suffered through. And they will show you, I think if you look at this, that in that community there was a rash of people burglarizing homes. And you know what else it's going to show you? It's going to show you that a lot of the people who were arrested for it, the only people who were found and arrested, were young black males.

We're going to talk about race in a little bit, too. But they're going to show you, and the reason why I mention that now is that we talked about assumptions, and what you sort of bring into your world when you come into our world. Because certainly you heard on the non-emergency call how George acted when he saw Trayvon Martin. We'll get to that in due time.

So what else do they have about George Zimmerman and his past that they bring to you? I think that's about it.

So, I would suggest that that's on the way towards absolute innocence. Why? Listen to the calls. Anger, frustration, hatred, ill will, spite? *Get out here and get these guys. I hate these young black males*? Or whatever is the absurdity that they want you to get from them. Listen to the calls. Do not allow them to give their words to your ears, rather than George's. Listen to what *he* said. Listen to the cadence of his voice. Listen to what he said.

Read those reports. Look at those people who lived through— OK, not many of them were home like Miss Bertalon, but what they came home to, and then wonder whether or not a frustration in Mr. Zimmerman's voice is inappropriate, or appropriate.

So that's his past.

So what have they shown you as to how he acted now, and how will I convince you of his absolute innocence?

Let's go to the 26th [of February]. On his way to Target. Undisputed. Does it, I think someone said, ... every Sunday. Just his regimen: makes his five sandwiches in their little plastic containers. That's what he does, so— by the way, as to absolute innocence, tell me the witnesses who said to you that George Zimmerman patrolled that neighborhood?... there is not a witness in there, not one – state's case – not one who will say to you, *Umm, George Zimmerman, yeah, the guy wandering around the neighborhood, looking around, talking about, "Hey, bring in your garbage cans"* or some absurdity like that. Not one witness to suggest that the guy who they want you to believe is The Neighborhood Watch Cop Wannabe/Crazy Liar, not one. They may want you to assume that, it would seem, and you would have to assume it, because you certainly can't find it. So you have to assume that this Neighborhood Watch guy was just some *crazy guy*, walking the neighborhood, looking for people to harass. Except, that's an assumption without any basis in fact whatsoever. Not one.

...

What do they really have? They have Miss Bertalon. He [Zimmerman] called Miss Bertalon and said, *Ugh.* He came over. *Heard what happened, really sorry. We just started this Neighborhood Watch.... [T]here's real problems with these sliding glass doors. Here's a lock. And you know what, my wife's home, she works, she's a nursing student,* or something. *She's around. She's home if you need to stop by.*

Innocence. Pure, unadulterated innocence, I would suggest that that shows to you, certainly as far as second-degree murder or anything like it.

So, in my quest to prove that he is innocent beyond a reasonable doubt: he is on his way to Target, and he sees somebody that was suspicious. So does he jump out of his car, unholster his weapon, track him down, shoot him in cold blood? No.

He does what he was told to do. He calls non-emergency. Not a big deal, not an emergency. But he did tell you, of course, in his statements at least, and you know because it's in those reports, that at that very same house, maybe coincidentally, Trayvon Martin [*sic*] was burglarized a few weeks before, with a window open and a door unlocked to the back. Is it inappropriate for that to become a concern to somebody who's concerned about his neighbors?

...

OK. Well, in this case he does what? He calls non-emergency, and he says, knowing full well that – give him the benefit of some of the history the state wants you to use to convict him – that he knows it was being recorded, ... so he says on the call what he says. I'm not going to play it for you again. You've heard it more times than most people. And he called him an "asshole." Actually, he didn't call him an "asshole"; he said "these assholes," but probably in his mind in that group of people who in the past had gotten away. So he called, and he spoke to the dispatch, and he went through it.

So, looking at the question of whether or not my client is completely innocent, provably innocent, what did he do?

He stayed on the phone, cursed – yeah, he definitely cursed. And he cursed towards those people, maybe including Trayvon Martin, by the way – at least to him, maybe, because he did match the description, unfortunately, and that's just maybe happenstance. We'll talk more about that, too. So, he calls it in, and stays on the phone, like he's supposed to. Does what he's supposed to. Describe him. *I think he's black*, after being asked, Black? White? Hispanic? So where is the— how do we move from *I'm looking at a suspicious guy, I'm not sure, it's raining out, he's obviously not coming in the main entrances, maybe that's an issue*. When you look at those reports, you'll see that there are ingress and egress points, at least there used to be, where some people do come in to do bad things. And he talks to non-emergency. And he basically stays on the phone all the way through.

So, where is the guilt? No, that's not my burden. Where is the non-guilt?

Well, he never screams [over the phone]. Mr. Guy screamed. Mr. de la Rionda screamed. George Zimmerman didn't scream on that call. Of course, then to cover up his non-scream, at one point Mr. de la Rionda suggested to you that ... what he did was, under his breath— what he wants you to assume within that context is he said it under his breath because he wanted to say it but he didn't want the non-emergency caller to hear it? And then he wants you to assume that what that means is guilt.

Seriously? Seriously?

Here's a way you do that. [*Points to temple and speaking in a near-whisper*] "F'ing punks." It's just— the fact that he was willing to say it on a recorded call to law enforcement is evidence of non-guilt. It is evidence that he *wasn't* saying it in a way laced with ill will, spite, hatred or anything else like that.

So, call continues. And now we have the call. Now we have our first very large graphic.

[*Presents a ten-foot timeline*] ... What this is is a graphic representation of the significant parts of the phone call that started at 7:09:34 that night. You will have this back with you, so you can sort of go through it. It doesn't include every word that was said back and forth because it would have been twenty feet long, but it does have, I would argue to you or submit to you, it has all of the significant words....

It starts:

Dispatcher: "Sanford PD. May I help you?"

And George says *Some suspicious guy*, whatever. Then he says— note down here that Trayvon Martin is on the phone with Rachel Jeantel. That's sort of significant ... we'll talk about it as we come down the line. "Now he's just staring at me."

7:10:21, so we're looking at it about a little bit less than a minute later: "Can you see what he's doing?"

"Yes he's near the clubhouse right now. Yeah, he's coming towards me."

... [T]his is when he was sitting at the clubhouse. You can see. It seems to be uncontroverted. And this is on here because the suggestion is that this cop wannabe was just so frustrated, so angry, so full of ill will and hatred, that finally he cracked. Finally he broke. And I want to ask when you go back to figure out where he broke. But maybe this is the spot. Maybe it was just after the dispatch says, "Ok, just let me know if he does anything else, ok?"

Now, they want you to really focus ... on the idea that [dispatcher] Sean Noffke said, "We don't need you to do that," and that was a *command* of law enforcement, and somehow he violated it. We'll get to that. But, they don't want you to focus on the fact that this same law enforcement officer says, "Let me know if he does anything else."

So, here's a thought. Let me know if I do anything else. [*Takes a sip of water, walks across the courtroom, pours more water from a pitcher, walks back across to the jury and sets the glass down.*] Have I done anything else?

"Please get an officer over here" is his response.

Evidence of the ill will and hatred necessary that you just want to go kill somebody because you hate him? "Please, please, get an officer over here." Twice.

"Let me know if he does anything else." Twice.

OK. Well, it makes sense. I think that's probably what they're supposed to ask. And then the person hearing that says, "OK," or does something to let them know if he does anything else.

"These assholes, they always get away."

Use his words, listen to the tape.... What really counts is the way Mr. Zimmerman said it. So listen to the tape, and, you know, see if in that you walk away, just at this point right here, you walk away with ill will, spite, hatred and just this animus towards Trayvon Martin.

"Shit, he's running." OK. And the next second, "Which way is he running?"... I would suggest that at this point this is a conversation. Don't forget, when they're doing this conversation they had no idea we were going to be here today. They had no idea that we would have a ten-foot graphic of every sentence that they talked about. They were just talking. *What's he doing? Let me know. Where is he now? Which way is he running?*

And he gets out of his car.

Now, at this point I think the state— maybe this is another break point. Maybe this is the break point where George said, what's the *Network* movie, "I've had it; I just can't take it anymore!" something like that? Maybe that's when it happened.

Well, let's see. No, maybe not. He gets out of the car, says, "Down towards the other entrance to the neighborhood." Listen to that; see if there's this, this crescendo of hatred in his voice.

"Which entrance?"

"The back entrance."

Then he says— we've just got so used to using this in front of regular people, it's just, you know what he said; I'm not going to use the words anymore. That's not oversensitivity to you or to pander to you, but we've used the words enough in this courthouse so far.

And then he [dispatcher] says, "Are you following him?" What does George say, in his anger and hatred and plan to track down and kill this unknown person? 'Unknown' is important because ill will and hatred and spite, it's difficult – don't you think? – to really gain that for somebody who you don't even know. How do you actually get to the level necessary for second-degree murder when you don't know the person? But anyway, ill will, spite and hatred, are they shown right here?

"We don't need you to do that." Is that when he says, *Screw you. I'm sick and tired. I'm not gonna take it anymore*? No.

What does he say? "OK."

... Was George Zimmerman tracking? Was he running after him? We know he was following him, because he said it. The question is, was he tracking him? And the wind noise, the running noise ... you guys get to decide that.

But what I really want you to focus on is where this ill will, spite and hatred comes in. So, does it come in here?...

Is there any piece of evidence that you have in this case that supports the contention that George Zimmerman ran anywhere, or that he ran after Trayvon Martin, after he said, "OK"?

I have another challenge for the state. Let them tell you about it. Let them show you in the record of this case that they have evidence that he ran after Trayvon Martin, walked after him, after he said "OK." Because if it's there, I missed it.

Presumption, assumption, connecting the dots, sure. But you've agreed not to do that, and don't let them let you do that.

... At this point, I think right around here [*pointing at the timeline*] is when he [the dispatcher] says, "Do you still want an officer?"

Yeah. "Yes." OK. "Where do you want me to meet him?" The clubhouse, they talked about. The truck, they talked about. And then, I guess, in the state's presentation to you they have said, and maybe will say again, that at that point, that's the ill will, spite and hatred – I guess, because at that point he says, *Ah, no no no no no. No, I'm going to go track him down and shoot him, or something, so just have him call me.* Now, don't forget sixteen months ago, a regular phone call for Sean Knoffke, sort of a regular phone call for George Zimmerman, and, um, "I'll tell you where I am."

...

We know— we don't know, the evidence seems to support that George was heading back towards his car, and they don't have one shred of evidence to suggest otherwise. And if they had it, I presume that they would have presented it.

...

I'm going to show you what Mr. de la Rionda mentioned. It's an animation. It's not evidence. It doesn't go back there with you. It's just an overview of some of the evidence and how it may look in the context of it.....

OK. A couple of assumptions and a couple of problems with this before we look at it. You see where they started I have Mr. Martin sort of approaching, coming down the sidewalk. There's questions or conflicts about that. Was it bushes, was it sidewalk, was it behind me? And of course you can see it. It's lit. If it was real weather and lighting conditions, we would be looking at a black screen. So some artificiality that I've had to include in the animation to show you is just things like that.

But what I want you to look at is how the event may have happened at the T intersection, and how things sort of progressed from there, and how that comports with some of the evidence.

[*plays animation, gives commentary*]

An animation of course is just that; it's somewhat made up. I mean, it wasn't that night. It wasn't a videotape, although George certainly hoped that there was – George Zimmerman, sorry, hoped that there was – but it does somewhat give an idea, a perspective, that is at least consistent with the evidence that was presented before you in the case, because it does show the probability, if not the exact certainty, that this event started at the T intersection or thereabouts, and it started with a shot to the face, Trayvon Martin against George Zimmerman. And then it traveled down those thirty feet or so. However they ended up there, we know that when they ended up there that the only one who was injured, at all, except for the gunshot, was George Zimmerman. And that the only other injury that Trayvon Martin had on him was what seemed to be a fight injury, from a couple of scrapes to the knuckle.

So, again in my quest, my dangerous quest, to prove my client's innocence beyond a reasonable doubt, now we get really into what happened. Because you can argue, and the state will, all you want that George wanted to be a cop, and George's calls to law enforcement in the past just had some seething anger build-up, but don't assume it. Prove it.... Don't prove it? It just doesn't exist. And don't connect those dots if they've not been connected to you beyond a reasonable doubt by the state.

So now let's look at what really happened that night.

... [W]hat were these people doing just before? Spend a moment on that, to start talking about my client's absolute innocence. There's about a minute and a half, something like that, after George's call, that he [Zimmerman] was doing something. Whether or not he was wandering up to Retreat View Circle to get an address; whether or not he had that flashlight on him, looking around a little bit; whether, as he said to the law enforcement officer, I do want to try and figure out where he is; I do want at least to keep a visual on him, whatever. That was about a minute and a half.

What's really interesting, as well, about the phone calls is what Trayvon Martin was doing.

Because we haven't spent a lot of time on that yet, but the evidence is sort of compelling as to what he might have been doing. We know that he was on the phone with Rachel Jeantel. And we know that that ended, we have the times, ... and that she said he was running. Which actually coincides pretty straightforward with when George said he was running.

There's some consistency there.

So, Trayvon Martin was running, and he was running at about, somewhere nearby 7:11:47. Keep that number in mind for a minute: 7:11:47. Because the altercation, according to Miss Lauer's phone call, if you sort of look at when her phone call started, back it up to when she heard what she heard, she called at 7:16:11. Give her thirty seconds or so to have started – all right, somewhere around there— [*looks at watch*]

We're going to take a break for a couple of minutes because I didn't realize I've been talking for an hour and twenty minutes, so we're going to take a break. But before we take a break, here is what I'm going to do.

We're going to sit tight. And we're not going to talk. And I'll tell you when we'll talk again, OK? So try not to do much. Starting now.

[*time clock at 9:50:54*]

[*time clock at 9:54:43*] That's how long Trayvon Martin had to run. About four minutes. When he said he was running, that's how long he had.

So, let's talk about who was doing what and when. [*sets up another chart*]

Chad [Joseph, son of Tracy Martin's fiancee], the first witness who we talked to, said he could probably throw a football from his backyard to the T intersection. We actually don't have evidence from the state as to how far that was, but ... nonetheless, [*pointing at diagram of crime scene area*] this is where he [Trayvon] was staying, this is where George's car was parked, this is the T intersection. Do you think Chad can throw a football— he actually probably can't throw a football that far, ... but there are some good football players who probably could.

He [Martin] had four minutes, and he told Rachel Jeantel that he was running. We sort of know for the most part what George was doing then [*inaudible*], but since this is the state's case and not mine, did they show you, tell you, explain to you, give you any insight whatsoever, about what Trayvon Martin was doing four minutes before that fight started at the T intersection? Do you have a doubt as to what happened and what Trayvon Martin was doing and what he must have been thinking for four minutes?

Maybe it's time for a break.

[*fifteen minutes later*]

Four minutes.

Did that feel like a long time to you before the break when we sat here and did *nothing*, for four minutes? You get to think what Trayvon Martin was doing. You get to try and figure out why when he said, George said, at 7:11:40, "he's running"; 7:15:43 when Rachel Jeantel tells you the phone call ended because of a – bump.

Four minutes, to do what?

To walk home? To run home? The four-minute mile was broken when I was, like, 12, by somebody, and I think he was in his teens.... I do know that you can run a mile in about four minutes if you're in decent shape. So we know, that with the opportunity to go home, that he did not. We know that....

So, let's talk about factual innocence of my client, then I'm going to finally leave this behind. You want to talk about factual innocence? *Somebody* decided that they were angry. *Somebody* decided that they were ticked off. Maybe *somebody* decided that they just had ill will, spite or hatred. But for whatever reason *somebody* did decide that it wasn't over with the running.

Because it wasn't, after all. It had only just begun, right? Isn't that really what happened here? It wasn't some cop wannabe. It wasn't some I've-learned-about-how-to-talk-about-self-defense (and, oh my God, he forgot to say Stand Your Ground on *Hannity*, let's convict him; he didn't tell Hannity he'd heard of Stand Your Ground).

The person who decided that this was going to continue, that it was going to become a violent event, was the guy who didn't go home when he had the chance to. It was the guy who decided to lie in wait, I guess; plan his move, it seems; decide what he was going to do. And when the state told you that he had no decisions! They dared to tell you that Trayvon Martin had no decisions, that my client planned this?! Really?

Four minutes.

Four minutes of planning, and they want you to ignore it. I guess, because if you don't ignore that: factual and undeniable innocence. Because with those four minutes, now let's use your common sense. Now let's decide what probably happened that night, because we know the result. Now let's try and figure out the why.

George Zimmerman: probably heading back to his car. Looking with his little baby flashlight for Trayvon Martin a little bit? Maybe. Maybe. Not proven, but maybe.

Trayvon Martin: four minutes, doing something. And we don't know. We really don't. We know he's on the phone. We know he's talking. We know what Rachel Jeantel said he was saying about whatever he called him [Zimmerman]. And I don't care that he called him some stupid name. He's 17 years old; they get to talk stupidly if they want. I'm OK with that. I'm OK with Rachel Jeantel being 16 or 18 or whatever. Who cares? She didn't want to be involved in this case. But, the reality of what happened is very straightforward. And it proves absolute innocence.

Because for four minutes Trayvon Martin did something that led to his confronting George Zimmerman. That, I would suggest— not because George Zimmerman said it; throw out everything George Zimmerman said, just forget it for a minute, just, it didn't exist.

[Pretend] he did what I probably would have told him to do if he had called me on the 26th, that night: "Shut up, and don't say a word to law enforcement. I'll see you there in half an hour." I would've thrown on a pair of jeans, said good-bye to my wife and gone out the door to see a potential new client. And I would've said, "Oh, no, no, no. You are not talking to law enforcement, particularly not looking like you look. And particularly not having just shot somebody, and I don't know anything about it, so hush up. And, now, tell me." So let's just make believe that happened. Let's just take all of his "self-serving" cop-wannabe-created statements and throw them out.

What do we have?

You've seen the picture a lot. You're going to see it again. What we do have, and thank God for Jenna Lauer, because when [Officer] Mike Wagner went to her, "Can you pick out the guy?" – the potential shooter – she said, *Nooo. Go get me a picture, and I'll look at the picture. But somebody who shot somebody, I don't want to go say I know who that is.*

So we have this. [*holds up enlarged photograph of Zimmerman bloodied]* Interestingly, and thankfully, we have this, because if we didn't have this, we would only have the cleaned-up photo, the one that doesn't show the significant injury. You know what I'm talking about: the one that says, you know, the nose is sort of back in shape. I don't know who put the nose back in shape. I don't know how it happened. But I do know it did look like that right afterwards.

So if Mr. Zimmerman just created all these statements and we throw them all out, we start with this. Because *this* is undeniable. This is significant injury. And then we have the back of his head, and you know all about that already. And, what else do we have?

We have forty [*sic*] seconds of screaming. When I first got this case, I thought it was going to come and go in twenty minutes. Because when I found out that there was a 911 call with somebody screaming on it, it was game over. Figure out who it is, and then we're done. Because the alternatives are it's Trayvon Martin screaming, and my guy is some horrible, extended, torturing, then eventual murderer. For forty-five [*sic*] seconds. If it was Trayvon Martin, something strange was happening for it to be him, some, some bizarre forty-five-second event where he would scream for help yet still be able to batter George Zimmerman.... Or it was George Zimmerman. And I could get this to whoever, FBI, let's say, do a little comparison, and we're done.

You heard from Dr. Nakasone, unfortunately, it couldn't be done. So, now we don't know. Now, as Mr. de la Rionda suggested, now you do get to decide – I guess. Or not, of course. Or not. You just simply get to decide that you can't decide. And then who gets the benefit of that? Mr. Zimmerman. So let's not forget about that standard as I'm wandering you down my little make-believe path of factual innocence.

...

So we have that evidence. We have [Officer] Smith, who says right away he told him he was screaming for help, twice. Then we go forward, we have the medical personnel. The screaming for help is fun, because now the state wants you to say, this mastermind criminal, this guilty-beyond-a-reasonable-doubt second-degree murderer *knew* at that precise moment that he darned well better say that he was the one screaming. Cause, after all, he had killed the guy who was screaming, in the state's theory, right? So he knew he took care of that problem. The real problem with that theory: unless the mastermind knew when [Officer] Singleton mentioned in her interview that Trayvon Martin had passed, George was affected. I guess it could be part of the mastermind criminal behavior that he learned in community college. I guess it could've been. But let me tell you: if you have a doubt as to whether or not that's true, you need to tell the state, *Don't ever come before us again with a case like this. Don't ever do this to us.*

Because what we really have is what I said a while ago: we have factual innocence. You could go back there right now, look at the facts of this case and say, *We're going to flip the standard upside down. We're not going to allow Mr. O'Mara to get an acquittal for his client simply because the state hasn't proven their case beyond a reasonable doubt. We're only going to allow Mr. O'Mara to get his acquittal if he proves to us, beyond a reasonable doubt, that his client is innocent.* And you could, because he is. Because he acted in self-defense. But it's not the standard.

...

I'm going to spend a moment on the witnesses, real quick.... [*begins Power Point presentation, with photographs of witnesses*]

Chad Joseph: Didn't have much to say.... could throw about a football.... You know him to be the sort of stepson of Trayvon [*sic*] Martin.

Andrew Gaugh [*7-Eleven clerk*]: 5'10". That's important, and we're going to get to that in a second. You saw him stand him next to me, and I did that on purpose....

Sean Noffke [*police dispatch operator*]: What did he say? Interestingly, because the first person who talked about talking to George was this guy, and what did he say? No anger, no animosity, no hatred, no anything in George's voice. Quite matter of fact – a person who's trained, by the way, to deal with stressful situations and to understand, and to dynamically interact with people on the other line, because sometimes these things turn serious quickly. And what did he say? Nope. He even accepted the reality that George may have misunderstood when he said, "Which way is he running?" that George Zimmerman may have thought, *I should go find out....*

Ramona Rumph [*SCSO deputy director of communications*]: She brought in the records [*inaudible*] for the five calls [Zimmerman's earlier calls to police]. She also brought in the record of the sixth call ... nothing to do with burglaries, just George Zimmerman being George Zimmerman.

Wendy Dorival [*SPD Neighborhood Crime Watch volunteer coordinator*]: Interesting witness. A lady who set up Neighborhood Watch a few months before because, as she said, they looked at the crime stats for that neighborhood and it was being assaulted by burglaries, and something needed to be done. So she went in, and she did something. And she told us, you know, who might be suspicious, in her experience and training.... Someone you don't know could be a reason for suspicion. A person walking in areas they don't belong, maybe. Someone walking in the rain without purpose. I don't want to just have you acquit my client because I can show you that Trayvon Martin did something bad, but I'm also not going to allow you, or the state, to ignore the realities of what actually happened that night.

And described Mr. Zimmerman, to her knowledge, as meek.

The other interesting thing about this cop wannabe. They have this Citizens on Patrol program, where you get a uniform; you get a car, with little yellow lights on it. They can't be blue lights, like we have for true law enforcement, but you get little yellow lights, and you get to drive around and act like a cop. And he said to that opportunity to be a cop wannabe in a cop uniform and a cop car with cop lights and probably a little cop computer in his car, or at least a cop clipboard, *No. Thanks, but no. I'm just— I got what I'm doing; I'm working; I'm going to school, got my wife. I don't want your cop car. I don't want your lights. And I don't need your uniform.* But this is the guy that the state is telling you, *Get ill will and hatred out of his cop wannabe-ism*? Really? Seriously?

Have they proven that to you? Have they come even close? Except for speculation? How many times did you hear an objection on the stand for speculation? Cause we're not allowed to do that in court. There can't be a witness up there and say, *What do you think, maybe?* Cause it's not evidence, and that's why. It's not evidence for you, cause you could go back there and say, *Well, John Doe speculated, and the judge allowed it; I guess we can speculate.*

Absolutely not, absolutely not.

Donald O'Brien [*Homeowner Association president*]: ... Cop wannabe? I don't know; he doesn't seem [to be] if he doesn't want the cop car. Involved citizen? Sure.

Any complaints, by the way, that the state brought to you about him [Zimmerman] towing cars away, ticketing people, knocking on doors – *Get your car off that yellow*— anything like that to foster their argument to you that he was doing something wrong?...

Mr. de la Rionada says to you Mr. Zimmerman was frustrated [because he had not been the one to capture a burglar earlier]. *Oooo; I wanted that one. Damn, darn, the Stucco guy got him instead! I'm not going to let that happen again.* Are you kidding me? Are you actually kidding me that the state attorney's office, representing the state, is making that allegation to you? That that's ill will, because somebody else caught a burglar? OK, great. Just tie it together, please. You got two dots, and they're this far away [*extending arms to each side*]. Just give me a line, give me something ... anything between besides speculation, assumption or idiocy? Anything?

Sgt. Anthony Raimondo [*SPD*]: I would want him coming to a car accident that I was involved in. What a guy. What a cop. Did everything that he could, and did it without even thinking about it. Great cop, likes his job.

Diana Smith [*SPD crime scene technician*]: There's problems with the evidence ... weather conditions wouldn't allow her to process the items, touched DNA could have been wiped away, firearm not given to her. I don't know that it turns out to a big deal, but there is the lack of evidence here ... and who gets the benefit, again, of lack of evidence? George Zimmerman.

Selene Bahadoor [*Retreat at Twin Lakes resident*]: ... You assign credibility to witnesses. You decide what to believe and who to believe, and whether or not they're credible. I would suggest that along this scheme as we're going, check out this woman's credibility before you accept what she said....

Jayne Surdyka [*Retreat at Twin Lakes resident*]: You know, so she heard three pops. Is she lying ... because she heard three pops? No. Let's get off this lying thing because you have slight inconsistencies. She heard, or thought she heard, what she thought she heard. OK.... She got it wrong. What else she got wrong was she thought the big guy was on top.... Actually, what she really thought was that Mr. Martin, Trayvon Martin, happened to move, cause she saw the whole thing, including the shot, which of course doesn't comport with the 911 call, but, again, a stressful time for everybody, and she seemed particularly affected by stress.... Saw the shot, shot was from the top, shot was through the back, and that he [Martin] never moved.

It just doesn't make sense. It's OK. That *Vantage Point* that Mr. Root talked about, that movie: I don't know if any of you have ever seen it, but it's a great movie.... One event happens – it's the president getting shot by a marksman – and there's eight different people, seven different people watching it. And everyone has a completely different story. They all view the same event, but they all viewed it with their history, with their life experiences, with what they were going through that day and with what perspective they had. And it's just different; that's OK. It happens.

Miss Manalo [*Jeanne Manalo, Retreat at Twin Lakes resident*]: She heard voices twenty or thirty feet to the right, seems to be consistent with it starting at the T intersection. And, of course, what she did is what we all do. I'm not going to assail her for that, but what she did was make some assumptions based upon some facts that she saw afterwards.... She was looking at pictures of Trayvon Martin when he was 12.... But the reality is that she just had this vantage point of a child at 12 years old getting, I guess, the heck beat out of him by the other guy who was on TV, this big, heavy picture of George Zimmerman....

And she acknowledged, ... now here's the ones [pictures] that I did look at and find out or think of Trayvon Martin being the small guy; now you show me these other pictures. I could have been wrong. Lying? Perjury? No, no, come on..... That's why you're here; you get to figure it out.

Rachel Jeantel [*Trayvon Martin's friend*]: Let me give you my perspective on Rachel Jeantel. She didn't want to be involved in the case. She didn't want to be involved in the depositions, and she didn't want to be involved in trial. I think what happened – and this is just conjecture, and I'm not supposed to conjecture too much – I think her mom got with Ms. Fulton and said, *Go tell that lady what happened to her son.* And she didn't really want to do that.... Interesting to me about Miss Jeantel, you know, if you asked me right now to explain to you the phone call that I had three weeks ago with my wife, four weeks ago with my sister, or last week with Mr. West, I can give you the idea ... no way do you have the recall. But if you're asked to have the recall – *Tell me what happened? Now did this happen? Didn't he say this? Didn't he say that? Well, he didn't say, "What are you talking about?"; he said, "What are you doing here?" – right? Oh, yeah, that too.*

Miss Jeantel didn't want to be here, and I am ... sorry that she had to involve her life in our lives in a way that she never wanted to be involved. Unfortunately, she was a witness, and we had to deal with it. And some of her frailties came out in the courtroom, on TV, that I'm sure she never wanted out.

And probably every other witness. You know, witnesses wanted to be anonymous; you know all that. They were concerned, and she's one of them.

Some of the stuff she said was that it was close to the dad's fiancee's place. I actually think probably she meant close as compared to the 711. It makes more sense. It took him forty-five minutes to go from the 711 home; probably, he was just hanging out at some mailbox ... between the two. Doesn't make any sense that he was hiding out at the mailbox at Retreat View Circle, but, whatever.

... I think the change [in her account] occurred because of the way her initial interview was handled by one of the attorneys. Horribly inappropriate to not get this person to law enforcement – almost as bad as to have the mom on the couch next to you crying when the state does their first interview of you. Their call, but, wow, to do it that way.

Of course, she even acknowledged that she was concerned about Ms. Martin's [*sic*] feelings, which is why she sort of modified or smoothed over some of the more colorful language in the events that happened. And that's OK. You're supposed to just tell the absolute truth here, but I'm not going to ask a, a p—, someone like Miss Jeantel to come in and just not acknowledge the sensitivities, why she may have made it sound a bit better when telling the story of her son's passing to Ms. Fulton.

...

Miss Lauer [*Jennifer Lauer, Retreat at Twin Lakes resident*]: Interesting about her because she sort of, without knowing about it, she gave some pretty good information.... That's where we got the movement down in the animation, by the way, because she said T intersection, down to the [*inaudible*] past me, and then, of course, John Good says that it happened in front.

And that there was only one person calling for help. That's significant because there is no evidence, none, to suggest that there was more than one person yelling for help....

Ms. Mora [*Selma Mora, Retreat at Twin Lakes resident*]: We talked about her. She heard what she heard, and then she saw what she saw....

...

John Good [*Retreat at Twin Lakes resident*]: We've talked about him a lot. I think he's a significant witness because he watched it for eight to ten seconds, and he was the basis for the animation and the information that came to you through the animation.

Manalo, Jonathan Manalo, same thing: *He looked like he got his butt beat....*

Ricardo Ayala, SPD: The hands under the body. You know, if that is a concern of yours, that my client dared to testify in his statement that he took his [Martin's] hands out out of fear for a weapon, and that that is contraindicated because Trayvon Martin's hands – you'll get the pictures, by the way, one hand is not really under him, but the other one seems to be – that that is some inconsistency from which you should impute ill will or hatred or spite, that's absurd, and Dr. Di Maio said it was....

Stacey Livingston, the EMT who was there: You heard all about the injuries and what she did.

Timothy Smith [*SPD*]: Important because, you remember, he was the person on the scene, took George Zimmerman into custody for his own protection. He was the one George Zimmerman talked to twice about screaming for help before he knew that there was any 911 call suggesting it.

Lindzee Folgate [*physicians assistant*]: You know about the medical records, and she was the first one to mention MMA [mixed martial arts] style.

Hirotaka Nakasone [*FBI voice expert*]: ... basically he said, *Can't tell you. Can't help you. Don't do it; don't even try* [to distinguish whose voice is crying for help]. Unfortunately, even the FBI couldn't help us out with that voice, so now it is sort of up to you on that.[1]

Doris Singleton [*SPD*]: ... what was significant about that [initial interview] was George Zimmerman's response to the Christian issue, and to the fact that she was the first person to tell him that Trayvon Martin had passed away. And the statements are what the statements are.

Chris Serino [*SPD*]: Again, what he stated was, in his opinion – and, again, he's the law enforcement officer in charge of the investigation – was that there weren't any significant inconsistencies in what he heard from George Zimmerman. Were there some? Yes. Were they significant in his mind, as to, that they were lies? No....

---

1 The state called Nakasone to testify on the background cries on the 911 tape. In pretrial hearings, prosecutors attempted to qualify the opinions of two acoustic analysts previously (and quite publicly) engaged by *The Washington Post* and the *Orlando Sentinel*, both of whom said they thought the voice was Martin's. In a Frye hearing on the scientific validity of their methods, the state called no independent experts to bolster the two's opinions or vouch for their methodology. At the Frye hearing the defense called Nakasone and three other experts, all of whom said any positive identification from so short a recording was scientifically impossible using generally accepted voice recognition methods. The court then found for the defense, excluding testimony by the newspapers' experts as unreliable. At trial, while ruling out scientific analysis, Nakasone testified that it might be possible for someone close to one of the parties to recognize the voice using "personal analysis." (Ed.)

The state said to you, George Zimmerman knew those video cameras weren't working. So, ha ha! It wasn't a bluff. It was, again, supercop, knowing everything, and just deciding, *I can get away with this*. Really? Really?... What [Serino] had said was the inconsistencies did not matter to him, and did not change his opinion....

Mark Osterman: Good buddy [of Zimmerman]. Don't think he would lie for his friend, but was the one who testified about the self-defense. And I think you remember his testimony, a little bit animated, but sort of told you all about everything he could about George Zimmerman that night, wrote a book about it. That his story is different from George's other stories, figure it out. And figure out how significant it is, and whether or not it suggests second degree or anything.

Dr. [Valerie] Rao [*medical examiner*]: I don't know what to say. Minimum of four hits [that Zimmerman suffered]. OK. You see the pictures. If you think George Zimmerman was only hit four times, fine.

Let's take a moment on those four hits. You're going to get the statute, you're going to get the jury instructions, and here's what they're going to tell you about the extent of the injuries that you have to find my client suffered at the time he decided to shoot, the significance of those injuries, how life threatening those injuries were, how soon my client presumed he was going to die from the injuries already inflicted upon him.

Are you ready? Zero. Zero. No injuries necessary to respond with deadly force, not a cut on a finger.

The statute is clear. Reasonable fear of bodily harm.... Do you need a cut on your finger? No. Of course, getting a cut on your finger doesn't allow you to just shoot somebody, unless you're in reasonable fear of ongoing great bodily injury. So the injuries: icing on the cake of self-defense. Has nothing to do with the substance of self-defense, not a thing.

You will not hear a word about inflicted injuries [in instructions]. You will only hear that you must look at George Zimmerman's state of mind, when he did what he did. So, even if I said to you, *I'll take Dr. Rao's testimony* – though, you can tell, I wasn't taking Dr. Rao's testimony, but let's just say I was – it doesn't matter.

Miss [Kristin] Benson, print expert: There wasn't a lot. Absence of prints doesn't mean no fingerprints or no touching, just that it's not there. Environmental factors such as rain could remove them.

...

Captain [Alexis] Carter: Criminal litigation coursework. He actually turned out to be a good expert to tell you what self-defense is, and how getting your butt beat is really probably a good indication that great bodily injury is coming, because it's already started. And, he says, not a good idea to wait.

...

Anthony Gorgone, FDLE [*Florida Department of Law Enforcement*]: Talking about DNA. The problem with part of that DNA: they got some; I think they missed a bunch, or at least some because of the way it was packaged. Significant? I don't know. I don't think it was that significant. There may have been more blood. I don't think that George Zimmerman was bleeding a lot that night. I don't think he was bleeding a lot *out* that night. I think he was probably bleeding a fair amount *in*, and then when he stood up, after the attack was over, yes, it started coming out of his nose. Not a lot of blood on Trayvon Martin, probably not a lot to be expected, and there was no injuries on Trayvon Martin until the gunshot, so you wouldn't imagine there would be any blood on George – sorry, on George Zimmerman's hands, or anyplace else on his body, because when Trayvon Martin was finally shot, he went up and over....

Ms. [Sybrina] Fulton: People asked why I even questioned her. How dare you question the mom of a passed away 17-year-old? Doctors cut people sometimes when they do their work, and that was something that I had to present to you, something about the way it happened and how it happened. And, you know, the impact and just how moms think about these things, both sides. Because I know that both moms believe with their heart, and with their soul, that that was their son screaming for help. You have to, and you want to, and it's just the way you get through it.

Jahvaris Fulton, the brother [of Trayvon]: He really didn't know. I think he told you in his testimony, when he was talking to the NBC affiliate, yeah, it could have been him [Trayvon screaming], not certain, might have been, I think it was. And now he's more certain. Well, again, I'm OK with that. I'm OK with people wanting to hear what they want to hear.

Dr. [Shiping] Bao [*medical examiner*]: ... He was the one who did the autopsy, so, although there was some interaction there that might have best been just redone, the reality is the only injuries were the injuries that we know about on Trayvon Martin, and that the wet clothes should not have been bagged in paper, and that the hands should have been bagged. And we'll talk about the hands in a little bit.

Ms. [Gladys] Zimmerman [*mother of George*]: Told you that it was her son [screaming on tape], as I'm sure you expected before she ever got on the stand.

Jorge Meza [*uncle of Zimmerman*]: Interesting, because that was unplanned by him, it would seem, if you believe his testimony. Said he had a computer, listening and then hearing in the background a voice that he knew without question and immediately to be that of his nephew, George Zimmerman. I think he came across very credibly. I think he came across as a man of his oath and of his word, and I would ask you to consider the testimony in that regard.

Mark Osterman, buddy of his [George Zimmerman]: Talked about the weapon use, how you holster a gun. He's good at what he does. He was helping George figure out how to fire a gun.

Sondra Osterman, friend: Definitely George Zimmerman screaming for help. And explained away some of what the state was trying to prove to you through the non-emergency call about the anger and hatred and all that that just isn't there.

Same thing with Miss Geri Russo: No question in her mind, George's voice.

Same thing with Leanne Benjamin: I've heard him scream and yell in campaigns, and that was George Zimmerman.

John Donnelly [*Vietnam combat medic*]: Was interesting, because I'm not sure if I had thought about trying to figure out who in the world talks to people they know and then hears them scream for their life. There's no profession that does that.... A medic in Vietnam, a person who hangs out during the day with his buddies ... [and then] he's the guy who grabs a medic bag and a rifle, I think he said, and heads out towards the screams, and that even before he gets there, sometimes, he knows who it is who's screaming. Wow. Didn't want to testify – I don't think a guy who's been in Vietnam wants to come before people and break down a little bit, but I think that his testimony was quite credible when he believed it was Mr. Zimmerman [screaming].

Doris Singleton and, by the way, Chris Serino both said the same thing.

Unfortunately, when Mr. [Tracy] Martin first heard the tape he said what he believed to be true then – it would seem from the officers – and that is "That's not my son's voice."[2] It just wasn't his voice to him, and his mind is changed now. But it is interesting if you consider, when you're trying to figure out that issue of who said what, and what witnesses said what, cause you're going to give them credibility, you're going to weigh them, you're going to decide to dismiss their testimony or to accept their testimony, and try and figure out, remembering always ... the doubt always goes to my

2 At trial, Tracy Martin testified, "[I] shook my head and said I can't tell. I never said that no, it was not my son's voice." Officer Serino, who testified that Martin had said "No," also testified that, when asked about the screams, George Zimmerman said, "That doesn't even sound like me." (Ed.)

client's benefit.

Adam Pollock [*gym owner*]: Animated. Good guy. *George is soft. He's a 1; I don't care that he's been here [at the gym] for a year.* I'm not sure that I would have actually advertised that I trained George Zimmerman for a year and brought him from a .5 to a 1, but he did it. He's [Zimmerman's] not a fighter, not even off a bag. So this "MMA" – you know, I think the state even said it was eighteen months that George was MMA training, three times a week, grrrrr. Really? Come on, really? In light of the testimony of the trainer, who said *I wouldn't even let him do anything but shadow box for fear the shadow might win.*

...

Chief Bill Lee [*former Sanford police chief*]: ... He was the officer who said, *Whatever you do, separate them* [members of Martin's family, when listening to 911 tape]. *Don't infect witness testimony with other witness testimony.* It is Cop 101. I understand the sensitivities of the family members listening to the possible voice of their son and definitely the gunshot that ended their son's life, but law enforcement, ongoing investigation, just put them in one at a time. The way it was handled infected the evaluation of that testimony horribly. And who gets the benefit of that? George Zimmerman.

Dr. Vincent Di Maio [*pathologist*]: Just a grandfather. He's done this his whole life.... What he's good at is gunshot wounds, and suggesting that it made perfect sense that the hand in the jacket would do what it did. Does it make anything less than perfect sense as to what happened? It's in there, and he's [Trayvon's] leaning over. And his loose, billowing shirt falls forward, and he gets shot. And it's contact to the fabric. It [the gun] is not pressed against the chest; I think that little play in opening statement has been dismissed. And it was four inches from his chest. As it turns out, the type of forensic evidence is fairly significant because it completely supports the contention that Mr. Zimmerman was on the bottom, Trayvon Martin leaning over the top when he got shot.

Now, here's a theory of guilt for you. You ready? Cause this is the state's presentation, so listen carefully. He might have been backing up. He *coulda* been backing up. Coulda been! If I was arguing that, I would be arguing to you reasonable doubt.... I almost made light of it when I said, well, he coulda been backing up to strike another blow, but the coulda beens don't belong in this courtroom. Proof beyond a reasonable doubt. Consistent with a reasonable hypothesis of innocence, he was leaning over him: nothing to suggest anything else but that. He coulda been leaning back? At some point, after forty-five seconds of attacking George Zimmerman for no other reason— let's not forget, he didn't back up when John Good told him to, right? So for some reason, just before the shot takes off, at that moment the state wants you to believe Trayvon Martin retreated. Really? Really?

One piece of evidence, just one I ask for. Just one piece of evidence that supports that contention. Where is it? Where's the eyewitness who said, "I saw him back up"? Where's the forensic evidence?... Where is one shred of evidence to support the absurdity that they're trying to have you buy? One. Mr. Guy can tell you about it when he closes, if it's there. Assumption, supposition, coulda been.

...

Ms. [Eloise] Dilligard [*Retreat at Twin Lakes resident*]: Nice lady. Didn't want to bring her here sick. Knows George Zimmerman. Saw him that night. Saw him beat up. Saw the picture. Or hit, I'm sorry, saw him hit. And that he has a light voice, and that it sounded like it was his voice.

Dennis Root [*use of force expert*]: ... Again, talk about the bizarro case. Now we have prosecutors attacking, sort of, impeaching lifetime law enforcement officers who have dedicated their life to the pursuit of perfection in law enforcement. Perfection, my God, he's trained in *everything*. He takes something on; he becomes a trainer. And now we have the state impeach you. *Well, wait a second here, coulda been this way, right?...*

Well, let me ask you this question, Mr. Guy says, *At that moment when George Zimmerman decided to shoot Trayvon Martin what other options did he have?* None. He had none – from a use of force expert who's been doing this his entire career, and who has become proficient in assisting others in how to use force, learning how not to use force and learning when to use force. And they asked him the question of whether or not George Zimmerman had alternatives.

Tell me the piece of evidence that contraindicates that? Just give me one. Give me a shred of evidence that contradicts that he had any other option. Because now we have an expert who's qualified, who gave you that opinion. Dismiss it if you want. The judge will tell you, just because they're experts doesn't mean it's gospel, that you have to listen to them. But if you believe 'em, if you think they're well qualified to give an opinion, if it's an area of inquiry which will help you, then accept it.

Miss [Olivia] Bertalan [*Retreat at Twin Lakes resident whose house was once burglarized*]: I hope that it does not come across that I was just seeking sympathy for this woman. But the reality is, I think, that when you put a face on what was happening at Retreat View, she's it. She really is. Because thank God nobody came upstairs [in her home invasion]. I'm not sure the scissors would have really helped. But that's the face— and I'll tell you this, I'll give you this much, that's the face of the frustration that I think George was feeling a little bit of. You know, that's something that he wanted to help out with. That's why he walked over and didn't say [*grunting*] "I'm gonna get that guy." No, that's why he said *Here's a lock for the back of your door, here's my telephone number, and here's my wife's number. You need our help? This is what we do. We help.*

...

Some of the things you ought to consider when you look at this case is the forensic evidence: what it does and doesn't support.

Here was an interesting thing that I didn't make a big deal about in the trial, but I want you to focus on because a lot has been said about the lack of blood, and what happened to the blood, and, well, if Trayvon Martin was doing what George Zimmerman says Trayvon Martin was doing, where's the blood, where's the anger, where does it show up on the hands?

State 28, gunshot wound [*shows picture*]. See the blood, trickling down and across the chest? See that three-inch swath of blood, all the way over there?

State 95, it's gone, not there [*shows another picture*]. Yet, everybody who handled that body said they didn't touch it, or they didn't wipe it.... And it was actually still oozing in this photograph.... The idea that they want you to assume, that they want you to believe, just connect the dots that there is no blood when there is no blood because *they* failed to properly preserve items like the sweatshirts, items like the body, it seems, items like the hands that were to be bagged but weren't. They don't have to prove beyond a reasonable doubt that they bagged the hands. That's not an element they have to prove, but if they're going to try and come up with conclusive evidence that supports no other reasonable hypothesis of innocence but guilt, then they have to have a better case....

A couple of graphics: George Zimmerman the way he was [*shows photograph*]. Travyon Martin the way he was [*shows photograph*]. Now let's do it life size [*presents two cut-out silhouettes*]. Trayvon Martin that night [*referencing the taller of the two*]. He was wearing shoes I have to show you. He had the hoody on.... This is from the picture that we showed you. It's not in evidence, just to have you look at it; don't even have to believe it's accurate; just take a look at it.... And then there's George Zimmerman. Look at how tall he is....

Relative physical abilities: that's what you have to look at and determine in a self-defense case. So, you look at this guy [Zimmerman] that night ... and how Trayvon Martin looked that day.

... November 15, 2011, about two months, three moths before Trayvon

Martin passed away [*presents a picture of Martin shirtless and wearing grills on his teeth, which O'Mara continues to hold up for over half a minute as he speaks*]. That's what he looked like. Just a young kid, nice kid, actually, if you look at the picture, not bad. The problem with it is that when we show you autopsy photographs, there are two things you need to know about autopsy photographs. One, they're horrific, and they're meant to have negative impact.... A dead person on a slab has an impact on you.... The other thing about autopsy photographs is that there's no muscle tone, because there's no nerves; there's no movement. He lost half his blood; we know that. So on that picture that we have of him on the medical examiner's table, yeah, he does look emaciated, but here's him three months before that night. So it's in evidence. Take a look at it, because this is the person, and this is the person [*holding up another photo*] who George Zimmerman encountered that night. This is the person who, on all of the evidence, attacked George Zimmerman, broke his nose or something close to it and battered him on something....

You know how dark it was that night; you've seen this before [*holding up an almost totally black photo*]. It was out of this darkness that Trayvon Martin decided to stalk, I guess, plan, pounce, I don't know. All I know is that when George Zimmerman was walking back to his car, out of the darkness – be it bushes or darkness or left or behind or somewhere – Trayvon Martin came towards George Zimmerman. Out of this [*waving the black photo*], and we know what happened. The big picture is what happened.

And it's supported by evidence. You know, we talked a moment ago about ignoring George's statements. You know what? Don't ignore them. Listen to them. Find inconsistencies in them, see what you think about them, take them in context of what he was going through that night, and how voluntary he gave all those statements, and decide whether or not, as Dennis Root said, as Chris Serino said, as I believe [Officer] Singleton said, if anyone is giving me the same exact story twice, they're probably lying. They're probably pathological liars. Because when you lie, I guess, since you're making up a fantasy, you can tell the fantasy twice, the same exact way. But if you get your nose smashed and your head smashed and you're trying to do what you can, and you're answering every question they ask of you, then, OK, deal with the inconsistencies however you want to.

...

If you lie, it's normally with intent to deceive, isn't it? Isn't that the essence of a lie? If George Zimmerman had the intent to deceive, why would he give six statements? If you're going to give him credit for anything about going to school, and going through legal studies, here's one: Miranda. He knows self-defense. He knows Stand Your Ground. He knows whatever the state wants you to think he knows, but he doesn't know Miranda? Or, no, he knows Miranda, but he was such the mastermind that he could, without knowing any of the evidence – who was watching, who was videotaping, who was doing anything – without knowing any of that, he had it all sussed. He had it all figured out. Really?

...

I almost wish – and I've never said this in a criminal trial before, I've never heard it being said before – I almost wish that the verdict had guilty, not guilty and completely innocent. Cause I would ask you to check that one. You gotta check the not guilty, but check the innocent then too.

...

Rules for you to deliberate under, and here they are. The case must be decided upon the evidence. Sort of makes sense. I started, I don't know, two and half, three hours ago, I started with the idea that you need to be very careful not to do the assumptions that you might otherwise do at the state's request. It is only the evidence and the witnesses that you can look toward.

Though you can bring your common sense, don't bring your assumptions, don't bring your presumptions.... You don't have that luxury in a criminal courtroom. You don't. You only get to decide it upon what you are certain of: something that you do not have a reasonable doubt about.

Don't do it because you feel sorry for anyone.... I said to you [in jury selection], you know, if the state doesn't prove their case, will you be able to say something, to announce a verdict of acquittal even though that verdict has to be heard by the Martin family? And you said you could.

I meant that for a very significant reason. It is a tragedy, truly, but you can't allow sympathy to feed into it. When I say that to you, someone should raise their hand and say, *Are you nuts? How dare you tell me to leave sympathy out of my life. How dare you tell me to leave all of my emotions besides. How dare you! I don't do that ever in my life.* Welcome to a criminal courtroom, because unfortunately you have to be better than your presumptions. You have to be better than what you do in everyday life. Better – at least different, at least unique.

Verdicts should not be influenced by feelings of prejudice, bias or sympathy. They must be based on the evidence and law, period. And the judge will tell you what the law is.

And now we have to talk for a moment about self-defense, because we've talked all around it.... A person is justified in using deadly force – force likely to cause death – if he reasonably believes that such force is necessary to prevent imminent death or great bodily harm to himself.

There are alternatives – death or great bodily harm – so I'm going to go through this and tell you that what you need to consider is whether or not George reasonably believed, had a reasonable fear of great bodily harm. He doesn't have to think he was going to die. He does not have to think he was going to die; he does have to think that he was going to be injured greatly....

... You must judge him by the circumstances which he was surrounded with at the time the force was used. The moment of using the force, what was happening?

The danger facing George Zimmerman need not have been actual. Now, getting beat up sort of takes that better in context, but it doesn't have to be actual. In effect, I guess, the knife coming at you could be rubber as long as you perceive it to be steel. Or the next blow of a fist could be a fake one, but as long as you perceive it to continue to be blow down upon blow down upon you, then that's enough.

The danger that George Zimmerman faced need not have been actual; however, to justify the use of deadly force the appearance of danger must have been so real that a reasonably cautious and prudent person under those circumstances ... – you gotta put yourself, in effect, in the mind of what George Zimmerman was going through, the circumstances that he was going through – and then decide yourself whether or not a reasonably cautious person under those circumstances would have believed the danger could only be avoided through the use of that force. Based upon appearances, George Zimmerman must have actually believed the danger was real.

In considering self-defense – and, again, it's called justifiable use of deadly force; we shorthand it to self-defense – you may take into account the relative physical abilities and capacities of George Zimmerman and Trayvon Martin. If in your consideration of the issue of self-defense you have a reasonable doubt on the question of whether George Zimmerman was justified in the use of deadly force, you should find George Zimmerman not guilty.

...

You're going to get all the law that applies in this case. Every shred of law that applies in this case you will have before you. What you won't have is any law that suggests something like following somebody is illegal, because it's not.

[*reading from another large graphic*] Following somebody in a car or on foot in order to report their whereabouts to the police is not unlawful activity under Florida law. If it was, you would be instructed on it. You would have a statute as part of your jury instructions that says something that George Zimmerman did was unlawful. And you won't have it, because it's just not there, because it's just not true.

...

I cannot imagine that I've actually been here for three hours, but I want to do a couple of quick things to show you, since this is the state's burden, what they haven't proven.... The fact that I had to call Tracy Martin.... I guess they didn't have to do that, but if you're really seeking justice, why have me do it? Why not even have [Officer] Serino testify? Why did I have to have him testify that Tracy Martin said it wasn't his son [screaming]? Why did I have to have [Officer] Singleton testify? Certainly they're available to me, and I did it, and, I guess, if I can do it the state doesn't have to, except, you know, it really is and always will be their burden and not mine.

They didn't tell you about all the other burglaries that happened at Retreat View. I did. They're there. I haven't highlighted them, but trust me, they're there.

Where's the expert on the counter use of force? Where's their guy? So all we have on use of force now is Dennis Root. Again, they don't have to bring a use of force expert. I did; they don't have to. But if that's their issue, where's their information?

The same thing with Dr. Di Maio. I guess they sort of had Dr. Rao, though not on the gunshot. Where is that? Again, they don't have to, but this is their case. It affects George Zimmerman, but it's their prosecution; it's their burden.

That he pushed the gun into Trayvon Martin's chest: you know, justice and emotions, you've got to be careful because we all have emotions as human beings, and then we have justice. And you sit back and you go, *What are they trying to do?*

Does it really help you decide this case when somebody who is not George Zimmerman's voice screams at you, or yells at you, and curses at you? No, I would contend. Listen to the tape; don't listen to Mr. Guy. I'm sure people say that I look like Joel Osteen; I think Mr. Guy was trying to sound like him, with his really loud "F-ing punks." You know, do we need that? I do it a little bit, I guess, but do we need that type of anger coming out from a prosecutor rather than from a defendant? Is that really the way we're going to present this case to a jury?...

One piece of evidence that my client attacked Trayvon Martin? Landed one blow, for that matter? Did anything to justify in any form or fashion the onslaught of injury perpetrated upon him by no one other than Trayvon Martin?

He actually had something else. Because George Zimmerman was, in fact, armed with a firearm – and we know that. We know he had the right to have it.

[*carrying a chunk of concrete to the front of the courtroom*] And then it was said – how many times was it said? – that Trayvon Martin was unarmed. Now, I'll be held in contempt if I drop this, so I'm not going to do some drama and drop it on the floor and watch it roll around. [*placing the concrete on the floor with a thud*] But that's cement. That is a sidewalk.

And that is not an unarmed teenager with nothing but Skittles trying to get home. That was somebody who used the availability of dangerous items, from his fist to the concrete, to cause great bodily injury ... against George Zimmerman.

And the suggestion by the state that that's not a weapon, that that can't hurt somebody, that that can't cause great bodily injury, is disgusting.

Even if we presume Rachel Jeantel was completely accurate in whichever version of what first happened you want to believe, what she said was that George Zimmerman said, "What are you doing around here?"

Let's just for a moment presume that we had that on audiotape. Let's just say they were recording their phone call and you heard ... George Zimmerman's voice on the tape that said, "What are you doing around here?"

What did Mr. Root say about that? What did the only expert who talks about the evolution of force tell us? Well, you say something like that, I might say, "Whatever I want" or "Who are you to ask?" or "What do you mean?" or "Get out of my face." But Dennis Root didn't say that the appropriate response is to break somebody's nose, did he? Did he suggest that that was even near the spectrum of violence allowed, the spectrum of force allowed, in a situation like that?

Unfortunately, you know, there was some anger and hostility and ill will and spite maybe that night. It just had nothing to do with George Zimmerman. Well, that's not true; it had something to do with George Zimmerman: he was the victim of it. Because you can't look at those pictures and say that what was visited upon George Zimmerman was not evidence of ill will, spite and hatred.

Had Trayvon Martin been shot through the hip and survived, what do you think he would have been charged with? Aggravated battery? Two counts?

The state has to convince you beyond a reasonable doubt – you have no doubt in your mind – that my client is guilty of anything.... I really feel that I may have convinced you beyond a reasonable doubt that Mr. Zimmerman is innocent, but of course we know that has nothing to do with it.

…

Here is the standard. You go back there. First thing you might want to consider doing: do you have a reasonable doubt that my client may have acted in self-defense? Go back there and say to yourselves, *Let's just talk, forget the crimes, let's just talk about self-defense. Do we think he might have acted in self-defense?* Not convinced, have some doubt, have some concern that he just *may* have acted in self-defense. And if you reach that conclusion, you get to stop. You really do. Why? Because self-defense is a defense to everything. To littering, to speeding, to battery, if it mattered to grand theft, to assault, to manslaughter, to second degree. You go no further than a determination that the state, now that we're done and there is no more evidence, that the state has not convinced you beyond a reasonable doubt that George Zimmerman did *not* act in self-defense.

It's an easy decision. And I don't say that out of hubris or just ego – ha ha ha – I'm saying it because of the facts of the case. You look at these facts, you look at all this evidence, and you have to say, *I have a reasonable doubt as to whether or not the state convinced me he didn't act in self-defense*. That's all you have to do. You don't have to write "Innocent" on the bottom of the verdict form. We don't go anywhere near those in this courtroom.

The state never, ever loses their responsibility to take away reasonable doubt from you. Don't let them do it with innuendo. Don't let them do it with sympathy. Don't let them do it with yelling. Don't let them do it with screeching. Because none of that matters. Because we have a definition of reasonable doubt, and now you do. You look at that definition, you go back to that room and say, *Let's talk first about self-defense. If I think George may have acted in self-defense, we are done.*

The Critical Role of Women in the Zimmerman Decision

Brenda E. Stevenson

On Saturday, July 13, 2013, the all-female jury in *Florida v. Zimmerman* found the defendant, George Zimmerman, not guilty on all charges in the shooting death of Trayvon Martin. Much of the months-long debate regarding Martin's death – whether Zimmerman should be arrested and tried, and for what crimes; if he should be found guilty or not guilty – has been cast as part of the running commentary we have in this country concerning race and whether it affects the justice that one seeks and receives in our society. Certainly race is at issue here: Trayvon Martin was black; George Zimmerman is white and Hispanic. There is a well-documented, lengthy history of great antagonism between blacks and whites in our country, as well as a more recent history of dislike, distrust and violence between blacks and Hispanics/Latinos, particularly in the urban arena. I also realize, however, as I did while writing about another controversial case in *The Contested Murder of Latasha Harlins: Justice, Gender and the Origins of the L.A. Riots*, that gender, intertwined with race and class, played a significant role in key aspects of *Florida v. Zimmerman*.

Soon Ja Du shot and killed Latasha Harlins in South Central Los Angeles on March 16, 1991. The outcome of *California v. Du* helped spark the Los Angeles riots of 1992, the deadliest and costliest in US history. In that case, the decedent, the defendant, the judge and the prosecuting attorney all were female. They also all were from different races or ethnicities, generations and social classes. Du was a 51-year-old Korean shopkeeper. Latasha was a 15-year-old African-American from a working-poor family. The judge, Joyce Karlin, was a 40-year-old Jewish woman from a wealthy family; her father had been president of Warner Brothers and of the Motion Picture Association of America. Along with the social distance between these females, gender played out in every aspect of this case; in the end, it was a deciding factor.

The jury found Soon Ja Du guilty of voluntary manslaughter, and the black female probation officer recommended to the court that the convicted felon receive the maximum sentence of sixteen years. The judge, however, decided that Du should serve no jail time for killing Harlins. Why? Because in weighing which person was really the victim – Latasha or Soon Ja – Judge Karlin decided that it was Soon Ja, a model, in the judge's eyes, of feminine vulnerability, compassionate motherhood and respectable womanhood.

In the hierarchy of women present in the case, Karlin had the power and the discretion to decide which of these females of "minority" racial status was guilty, and which was not. She determined that the black girl, although dead from a single gunshot wound to the back of her head, was more aggressor than victim, more guilty than Du, whom the jury already had convicted of murder.

In *Florida v. Zimmerman*, women again had extremely important roles to play in determining the outcome of the case. Despite the fact that Martin and Zimmerman were both men (as were the lead defense and prosecuting attorneys), the judge, Debra Nelson, the special prosecutor, Angela Corey, and the jury were all women. Women, therefore, determined the key decisions that led to Zimmerman's acquittal.

Special prosecutor Corey decided that Zimmerman should be charged with second-degree murder, after the male police chief in Sanford, Bill Lee, concluded that Zimmerman had acted in self-defense and should not be arrested.

Judge Debra Nelson made essential rulings on evidence and other aspects of the case. She decided that the prosecution should have access to Trayvon Martin's text messages and social media files but that the jury should not. Before the trial, she excluded the prosecution's expert witnesses regarding the voice heard screaming on the 911 tape. In her instructions to the jury following closing arguments, Nelson allowed the jury to consider the lesser charge of manslaughter. She also decided that the jury should be sequestered for the duration of the trial and mandated the quick pace of trial proceedings.

The all-female jury was left to resolve the question of who was the true victim – George Zimmerman or Trayvon Martin. While evidence was scanty on both sides of the aisle, one of the central queries that dominated the issue of victimization was the identity of the person pleading for assistance on the 911 tape. Trayvon's mother, Sybrina Fulton, testified that it was her son. George Zimmerman's mother, Gladys Zimmerman, then testified it was her son's voice. Whose mother was more convincing to this jury?

When given the task of sentencing Du, the judge chose to underscore the victimization of the woman whose "womanhood" was most like hers. Did the jury of six women, five of whom were mothers, in *Florida v. Zimmerman*, choose to believe the mother whose life, culture and son were most like theirs? Like Judge Karlin in *California v. Du*, the mostly white female jury was in the position of assessing the victim status of women of color and, in this case, their sons.

It has been only in the last fifty years or so that women have gained such significant presence as lawyers, prosecutors and jurists. It will become increasingly important, therefore, that we understand the kinds of histories and socializations of females in our society that they bring into the courtroom; that weighs in when they consider the evidence, victims and defendants before them. Do these women act as those who, historically, have dominated the courtroom – white men of status? Or are their experiences, expectations, insights and miscalculations unique because of their gender? Gender certainly held influence in *California v. Du*. It did so, no doubt as well, in *Florida v. Zimmerman*.

White Women in the Jury Box

Monica J. Casper

During the trial of George Zimmerman for the murder of Trayvon Martin, considerable media coverage surrounded the selection of six women for jury duty. Perhaps, some speculated, an all-woman jury would be more sympathetic to the Martin family, recognizing the profound loss of a dead child. Or perhaps women are the "fairer" sex and would be able to deliberate more humanely about the details of the case. Or perhaps selecting six women might compensate for the glaring absence of any black jury members.

*B51 was once a real estate agent in Atlanta, and she ran a call center with 1,200 employees in Brevard County, Florida. Described as an older white woman, B51 has a dog and a cat. She told the court that though she knows a bit about the case, she's not "rigid in [her] thinking."**

Of course, none of those gendered speculations mattered: a jury of six women, five of them white and none of them black, found Zimmerman not guilty. Seemingly unaware of the furor invoked by the decision, Juror B37 – who wished to remain anonymous but nonetheless conducted a public interview and signed (then canceled) a book deal – stated, "All of us thought race did not play a role." This was the same juror who, during jury selection, referred to Trayvon Martin as a "boy of color" whose murder was "an unfortunate incident."

This juror, like so many white people, likely doesn't see herself as a racist. This is how invisible ideologies work. So let's talk about racism, and specifically the historical, systemic racism of white women.

B76 has a 28-year-old son who is an attorney in Seminole County. The white, middle-aged woman also has a daughter who is 26 years old. She didn't know much about the Zimmerman case, but told attorneys that the defendant "had an altercation with a young man" and during the struggle, the gun went off. Though she doesn't work currently, she used to work for her husband's construction company. They've been married for thirty years.

One of the most widely circulated photographs of lynching in America shows the murder by hanging of Rubin Stacy in Fort Lauderdale, Florida. Stacy was falsely accused and lynched for harming a white woman, Marion Jones. In the photograph, Stacy's lifeless body, clad in overalls and with bound hands, hangs from a tree – "strange fruit" – while a crowd of white people looks on. A man in a straw hat stands with his arms crossed, a woman behind the tree appears to be inching closer to Stacy's body to gaze curiously, and a young girl in the foreground ... smiles.

On the young girl in the photo, we see the "angelic" visage of a racist childhood, the seeds of white supremacy defined as outdoor adventure. Historian Amy Louise Wood, in *Lynching and Spectacle,* writes, "The cultural power of lynching – indeed, the cultural power of white supremacy itself – rested on spectacle: the crowds, the rituals and performances, and their sensational representations in narratives, photographs, and films." Lynching lies at the historical intersection *and construction of* white supremacy, white Southern womanhood and white and black masculinity, the latter framed always as pathological in direct relation to the "purity" of white womanhood. As Wood also notes, "Lynching was thus more than a white prerogative; it was a patriarchal duty through which white men restored their masculine dominance."

B37 is described as a middle-aged white woman who owns many pets. She worked for a chiropractor for sixteen years and has two children – a 24-year-old dog groomer and a 27-year-old who attends the University of Central Florida. Both are girls. Her husband has a concealed weapons permit, and while she used to have one, she let it expire.

You might ask, What does lynching have to do with the George Zimmerman trial? Quite a lot, actually. Just as lynching was a potent and effective racial technology fostering white supremacy, so too is the American justice system a racial technology for fostering white supremacy, as Angela Davis, Ruth Wilson Gilmore and others have argued. In the land of the free, we disproportionately imprison people of color and specifically black men; African-Americans make up almost half of all people imprisoned, and are incarcerated at almost six times the rate of whites. And racial bias permeates every level of the criminal justice system, from racial profiling to Stand Your Ground laws, to arrests, to trials, to sentencing, to imprisonment, to the death penalty.

With patterns like these, is it any wonder that black boys (and increasingly black girls) are criminalized almost from birth? From the transcript of Zimmerman's call to the police, his responses to the dispatcher's anodyne questions reveal his criminalization of Martin on the basis of race:

"He looks black."

"a dark hoodie, like a grey hoodie"

"...looking at all the houses"

"Now he's just staring at me."

"He's got his hand in his waistband. And he's a black male."

"Something's wrong with him. Yup, he's coming to check me out, he's got something in his hands."

"These assholes, they always get away."

Race, gender and criminality, all woven into one "suspicious" package: a young, unarmed black boy carrying a bag of candy.

Sanford, Florida, where the racial profiling and murder of Trayvon Martin occurred, has its own foul racist history. From 1882 to 1930, Florida had the highest number of lynchings per capita in the nation. Three lynchings occurred in the 1940s, one as late as 1943. In his autobiography, baseball legend Jackie Robinson described his horror at the level of racism directed toward him and his new wife, Rachel, from local whites in Sanford in 1946 – painful experiences that led him to a lifetime of social justice work.

The Hispanic nurse serving on the jury didn't even live in Sanford at the time of the shooting – she was residing in Chicago with her several children and husband. She also hates watching the news, telling the court during pretrial publicity questioning that she really loves her reality television shows (like Bad Girls Club*).*

Much has been written about negative representations of Trayvon Martin during the trial, and about the ways the trial was very much about race in America, including the absurd white supremacist fantasy that we live in a post-racial nation. Much less has been written about race, gender and the six jurors.

It is striking that in her post-verdict interview, juror B37 – from whom four of the other jurors distanced themselves in a statement on July 16 – revealed that she sympathized with both Zimmerman and Martin. She stated, "I feel sorry for both of them. I feel sorry for Trayvon, in the situation he was in. I feel sorry for George because of the situation he got himself in." The same juror confided, "Both were responsible for the situation they had gotten themselves into." She believes that Zimmerman has learned an important lesson, and she feels he can safely go back to community policing: "I think he just didn't know when to stop. He was frustrated, and things just got out of hand." By "things just got out of hand" surely she must have meant, "George Zimmerman shot and killed an unarmed child."

E40 may have a different kind of perspective on the Zimmerman case. She describes herself as a "safety officer" who is well versed in cell phone technology. Described as a white woman in her 60s, E40 loves football and is married to a chemical engineer. Her 28-year-old son is out of work.

There is only one system of logic by which juror B37's statements, and the verdict, even make sense. That is the "logic" of white racism, and specifically white female racism. Rather than seeing Trayvon Martin as somebody's child, as the son of Tracy Martin and Sybrina Fulton, as a child buying candy, as just another teenage boy, the non-black jury saw him instead as a thug. And nothing in the prosecution's clumsily argued case dispelled the jurors' fundamental cultural presumption of black criminality.

Juror B37 was clearly persuaded by the defense team's portrayal of Martin as suspicious – in her words, "cutting through the back, looking into houses ... it was late at night, dark at night, raining." Where Trayvon Martin's friend Rachel Jeantel described him as a young man out alone at night, afraid of the man following him, clearly the women jurors did not *see* this particular Trayvon Martin. They did not *see* a vulnerable teenager, alone at night walking through a neighborhood with a stranger, possibly a sexual predator, on his trail. No, what they saw – and what juror B37 described seeing – was a "thug" up to no good; and a man, Zimmerman, who was "no doubt," according to the juror, fearing for his life:

> a man whose heart was in the right place, but just got displaced by the vandalism in the neighborhoods, and wanting to catch these people so badly that he went above and beyond what he really should have done. [Emphasis added.]

Right, because Zimmerman should not have followed Trayvon Martin, nor should he have killed the unarmed youth. Here we see a representation of George Zimmerman as the (armed) Good Guy, whose apparent decency was led astray by persistent black criminality (e.g., "the vandalism in the neighborhood").

When E6 learned about the Zimmerman case, she used it as an example for her two adolescent children, warning them not to go out at night. She is married to an engineer who owns guns and has lived in Seminole County for eight years.

I had a telling encounter with a friend the other day, a white woman who is a mother to three children and a proverbial pillar of the community. When I expressed my feelings about the Zimmerman verdict – that it was wrong on many levels – on the assumption that she would agree with me, her facial expression immediately told me I was mistaken. "We need to trust the justice system," she said, noting that "this was a case we never should have known about.... it was blown up by the media and it never even should have come to trial." I was most struck by the 'we' in her words, because clearly *we* had starkly different feelings about the trial and whether any sort of justice was served. The term 'we' is one of inclusion as often as it is of exclusion, and I wanted no part of it.

Critics and detractors of my argument – and I suspect there will be many who will claim that I'm manufacturing racism where there was simply not enough reasonable doubt to convict – will likely point out that I have no way of knowing whether these six jurors are, in fact, racist. As if racism is only an internal belief system and does not manifest itself in life's decisions and actions, including jury deliberations. Was the little white girl smiling in the Rubin Stacy lynching photograph *really* racist? Were the white women jurors in the George Zimmerman trial *really* racist? In some ways, it doesn't matter, because their very presence *as white girls and women* is already unequivocally implicated in the machinations of white supremacy. Indeed, the architecture of white supremacy is crafted from the bricks and mortar of racism and patriarchy.

The Zimmerman trial has demonstrated viscerally that the knot of racism, white womanhood, black male pathology and "justice" is cinched as tightly as ever in this "post-racial" century. And black bodies – even when they are the victims – are still criminalized.

**Italicized juror bios are all taken verbatim from a July 2013 report by Christina Coleman for Global Grind, titled "Jury Duty! Who Are the Women That Will Determine George Zimmerman's Fate?"*

Perversities of Justice

Linn Washington, Jr.

I received the text message from my buddy blasting the acquittal of George Zimmerman minutes before I boarded an airplane in London en route to South Africa.

Part of me wanted to side with my buddy's ire over Zimmerman's not even getting a wrist-slap conviction on a lesser charge for his punkish admission that he killed a much smaller kid who he said beat him up during a scuffle. But another side of me remained detached, reminded as I was of the details in so many stories that I've covered during my thirty-plus years of journalism.

I've seen too many juries render acquittal verdicts in too many race-tainted cases where clear evidence of the white defendant's guilt existed – guilt obscured by lackluster prosecution and other perverse judicial system procedures.

I remember writing about a black teen in Philadelphia who spent a year in adult prison awaiting trial for rape because lazy police and prosecutors didn't review an easily obtainable security camera video that eventually freed that teen. And I remember writing about a Philadelphia judge who gave big breaks to the white teens charged with raping an 11-year-old black girl at the city's baseball stadium months after that black teen's release. Those white teens did not endure pretrial detention, like that black teen. And those white teens, once convicted, were sentenced to treatment, not custody – treatment that lasted less than a year.

Interestingly, lackluster prosecutions and judicial system perversities don't seem to affect the successful prosecution of minorities, particularly blacks. Blacks and Hispanics, for example, constitute more than half of the inmates in Florida's prison system, despite those two groups' accounting for slightly more than a third of Florida's population. Do blacks commit crimes, disproportionately? Yes. But mass incarceration of minorities defies the fact that whites also commit crimes disproportionately yet do not end up in dungeonlike prisons.

One of the first race-roiling stories I remember covering involved a white teen charged with killing a 3-year-old black child in the mid-1970s. That teen had recklessly sped up a small street in South Philadelphia – driving in reverse and driving drunk – running over the child and then fleeing the scene. The child had angered that teen by spilling cookies and milk on his car.

Like the Trayvon Martin murder (and it was murder, despite the jury's misapplication of law and logic), it took public outrage to push prosecutors to haul that drunk-driving, hit-and-run teen into court. And, like the Martin murder, lackluster prosecution laid the groundwork for that teen's acquittal by an all-white jury.

While that white teen defendant did not present a conflicted self-defense claim, as Zimmerman did, his attorney (a former Philadelphia DA) did play a warped defense card. Basically, that teen's defense was: Oops – I made a stupid, alcohol-soaked mistake...I'm sorry...Kinda...Please don't send me to jail with all those Nig...I mean, Negroes, who are real criminals. And that BS worked.

The case presented by prosecutors in Zimmerman's trial was so muddled it made reasonably competent lawyers cringe. And, yes, that muddled prosecution aided efforts by the defense in snowing the jury on Zimmerman's asserted (and evidence-challenged) claim of innocence of any wrongdoing.

Could an aggressive black prosecutor have done a better job than the dumb & dumber team assigned to prosecute Zimmerman? That's debatable. However, what is beyond debate is that few non-white prosecutors worked in the prosecutor's office covering Sanford, Florida, when Zimmerman killed Martin. The office contained nearly three dozen prosecutors, yet non-white prosecutors there could be counted on one hand with fingers left over. I found that out from court administration officials in the Sanford area while seeking such fairness-illuminating information – information evidencing debilitating structural deficiencies that the mainstream media (conservative and liberal) persistently overlook.

Remember, prosecutors in Sanford initially backed the city's top police, who reflexively accepted Zimmerman's self-defense claim. Neither the legislative intent nor court interpretations of Florida's controversial Stand Your Ground law authorize a person to initiate a confrontation, lose that confrontation and then shoot the victim of his aggression, proclaiming it a lawful act of self-defense.

A 2008 report by the Florida Supreme Court faulted the continuing lack of diversity among prosecutors, judges, court staffs and attorneys across the Sunshine State as both contributing to bias and diminishing "the concept of fairness."

That 2008 report was a follow-up to the same court's seminal 1990 report examining race bias in Florida's justice system, which criticized the fact that minorities were "underrepresented" among judges in the state. Only one minority (a Hispanic) served among the sixteen judges working in the judicial district encompassing Sanford when Zimmerman killed Martin.

A comment contained in that 2008 high court report chillingly foreshadowed the acquittal of Zimmerman. A civil rights activist from a town near Sanford told Florida Supreme Court examiners that most Florida blacks believe that "if you are white and kill a black, there is a very slim chance that you will be punished."

It's no surprise that American society perniciously denies the role of race in its body politic. In an ebook defending his son, Zimmerman's father, a former magistrate judge in Virginia, a core state of the Confederacy, writes that he believed racism was a thing of the past until he rudely discovered real racists assailing his son: the NAACP (America's oldest civil rights organization) and the Congressional Black Caucus.

The elder Zimmerman's misperceptions about, or failure to see, persistent race prejudice is offensively systemic. Florida judges similarly denied that racism is an element operative in that state's courts when they responded to investigators for the high court's 2008 report.

In answering a survey question, 70 percent of white judges in Florida insisted that courts in their state treated whites and blacks alike – an opinion inconsistent with the findings of Florida Supreme Court investigative reports released in 1990, 2000 and 2008.

Although racially separate water fountains are now a thing of America's segregationist past and the US twice elected a black man as president, separate and unequal justice too often remains the rule, not the exception.

Americans like to condemn South Africa for its old system of apartheid, blissfully unaware that the architects of apartheid defended their system as modeled on American practices.

'No Rights That Any White Man Is Bound to Respect'

What It Feels Like to Be Black in America

Kevin Alexander Gray

Seminole County, Florida ~ named for the Seminole people, who once lived throughout the area. The term 'Seminole' comes from the Creek word 'semino le,' which means 'runaway,' and the Spanish word 'cimarrón,' which means 'runaway slave.' While the logo of the Florida State University Seminoles is that of a white man, Thomas Wright, a longtime music professor at the school with a lifetime pass to all athletic events, says Seminole is the collective name given to the amalgamation/intermixing of various groups of native peoples and runaway ex-enslaved Africans who settled in Florida in the early eighteenth century and fought three wars against the United States. The first Seminole War was from 1814 to 1819; the second, from 1835 to 1842; and the third, from 1855 to 1858. In 1817, future President Andrew Jackson, called the Extermination President for his savagery against the native population, invaded then-Spanish Florida and defeated the Seminoles in the first war. After defeating US forces in early battles of the second war, Seminole leader Chief Osceola was tricked, then captured, on October 20, 1837, when US troops said they wanted a truce to talk peace. Almost 100 years later, Jackie Robinson couldn't stay with teammates in a white-owned hotel in Sanford and was forced to flee the town in the middle of the night to avoid being lynched by local whites opposed to the desegregation of baseball. On Christmas night 1952, NAACP leader Harry T. Moore and his wife, Harriette, were killed when the Ku Klux Klan blew up their home in Seminole County. The closest hospital was thirty-five miles away, in Sanford. There was a delay in getting the couple to the hospital and getting a black doctor to attend to them. They both died in Sanford. No one spent a day in jail for their murders. Today the racial make-up of the county is 82.41 percent white, 9.52 percent black, 11.15 percent Hispanic or Latino, 0.30 percent Native American, 2.50 percent Asian, 0.04 percent Pacific Islander, 3.06 percent "other" and 2.18 percent from two or more races. Out of a population of 54,000, about 57 percent of Sanford city residents are white, and 31 percent are black.

A friend asked me if I'd been keeping up with the George Zimmerman trial. My immediate answer was "Not really. Watching it was really angering me." But then I admitted I was lying. I had hedged to temper my anger. I also didn't want to try to explain to the white person on the other end of the phone how it feels being black in the USA these days.

Like many others, I believe that Zimmerman is a liar, a racist and a murderer (with the understanding that 'murder' is a *legal* term). I believe that Zimmerman profiled Martin.

And I believe that Martin had every right, even a greater right, to fight for his life with all the strength he could muster. He lost the fight because his killer had a gun, and Martin had only a can of Arizona iced tea and a bag of Skittles.

Yet if you didn't know any better, you'd think Trayvon Benjamin Martin was on trial, and George Zimmerman the victim.

After the five white, one Latina, all-female jury found Zimmerman not guilty, it occurred to me that Martin had been subjected to worse treatment over the airwaves than Adam Lanza, the perpetrator of the Newtown school killings in the fall of 2012.

I was disappointed with the verdict. I think my disappointment is related to the reason blacks are so overwhelmingly in support of Barack Obama. With all the unfairness that comes with living in an environment of pervasive racism and white skin entitlement, blacks still consciously and subconsciously desire white acceptance; to many blacks Obama represents that acceptance. So, though experience told me it was a done deal from the start of the trial, I had hoped that a white judge, white prosecutors and, for the most part, white jury would be just.

I make no apology for my bias against racists and racism. Oftentimes when I'm speaking to a crowd I'll introduce myself as a father and a grandfather, followed by "they can take your car, house, job; a spouse can kick you to the curb, but being a parent and grandparent is something they can't take from you." I was a young black boy at one time, and I've raised black boys. I know what they face. I know that white supremacy does take us out at will.

When I was coming up, I would hear a young white man proclaim, "I'm free, white and 21," and that meant the world was his. For black males the benchmark is "35 and still alive."

So, in all honesty, I despise Zimmerman and every racist thing he and his supporters stand for. That's the feeling I get by just seeing his image online or in the courtroom, or even hearing his voice. I've seen too many victims of raw, racist power wielded by fools. No court proceeding or verdict is going to change that *feeling* in me, or that *reality* for black males.

My friend, knowing me as well as she does, never took my "not really" seriously and pressed on until I told her that I had watched most of the prosecution's case, including Don West and Mark O'Mara's cross-examination of prosecution witnesses. I watched most if not all of the testimony of Martin's mother and father, Sybrina Fulton and Tracy Martin, and of his brother, Jahvaris Fulton. I saw a good deal of the medical examiner, Dr. Shiping Bao, who conducted Martin's autopsy. I watched Alexis Carter, the instructor who taught Zimmerman's criminal litigation class and instructed him on Florida's self-defense laws. And I watched prosecutors Richard Mantei, Bernie de la Rionda and John Guy. I saw very little of the defense's case other than a couple of minutes of testimony from Zimmerman's mother, Gladys, and O'Mara's closing. I didn't want to waste time or emotional capital; basically, I saw what I expected to see in the defense attorney's cross-examinations. To me, any witness they put up only served to bolster Zimmerman's lies.

I went on to tell my friend how excruciating it was to hear the defense argue that Zimmerman, against the instructions of the police, initiated a pursuit of a stranger who was not committing a crime, and that Zimmerman had a greater right of self-defense than his victim. That Martin's fists and the concrete sidewalk were his deadly "weapons." That Martin was basically a homicidal maniac.

For all Trayvon Martin knew, Zimmerman could have been a Jeffrey Dahmer-type. Yet many Zimmerman supporters will ever only see black boys and men as "dope smoking," "gang-banging" "thugs" and "low-lifes" with no right to exist.

That's what Zimmerman's father, brother and backers were saying before the start of the trial. They hired attorneys to advance their racism and assert their demand for white privilege. They even found Chana Lloyd, a young black, attractive female third-year law student to sit behind them in court. Lloyd claimed in an interview that she had asked O'Mara, "Is George a racist?" to which he responded, "I wouldn't work for him if he was." I won't be surprised if one day Lloyd lands a spot on Fox News, where Zimmerman has said he also hopes to be.

Obviously, knowing history is not a requirement for a law degree. If it were, Lloyd would have had to recognize O'Mara's Klan defense strategy: that Zimmerman was protecting white womanhood. That's why in his closing argument he emphasized for the jury of six women a picture of

Zimmerman's white woman neighbor, defense witness Olivia Bertalan, about whom he said, "When you put a face on what was happening at Retreat View, she's it." The defense invoked the same justification for the killing of Martin that the Ku Klux Klan used to lynch black men in the past.

O'Mara held up a picture of Martin shirtless and wearing a gangsta grill in his teeth. The implicit message: George Zimmerman was protecting not just himself but white womanhood from this vicious black thug. When he held up a big chunk of concrete all I could think about was the old racist joke where the white sheriff and his deputies pull the body of a black man killed by the Klan out of the lake wrapped in chains and says: "See boys! Just like a nigger. Stole more chains than he could carry."

In the months leading up to the trial, Robert Zimmerman, Sr., the father of the accused, said, "Racism is flourishing at the insistence of some in the African-American community." He called the Congressional Black Caucus "a pathetic, self-serving group of racists ... advancing their purely racist agenda." He said, "All members of Congress should be ashamed of the Congressional Black Caucus, as should be their constituents," adding, "They are truly a disgrace to all Americans." He called then-NAACP president Benjamin Jealous "a racist," said his organization "simply promotes racism and hatred for their own, primarily financial, interests" and declared, "Without prejudice and racial divide, the NAACP would simply cease to exist."

Like father like son, Robert Zimmerman, Jr., the defendant's brother, sent out a series of racist Tweets and photos before the trial. He compared Trayvon Martin with De'Marquise Elkins, a 17-year-old detained in the murder of a Georgia infant. Both pictures feature the young men flipping the bird at the camera, with the caption: "A picture speaks a thousand words ... Any questions?" In another Tweet he wrote, "Lib media shld ask if what these 2 black teens did 2 a woman&baby is the reason ppl think blacks mightB risky."

Frank Taaffe, outspoken defender of Zimmerman, has been all over the media spewing just about any racist thing he wants to spew. In one CNN interview he let loose, "Neighbor-*hood*, that's a great word. We had eight burglaries in our neighborhood, all perpetrated by young black males in the fifteen months prior to Trayvon being shot.... You know, there's an old saying that if you plant corn, you get corn." So in Taaffe's white supremacist world black people should expect to take a bullet for another black person's actions even if there's no connection between them.[1]

---

1 In May of 2014, Taafee told television reporter John Davis of Orlando's News 13 that he was "getting right with God" and now believes Zimmerman should have been found guilty: "What I know of George and his tendencies and also my opinion is that he racially profiled Trayvon Martin that night, because if that had been a white kid on a cell phone, walking through our neighborhood, he wouldn't have stayed on him the way he did, and that's a fact, and I

For the people on Fox News it seems that the only thing a black person can do to make them happy (unless you're against Obama, a hawk, fundamentalist Christian xenophobe, Republican, quasi-libertarian or into self-hate for the money) is somehow to move to another planet. One of their news hosts, Gregg Jarrett, suggested that Zimmerman might have been justified in killing Martin because the teen "may have been violent" from smoking marijuana. I thought, the eighteen states and the District of Columbia where medical marijuana is legal must not have got the memo. Ironically, it's mainly whites leading marijuana legalization efforts and smoking more pot than blacks. Yet whites, and white youth in particular, are not criminalized like blacks kids in the ongoing war on drugs.

When Judge Debra Nelson allowed Martin's drug test into evideence, it was a "tell" on the way the trial would unfold. How could the prosecutors wholeheartedly argue against the ridiculous claim that pot makes a person violent, or at least suspect, when the majority of the people that they prosecute and imprison are for marijuana possession charges? Pot arrests and adjudications are the feeding trough of the criminal justice system. It's the essence of what Michelle Alexander and others call the New Jim Crow. The police, prosecutors, judges and defense lawyers are all complicit in that system; they are not going to contradict one another.

Early on in the trial, before Nelson allowed Martin's drug test results in, my wife, who works at one of the big department stores, was in the break room on her job. The news played on the television set in the background as she chitchatted with about five co-workers, all black women of various ages, most either mothers or grandmothers. As she tells the story: into the room comes a middle-aged, 50-ish white female employee, who just starts up talking about the trial. There was no invitation for her to strike up a conversation, nor care or awareness as to whom she was addressing; just her arrogant, know-it-all, intrusive whiteness sucking the air out the room. Or as my wife put it, "She was talkin' at us."

From the beginning, the white woman goes in on Martin, saying, "Well, you know he smoked that marijuana!" At that point, the black women all get up and leave the room. Once past the cussing-the-woman-out range, this is how the conversation goes:

"White people think they can say and do anything."

"He [Zimmerman] had no business following that boy."

"What's smoking pot got to do with anything?"

"He had no right to shoot that boy."

---

believe that in my heart." (Ed.)

"I was about to lose my job."

"Me too!"

"Me too!"

"Me too!"

As I told that story to my friend, she became quiet. I joked: didn't that white woman know she was talking to a group of *black mothers*? Then I mentioned Trayvon's mother, Sybrina Fulton. Many blacks are extremely proud of the way she and her ex-husband, Tracy Martin, have taken the high road throughout this ordeal. 'Dignified' is the word most often used. They have let their attorney, Benjamin Crump, do the attacking. Crump has repeatedly expressed what most blacks feel: "If Zimmerman had been killed, Trayvon Martin would have been drug-tested, immediately jailed without bond and put on trial for first-degree murder facing the death penalty." Tracy Martin may have let down his guard once in the courthouse, if one believes Zimmerman's crew. On the first day of the trial Zimmerman supporter Tim Tuchalski claimed Martin called him a "motherfucker." If it happened, he's lucky that's all he was called.

For her part, Sybrina Fulton has become somewhat of an icon to many black people, much as happened with Mamie Till, the mother of Emmett Till. For many blacks, Sybrina represents how they view black mothers and wives. And many black women view themselves going through hell or high water for their kids, as she has done. With her strong bearing, dark skin, motherly but attractive and sensual look, she is the kind of woman that many Southern black men married. Women like her had our kids and raised our families. For those who would denigrate dark-skinned women, the response has long been "the blacker the berry the sweeter the juice."

Tracy Martin, though divorced, maintained a close relationship with his son and a respectful relationship with his ex-lover, ex-wife and mother of his child. He wasn't an absentee father. He seemed to be a good parent. But you just *knew* that a white man was going to play the irresponsible black parent game. The conservative online magazine Frontpage suggested that the father was once a gang member, and posted pictures of him with friends supposedly flashing a Crips' gang sign. The writer went on to say that "Trayvon Martin's family background was not particularly conducive to not acting like a thug." Another conservative writer basically said that Tracy Martin didn't even know his son was not in his girlfriend's apartment and didn't call police until twenty-four hours after he'd gone missing. The general notion is that black fathers are irresponsible, absent or don't care about their children. Kind of what Obama suggests from time to time, even though a Boston College study done a couple of years back revealed

– surprisingly to some – that black fathers not living in the same domicile as their children are *more* likely to have a relationship with their kids than white fathers in similar circumstances.

I found myself posting photos of the parents and their sons on social media throughout the trial. I wanted to remind myself and others what the trial was really about. And instead of getting angry at the mere sight of Zimmerman, I wanted to focus instead on the strength of Trayvon Martin's parents. I used words like 'respect' and 'strength' as captions to cut through efforts to dehumanize and denigrate the family and their slain son. Zimmerman's team wanted words like 'gang,' 'gang-related,' 'gun' or 'drug-related' added to the story because they know that most of the time it strips "the accused" of his human rights and humanity. They know that if some black kid's face is on the news and the word 'gun' or 'drug' is mentioned, even blacks, unless they're family members, most often don't really care what happens to him. The defense's goal was to flip the script and make Martin the accused.

The defense couldn't put the gun in Martin's hands, so they did the next best thing, advancing the old Reefer Madness myth. Back in the 1980s and '90s, usually after a cop shot someone, authorities would say that the shooting victim was on PCP (angel dust) or crack and that the drug gave them superhuman strength. I haven't seen many superstrong crack heads in my lifetime, but I've seen a lot of them wasting away. I haven't seen all that many superstrong potheads either.

Painful as it was, as I told my friend, I did watch defense attorney Don West attempt to tar 19-year-old prosecution witness Rachel Jeantel as a stupid liar. Jeantel was the last person Trayvon spoke to. He told her he was being followed by a "creepy-ass cracker." Her testimony sparked a courtroom, online and television argument, and a trumped-up controversy with the premise that Martin calling Zimmerman a cracker made *Trayvon* the racist.

Then Jeantel came under attack from the "Precious"-ghetto-big-black-girl-"mammy"-bashing crowd – both black and white. On the side of white privilege against Jeantel was Don West's daughter Molly, who posted an Instagram photo showing the family enjoying ice cream after West's contentious and contemptuous cross-examination of Jeantel. Molly West's picture was accompanied by the description, "We beat stupidity celebration cones ... #dadkilledit." Others criticized Jeantel for the way she looked, the way she talked.

In response, someone posted online a quote by James Baldwin: "It is not the black child's language that is in question; it is not their language that is despised: it is their experience."

On the black side of the attack – perhaps unwittingly injecting light-skin, "high-yella" privilege into the mix – was Olympian Lolo Jones, who's had past public problems with dark-skinned women who are more talented runners but are ignored by the media for reason of their complexion. Jones compared Jeantel to Tyler Perry's character Madea, tweeting: "Rachel Jeantel looked so irritated during the cross-examination that I burned it on DVD and I'm going to sell it as Madea goes to court." Like many others, I went to Jones's website, Twitter and Facebook pages to post *Shame!*

Coming on the heels of the Paula Deen "n-word" blow-up, CNN devoted airtime to debate "Does 'cracker' = 'nigger'?"

I laughed sardonically as I told my friend, "A cracker cracks the whip that some poor nigger is at the business end of."

I posted the Last Poets' "Niggers Are Scared of Revolution" to the Facebook page of CNN's Don Lemon as an example of one appropriate use of the word. I added: Why should blacks (or whites or any other racial or ethnic group for that matter) buy into the idea that there's a *word* that has so much power that when said by anyone of another racial or ethnic group it causes one to take leave of their senses? Why should a *word* be a prelude to a fight? have the power to make people act against their interest? provoke a response that fortifies the stereotype that "these people are guided by emotion versus reason"? How can a *word* be an excuse to forgive violence? It can and does signal bigotry, and if the bigot is one's employer, it can signal and unveil discriminatory employment practices. For the racist, 'nigger' means the same as 'subhuman,' or having no rights that any white man is bound to respect. You wanna talk about power? That word already has power. Banning it just gives it *more* power. I think it's better to teach, "Sticks and stones may break my bones, but words can never hurt me." That's what I've told my kids through the years.

There are some who disagreed with me online. One person suggested that there are such things as "fighting words" that ought to be prohibited or made subject to a hate speech code of conduct. On Lemon's show Columbia University professor Marc Lamont Hill said it is perfectly fine for black people to use the word but not whites: "You just have to accept that there are some things in the world, just, at least one thing, that you can't do that black people can! That just might be OK."

I was listening to my young (20-something) neighbor's music the other night: the song "My Nigga," by YG, Young Jeezy and Rich Homie Quan, three Southern rappers out of Atlanta. To me, the use of the term 'my nigger' among black people can mean 'I love (or regard) you even though others think you're nothing.' It's solidarity among "the damned and despised." Obviously, it's hard to be in the damned and despised group when you're doing all the damning and despising, thus whites using the word has been culturally verboten. Still, there are plenty of whites, often in the same socioeconomic class, who grew up around blacks in an intimate way, who faced similar experiences as their black neighbors and are called "nigger" (to their faces) by blacks. They take the moniker as a badge of acceptance, though they rarely reciprocate. It was even that way when I was growing up. That said, 'My nigger' can also have a slavery connotation, as in 'My boy.'

Late in the evening on the Fourth of July I went outside to sit on the front porch. I was drinking a little rum, puffing on a birthday joint, just thinking about things. Things like the trial, "creepy-ass cracker(s)," the n-word, the announced death of the Voting Rights Act, the split decision on affirmative action, Paula Deen, politicians talking about building a higher, longer wall on the border with Mexico and sending a "surge" of 20,- to 30,000 additional troops to guard it, the black unemployment rate continuing to rise and what it was doing to those around me. It *all* seemed bad. Just a ton of bullshit, poison and ill will, all aimed at black people and people of color in the "color-blind," "post-racial" "new normal." It had rained on and off most of the day, but it cleared up around 9ish. Fireworks and gunshots rang out continuously for more than an hour. I took it all in from my perch in the middle of a very black Southern neighborhood. I could hear a helicopter in the distance. Folks were back on the grills they had abandoned earlier due to the rain. Across the railroad tracks from me (maybe 200 yards through the woods and what's left of an old cemetery where blacks committed to the state mental asylum were buried) someone had the music turned up really, really loud. Cutting through the smoke, dampness and fog of the night was "My Nigga." I laughed out loud thinking the "sweet smelling" black folks and white people would love this scene. The scent of barbecue and marijuana mixed together, gunshots, helicopter, black neighborhood, loud music. I was also thinking that CNN and Don Lemon need to come talk to the folk back in the cut. Just about then, some older person must have taken over the DJ duties. Frankie Beverly and Maze singing "Happy Feelings" took over the air and played for a long while.

I went back in the house, jumped online to see what was in my news feed, and there was a *New York Times* headline on the trial, "Race is an undertone of trial..." *Undertone!* Wow. How about "White supremacy and race privilege is everything America is?"

People, such as that headline writer, substituting the word 'race' for 'racism' to soften its meaning, and meanness, always gets to me.

Drug-testing Martin after the killing and not testing Zimmerman is just one of many privileges of racism and white supremacy granted to Zimmerman before a single charge was filed against him. I watched trial video of Zimmerman riding in a cop car after the killing and taking the detective on a tour of the crime scene while crafting his lies. No handcuffs. Front seat. Again I thought, "Wow, they'd never let a *black* person do such a thing."

I believe the Zimmerman trial is of greater racial and civil significance for blacks than the O.J. Simpson trial. First of all, there's no epidemic of aging black ex-football player movie stars (allegedly) killing their young white wives and their boyfriends. What Zimmerman did was to use deadly force even when his life was not in danger, and his victim was unarmed: the same thing police are often guilty of, denying people of color due process and equal treatment with their disparate use of official violence. According to data collected by the Malcolm X Grassroots Movement, a black man, woman or child died at the trigger of law enforcement or those acting "under the color of law" every twenty-eight hours in 2012.

That's not to ignore the fact that black people kill other black people. According to the Justice Department, 93 percent of black victims were killed by other black people, and 84 percent of white victims were slain by other white people. A majority – 51 percent – of the black murder victims are young, between 17 and 29. Comparatively, just over a third – 37 percent – of white people murdered are between the ages of 17 and 29. That tells us a couple of things. First, in the main, blacks don't kill whites and vice-versa, but laws like Stand Your Ground might change that. Already, white defendants who assert Stand Your Ground as a justification for their violent acts are more likely to prevail if the victim is black: 73 percent of those who killed a black person faced no penalty, compared with 59 percent of those who killed a white. Second, we need to deal with the issues that create the conditions for societal violence. Approximately forty-six murders are committed each day in the US, and twenty-seven of those involve a gun. That's a total of about 16,700 gun murders each year. What we don't need are laws that only *increase* that number.

Years ago someone said to me: "White folk believe that most blacks are criminals even if they haven't ever been charged with a crime or haven't done time in jail. They just haven't been caught." Or as my lawyer friend Efia Nwangaza put it: "To a racist, the average cop and even the courts, most blacks are either busted or bustable. In a nutshell, racial profiling takes away the benefit of a doubt."

It's not so hard to imagine that Zimmerman's not guilty verdict might just give any white stranger the ammunition (pun intended) or gumption to approach any black stranger on the street and ask him anything. Blacks now face a civilian version of the NYPD's dreaded stop-and-frisk in states with Stand Your Ground laws. It's tantamount to deputizing the 6 million conceal/carry permit holders.

It doesn't take much to imagine questions like *What are you doing? Where are you going? Why are you here? Let's see some ID?* And what if the stranger black man tells his stranger white inquisitor to "back off" – with or without vulgarities – and the white man he doesn't know responds in a menacing way, or tries to detain him, or attempts to lay hands on him, and the black fellow does anything other than surrender himself to the stranger? How is it that *he* becomes the criminal, and the stranger white man has the right to take his life?

It's nullification of the social contract between blacks and whites, especially men – "You go your way, I'll go my way" – that was established after Jim Crow. In Jim Crow days, if a white man was walking on a sidewalk and a black person was walking toward him on the same sidewalk, the black person had to step into the ditch or road and give the white man the *whole* sidewalk to pass. It was a time when, living out the words of the *Dred Scott* decision, "blacks had no rights which the white man was bound to respect." But as Vernon Johns, the preacher who preceded Martin Luther King at Dexter Avenue Church in Montgomery, once said, "You have to have a license to hunt rabbits in the state of Alabama, but niggers are always in season."

It's really not so far-fetched that this nation is publicly ruminating on such things now. The disjunction between who has the right to take a life and who bears the burden sounds a lot like the way the United States has treated the Iraqis and the Afghanis and those it has labeled terrorists. Then again, as someone said to me as we talked about the war on people of color, here and abroad, "To call a nigger a terrorist is redundant."

I've spoken with some black folks at various points during this tragedy who are quite open about protecting their children, homes and themselves. They say, "We got guns, too." They aren't gangbangers. Most are working-class homeowners, prior military, rural, many in the vein of Robert Williams, Jr., former president of the North Carolina NAACP, who wrote a book called *Negroes With Guns*, about the right of self-defense for black families in the South.

One young family man, who is not supposed to have a gun or be around one because he has a couple of drug felonies on his record, told me something often said by Second Amendment supporters: "Look, if it's about protecting myself or my family, and I need or have to use a gun, I'd rather be judged by twelve of my peers than carried by six."

As I was talking to some young brothers the other night, they joked that "if Zimmerman had killed a white man, they'd drop the 'white' from the 'white Hispanic' description of him, and he'd be just another mistreated Hispanic instead of being able to pimp off playing white."

If Martin had been a female teen of the same age lying dead in the grass (the race of the victim would have also played a part), Zimmerman would have been charged with a crime on the spot.

Despite my contempt for Zimmerman, I still supported the idea that he was innocent until proven guilty, or as the jury decided "not guilty." Especially in the face of a criminal justice process that is routinely and institutionally unfair to people of color, protecting the theory is a good thing. In a progressive framework, the system should protect the rights of the accused, whether we like the defendant or not. And it shouldn't be a system of revenge.

Revenge is the final, worrisome reaction to this trial. All one has to do is check out the comments in almost any article about Zimmerman posted on black-oriented media outlets and it's clear that a lot of people wish him dead, and many have stupidly and publicly offered to kill him. Back in the period between the shooting and arrest, former heavyweight boxing champ Mike Tyson (who in 1992 was convicted of raping Desiree Washington, a beauty pageant contestant, and served three years in an Indiana prison) offered a death wish for Zimmerman:

> It's a disgrace that man hasn't been dragged out of his house and tied to a car and taken away. That's the only kind of retribution that people like that understand. It's a disgrace that man hasn't been shot yet. Forget about him being arrested – the fact that he hasn't been shot yet is a disgrace. That's how I feel personally about it.

Most of the death threats are probably not serious, but a few might be.

One young brother was trying to convince me that had it been his child murdered, he would have gone up in the courtroom after Zimmerman. I told him he was talking nonsense and asked was he willing to harm or kill people that did him no harm just to get Zimmerman? I suggested that it would make him as bad as or worse than Zimmerman. Someone else asked about the New Black Panthers' offer of a $10,000 bounty for the capture of Zimmerman back in March 2012 and their facing off with police on the protest lines in Sanford. I said, "What they gonna do? Provocative pictures with members wearing bulletproof vests standing face-to-face with police – what can they do beyond pose?"

One Zimmerman hater wrote: "He has proven that he fears blacks and will kill them because of that fear. He's a danger to black people, and blacks would be within their right to shoot him in self-defense."

After the verdict Atlanta Falcons wide receiver Roddy White tweeted that the jurors should "kill themselves." He backtracked the next day, was did many other football players who in anger expressed violent sentiments – which is pretty much what one would expect from employees in the soft-core violence industry.

I think Zimmerman should be in jail, though that would be a *very* dangerous place for him. Still, I do have the compassion to fear for his life. I don't support the death penalty by the government or by revenge-seekers. To me, that's one of the things that being *civilized* is all about.

It's very easy to kill a person. As Michael Corleone says to Tom Hagen in *The Godfather II*, "If anything in this life is certain – if history has taught us *anything* – it's that you can kill *anybody*."

Worldwide an estimated 520,000 people are murdered each year. That's an average of 1,477 per day. Two-fifths of them are young people between the ages of 10 and 29, killed by other young people. That doesn't include those killed in war – like those murdered by US soldiers in Iraq and Afghanistan, or those like 16-year-old Abdulrahman al-Awlaki, killed by an Obama-ordered drone strike in Yemen in 2011. Abdulrahman was a US citizen, the son of Anwar al-Awlaki, an American al Qaeda propagandist, also assassinated by drones. Neither of those killings is recorded as a murder. Not so ironically, Robert Gibbs, former White House press secretary, sounded a lot like Zimmerman's defenders attacking Tracy Martin as another irresponsible black father. Gibbs said Abdulrahman should have had a "more responsible father." Gibbs also said the Colorado-born teen happened to be "in the wrong place at the wrong time," another phrase echoed by Martin's accusers. I mention Abdulrahman al-Awlaki here to remind people that President Obama did essentially the same thing to him that Zimmerman did to Trayvon Martin. He could hardly condemn Zimmerman and the outcome of the trial when he condemns strangers to death every Tuesday.

It's easy to kill, but to be civilized is to help people live and to seek ways to end animosity and needless killing. And it's a parent's and adult's duty to help young people get through the dangerous and stupid periods of their lives, where little things can become life-altering or ending events. One can't fall into the trap of criminalizing youth or youthful behaviors and fads. Or using blanket stereotypes. Or fearing and wanting to kill someone because they don't *look* like you.

On the night prior to the verdict my friend Tony dropped by, and the television was on with trial coverage playing in the background. Tony, who manages a gospel radio network here in South Carolina, has twin 13-year-old sons. He relays to me that his sons have kind of followed the trial, as kids tend to do. They're not glued to the tube, but they're watching the process. So Tony says: "Andrew asks me 'Dad, what's happening with Zimmerman?' And I say it's with the jury. He responds, 'We gotta wait?' It was then I realized that this is shaping their reality. They have white friends that they hang out with, and now all this goes into their mix."

A number of people have called or emailed or stopped by or asked me to stop by to help them sort out what they feel. Black kids have had their world shaken up by this verdict. They understand it wasn't just a court case but a referendum on their value as human beings, and they lost.

I was talking to my son as his neighbor was walking up the street with his daughter. They heard our conversation on the decision and stopped. The man said he had to talk to his daughter, who couldn't have been more than 10 or 11. She was visibly sad. Yet it was beautiful to see a young father walking with his young daughter talking about something important albeit tragic. And their stopping to share their experience with my son and me was cool as well. That's been the positive thing coming out of this tragedy. People are talking to one another in a different way: children facing the prospect of early mortality; parents responding in lots of ways, but *having* to respond. And this doesn't apply just to blacks. Yet for the most, blacks are unified on the wrongness of it all. It's white people who are divided.

As I struggled to finish this record of observations, a young father stopped by my house late in the evening. His 14-year-old son had said in response to the verdict, "Daddy that's messed up. What we gonna do?" The father said he was trying to figure out a way to make his boy feel more secure and able to take care of himself. He says he is putting his son in a self-defense class and enrolling him in a gun training and safety class.

As I said from the start, I have a rock-hard bias against Zimmerman. But my anger isn't just about him. It's about the repulsive and dangerous swirl of racism that is in the air right now in America. It's shaping future generations in a very bad way.

Fulton and Martin plan to file a wrongful death civil case. I did a radio show with their attorney, Benjamin Crump, after the verdict in which he reminded listeners that the case would be heard in Seminole County, in the very same courthouse. In the meantime, the NAACP and others are pressing the Department of Justice to bring a federal civil rights case against the freed killer. Al Sharpton is trying to corral the rage over the verdict in support of the 50th Anniversary March on Washington in late August. I hope this isn't more of "the best way to control the opposition is to lead it." The last Trayvon Martin rally I attended in Columbia was organized by black Tea Partiers, and the main speakers were a black Democratic representative who supports Stand Your Ground and a young wannabe politician who was running for office and using Martin's death as a platform for his own aims.

Stevie Wonder has said he'll no longer play states with Stand Your Ground laws, but that will mean he'll be mostly playing in Europe. In addition to Florida at least thirty-three other states (and counting) now have a similar law (also called Line In The Sand, Make My Day, Kill at Will or No Duty To Retreat), language and all. Those other states are: Alabama, Arizona, Connecticut, Georgia, Hawai'i, Idaho, Illinois, Indiana, Iowa, Kansas, Kentucky, Louisiana, Michigan, Mississippi, Montana, Missouri, Nevada, New Hampshire, North Carolina, North Dakota, Ohio, Oklahoma, Oregon, Pennsylvania, Rhode Island, South Carolina, South Dakota, Tennessee, Texas, Utah, Washington, West Virginia and Wisconsin. Instead of not going to those states, Stevie ought to come in and help mobilize against the law – not as an entertainer but as a citizen.

Racism is a hard nut to crack. Yet at the very least, maybe the groundswell of public pressure in support of Trayvon's parents that forced Zimmerman's indictment will spread beyond his trial into a grassroots state-by-state movement to repeal Stand Your Ground laws and reign in the police. And as people organize against the measures and mores that doubtless emboldened Zimmerman's brand of vigilantism, maybe they'll stay organized to take on what is happening with voting rights, Medicaid funding, aid to the poor, drug and prison policies and a host of issues that we should have been fighting off or fighting for.

One can hope.

But right on cue: the day after the verdict, hundreds of miles away from Florida, at Benny's Burritos on Greenwich Avenue and 12th Street in New York City, a drunken white Goldman Sachs employee, reportedly "angry at both his job and his dissolving marriage," was passing a black couple when he stumbled into their table. Douglas Reddish, 25, tried to help the man regain his balance, when the drunken man lashed out at him, "This nigger wants to fight me!" And, "You niggers are why I lost my job." Shortly after that, Reddish punched the white guy in the face, knocked him out cold. The man hit his head on the curb. Paramedics arrived and rushed the man to Beth Israel Medical Center with brain trauma. Reddish took off after the assault but was later arrested. He was arraigned in Manhattan Criminal Court for misdemeanor assault. He was released on his own recognizance. The other man remains in critical condition, as does America.

Aftermath

A Memory: Poem about Police Violence

June Jordan

Tell me something
what you think would happen if
everytime they kill a black boy
then we kill a cop
everytime they kill a black man
then we kill a cop

you think the accident rate would lower
subsequently

sometimes the feeling like amaze me baby
comes back to my mouth and I am quiet
like Olympian pools from the running the
mountainous snows under the sun

sometimes thinking about the 12th House of the Cosmos
or the way your ear ensnares the tip
of my tongue or signs that I have never seen
like danger women working

I lose consciousness of ugly bestial rapid
and repetitive affront as when they tell me
18 cops in order to subdue one man
18 strangled him to death in the ensuing scuffle (don't
you idolize the diction of the powerful: *subdue* and
scuffle my oh my) and that the murder
that the killing of Arthur Miller on a Brooklyn
street was just a "justifiable accident" again
(again)

People been having accidents all over the globe
so long like that I reckon that the only
suitable insurance is a gun
I'm saying war is not to understand or rerun
war is to be fought and won

sometimes the feeling like amaze me baby
blots it out/the bestial but
not too often

tell me something
what you think would happen if
everytime they kill a black boy
then we kill a cop
everytime they kill a black man
then we kill a cop

you think the accident rate would lower
subsequently

(late 1970's)

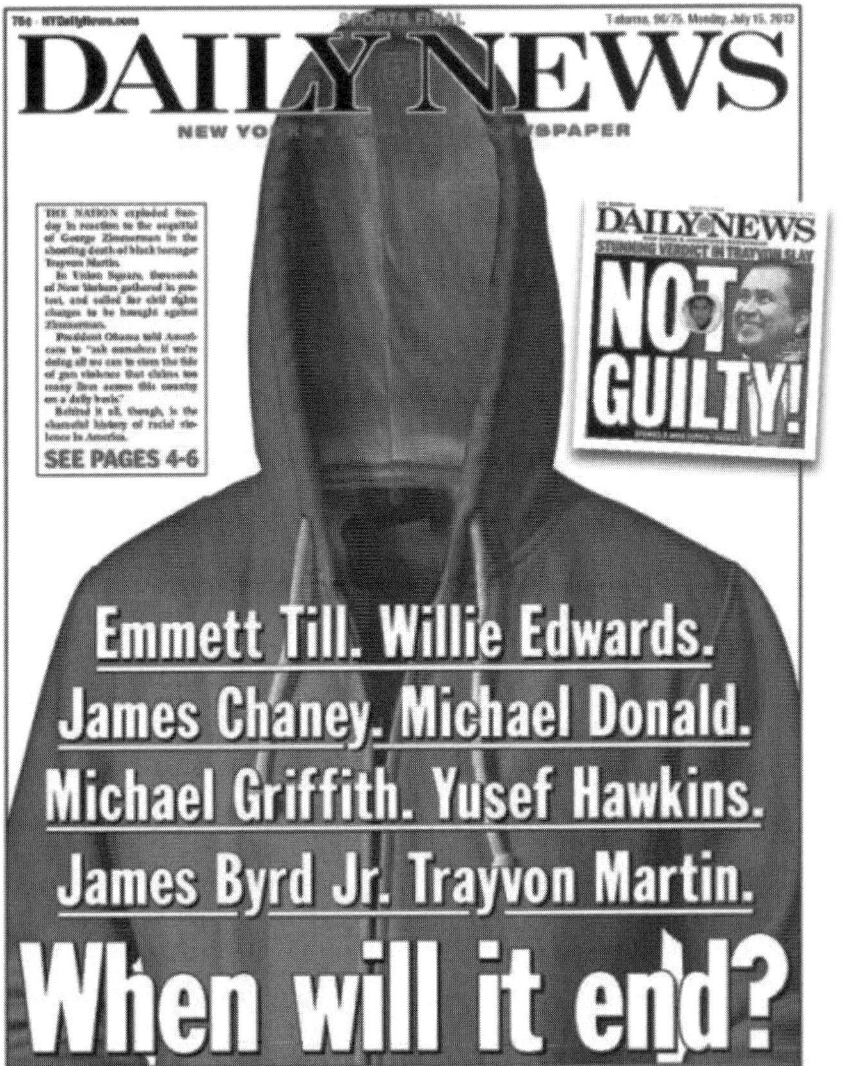
DAILY NEWS
SEE PAGES 4-6
DAILY NEWS
NOT GUILTY!
Emmett Till. Willie Edwards.
James Chaney. Michael Donald.
Michael Griffith. Yusef Hawkins.
James Byrd Jr. Trayvon Martin.
When will it end?
FULL COVERAGE OF THE VERDICT THAT SHOCKED AMERICA
NYDN

How the System Worked
The US v. Trayvon Martin

Robin D.G. Kelley

In the aftermath of the Sandy Hook Elementary School massacre, Texas Congressman Louie Gohmert, Virginia Governor Bob McDonnell, Senator Rand Paul, Florida State Representative Dennis Baxley (also sponsor of his state's Stand Your Ground law), along with a host of other Republicans, argued that had the teachers and administrators been armed, those twenty little kids whose lives Adam Lanza stole would be alive today. Of course, they were parroting the National Rifle Association's talking points. The NRA and the American Legislative Exchange Council (ALEC), the conservative lobbying group responsible for drafting and pushing Stand Your Ground laws across the country, insist that an armed citizenry is the only effective defense against imminent threats, assailants and predators.

But when George Zimmerman fatally shot Trayvon Martin, an unarmed, teenage pedestrian returning home one rainy February evening from a neighborhood convenience store, the NRA went mute. Neither NRA officials nor the pro-gun wing of the Republican Party argued that had Trayvon Martin been armed, he would be alive today. The basic facts are indisputable: Martin was on his way home when Zimmerman began to follow him – first in his SUV and then on foot. Zimmerman told the police he had been following this "suspicious-looking" young man. Martin knew he was being followed and told his friend Rachel Jeantel that the man might be some kind of sexual predator. At some point, Martin and Zimmerman confronted each other, a fight ensued and in the struggle Zimmerman shot and killed Martin.

Zimmerman pursued Martin. This is a fact. Martin could have run, I suppose, but every black man knows that unless you're on a field, a track or a basketball court, running is suspicious and could get you a bullet in the back. The other option was to ask this stranger what he was doing, but confrontations can also be dangerous – especially without witnesses and without a weapon besides a cell phone and his fists. Florida law did not require Martin to retreat, though it is not clear if he had tried to retreat. He did know he was in imminent danger.

Where was the NRA on Trayvon Martin's right to stand his ground? What happened to its principled position? Let's be clear: the Trayvon Martins of the world never had that right, because the "ground" was never considered theirs to stand on. Unless black people could magically produce some official documentation proving that they are not burglars, rapists, drug dealers, pimps, prostitutes or intruders, they are assumed to be "up to no good." (In the antebellum period, such documentation was called "freedom papers.") As Wayne LaPierre, the NRA's executive vice president, succinctly explained his organization's position, "The only thing that stops a bad guy with a gun is a good guy with a gun." Trayvon Martin was a bad guy, or at least looked and acted like one. In our allegedly post-racial moment, where simply talking about racism openly is considered an impolitic, if not racist, thing to do, we constantly learn and re-learn racial codes. The world knows that black men are criminal, that they populate our jails and prisons, that they kill each other over trinkets, that even the celebrities among us are up to no good. Zimmerman's racial profiling was therefore justified, and the defense consistently employed racial stereotypes and played on racial knowledge to turn the victim into the predator, and the predator into the victim. In short, it was Trayvon Martin, not George Zimmerman, who was put on trial. He was tried for the crimes he may have committed and the ones he would have committed had he lived past 17. He was tried for using lethal force against Zimmerman in the form of a sidewalk and his natural athleticism.

The successful transformation of Zimmerman into the victim of black predatory violence was evident not only in the verdict but in the stunning Orwellian language defense lawyers Mark O'Mara and Don West employed in the post-verdict interview. West was incensed that anyone had the audacity even to bring the case to trial, suggesting that no one need be held accountable for the killing of an unarmed teenager. When O'Mara was asked if he thought the verdict might have been different if his client had been black, he replied, "Things would have been different for George Zimmerman if he was black for this reason: he would never have been charged with a crime." In other words, black men can go around killing indiscriminately with no fear of prosecution because there are no civil rights organizations pressing to hold them accountable.

And yet, it would be a mistake to place the verdict at the feet of the defense for its unscrupulous use of race, or to blame the prosecution for avoiding race, or the jury for insensitivity, or even the gun lobby for creating the conditions that have made the murder of young black men justifiable homicide. The verdict did not surprise me, or most people I know, because we've been here before. We were here with Latasha Harlins and Rodney King, with Eleanor Bumpurs and Michael Stewart. We were here with Anthony Baez, Michael Wayne Clark, Julio Nunez, Maria Rivas, Mohammed Assassa. We were here with Amadou Diallo, the Central Park Five, Oscar Grant, Stanley "Rock" Scott, Donnell "Bo" Lucas, Tommy Yates. We were here with Angel Castro Jr., Bilal Ashraf, Anthony Starks, Johnny Gammage, Malice Green, Darlene Tiller, Alvin Barroso, Marcillus Miller, Brenda Forester. We've been here before with Eliberto Saldana, Elzie Coleman, Tracy Mayberry, De Andre Harrison, Sonji Taylor, Baraka Hall, Sean Bell, Tyisha Miller, Devon Nelson, LaTanya Haggerty, Prince Jamel Galvin, Robin Taneisha Williams, Melvin Cox, Rudolph Bell, Sheron Jackson. And Jordan Davis, killed in Jacksonville, Florida, not long after Trayvon Martin. His murderer, Michael Dunn, emptied his gun into the parked SUV where Davis and three friends sat because they refused to turn down their music. Dunn is invoking Stand Your Ground in his defense.[1]

The list is long and deep. In 2012 alone, police officers, security guards or vigilantes took the lives of 136 unarmed black men and women – at least twenty-five of whom were killed by vigilantes. In ten of the incidents, the killers were not charged with a crime, and most of those who were charged either escaped conviction or accepted reduced charges in exchange for a guilty plea. And I haven't included the reign of terror that produced at least 5,000 legal lynchings in the United States, or the numerous assassinations – from political activists to four black girls attending Sunday school in Birmingham fifty years ago.

The point is that justice was always going to elude Trayvon Martin, not because the system *failed* but because it worked. Martin died and Zimmerman walked because our entire political and legal foundations were built on an ideology of settler colonialism – an ideology in which the protection of white property rights was always sacrosanct; in which predators and threats to those privileges were almost always black, brown and red; and whereby the very purpose of police power was to discipline, monitor and contain populations rendered a threat to white property and privilege. This has been the legal standard for African-Americans and other racialized groups in the US long before ALEC or the NRA came into being. We were rendered property in slavery, and a threat to property in freedom. And during the brief moment in the 1860s and '70s when former slaves participated in democracy, held political offices and insisted on the

1 In the end Dunn, like Zimmerman, invoked ordinary self-defense, saying he believed his life was in danger. On February 15, 2014, a jury in Jacksonville convicted him of three counts of attempted second-degree murder, but deadlocked on the murder charge. Dunn is to be retried for first-degree murder in late September 2014.

rights of citizenship, it was a well-armed (white) citizenry that overthrew democratically elected governments in the South, assassinated black political leaders, stripped African-Americans of virtually all citizenship rights (the franchise, the right of habeas corpus, right of free speech and assembly, etc.), and turned an entire people into predators. (For evidence, read the crime pages of any urban newspaper during the early twentieth century. Or just watch the hot new show *Orange Is the New Black*.)

If we do not come to terms with this history, we will continue to believe that the system just needs to be tweaked, or that the fault lies with a fanatical gun culture or a wacky right-wing fringe. We will miss the routine character of such murders. And we will miss how this history of routine violence has become a central component of the US drone warfare and targeted killing. What are signature strikes if not routine, justified killings of young men who *might* be Al-Qaeda members or *may* one day commit acts of terrorism? It is little more than a form of high-tech racial profiling.

In the end, we should be able to prevent another Sandy Hook school tragedy – and the $7.7 million that poured into Newtown on behalf of the victims suggests a real will to do all we can to protect the innocent. But, sadly, the trial of Trayvon Martin reminds us, once again, that our black and brown children must prove their innocence every day. We cannot change the situation by simply finding the right legal strategy. Unless we challenge the entire criminal justice system and mass incarceration, there will be many more Trayvon Martins and a constant dread that one of our children might be next. As long as we continue to uphold and defend a system designed to protect white privilege, property and personhood, and render black and brown people predators, criminals, illegals and terrorists, we will continue to attend funerals and rallies; watch in stunned silence as another police officer or vigilante is acquitted after taking another young life; allow our government to kill civilians in our name; and inherit a society in which our prisons and jails become the largest, most diverse institutions in the country.

Investigate the Racial Context Behind Trayvon Martin's Death

Rev. Jesse L. Jackson

If Trayvon Martin were not a young black male, he would be alive today. Despite the verdict, it's clear that George Zimmerman would never have confronted a young white man wearing a hoodie. He would, at the very least, have listened to the cops and stayed back. Trayvon Martin is dead because Zimmerman believed that "these guys always get away" and chose not to wait for the police.

Trayvon Martin's death shatters the convenient myths that blind us to reality. That reality, as the Chicago *Sun-Times* editorial board wrote, is that "black men carry a special burden from the day they are born."

Both the prosecutor and the defense claimed that the trial was not about race. But Trayvon Martin was assumed to be threatening just for walking while being young, black and male.

That is the reality that can no longer be ignored. Through the years, gruesome horrors – the murder of Emmett Till, the shooting of Medgar Evers in his front yard – have galvanized African-Americans and public action on civil rights. Trayvon Martin's death should do the same.

What it dramatizes is what Michelle Alexander calls the New Jim Crow. Segregation is illegal; scurrilous racism, unacceptable. But mass incarceration and a racially biased criminal justice system have served many of the same functions. Since 1970, we've witnessed a 600 percent increase in the number of people behind bars, overwhelmingly due to the War on Drugs. Those imprisoned are disproportionately African-Americans. The US now imprisons a greater percentage of its black population than South Africa did at the height of apartheid.

Drug usage is not dramatically greater in the black community. But young black males are racially profiled, more likely to be stopped and frisked, more likely to be arrested if stopped, more likely to be charged if arrested, more likely to be jailed if charged. In schools, zero tolerance – once again enforced disproportionately against people of color – results in expulsions, creating a virtual pipeline to prison.

The results are devastating. Young fathers are jailed. Children grow up in broken homes, in severe poverty, since those convicted never really leave prison. They face discrimination in employment, in housing, in the right to vote, in educational opportunities, in food stamps and public support. As Alexander argues, the US hasn't ended the racial caste system; it has redesigned it.

As Trayvon Martin's death shows us, the norm increasingly is to police and punish poor young men of color, not educate or empower them. And that norm makes it dangerous to be young, black and male in America.

There are three possible reactions to this reality. African-Americans can adjust to it, teaching their children how to survive against the odds. We can resent it, seething in suppressed fury until we can't stand it anymore. Or we can resist, assert our rights to equal protection under the laws, and challenge openly the new reality.

We need a national investigation of the racial context that led to Trayvon Martin's slaying. Congress must act. And it's time to call on the United Nations Human Rights Commission for an in-depth investigation of whether the US is upholding its obligations under international human rights laws and treaties. Trayvon Martin's death demands much more than a jury's verdict on George Zimmerman. It calls for us to hear the evidence and render a verdict on the racial reality that never had its day in court.

Tried for His Own Death

Jesmyn Ward

When I heard the Trayvon Martin verdict last month, I was astonished. I shouldn't have been, but I was. I grew up in Mississippi in the 1980s, and my entire family has lived here in the South for generations, so I should have known that George Zimmerman would be found not guilty. I saw that Trayvon Martin was, in some ways, tried for his own death, that the subtext in the courtroom and in the court of public opinion was: he was a thug; he was a threat; he was a violent menace; he deserved it. That in some ways, little baby-faced Trayvon went on trial for being young and black and male. I know this country is rife with racism. I didn't have the heart to actually watch the trial proceedings or any commentary on the case, so I was following all of it on Twitter. When I read that verdict, I was moved to tears, but something about the outcome felt expected. I felt surprise and knowing all at once.

And then my chest tightened and I wondered if those involved in the case, the lawyers and judge and jury, understood what kind of message they'd just delivered to young black people across the country. Because they did deliver a message. That message was this: your skin and your hair and your blood and your bones are worth nothing. You are worth nothing. The subtext was clear: because you are black, your lives are worth less, as are your deaths. I'm familiar with that message. It has dogged me every day of my life. I've grown up with stories of the different ways that message has been delivered. My great-great-grandfather was killed by a group of white men, and of course no one was ever convicted of the crime of his murder. He was working his liquor stills in the woods, and when they came upon him there, they shot him and let him bleed out in the pine straw like a wild animal deemed too dirty to eat: a possum or an armadillo. My grandmother had to hide in the boot of a car along with her brothers and sisters as a child because it wasn't safe for someone of her complexion to be outside in the area where the Ku Klux Klan was so active. My mother integrated her elementary school, and the teachers, she said, treated her and the other black children like a disease.

During my 20s, when I was young and still coasting out of my teenage years, I thought, with the blind certainty that most young people feel, that nothing bad would ever come to me and the people I loved. In the fall of 2000, my younger brother died. He was on his way home from work, and he was hit from behind by a white drunk driver who was speeding more than 80 miles per hour. The drunk driver left the scene of the crime, and in the end, that's all he was charged with: not manslaughter, not vehicular manslaughter, but leaving the scene of an accident. He was sentenced to five years, served three and a few months, and is now free and alive and healthy and happy, able to wake up and eat breakfast and walk out of his front door into the green, great world as he approaches middle age. My brother was 19 and black and poor, his parents a maid and a jack-of-all trades, and therefore, it seems, not such a great loss if he is not able to see middle age. And then within the next four years, from 2000 to 2004, I lost four of my friends, all young and black and male, all members of my poor and black community in the rural South, where people keep goats and chickens and horses and are particularly vulnerable to bad luck as the inheritors of over 500 years of systematic racism. So many young black men, dying without cause, from drug overdose and suicide and murder and car accidents. No one is talking about it, here and in the North and the East and the West, unless the families, who feel the loss keenly, speak out.

And that's why I found myself, angry as I was, reading commentary on Twitter about the verdict, because it seemed that not enough people were openly acknowledging the fact that there was indeed a message delivered that night. That black people are told again and again – by media and political doublespeak, by the fact that it's damn near impossible to get good medical care or psychiatric help, by the lack of positive, empowering, beautiful images of ourselves and our black bodies on television – that we are worth nothing. And this message resounds loudest with those left behind to hear it: with the mothers and the fathers and the sisters and the brothers of those dead, the message that their dead are worth only the caskets they are buried in.

Extract: 'We Will Not Be Moved'

Phillip Agnew

From a speech given at a rally outside the Capitol in Tallahassee, Florida, July 19, 2013. Transcribed by Leah Weston.

Now, we have been here since Tuesday, and some of our students from Florida State and Florida A&M University have been here since Saturday. And for some of us, ... we've been here since 2006, when Martin Lee Anderson was murdered here at a Bay County boot camp.

And so, what I'd like to do today is not offer a fiery speech, but to clarify a few things on the record about who we are, why we're here, what we want, and our vision for a way forward.

First, who we are.

We are the Dream Defenders. We are a multiracial human rights organization dedicated to defeating systemic inequality in our communities through direct action, through nonviolent civil disobedience and through relational organizing. We are a network of youth and students from around the state, right now at colleges and universities around the state, from Tallahassee to Gainesville to Orlando to Tampa to Boca Raton and to Miami, and we are building.

I'd like to correct a few things that have been inconsistent in the presentation of who we are. We are not protesters. The verdict has been read. We are here presenting a way forward. We are not activists. We are not here for the theater that this presents. We are not demonstrators. We're not here to perform a show for anybody. We are an organized student and youth resistance, standing against what seems to be to many an unmovable object. And we are here, excited to see what happens when an unmovable object meets a seemingly unmovable object.

I'd like to talk about why we are here. We are here, indeed, because our hearts were crumbled when we heard a "not guilty" verdict last Saturday evening. We are not here to re-try George Zimmerman. What we are here to do is to express our anger, our angst, our disappointment at the governor, at this state, for what happened under his watch, for what happened under his regime, under his administration – in a constructive way, in a way of peace and love but in a way, as I said before, that is unmovable.

We are here to prevent any more instances like the one we saw on a rainy night in Sanford a year ago. And we are here to produce a solution.

I'd like to tell you a little bit more about why we're here. We are here to present the Trayvon Martin Civil Rights Act. The Trayvon Martin Civil Rights Act is the result of *our* determination, of the environment and the circumstances that led to that rainy night a little over a year ago. We decided to make it simple for everyone.

The first pillar in the three pillars of our Trayvon Martin Civil Rights Act is an end to racial profiling. Now, what we've done is laid out an agenda that leaves room for our lawmakers to do what they do best and present innovative ideas to tackle the issues. We've done a little bit of the work, but there's much work to do. So the first pillar is to remove and eradicate the scourge of racial profiling from our police forces, from our Neighborhood Watchmen and from anybody that seeks to judge someone for the color of their skin.

Now, the second pillar – the second pillar is an end to the school-to-prison pipeline. Now, for anybody that may be wondering what that is, it is, as it states, a prevalent and corrosive list of policies and disciplinary procedures that funnel disproportionately our black and our brown and our poor children out of schools and into prisons. And what is perpetuated by these policies is a generation of second-hand citizens who in Florida – before they reach high school – have already caught a felony.

And in Florida, because of their inability to see the light, if you have a felony in the State of Florida, you are rendered a second-class citizen. It is legal for anyone to discriminate against you in housing, in employment, and you cannot vote. That means you have no say over your future. So we're producing a generation of young people – before they reach eighth grade – who have no choice, no voice over their future. And so we're here today to present a unified student resistance, not to demonstrate to you, not to protest what has happened in the past, but to present a way forward for our state.

The third pillar is an end to Stand Your Ground.

I'd like to tell you a little bit more about what we will not do. We will not be silenced. We will not be stopped. We will not be bought. We will not be co-opted. No one will speak for us. We do not hear the words of politicians who only seek to pander to us. We do not honor the results of a task force that honors and upholds a law that eradicates us based on fear and out of emotion. We will not be silenced, and as I said at the beginningof my remarks, we will not be moved.

We make a call to all young people in the State of Florida, because what we are presenting today is a new way forward. You cannot confront the world as it is without presenting a vision of the world as it should be and as it could be: an image of Florida and the world that presents a generation that acknowledges race, confronts race but is not shackled by race – that accepts our differences, that embraces our similarities, that stands tall and says something whenever we see something that's a little bit incorrect.

I'd like to say something that may be perceived by a few as controversial. But the Dream Defenders and Power U and youth groups around the country are standing up because you left us with nothing. We've had to make something out of nothing. The last fifty years have seen a systematic rollback in the victories of the civil rights movement. We have not forgotten what you have done. In fact, we are building on the blueprint. History is our compass. We are creating new ways to do what you've done before. We admit, we concede – and the only time we will concede – that we are not reinventing the wheel. But what we are doing is updating. What we are doing is speaking from our hearts and using our minds.

... I must tell you at the first sign of anybody speaking for young people: this cannot work. There must be unity. There must be an equal exchange of experience and energy. We must do this together. We must shun organizational affiliations. We might have to shun a few mission statements. We might have to shun a few boards of directors. We might have to shun a few funders and fundraisers. We might have to shun a few reporters. We might have to shun a few of our parents. But we must do this together. It is, indeed, the only way.

We do not purport to speak for the youth. There are youth groups around the country – if any of you all are paying attention in New York, and in Ohio, and in North Carolina, and here in Florida, and in California, and in Oregon, and in Colorado, and in Vermont – who are moving. We are part of a growing student movement. And even here in Florida, there are a number of groups working for the betterment of our Florida.

The Bible says, "O, come let us gather together." There's a scripture that says, "Now faith is the substance of things hoped for, the evidence of things not seen." Last night, the governor told us we had big dreams, big goals. Our contention is, if it's not big, you can't call it a dream or a goal. And so we are here in solidarity with you. Not in spite of you but because of you. We have not forgotten, but, as in everything, we must evolve – to be faster, stronger, better. And then we will really, truly see what it's like when a seemingly unmovable object meets a truly unified, colorless, ageless, powerful, energized, experienced, unmovable object.

Thank you all for being here in support of us. Thank you all for standing with us. And if you really wanna be down with us, be here at 4 o'clock and get shut in with us cause we'll be here all weekend.

An Open Letter to White People About Trayvon Martin

Kyle 'Guante' Tran Myhre

In the next few days, there are going to be a lot of essays and op-eds attempting to make sense of, or grapple with, or process the Zimmerman verdict from writers who are better than me. So I want to talk about this from a very specific angle.

This is an open letter to white people, especially to those white people who understand that something terrible has happened, and has been happening, and will continue to happen, but don't know what to do.

Clearly, something needs to change. But not every problem has a clear-cut, run-out-the-door-and-do-something solution. If you're angry, or sad, take a second to process. Think about where you fit into this injustice, how you benefit from it, how you're hurt by it. If that involves prayers, or posting links on Twitter, or having hard conversations, or writing poems, do that. Process.

But it can't end with "processing."

If you're someone who has avoided thinking about white privilege – the unearned advantages that white people benefit from because of how institutions are set up and how history has unfolded – now is a great time to unstick your head from the sand. If Trayvon Martin had been white, he'd still be alive. What better real-world example of white privilege is there? Grappling with how privilege plays out in our own lives is a vital first step to being able to understand what racism is.

But it can't end with "thinking about our privilege."

We also need to act on those thoughts, to cultivate an awareness that can permeate our lives and relationships. When people of color share personal stories about racism, our immediate response has to stop being "but *I'm* not like that." Just listen. Don't make someone else's oppression about you and your feelings. When people of color are angry, we need to stop worrying about the "tone" of their arguments, or trying to derail the conversation with phrases like "it's not just about race," or contribute meaningless abstractions like "let's start a revolution." When we see unjust or discriminatory practices or attitudes in our workplaces, schools, families or neighborhoods, we need to step up and challenge them. We need to take risks. We need to do better.

But it can't end with "striving to be a better individual."

Times like this can feel so hopeless, but it's important to remember that people are fighting back, and have *been* fighting back. Racism doesn't end when you decide to not be racist. It ends when people come together to organize, to work to reshape how our society is put together.

Check out organizations that are doing racial justice work, community organizing trainings, work with youth and more: the Organizing Apprenticeship Project, MN Neighborhoods Organizing for Change, the Hope Community Center, TruArtSpeaks, Juxtaposition Arts, Justice for Terrance Franklin, Justice for Fong Lee, Communities United Against Police Brutality. There are certainly others. Google stuff. Talk to people. Figure out where and how you can plug in.

As a white person, that can be hard. The leaders of any racial justice movement will be, and should be, the people who are most affected by the problem. But that doesn't mean that white folks should sit by and watch. Some of the organizations listed above may have ways for you to get involved; some may not. But there's always something you can do. Organize a discussion group. Learn about good ally behavior. Challenge your Facebook friends. Challenge yourself. Join an organization. Infuse social justice principles into your workplace, or place of worship, or school, or neighborhood. Listen. Understand that Trayvon Martin's murder was not an isolated incident; start seeing the racism all around you, and start doing something about it.

Above all, stay engaged. As white people, we have the option of not caring. Many don't.

Obama Dog-Whistles Over Trayvon

Margaret Kimberley

There is an understanding, like the instinct that tells birds where and when to migrate, that tells white people that they ought to rule black people. They profit from white supremacy quite literally, and it is part of their natural order. It is accepted, and it continues like mass psychosis. It isn't questioned and keeps black people locked up in jail and unemployed, and every year it kills more than 300 black people at the hands of cops, security guards and Zimmerman-like vigilantes.

President Barack Obama surely understands this phenomenon. He has made a career out of speaking to white people while pretending to speak to black people. He would never have become president had he not mastered this skill. During his 2008 campaign he never passed up an opportunity to assure white people that their natural order was safe. He ranted that black men were terrible fathers, claimed that the country is "90 percent of the way" toward equality, called Jeremiah Wright an old crank who should shut up about racism, and so on.

In the wake of the raw anger and grief that black people felt about the Zimmerman verdict, the president was true to form. He spoke right over the heads of black people, directly to white people, once again engaging in "dog whistle" politics. Just as there are sounds that can be heard only by the canine ear, there is language that can be heard only by specific constituencies, though the words may appear to have been crafted for others. While black people waited anxiously to hear a statement from the president, his words regarding the verdict were tailor made for white America:

> The death of Trayvon Martin was a tragedy. Not just for his family, or for any one community but for America. I know this case has elicited strong passions. And in the wake of the verdict, I know those passions may be running even higher. But we are a nation of laws, and a jury has spoken. I now ask every American to respect the call for calm reflection

> from two parents who lost their young son. And as we do, we should ask ourselves if we're doing all we can to widen the circle of compassion and understanding in our own communities. We should ask ourselves if we're doing all we can to stem the tide of gun violence that claims too many lives across this country on a daily basis. We should ask ourselves, as individuals and as a society, how we can prevent future tragedies like this. As citizens, that's a job for all of us. That's the way to honor Trayvon Martin.

His seemingly nonsensical statement made perfect sense to its intended audience. "A jury has spoken." In other words, shut up, get over it and don't complain. To say that Martin's death was a tragedy not just for his or for any one community is an outright lie. His death is a tragedy and a trauma more for black people than for any other group. Not only was his death not tragic to millions of Americans but some were quite happy that Martin was killed, and were happy when his murderer went free. "Tide of gun violence" meant only one thing. The president was in agreement with the white people who minimized Trayvon's death by constantly bringing up violence within the black community. The 'black-on-black violence' trope was intended to silence the outrage directed at Zimmerman's slave patroller-style murder.

Many people asked themselves why Obama said anything at all, given that the Department of Justice announced it would investigate whether to file federal charges in the case. Those people miss the point entirely. He felt it important to speak to his people in the language they understand. The dog whistle range was clearly understood by the people he wanted to hear it.

In 2012 when the story of Martin's death first became widely known, Obama was caught off guard and had to throw black people a bone. He was forced to point out that if he had a son "he would look like Trayvon." That was the last time he would publicly make a connection between himself and Trayvon Martin – all the more reason to blow the dog whistle at the opportune moment.

The crises facing black America did not become more acute when the verdict was announced. They were simply brought to the fore where they couldn't be ignored. Times of crisis bring clarity. The clarity of the Zimmerman verdict is an ugly one. The verdict tells us that we remain defeated, an oppressed people surrounded by but dependent upon enemies. Our past victories are constantly undermined, and we live a precarious existence.

We don't honor Trayvon Martin by shutting up and pretending that there is some mystery involved in preventing future hate crime murders.

We honor him and ourselves by demanding justice. A few prominent cases of Zimmerman-style vigilantes going to jail will prevent more killing. Obama and Attorney General Eric Holder shouldn't be let off the hook because they investigate this case. They must investigate all of them and use their power to end Stand Your Ground laws, which are a license for racist murder. If we demand anything less, we are just helping to blow the dog whistle.

George Zimmerman Is Entitled to Civil Rights Protections, Too

Michael Meyers

No compendium on the killing of Trayvon Martin is complete without asking and answering the question, Since when did civil rights activists not care about due process and a fair trial for the accused?

With few exceptions, civil-righters labeled George Zimmerman a white murderer and pronounced him guilty of racial profiling, a charge usually associated with police behavior. Many accused him of being a "trigger-happy" vigilante. On TV and elsewhere the Rev. Al Sharpton and his ilk summoned rabble-rousers to demand "justice" for Trayvon Martin – i.e., for the arrest of George Zimmerman for his having "murdered" Martin in cold blood. They were especially mad because on the night and days after the shooting, Zimmerman was set free by the local police. The rhetoric invoked had a familiar ring: the lives of black boys are held cheap by whites, including "white" Hispanics, and particularly by local cops in the South.

I was especially taken aback by the ACLU's fomenting tone. The nation's supposed guardian of civil liberties immediately forsook its mission by joining the Sharpton clan's call for punishment. In a speech to Rev. Al's National Action Network convention, Laura Murphy, director of the ACLU's Washington legislative office, shared her personal fears for her own African-American son. The Murphys live in a predominantly white, upper-middle-class community, and she recounted how she had emailed her neighbors not to panic when they eyed a black man in the neighborhood; that young black man would be her son, back home from boarding school. Murphy had lamented, without evidence, that Martin had been racially profiled by Zimmerman. The ACLU also urged the US Justice Department to enter the investigation of Trayvon Martin's killing. Against the backdrop of the national outcry over Trayvon Martin's tragic death, the ACLU issued demands for passage of the End Racial Profiling Act; and when Zimmerman was acquitted by a jury of his peers, the ACLU urged a federal civil rights prosecution of Zimmerman.

The ACLU's joining the chorus for a federal prosecution of George Zimmerman – a second trial, in effect – violated the ACLU's longstanding policy against double jeopardy. The ACLU defines 'double jeopardy' as a second criminal trial, by any sovereignty, once the accused has been acquitted of a crime such as murder. Rather than defend its principles, the ACLU pandered to racial hucksters and to those among its "constituents" who felt George Zimmerman's acquittal was a miscarriage of justice.

It is a civil rights principle that the government does not get two bites; it doesn't get to try the accused again for the same crime once the accused has beaten the charges. Either the feds should have gone first on civil rights charges – which they admitted they had no evidence to do following their initial investigation – or they should have announced declaratively that in America we do not put one in double jeopardy of losing his liberty. The Obama Justice Department, instead, played the racial politics game. Perhaps worried about disorders, it insisted that its investigation is "open" and ongoing.

The ordinary advocates and guardians of civil rights sunk to the lowest common denominator – demanding conviction before, during and after the trial. It was a field day for hotheads. On local and national TV shows, shrill commentators accused George Zimmerman of murder, of a lynching. The esteemed historian Doris Kearns Goodwin even compared the circumstances of Trayvon Martin's death to the 1955 murder of 14-year-old Emmett Till. Ordinarily sober heads spun into an Orwellian universe of spitting out nonsensical epithets and outrageous calumny about the racist character of modern America. It was the right time for the ACLU to speak truth about law, about due process, about double jeopardy, about what is and what is not a civil rights crime under Florida and federal laws. Instead, the ACLU's chieftains "went there" – to the side of Al Sharpton and stoked the flames of racial upset.

One might have thought that Laura Murphy's superiors would have reprimanded her, or at the very least corrected her misstatement of policy. Rather, her racial paranoia was indicative of the viewpoint of the ACLU's executive director, Anthony Romero. Not until the ACLU's hypocrisy was exposed in Politico (with quotes from me) did the ACLU remove from its website its previous support for a federal civil rights probe of George Zimmerman, and finally explicate its true position on double jeopardy in a letter to the Justice Department. It did not have the *cojones*, however, to issue a press release correcting its prior statements.

The ACLU's dissembling is the kind of trouble civil rights activists fall into whenever they allow passion and prejudice to dictate bottom lines instead of hard evidence and principle. As I have often pointed out, just about every cop that was ever indicted by Al Sharpton has walked free. Chants of "No justice, no peace" do not a criminal prosecution make – and they never satisfy the burden of proof beyond a reasonable doubt.

To those who, like me, watched every day of George Zimmerman's public trial, the State of Florida messed up big-time. It simply had or presented a very weak case. There was hardly convincing proof of Zimmerman having committed murder. Indeed, the state's own witnesses undermined and torpedoed the prosecution of George Zimmerman. The judge's bias showed – allowing lesser charges to go to the jury – and, still, the jury came back with acquittals. Not guilty of murder or any lesser charge, Zimmerman walked out of that Florida courtroom because the prosecution did not meet its burden, not because the jury or America was racist.

Nothing I heard in that trial convinced me of Zimmerman's guilt. According to the best evidence of the race hucksters, however, any Hispanic white who associates with white people, by living in a mostly white neighborhood – no matter that he took a black girl to the prom, that he mentored black kids, that he stepped in to stick up for a black man who was being harassed by the local police – has got to be a racist. They have come to that conclusion because their instincts, and the likes of Al Sharpton and Doris Kearns Goodwin, tell them that he must be.

I don't believe that, and, more important, the facts of the case don't support a federal civil rights prosecution. Did George Zimmerman so hate black youths that he deliberately set out to kill one of them? That's what a federal civil rights violation and trial mean.

To win a federal criminal civil rights case, the Justice Department would have to prove that Zimmerman acted out of hatred for Trayvon Martin because of Trayvon's race. "Negligence, recklessness, mistakes and accidents are not prosecutable under the federal criminal civil rights laws," as the department itself has stated clearly. Meaning, the feds would face a burden far stiffer than the Florida prosecutor did.

Yet instead of telling the race activists, including the NAACP and its allies, "you're nuts" – which would have been the responsible reaction – the Justice Department refused to slam the door on a federal civil rights prosecution. That's how the government often plays it, and plays us.

I always thought justice was giving a guy a fair trial. Apparently not any more.

This nation needs urgently to be re-schooled about liberty and fairness. I used to think there was common agreement that civil rights included due process and civil liberties, and that keeping the mob out of the courthouse was a fundamental protection for the guy "everybody knows" killed one of their own.

Now civil rights are apparently whatever some activists say they are. They make errant analogies, such as comparing the shooting of Trayvon Martin to the racist pummeling and murder of young Emmett Till, whose offense in the Old South was to whistle at a white woman.

That was racist violence.

It's not a federal case, much less a civil rights violation, when a black teen dies tragically and his Hispanic shooter is found not guilty. Al Sharpton is no fair judge.

I don't want another national conversation about race around this incident. That's bunk. We will never persuade the race hucksters either of America's progress or that race ain't what it used to be. The fact is, most Americans do not fear black youths because of their skin color or because we have hatred in our hearts. When we are afraid, it is for far more complex reasons. Even Jesse Jackson once admitted to his own fears of young black males approaching him. Was Jackson racially profiling? Is he, too, a racist?

Come on. Black, white or Hispanic, neighbors in gated and other communities fear crime and criminals of whatever hue or ethnicity; they fear break-ins like the one that occurred in the home of one of Zimmerman's neighbors. The jurors got that. Why can't we?

I, for one, accept the jury's verdict.

Trayvon and White Madness

Glen Ford

When Trayvon Martin was murdered by a "creepy-ass cracker" in February 2012, an outraged black America mobilized to force the State of Florida to put the perpetrator on trial. Seventeen months later, in the words of President Obama, "a jury has spoken," affirming Florida's original contention that Trayvon's death was not a criminal act.

The White House also wanted Trayvon to be forgotten. Three weeks after the shooting, speaking through his press secretary, the president declared, "Obviously we're not going to wade into a local law-enforcement matter." A few days later, Obama sought to placate black public opinion with a statement of physical fact: "If I had a son, he'd look like Trayvon."

In the wake of the acquittal, Obama's press people have announced he'll stay out of the case while Attorney General Eric Holder pretends to explore the possibility of pursuing civil rights charges against George Zimmerman. Holder told the sorority sisters of Delta Sigma Theta that Martin's death was "tragic" and "unnecessary," but a federal prosecution of Zimmerman is highly unlikely. The government would have to prove that Zimmerman was motivated by racial animus – a fact that is as obvious to black America as a mob lynching at high noon in Times Square. However, except for the fact that he murdered a teenager, George Zimmerman is no more provably racist in a US court than most white Americans – which is why the Florida cops and prosecutors initially refused to arrest him, why the jury acquitted him and why the bulk of the corporate media empathized with the defense.

The white public at large shares with Zimmerman the belief – a received wisdom, embedded in its worldview – that young black males are inherently dangerous. From this "fact" flows a reflex of behaviors that, to most whites, are simply commonsensical. If young black males are inherently dangerous, they must be watched, relentlessly. Black hypersurveillance is the great intake mechanism for mass black incarceration. Zimmerman, the self-appointed Neighborhood Watchman, was acting on the same racist assumption that motivates police across the country, which is why the cops in Zimmerman's trial were more valuable to the defense than to the prosecution. The same goes for the prosecutors and judge, much of whose daily lives are organized around the inherent dangerousness of young black men.

Naturally, the cops testified that they saw no racial animus in Zimmerman's actions, just as they would deny that their own hyper-surveillance of black communities is motivated by animus. The jury, like the vast majority of white Americans, approves of the black surveillance regime. As juror B37 put it, something "just went terribly wrong" – meaning, she saw Zimmerman's profiling and pursuit of Trayvon as well-intentioned and civic-minded, clearly not malicious; an unfortunate turn of events but not a crime. The unanimous verdict shows the other jurors also perceived no malice – no racial motivation – by Zimmerman.

In fact, white folks in general do not think it is racist or evidence of malice to believe that black males are a prima facie threat; it's just a fact. Therefore, it is "reasonable" that civilians, as well as cops, be prepared to use deadly force in confrontations with black males.

The answer to the question What would a reasonable person do? is essential to American law. Police, prosecutors, judges and jurors base their decisions on their own subjective perception of the state of mind of people who harm or kill, and the reasonableness of their actions. To most white people, it is reasonable to suspect young black males of having criminal intent reflexively, and reasonable to fear for one's life in a confrontation with such a person. "Not guilty" is reasonable when everyone that counts shares the same assumptions as the perpetrator.

Black people cannot fix that. We cannot change white people's warped perceptions of the world, although, Lord knows, we've tried. It has been forty-five years since passage of the last major civil rights bill, the Fair Housing Act, yet housing segregation remains general, overwhelmingly due to white people's decisions in the housing market, based on their racial assumptions. So powerful is the general white racist belief in black criminality and inferiority, the mere presence of African-Americans on or near property devalues the land. This is racism with the practical force of economic law. The same "law" has locked black unemployment at roughly twice that of whites for more than two generations – an outcome so consistent over time it must be a product of the political culture rather than the vicissitudes of the marketplace.

The *Brown v. Board of Education* Supreme Court decision is nearly sixty years old, yet school segregation is, in some ways, more entrenched than ever – again, because of white peoples' decisions. Not only is school segregation on the rise but charterization is creating an alternative publicly financed system designed primarily for black and brown kids. In many cities whites can be retained in the public schools only by offering them the best facilities and programs. School desegregation has largely been abandoned as a lost cause because of the whites' "intransigence," a euphemism for enduring racism: a refusal to share space with black people.

But the criminal justice system is white supremacy's playground, where racial hatreds, fears and suspicions are given free rein. One out of eight prison inmates on the planet is African-American, proof of the general white urge to purge blacks from the national landscape. Trayvon Martin fell victim to the extrajudicial component of the black-erasure machine.

White people don't think they are malicious and racist; rather, they are simply defending themselves (quite reasonably, they believe) from black evildoing. That whites perceive themselves as under collective attack is evident in the results of a Harvard and Tufts University study, which shows majorities of whites are convinced they are the primary victims of racial discrimination in America. Such mass madness is incomprehensible to sane people, but racism is a form of mental illness, in which the afflicted perceive things that are not there, and are blind to that which is right in front of their eyes.

To live under the sway of such people is a nightmare. Most of African-American history has been a struggle to mollify or tame the racist beast, to find a way to coexist with white insanity, possibly to cure it, or to make ourselves powerful and independent enough that the madness cannot harm us too badly. George Zimmerman's acquittal is so painful to black America because it signals that our ancient enemy – white supremacy – is alive and raging, virtually impervious to any legal levers we can pull. The feeling of impotence is heightened by the growing realization that the black president – a man who, in his noxious "Philadelphia speech" on race in 2008, denied that racism had ever been endemic to America – cannot and will not make anyone atone for Trayvon.

We have been in this spot before – or, rather, we have always been in this spot, but have for the past forty years been urged to imagine that something fundamental had changed among white Americans. Trayvon smacks us awake.

We must organize for self-defense, in every meaning of the term, and create a black political dynamic – a movement – that will make our enemies fear the consequences of their actions.

'Sometimes You Have to Shout to Be Heard'

Rodolfo Acuña

Why should Latinos support justice for Trayvon Martin? It is not the first time that I have been asked such a question about another group. Take care of the family first.

Through the years, people have questioned why I opposed capital punishment and supported cases such as that of Mumia Abu-Jamal, a black journalist sentenced to death in 1981 for the murder of Philadelphia police officer Daniel Faulkner.

I got involved in that case through my friend attorney Elliot Grossman, who enlisted me during his appeal of the conviction of Manuel Salazar, a young Chicano artist on death row in Illinois, who had been sentenced for the 1984 murder of a white Joliet police officer. Salazar was freed after Republican Governor George Ryan declared a moratorium on executions in January 2000. Ryan's action led to the exoneration of thirteen death row inmates. The most prominent was Rolando Cruz, who had been on the row for twelve years for the 1983 murder and rape of a 10-year-old girl. A repeated sex offender and murderer named Brian Dugan confessed to the crime; it was corroborated by DNA testing. For a time, Elliot was Mumia's attorney.

When people asked me why we were supporting a black man instead of concentrating on Chicanas/os, my first reaction was flippant (*porque me da la chingada gana*), but after I thought it over my response changed and was similar to the one I have about the Trayvon Martin case: "It is not only Trayvon Martin who was wronged, it was society. The law is bad and encourages this behavior toward people who look different. Look at the attacks and murders of undocumented immigrants." In supporting Mumia or Trayvon Martin, we are fighting so that this injustice will not spread.

I feel almost certain that if Trayvon did not look *different* he would be alive today. I also reject the argument that George Zimmerman should be supported because he is Latino. Incidentally, he never identified as a Latino, and he obviously identified as white. The Huffington Post's Gene Demby dug into his past and came up with an old MySpace page belonging to Zimmerman. In it, he made disparaging comments about Mexicans, and he bragged about a 2005 criminal case against him.

On MySpace, Zimmerman explained why he did not miss his former home in Manassas, Virginia:

> I dont miss driving around scared to hit mexicans walkin on the side of the street, soft ass wanna be thugs messin with peoples cars when they aint around (what are you provin, that you can dent a car when no ones watchin) dont make you a man in my book. Workin 96 hours to get a decent pay check, gettin knifes pulled on you by every mexican you run into!

That same year, he was arrested and charged after an altercation with a police officer, and his fiancée at the time got a restraining order against him.

It doesn't take a genius to recognize that Mexicans and other Latinos are also profiled, and not only by police agencies. Florida's Stand Your Ground laws encourage rampant racial profiling. Zimmerman's postings take on many levels. Even so, his supporters try to portray him as the victim, a peace-loving citizen who was trying to protect his neighborhood, forgetting that Trayvon's father was also a neighbor. The facts say that Zimmerman was a racist *before* he killed and *when* he killed Trayvon Martin.

So why are people taking to the streets? It is too hot to be walking around in the sun. The simple answer is "Sometimes you have to shout to be heard!"

Henry David Thoreau in *Civil Disobedience and Other Essays* wrote:

> Unjust laws exist; shall we be content to obey them, or shall we endeavor to amend them, and obey them until we have succeeded, or shall we transgress them at once? Men generally, under such a government as this, think that they ought to wait until they have persuaded the majority to alter them. They think that, if they should resist, the remedy would be worse than the evil. But it is the fault of the government itself that the remedy is worse than the evil. It makes it worse. Why is it not more apt to anticipate and provide for reform? Why does it not cherish its wise minority? Why does it cry and resist before it is hurt? Why does it not encourage its citizens to be on the alert to point out its faults, and do better than it would have them?

Because of civil disobedience, injustices such as slavery were kept in wide public view and consciousness. Just in my lifetime I have seen countless examples of interracial solidarity and the effectiveness of civil disobedience: the civil rights movement, the anti-war movements, stopping the US from the use of nuclear weapons, the movements for Chicana/o studies, the LBGT movements, just to name a few. People were not quiet in those instances, and we are a better society because people shouted.

Unfortunately, I think many of us are forgetting history. Nothing comes without struggle. As Thoreau also wrote:

> Must the citizen ever for a moment, or in the least degree, resign his conscience to the legislator? Why has every man a conscience then? I think that we should be men first, and subjects afterward. It is not desirable to cultivate a respect for the law, so much as for the right. The only obligation which I have a right to assume is to do at any time what I think right.

Trayvon Martin was a 17-year-old kid who is no more because Zimmerman saw him as different.

Extract: 'Just Being a Regular Teenager'

An interview with bell hooks, by Quassan Castro

The growing number of gated communities in our nation is but one example of the obsession with safety.... The person who is really the threat here is the home owner who has been so well socialized by the thinking of white supremacy, of capitalism, of patriarchy that he can no longer respond rationally.

White supremacy has taught him that all people of color are threats irrespective of their behavior. Capitalism has taught him that, at all costs, his property can and must be protected. Patriarchy has taught him that his masculinity has to be proved by the willingness to conquer fear through aggression; that it would be unmanly to ask questions before taking action. Mass media then brings us the news of this in a newspeak manner that sounds almost jocular and celebratory, as though no tragedy has happened, as though the sacrifice of a young life was necessary to uphold property values and white patriarchal honor.... This is what the worship of death looks like.

– bell hooks, All About Love: New Visions, *2001*

Quassan Castro: What are some of the solutions to these injustices that keep arising in our community and around the world?

bell hooks: We can't combat white supremacy unless we can teach people to love justice. You have to love justice more than your allegiance to your race, sexuality and gender. It is about justice. That's why Dr. King was so vital, because he used the transformative power of love as a force for justice.

Castro: Wow! African-American parents are mortified for the safety of their children as they leave the house into a world that has shown it devalues blackness, but also a system exists that does not protect our beloved children. What should these parents say to their children?

hooks: First of all, black children in this country have never been safe. I think it's really important that we remember the four little black girls killed in Birmingham and realize that's where the type of white supremacist, terrorist assault began. That killing sent a message to black people that our children are not safe. I think we have to be careful not to act like this is some kind of new world that's been created but that this is the world we already existed in. I think we should honor the fact that people do amazing parenting of black children in the midst of white supremacist culture. Partially, it is by creating awareness and creating an activist mentality in children at a very early age. When we lived in the time of separate but (not) equal or coloreds only, black parents had to explain the reality to children who did not understand what was taking place. The work of parenting for justice, black parents have always done. Many white people have much to learn from progressive black people about how to parent for justice. I was just talking with a friend about a little black boy in Kentucky who was being told that the other kids didn't want to play with him or touch him because he was black. When parents parent for justice, a child knows how to respond. The boy knew how to deal with the situation; he knew they were being ridiculous. That is what conscious parenting is all about.

Castro: What would you say to George Zimmerman if you were able to speak to him face to face?

hooks: That's a difficult question because I believe that he's such a hater that it's impossible to speak to him through the wall of hate. Just think, if Zimmerman had never gotten out the car, Trayvon would be alive today. Trayvon was no threat to Zimmerman. A lot of hate had to be inside of Zimmerman, to get him out of the car, stalk Trayvon and execute him. It's impossible to answer that. Really, we can only be similar to the Amish and ask for forgiveness of his sins. Some black people might feel the urge to stalk Zimmerman and execute him. I think that's a real shift in many people's response to racialized aggression; it has to do with the feeling of powerlessness in the face of justice not prevailing.

Castro: Why should Stand Your Ground not exist?

hooks: Let's go back to the co-murderers of Trayvon Martin, because they are the white people in Tallahassee who are so obsessively supportive of Stand Your Ground. It is that law that gives the license to kill and that encourages white people to become predators of people of color. We have to look even before Stand Your Ground; white people have always used Private Property signs and No Trespassing signs as a way to kill people who are not like themselves. Florida has been the site of this madness; remember the Asian who was just looking for directions and was blown away by the white man who answered his door. There was a No Trespassing sign, so he was not seen as a murderer. Everybody is saying the decision for Zimmerman was all about the law, and we are a country of the law. Well, the laws in this country have always been anti-black people and people of color. It's yet another white supremacist attempt at mind distortion, like suddenly we have a pure law on behalf of justice when everyone knows that's not so.

Castro: Juror B37 said that Trayvon Martin played a role in his death to Anderson Cooper during an exclusive interview. How do you respond to her statement?

hooks: You know what's amazing about Trayvon Martin is that he was behaving like any teenager in our society would behave, in a normal teenage way. To say that he played a role in his death is to not acknowledge the amazing fact that despite imperialist white supremacist capitalist patriarchy, Trayvon was just being a regular teenager, causing harm to no one. People who want to believe that he played a role in his death are the same people that want to believe that black children are mini-adults, as if they are threats to the power of whiteness.

No Innocence Left to Kill

Explaining America to My Daughter

Tim Wise

You remember, forever and forever, that moment when you first discover the cruelties and injustices of the world, and having been ill-prepared for them, your heart breaks open.

I mean *really* discover them, and for yourself: not because someone else told you to see the elephant standing, gigantic and unrelenting, in the middle of your room but because *you* saw him, and now you know he's there, and will never go away until you attack him, and with a vengeance.

Last night, and I am writing it down so that *I* will not forget - because I already know she will not - my oldest daughter, who attained the age of 12 only eleven days ago, became an American. Not in the legal sense. She was already that, born here, and - as a white child in a nation set up for people just like her - fully entitled to all the rights and privileges thereof, without much question or drama. But now she is American in the fullest and most horrible sense of that word, by which I mean she has been truly introduced to the workings of the system of which she is both a part and, at the same time, merely an inheritor. A system that fails - with a near-unanimity almost incomprehensible to behold - to render justice to black peoples, the family of Trayvon Martin being only the latest battered by the machinations of American justice.

To watch her crumble, eyes swollen with tears too salty, too voluminous for her daddy to wipe away? Well now *that* is but the latest of *my* heartbreaks; to have to hold her, and tell her that everything will be OK, and to hear her respond, "No it *won't* be!" Because, see, even though she learned last night about injustice and even more than she knew before about the racial fault lines that divide her nation, she is still a bit too young to comprehend fully the notion of the marathon as opposed to the sprint; to understand that this is a very long race, indeed that even 26.2 miles is but a crawl in the long distance struggle for justice. And that if she is as bothered by what she sees as it appears, well now she will have to put on some incredibly strong running shoes, because *this*, my dear, is the work.

And, yes, I am fully aware that there are still those who would admonish me for even suggesting this case was about race. Not just the defenders of George Zimmerman, with whom I shall deal in a moment, but even the state, whose prosecutors deracialized this case to a point that frankly was as troubling as anything the defense tried to do. Maybe more. I mean, the defense attorneys' *job* is to represent their client, and I cannot fault them for having done so successfully. But the prosecution's job is to make it clear to the jury what the defendant did and preferably why he did it. By agreeing to a fundamentally color-blind "this isn't about race" narrative, they gave away the best part of their arsenal before the war had really started.

Because anyone who still believes that this case had nothing to do with race – or, worse, that it was simply a tragedy, the racial meaning of which was concocted by those whom they love to term "race hustlers" – are suffering from a delusion so profound as to call into question their capacities for rational thought. And yet, still, let us try to reason with them for a second, as if they were capable of hearing it. Let's do that for the sake of rational thought itself, as a thing we still believe in; and for our country, which some of us still believe – against all evidence – is capable of doing justice and living up to its promises. In short, let's give this *one more shot*.

Those who deny the racial angle to the killing of Trayvon Martin can do so only by a willful ignorance, a carefully cultivated denial of every logical, obvious piece of evidence before them, and by erasing from their minds the entire history of American criminal justice, the criminal suspicion regularly attached to black men, and the inevitable results whenever black men pay for these suspicions with their lives. They must *choose* to leave the dots unconnected between, for instance, Martin on the one hand and then, on the other, Amadou Diallo, or Sean Bell, or Patrick Dorismond, or any of a number of other black men whose names – were I to list them – would take up page after page, and whose names wouldn't mean shit to most white people even if I did list them, and *that* is the problem.

Oh, sure, I've heard it all before. George Zimmerman didn't follow Trayvon Martin because Martin was black; he followed him because he thought he might be a criminal. Yes, *precious*, I get that. But what *you* don't get – and by not getting it, while still managing somehow to hold down a job and feed yourself, *scares the shit* out of me – is far more important. Namely, if the presumption of criminality that Zimmerman attached to Martin was so attached *because* the latter was black – and would not have been similarly attached to him had he been white – then the charge of racial bias and profiling is entirely appropriate.

And surely we cannot deny that the presumption of criminality was dependent on this dead child's race, can we? Before you answer, please note that even the defense did not deny this. Indeed, Zimmerman's attorneys acknowledged in court that their client's concerns about Martin were connected directly to the fact that young black males had committed previous break-ins in the neighborhood.

This is why it matters that George Zimmerman justified his following of Martin because, as he put it, "these assholes," these "fucking punks," always get away. In other words, Zimmerman saw Martin as just another "fucking punk" up to no good, similar to those who had committed previous break-ins in the community. But why? What behavior did Martin display that would have suggested he was criminally inclined? Zimmerman's team produced nothing to indicate anything particularly suspicious about Martin's actions that night. According to Zimmerman, Martin was walking in the rain, "looking around," or "looking at the houses." But not looking in windows, or jiggling doorknobs or porch screens, or anything that might have suggested a possible burglar. At no point was any evidence presented by defense attorneys to justify their client's suspicions. All we know is that Zimmerman saw Martin and concluded that he was just like those other criminals. And to the extent there was nothing in Martin's actions – talking on the telephone and walking slowly home from the store – that would have indicated he was another of those "fucking punks," the only possible explanation as to why George Zimmerman would have seen him that way is because Martin was presumed to be a likely criminal, and for no other reason, ultimately, but color.

Which is to say, Trayvon Martin is dead because he is black and because George Zimmerman can't differentiate – and didn't see the need to – between criminal and non-criminal black people. Which is to say, George Zimmerman is a racist. Because if you cannot differentiate between black criminals and just plain kids, and don't even see the need to try, apparently, you *are* a racist. I don't care what your Peruvian mother says, or her white husband, or your brother, or your black friends, or the black girl you took to prom, or the black kids you mentored. If you see a black child and assume "criminal," in the absence of any behavioral evidence at all to suggest such a conclusion, you are a racist. No exceptions. That goes for George Zimmerman and for anyone reading this.

And here's the thing: even in the evidentiary light most favorable to George Zimmerman this would remain true. Because even if we believe, as the jury did, that Zimmerman acted in self-defense, there can be no question that were it not for George Zimmerman's unfounded and racially biased suspicions that evening, Trayvon Martin would be alive, and Zimmerman would be an entirely anonymous, pathetic wannabe lawman about whom no one would much care. It was he who initiated the drama that night. And even if you believe that Trayvon Martin attacked Zimmerman after being followed by him, that doesn't change.

But apparently that moral and existential truth mattered little to the jury, or to the white reactionaries so quick to praise their decision. To them, the fact that Martin might well have had reason to fear Zimmerman that night, might have thought he, Martin, was standing *his* ground, confronted by someone who himself was "up to no good," is irrelevant. They are saying that black people who fight back against someone whom they think is creepy, who is following them and who might intend to harm them, are more responsible for their deaths than those who ultimately kill them. What they have said, and make no mistake about it, is that any white person who wants to kill a black person can follow him, confront him, maybe even provoke him – and as soon as that black person takes a swing at his pursuer, or lunges, the white person can pull his weapon, fire and reasonably assume that he will get away with this act. I can start drama, and if you respond to the drama I created, *you* are to blame, not me.

We know, if we are remotely awake, that this same logic would never be used to protect a black person accused of such an act. Let's travel back to 1984, shall we, and hypothetically apply this logic to the Bernhard Goetz case in a little thought experiment so as to illustrate the point.

Goetz was the white man who, afraid of young black men because he had been previously mugged, decided to shoot several such youth on a New York City subway. They had not threatened him. They had asked him for money, and apparently teased him. But at no point did they threaten him. Nonetheless, he drew his weapon and fired several rounds into them, even (according to his own initial account, later recanted), shooting a second time at one of the young men, after saying, "You don't look so bad; here, have another."

The majority of the nation's whites, if polls and anecdotal evidence are to be believed, saw Goetz as a hero. He was a Dirty Harry-like vigilante, fighting back against crime, and more to the point, black crime. Ultimately, he too would successfully plead self-defense and face conviction only on a minor weapons charge.

But let us pretend for a second that after Goetz pulled his weapon and began to fire at the young men on that subway, one of them had pulled his own firearm. Now, as it turns out, none of the boys had one, but let's just *pretend*. And let's say that one of them pulled a weapon precisely because, after all, he and his friends were being fired upon and so, fearing for his life, he opted to defend himself against this deranged gunman. And let's pretend that the young man managed to hit Goetz, and perhaps paralyzed him, as Goetz did, in fact, to one of *his* victims. Does anyone seriously believe that that young black man would have been able to press a successful self-defense claim in court the way Goetz did? Or in the court of white public opinion the way Zimmerman has? If you would answer yes to that question, you are either engaged in an act of self-delusion so profound as to defy imagination, or you are so deeply committed to fooling others as to make you truly dangerous.

But we are not fooled.

We don't even have to travel back thirty years to the Goetz case to make the point. We can stay here, with this case. If everything about that night in Sanford had been the same, but Martin, fearing this stranger following him – the latter not identifying himself at any point as Neighborhood Watch – had pulled a weapon and shot George Zimmerman out of a genuine fear that he was going to be harmed (and even if Zimmerman had confronted him in a way so as to make that fear more than speculative), would the claim of self-defense have rung true for those who are so convinced by it in Zimmerman's case? Would this jury have likely concluded that Trayvon had a right to defend himself against the perceived violent intentions of George Zimmerman?

Oh, and would it have taken so long for Martin to be arrested in the first place, had *he* been the shooter? Would he have been granted bail? Would he have been given the benefit of the doubt the way Zimmerman was by virtually every white conservative of note in America? And, remember, those white folks were rushing to proclaim the shooting of Martin justified even before there had been *any* claim made by Zimmerman that Trayvon had attacked him. Before anyone had heard Zimmerman's version of the story, much of white America, and virtually its entire right flank, had already decided that Martin must have been up to no good because he wore a hoodie (in the rain, imagine), and was tall (according to the coroner, he was 5'11", not 6'2"or 6'4" as some have claimed), and that, considering those previous break-ins, Zimmerman had every right to confront him.

No, Martin-as-shooter would never have benefited from these public pronouncements of innocence the way Zimmerman did.

Because apparently black people don't have a right to defend *themselves*. Which is why Marissa Alexander, a woman who had suffered violence at the hands of her husband (by his own admission, in fact), was recently sentenced to twenty years in prison after firing a warning shot into a wall when she felt he was about to harm her yet again.

And so it continues. Year after year and case after case it continues, with black life viewed as expendable in the service of white fear, with black males in particular (but many a black female as well, and plenty of Latino folk too) marked as problems to be solved rather than as children to be nurtured. And tonight their parents will hold them and try to assure them that everything is going to be OK, even as they will have to worry again tomorrow that their child may represent the physical embodiment of white anxiety, and pay the ultimate price for that fact, either at the hands of a random loser with a law enforcement jones, or by an actual cop doing the bidding of the state. In short, they will hold their children and lie to them, at least a little – and to themselves – because who *doesn't* want their child to believe that everything will be alright?

But in calmer moments those parents of color will also tell their children the truth: that in fact everything is *not* going to be OK, unless we make it so; that justice is not an act of wish fulfillment but the product of resistance. Because black parents know these things like they know their names, and as a matter of survival they make sure their children know them, too.

And if *their* children have to know them, then *mine* must know them as well.

And now they do.

If their children are to be allowed no innocence free from these concerns, then so too must mine sacrifice some of their naiveté upon the altar of truth.

And now they have.

So to the keepers of white supremacy, I should offer this final word. You can think of it as a word of caution. My oldest daughter knows who you are and saw what you did. You have made a new enemy. One day, you might wish you hadn't.

A Symphony for Trayvon Martin

Yotam Marom

I had been in Atlanta before, running trainings with Occupy Our Homes Atlanta as part of the Wildfire Project. But until Saturday, July 13, 2013, I had never *been in Atlanta*. That was the day George Zimmerman was acquitted of the murder of Trayvon Martin.

In some ways, it was strange to be away from New York when it happened – the city whose streets I've got used to marching in, the people I've struggled alongside for years, the cops I've learned so well. But in many ways, being in Atlanta felt lucky – away from the shiny glass of Wall Street, the manufactured dreams of Times Square, even the quiet Park Slopes that blur our vision and obscure hard truths. Instead, I was in a place where slave-owning Confederate generals still stand chiseled into the sides of mountains commemorating them, where a sizable majority of the population is descended from people kidnapped, enslaved and brutalized ever since. Being in the South felt somehow closer to the truth. But you know what Malcom X said: "Long as you south of the Canadian border, you're South."

The first night after the verdict came, we marched in the streets, and the march grew with the very real anger and sadness and fear and hope drawing people out to join. The next day was even bigger, in the thousands. We must have marched five miles, much of it in the pouring rain. The city erupted in a symphony of car horns honking in solidarity, echoed by people cheering and clapping from their windows, emboldened by thousands of people stopping on every sidewalk with their fists up, and strengthened by people jumping out of homes, restaurants and cars to join. The music was loud – genuine mourning, righteous fury and deep purpose. I remember thinking, while marching to the beat, this is the kind of music that revolutions come from.

The sound of the car horns struck me most – honked in anger, but not anger that they couldn't get through, all in solidarity and encouragement.

I heard from friends in New York who were part of the demonstrations that took over Times Square that even there, in a city where people are so stressed they eat while walking, the honking was supportive. Tens of thousands were in the streets in dozens of cities across the country, and the media couldn't help reporting on it. Friends and family who have never identified themselves as political or radical were furious, and many of them took their first steps into a march. Maybe people have had it. Maybe the music is finally getting loud enough.

I suppose it's like Aura Bogado wrote in *The Nation*: the question is not whether the Zimmermans of the world (or the rest of us) are white, brown or black; the question is whether we uphold white supremacy or fight to dismantle it. Oddly enough, in this sense, this case *is* black and white. In a country where a black person is killed by a cop or vigilante virtually every day, where more black men are in prisons today than were enslaved just before the Civil War, where drones come home to rest after bombing people of color all across the world in the service of US imperialism, you are either for white supremacy or against it.

The honking horns seemed to compel us – white, black and anyone else – to choose a side. They pierced through the wall of white guilt that threatens to handicap some of us, booming: *Yes, you are different, your experience in this country is different, and your role in the struggle is different – but you, too, can choose a side.*

Rather, *you* must *choose a side.*

As the march snaked through downtown Atlanta, the protesters flooded around cars like water. The drivers – the musicians of the day – sat with their windows down, high fiving or clenching a fist in the air. And every so often a marcher would stop at an open window, have a conversation and take down the driver's phone number to put it on a list for future organizing. At moments like those I was reminded that people don't march forever, that crisis moments pass and we must always think of tomorrow today.

The sight of a young woman taking down people's numbers reminded me how too often we tell ourselves the myth of spontaneity to avoid the hard work of organizing. There is nothing spontaneous about people streaming into the streets. It comes from a rage that builds over years and centuries, the hard work of shifting narratives and raising consciousness, the organizing to bring people in and connect groups to one another, the movement-building to create structures to carry us as we fight. And, of course, people join only when an organized community is willing to step off the curb in the first place, ready to go into motion when confrontations are thrust on us and lines are drawn in the sand.

I drifted back into the music, an epic score dedicated not just to Trayvon Martin but also to all the kids carried through the streets those nights by their parents, whose raised fists seemed to declare that they would no longer permit a world in which they were forced to fear for their children's lives. The horns – and the rest of the music that gives life to our struggles – blasted through Atlanta and all across the country. The tune was unmistakable: choose your side, organize and take to the streets.

Am I a Race Traitor?

Trayvon Martin, Gender Talk and Invisible Black Women

Jasmine Nicole Salters

Because of the continuous battle against racial erasure that Black women and Black men share, some Black women still refuse to recognize that we are also oppressed as women, and that sexual hostility against Black women is practiced not only by the white racist society, but implemented within our Black communities as well. It is a disease striking the heart of Black nationhood, and silence will not make it disappear.

– Audre Lorde, Sister Outsider, *1984*

Despite Audre Lorde's call for Black women to speak, there has been an even louder call from various segments of our community to remain silent, and if we persist in naming our problems we are often labeled race traitors.

– Johnnetta B. Cole and Beverly Guy-Sheftall, Gender Talk, *2000*

These past few days, I have found myself questioning my blackness. My racial loyalty. My allegiance to racial progress. Every time I scroll my Facebook newsfeed or Twitter timeline and am met with links to articles on Trayvon Martin and the devaluation of black boys and men in America, or photos of rallies and protests in honor of the slain 17-year-old whose unjust death was deemed well-grounded by the criminal (in)justice system, I cannot help thinking, *But what about black girls and women?* Each time I see the "long list of African-American men and boys whose non-black killers escaped justice in America's courts – a list that runs from Emmett Till to Amadou Diallo to Oscar Grant to Sean Bell,"[1] I cannot help thinking, *What*

1 Nicole Austin-Hillery, "When blacks killed by non-blacks, justice rarely served," CNN, July 15, 2013 (http://www.cnn.com/2013/07/15/opinion/austin-hillery-Blacks-justice/)

about Rekia Boyd, Kasandra Perkins, Aiyana Stanley-Jones and Deanna Cook?

Yes, I, too, have vocalized my thoughts on America's mistreatment of black men. And I, too, have worn dark hoodies in Travyon's honor. And I, too, called my little black brother upon hearing the Zimmerman verdict to tell him how much I loved him and to express my fears as to what that verdict means in terms of the devaluation of young black male bodies in the United States.

But I, too, unlike the majority of America, also expressed my concerns and fears about the lives of black girls and women. Prior to the announcement of the not-guilty verdict, I wrote in the Huffington Post, "Why are black girls not 'our daughters' the same way that Trayvon Martin is 'our son'?"[2] In that article I question the continual erasure of black women's voices and victimization from dominant discourses, and the subordination of gender to race. I ask:

> Why were there no "I am Rekia Boyd" placards held in honor of the unarmed 22-year-old black woman killed by an off-duty Chicago police officer less than one month after Trayvon was murdered?[3] When will President Obama speak out on behalf of 26-year-old Tarika Wilson, who was shot and killed (and her 1-year-old son shot and injured) by a Lima police officer in 2008,[4] or 17-year-old Kiyanna Salter, who was fatally shot on a Chicago Transit Authority bus the same year?[5] When will there be another Million Woman March for all of the black girls and women continually murdered, assaulted, raped, demeaned, invisibilized, and shamed in our own backyard?

While I received a fair amount of positive feedback – supportive and appreciative comments and emails from friends, colleagues and strangers – like other black feminists, I was also derided: called divisive and self-indulgent for choosing to speak out publicly against self-inflicted gender inequities and to call for equality rather than focus solely on the dominant "endangered black male" synecdoche for the overall black experience; labeled a race traitor for my inability to support retrogressive politics that function to maintain gender hierarchies and repressive, patriarchal imperatives.[6] I cannot ignore the facts of systemic inequality,

2 J.N. Salters, "Trayvon Martin Is Still 'Our Son,' But What About Our Daughters?" Huffington Post, June 9, 2013 (www.huffingtonpost.com/jn-salters/trayvon-martin-is-still-our-son_b_3405835.html)

3 "Rekia Boyd Death: Months After Unarmed Woman Killed By Police, Family Has Few Answers," Huffington Post May 7, 2012 (www.huffingtonpost.com/2012/05/07/rekia-boyd-death-months-a_n_1496001.html)

4 Christopher Maag, "Police Shooting of Mother and Infant Exposes a City's Racial Tension," *New York Times*, January 30, 2008 (www.nytimes.com/2008/01/30/us/30lima.html?_r=0)

5 "Police Release Pictures of Suspect in Teen's Death," ABC7 Eyewitness News, October 6, 2008 (http://abclocal.go.com/wls/story?section=news/local&id=6433908) [Of those others named in this piece, Kasandra Perkins, 22, was killed in 2012 by her boyfriend, Kansas City Chiefs linebacker Jovan Belcher, before he killed himself. Aiyana Stanley-Jones, 7, was killed by a gunshot to the head when Detroit police stormed her grandmother's flat in 2010. Deanna Cook, 32, called 911 while begging for her life in her Dallas home, but her desperation was met with no urgency by dispatcher or police, who arrived after she'd been killed. Ed.]

6 Catherine Squires, "Popular Sentiments And Black Women's Studies," *Black Women, Gender, and Families* 1, no. 1 (2007): 74-93

sexism and imperialism within and outside black liberation struggles so that black men might affirm their manhood under "white supremacist capitalist patriarchy."[7]

With so much talk of *race*-ism, *race*-ial profiling, *color*-blindness and being post-*race*, we continually erase those at the intersection, those who must deal with multiple categories of oppression, such as race, gender, class and sexual orientation, which intersect and reinforce one another. Akin to the black liberation movements and women's movements, all of which obscured the intersectionality of race and gender and black women's identities, we continue to ignore, trivialize and marginalize the discrimination and violence against black women. A similar point has been compellingly made by bell hooks: "No other group in America has so had their identity socialized out of existence as have Black women. We are rarely recognized as a group separate and distinct from Black men, or a present part of the larger group 'women' in this culture.... When Black people are talked about the focus tends to be on Black men; and when women are talked about the focus tends to be on white women."[8] The ideological position of "race first, gender second" still renders the lives of black girls and women less important and fails to hold black men accountable for the oppression of black women. And we, black women, are still expected to sacrifice our own well-being in the interest of (male-dominated) race unity.

For instance, black women remain disproportionately victims of rape and assault, domestic violence and mass incarceration. We are murdered at a rate more than two and a half times higher than that of white women.[9] According to an ongoing study conducted by Black Women's Blueprint, 60 percent of black girls have experienced sexual abuse before the age of 18.[10] We are also the fastest growing segment of the criminal justice population. Yet, there are no national news stories, no marches, no collective outcry. Rather, black women are expected to put their race before their gender, to choose between their dual identities ("black" or "woman") at the expense of their full humanity. We are considered race traitors when we internally critique, "air dirty (colored) laundry" in public, break the silence around intracommunity issues such as the sexual hostility against black women often implemented within our own neighborhoods. We are taught to combat racism and fight for the redemption of black manhood at the expense of combatting sexism and fighting for the liberation of black women, to worry about our husbands and sons at the expense of daughters and ourselves. We

7 bell hooks, *Outlaw Culture: Resisting Representations* (Routledge: New York, 1994): 116

8 bell hooks, *Ain't I a Woman* (Boston: South End Press, 1981): 7

9 Violence Policy Center, "Black Women Are Most Often Killed By A Gun And Almost Always By Someone They Know," *Violence Policy Center*, September 25, 2013 (http://www.vpc.org/press/1309dv2.htm)

10 Terrell Jermaine Starr, "STUDY: More Than Half Of Black Girls Are Sexually Assaulted," *NewsOne*, December 2, 2011 (http://newsone.com/1680915/half-of-Black-girls-sexually-assaulted/)

are expected to rally for unarmed Trayvon Martin and Sean Bell, yet black men are not expected to rally for unarmed Rekia Boyd and Aiyana Stanley-Jones.

And this, I cannot stand for.

We, too, needlessly suffer simply for being born into a world in which the color of our skin determines the degree of our humanity. We, too, are not meant to survive – amidst stray bullets, a war on blackness and a patriarchal capitalist system built on our free labor and sexual exploitation. We, too, are victims of "the race problem," of media (in- and hyper-) visibility, forgottenness, temporality and apathy. And until the killing, assault and devaluation of black girls and women is as prominent on "the black agenda" as the murder, racial profiling and incarceration of black boys and men, we, as a whole, will continue to suffer at the hands of one overarching structure of domination.

So, to answer my own question, no, I am not a race traitor. I am a black woman who, thanks to my black feminist foremothers such as Audre Lorde, bell hooks, Toni Morrison, Angela Davis, Johnnetta Cole and Beverly Guy-Sheftall, recognizes that our silence will not protect us. I am a black woman who is tired of putting the needs of the "community" before my own, tired of suffering in silence from the physical and psychological abuse imposed by sexism manifested within my own backyard. I am a black women who seeks to protect what our dominant culture has little to no respect and value for – black womanhood.

Extract: On Second Thought

President Barack Obama

July 19, 2013. The reason I actually wanted to come out today is not to take questions but to speak to an issue that obviously has gotten a lot of attention over the course of the last week: the issue of the Trayvon Martin ruling. I gave a preliminary statement right after the ruling on Sunday. But watching the debate over the course of the last week, I thought it might be useful for me to expand on my thoughts a little bit.

First of all, I want to make sure that, once again, I send my thoughts and prayers, as well as Michelle's, to the family of Trayvon Martin, and to remark on the incredible grace and dignity with which they've dealt with the entire situation. I can only imagine what they're going through, and it's remarkable how they've handled it.

The second thing I want to say is to reiterate what I said on Sunday, which is there's going to be a lot of arguments about the legal issues in the case – I'll let all the legal analysts and talking heads address those issues. The judge conducted the trial in a professional manner. The prosecution and the defense made their arguments. The jurors were properly instructed that in a case such as this reasonable doubt was relevant, and they rendered a verdict. And once the jury has spoken, that's how our system works. But I did want to just talk a little bit about context and how people have responded to it and how people are feeling.

You know, when Trayvon Martin was first shot I said that this could have been my son. Another way of saying that is Trayvon Martin could have been me thirty-five years ago. And when you think about why, in the African-American community at least, there's a lot of pain around what happened here, I think it's important to recognize that the African-American community is looking at this issue through a set of experiences and a history that doesn't go away.

There are very few African-American men in this country who haven't had the experience of being followed when they were shopping in a department store. That includes me. There are very few African-American men who haven't had the experience of walking across the street and hearing the locks click on the doors of cars. That happens to me – at least before I was a senator. There are very few African-Americans who haven't had the experience of getting on an elevator and a woman clutching her purse nervously and holding her breath until she had a chance to get off. That happens often.

And I don't want to exaggerate this, but those sets of experiences inform how the African-American community interprets what happened one night in Florida. And it's inescapable for people to bring those experiences to bear. The African-American community is also knowledgeable that there is a history of racial disparities in the application of our criminal laws – everything from the death penalty to enforcement of our drug laws. And that ends up having an impact in terms of how people interpret the case.

Now, this isn't to say that the African-American community is naïve about the fact that African-American young men are disproportionately involved in the criminal justice system; that they're disproportionately both victims and perpetrators of violence. It's not to make excuses for that fact – although black folks do interpret the reasons for that in a historical context. They understand that some of the violence that takes place in poor black neighborhoods around the country is born out of a very violent past in this country, and that the poverty and dysfunction that we see in those communities can be traced to a very difficult history.

And so the fact that sometimes that's unacknowledged adds to the frustration. And the fact that a lot of African-American boys are painted with a broad brush and the excuse is given, *Well, there are these statistics out there that show that African-American boys are more violent* – using that as an excuse to then see sons treated differently causes pain.

I think the African-American community is also not naïve in understanding that, statistically, somebody like Trayvon Martin was statistically more likely to be shot by a peer than he was by somebody else. So folks understand the challenges that exist for African-American boys. But they get frustrated, I think, if they feel that there's no context for it and that context is being denied. And that all contributes, I think, to a sense that if a white male teen was involved in the same kind of scenario, that, from top to bottom, both the outcome and the aftermath might have been different.

Now, the question for me at least, and I think for a lot of folks, is where do we take this? How do we learn some lessons from this and move in a positive direction? I think it's understandable that there have been demonstrations and vigils and protests, and some of that stuff is just going to have to work its way through, as long as it remains nonviolent. If I see any violence, then I will remind folks that that dishonors what happened to Trayvon Martin and his family. But beyond protests or vigils, the question is, Are there some concrete things that we might be able to do?

I know that Eric Holder is reviewing what happened down there, but I think it's important for people to have some clear expectations here. Traditionally, these are issues of state and local government, the criminal code. And law enforcement is traditionally done at the state and local levels, not at the federal levels.

That doesn't mean, though, that as a nation we can't do some things that, I think, would be productive. So let me just give a couple of specifics that I'm still bouncing around with my staff, so we're not rolling out some five-point plan, but some areas where I think all of us could potentially focus.

Number one, precisely because law enforcement is often determined at the state and local level, I think it would be productive for the Justice Department, governors, mayors to work with law enforcement about training at the state and local levels in order to reduce the kind of mistrust in the system that sometimes currently exists.

When I was in Illinois, I passed racial profiling legislation, and it actually did just two simple things. One, it collected data on traffic stops and the race of the person who was stopped. But the other thing was it resourced us training police departments across the state on how to think about potential racial bias and ways to further professionalize what they were doing.

And initially, the police departments across the state were resistant, but actually they came to recognize that if it was done in a fair, straightforward way that it would allow them to do their jobs better and communities would have more confidence in them and, in turn, be more helpful in applying the law. And obviously, law enforcement has got a very tough job.

So that's one area where I think there are a lot of resources and best practices that could be brought to bear if state and local governments are receptive. And I think a lot of them would be. And let's figure out, are there ways for us to push out that kind of training?

Along the same lines, I think it would be useful for us to examine some state and local laws to see...if they are designed in such a way that they may encourage the kinds of altercations and confrontations and tragedies that we saw in the Florida case, rather than defuse potential altercations.

I know that there's been commentary about the fact that the Stand Your Ground laws in Florida were not used as a defense in the case. On the other hand, if we're sending a message as a society in our communities that someone who is armed potentially has the right to use those firearms even if there's a way for them to exit from a situation, is that really going to be contributing to the kind of peace and security and order that we'd like to see?

And for those who resist that idea that we should think about something like these Stand Your Ground laws, I'd just ask people to consider, if Trayvon Martin was of age and armed, could he have stood his ground on that sidewalk? And do we actually think that he would have been justified in shooting Mr. Zimmerman who had followed him in a car because he felt threatened? And if the answer to that question is at least ambiguous, then it seems to me that we might want to examine those kinds of laws.

Number three – and this is a long-term project – we need to spend some time in thinking about how do we bolster and reinforce our African-American boys. And this is something that Michelle and I talk a lot about. There are a lot of kids out there who need help who are getting a lot of negative reinforcement. And is there more that we can do to give them the sense that their country cares about them and values them and is willing to invest in them?

I'm not naïve about the prospects of some grand, new federal program. I'm not sure that that's what we're talking about here. But I do recognize that, as president, I've got some convening power, and there are a lot of good programs that are being done across the country on this front. And for us to be able to gather together business leaders and local elected officials and clergy and celebrities and athletes, and figure out how are we doing a better job helping young African-American men feel that they're a full part of this society and that they've got pathways and avenues to succeed – I think that would be a pretty good outcome from what was obviously a tragic situation. And we're going to spend some time working on that and thinking about that.

And then, finally, I think it's going to be important for all of us to do some soul-searching. There has been talk about, should we convene a conversation on race? I haven't seen that be particularly productive when politicians try to organize conversations. They end up being stilted and politicized, and folks are locked into the positions they already have. On the other hand, in families and churches and workplaces, there's the possibility that people are a little bit more honest, and at least you ask yourself your own questions about, *Am I wringing as much bias out of myself as I can? Am I judging people as much as I can, based on not the color of their skin but the content of their character?* That would, I think, be an appropriate exercise in the wake of this tragedy.

And let me just leave you with a final thought that, as difficult and challenging as this whole episode has been for a lot of people, I don't want us to lose sight that things are getting better. Each successive generation seems to be making progress in changing attitudes when it comes to race. It doesn't mean we're in a post-racial society. It doesn't mean that racism is eliminated. But when I talk to Malia and Sasha, and I listen to their friends and I see them interact, they're better than we are – they're better than we were – on these issues. And that's true in every community that I've visited all across the country.

And so we have to be vigilant and we have to work on these issues. And those of us in authority should be doing everything we can to encourage the better angels of our nature, as opposed to using these episodes to heighten divisions. But we should also have confidence that kids these days, I think, have more sense than we did back then, and certainly more than our parents did or our grandparents did; and that along this long, difficult journey, we're becoming a more perfect union – not a perfect union but a more perfect union.

Thank you, guys.

Extract: 'President Obama Is a Global George Zimmerman'

An interview with Dr. Cornel West, by Amy Goodman

Amy Goodman: President Obama surprised not only the press room at the White House, but the nation, I think, on Friday, in his first public remarks following the George Zimmerman acquittal. What are your thoughts?

Dr. Cornel West: Well, the first thing, I think we have to acknowledge that President Obama has very little moral authority at this point, because we know anybody who tries to rationalize the killing of innocent peoples is a criminal – George Zimmerman is a criminal, but President Obama is a global George Zimmerman, because he tries to rationalize the killing of innocent children, 221 so far, in the name of self-defense, so that there's actually parallels here.

Goodman: Where?

West: In Pakistan, Somalia, Yemen. So when he comes to talk about the killing of an innocent person, you say, "Well, wait a minute. What kind of moral authority are you bringing? You've got a $2 million bounty on Sister Assata Shakur. She's innocent, but you are pressing that intentionally. Will you press for the justice of Trayvon Martin in the same way you press for the prosecution of Brother Bradley Manning and Brother Edward Snowden?" So you begin to see the hypocrisy.

Then he tells stories about racial profiling. They're moving, sentimental stories, what Brother Kendall Thomas called racial moralism, very sentimental. But then, Ray Kelly, major candidate for Department of Homeland Security, he's the poster child of racial profiling. You know, Brother Carl Dix and many of us went to jail under Ray Kelly. Why? Because he racially profiled millions of young black and brown brothers. So, on the one hand, you get these stories, sentimental–

Goodman: Ray Kelly, the former police chief of New York City.

West: That's right.... And, in fact, he [President Obama] even says Ray Kelly expresses his values: *Ray Kelly is a magnificent police commissioner.* How are you going to say that when the brother is reinforcing stop-and-frisk? So the contradictions become so overwhelming here.

Goodman: But President Obama, speaking about his own life experience, going from saying, "Trayvon Martin could have been my child," to "Trayvon Martin could have been me"?

West: Well, no, that's beautiful. That's an identification. The question is, Will that identification hide and conceal the fact there's a criminal justice system in place that has nearly destroyed two generations of very precious poor black and brown brothers? He hasn't said a mumbling word until now. Five years in office and can't say a word about the New Jim Crow.

And at the same time, I think we have to recognize that he has been able to hide and conceal that criminalizing of the black poor, as what I call the re-niggerizing of the black professional class. You've got these black leaders on the Obama plantation, won't say a criminal word about the master in the big house, will only try to tame the field folk so that they're not critical of the master in the big house. That's why I think even Brother Sharpton is going to be in trouble. Why? Because he has unleashed – and I agree with him – the rage. And the rage is always on the road to self-determination. But the rage is going to hit up against a stone wall. Why? Because Obama and Holder, will they come through at the federal level for Trayvon Martin? We hope so. Don't hold your breath. And when they don't, they're going to have to somehow contain that rage. And in containing that rage, there's going to be many people who say, *No, we see, this president is not serious about the criminalizing of poor people.* We've got a black leadership that is deferential to Obama, that is subservient to Obama, and that's what niggerizing is. You keep folks so scared. You keep folks so intimidated. You can give them money, access, but they're still scared. And as long as you're scared, you're on the plantation.

Goodman: Let's talk about that issue of the civil rights charges.

West: Yes.

Goodman: During his remarks on Friday in the White House press room, President Obama addressed the calls for the Justice Department to file civil rights charges against George Zimmerman.

President Obama (*on tape*): I know that Eric Holder is reviewing what happened down there, but I think it's important for people to have some clear expectations here. Traditionally, these are issues of state and local government, the criminal code. And law enforcement is traditionally done at the state and local levels, not at the federal levels.

...

West: That was him saying, *Keep your expectations low. Sharpton, don't get them too fired up. Keep the rage contained*. We know, when it comes to the history of the vicious legacy of white supremacy in America, if the federal government did not move, we would still be locked into state's rights. And state's rights is always a code word for controlling, subjugating black folk. That's the history of the black struggle, you see. So what he was saying was *Don't expect federal action*. Well, Sharpton is going to be in trouble. Marc Morial, two brothers, they're going to be in trouble.

Goodman: Urban League.

West: The Urban League, absolutely. Ben Jealous – God bless the brother – he's going to be in trouble. He's getting folk riled up to hit up against this stone wall. The next thing, they'll be talking about, *Well, maybe we ought to shift to gun control*. No, we're talking about the legacy of white supremacy. We're talking about a criminal justice system that is criminal when it comes to mistreating poor people across the board, black and brown especially. And let us tell the truth and get off this Obama plantation and say, "You know what? We're dealing with criminality in high places, criminality in these low places, and let's expose the hypocrisy, expose the mendacity, and be true to the legacy of Martin." You know there's going to be a march in August, right? And the irony is, the sad irony is—

Goodman: This is the march of the – honoring the 50th Anniversary of the "I Have a Dream" speech.

West: And you know what the irony is, Sister Amy? Brother Martin would not be invited to the very march in his name, because he would talk about drones. He'd talk about Wall Street criminality. He would talk about the working class being pushed to the margins as profits went up for corporate executives in their compensation. He would talk about the legacies of white supremacy. Do you think anybody at that march will talk about drones and the drone president? Do you think anybody at that march will talk about the connection to Wall Street? They are all on the plantation.

Goodman: Are you invited?

West: Well, can you imagine? Good God, no. I mean, I pray for him, because I'm for liberal reform. But liberal reform is too narrow, is too truncated. And, of course, the two-party system is dying, and therefore it doesn't have the capacity to speak to these kinds of issues. So, no, not at all.

Goodman: So you're saying that President Obama should not only say, "I could have been Trayvon Martin," but "I could have been, for example, Abdulrahman al-Awlaki," the 16-year-old son—

West: Yes.

Goodman: Of Anwar al-Awlaki, who was killed in a drone strike.

West: Or the name of those 221 others, precious children, who are – who were as precious as the white brothers and sisters in Newtown that he cried tears for. Those in Indian res`and pervasive criminality in high places. That's why Brother Snowden and Brother Manning are the John Browns of our day, and the Glenn Greenwalds and the Chris Hedges and Glen Fords and Bruce Dixons and Margaret Kimberleys and Nellie Baileys are the William Lloyd Garrisons of our day, when we talk about the national security state.

Goodman: Clearly, the power of the personal representation is what grabbed people on Friday.

West: Absolutely.

Goodman: You also had Attorney General Eric Holder doing the same thing—

West: The same thing.

Goodman: When he was speaking at the NAACP convention on Tuesday...

> **Attorney General Holder** (*on tape*): The news of Trayvon Martin's death last year and the discussions that have taken place since then reminded me of my father's words so many years ago. And they brought me back to a number of experiences that I had as a young man – when I was pulled over twice and my car searched on the New Jersey Turnpike, when I'm sure I wasn't speeding; or when I was stopped by a police officer while simply running to catch a movie at night in Georgetown in Washington, DC. I was, at the time of that last incident, a federal prosecutor.
>
> Trayvon's death last spring caused me to sit down to have a conversation with my own 15-year-old son, like my dad did with me. This was a father-son tradition I hoped would not need to be handed down. But as a father who loves his son and who is more knowing in the ways of the world, I had to do this to protect my boy. I am his father, and

it is my responsibility not to burden him with the baggage of eras long gone but to make him aware of the world that he must still confront. This – this is a sad reality in a nation that is changing for the better in so many ways.

...

West: There's no doubt that the vicious legacy of white supremacy affects the black upper classes; it affects the black middle classes. But those kinds of stories hide and conceal just how ugly and intensely vicious it is for black poor, brown poor.... Why hasn't the New Jim Crow been a priority in the Obama administration? Why has not the New Jim Crow been a priority for Eric Holder? If what they're saying is something they feel deeply, if what they're saying is that they – themselves and their children – have the same status as Brother Jamal and Sister Latisha and Brother Ray Ray and Sister Jarell, then why has that not been a center part of what they do to ensure there's fairness and justice?

Well, the reason is political. Well, we don't want to identify with black folk, because a black president can't get too close to black folk, because Fox News ... will attack them, and that becomes the point of reference? No. If they're going to be part of the legacy of Martin King, Fannie Lou Hamer and Ella Baker and the others, then the truth and justice stuff that you pursue, you don't care who is coming at you. But, no, this black liberal class has proven itself to be too morally bankrupt, too hypocritical and indifferent to criminality – Wall Street criminality, no serious talk about enforcement of torturers and wiretappers under the Bush administration. Why? Because they don't want the subsequent administration to take them to jail. Any reference to the hunger strike of our brothers out in California [prisons] and other places, dealing with torture? Sustained solitary confinement is a form of torture. And we won't even talk about Guantánamo. Force-feeding, torture in its core – didn't our dear brother Yasiin Bey point that out, the former Mos Def? God bless that brother. Jay Z got something to learn from Mos Def. Both of them lyrical geniuses, but Jay Z got a whole lot to learn from Mos Def.

Goodman: Explain that. Yasiin Bey actually underwent force-feeding –

West: Yes, he did.

Goodman: To see how it felt, and broke down and started screaming, "Stop! Stop!" in the middle of it, and it was a videotape that went viral.

West: And it happens twice a day for those precious brothers in Guantánamo Bay. And, of course, that's under Bush. People say, "That's under Bush." OK, Bush was the Capture-and-Torture President. Now we've got the Targeted-Killing President, the Drone President. That's not progress.

That's not part of the legacy of Martin King. That's not part of the legacy of especially somebody like a Dorothy Day and others who I think ought to be at the center of what we're all about, you see.

Goodman: ...Near the end of his speech on Friday, President Obama said the nation should be doing a better job helping young African-American men feel that they are a fuller part of society.... How would you do this?

West: Well, when I heard that, I said to myself, "Lord, he came to New York City and said Michael Bloomberg was a terrific mayor." Well, this is the same mayor who, again, nearly four-and-a-half million folk have been stopped and frisked. What's terrific about that, if you're concerned about black boys being part of society? No, no, I would say we're going to have to talk seriously about massive employment programs; high-quality public education, not the privatizing of education; dealing with gentrification and the land grab that's been taking place; ensuring that young black boys – and I want to include all poor boys, but I'll begin on the chocolate side of town, there's no doubt about that – that ought to have access to a sense of self-respect and self-determination, not just through education and jobs but through the unleashing of their imagination, more arts programs in the educational system. They've been eliminated, you see. Those are the kind of things hardly ever talked about. But, oh, we can only talk about transpartnerships in terms of global training for capital and multinational corporations and big banks. That's been the priority, the Wall Street-friendly and the corporate-friendly policies that I think are deeply upsetting for somebody like myself vis-à-vis the Obama administration.

...

If you're concerned about poor black brothers, then you make it a priority. It's the first time he spoke publicly about this in five years, so it's clear it's not a priority. When he went down to Morehouse [College], it was more scolding: "No excuses." Went to NAACP before: "Quit whining." No, we're wailing; we're not whining. So, to say to the country, *Well, we need to talk about caring,* well, you've got to be able to enact that, you see. And for those of us who spend a lot of time in prisons, those of us at Boys Clubs, all the magnificent work that various churches and civic institutions do in the black community – and it cuts across race, of course, you've got a lot of white brothers and sisters and brown and others who are there, as well – the question is, Since when has it been a priority in this administration at all? So that language begins to ring very, very hollow. Because he's right: we've got to love; we've got to care for our poor brothers and sisters, and especially our black and brown brothers and sisters, because they're lost, they're confused, they're desperate, they're unemployed, they're too uneducated, and they turn on each other – because when you criminalize poor people, and criminalize poor black people, we turn on each other. There's no doubt about that. Can you imagine if the creativity and intelligence that goes into turning on each other is turned on the system – not any individual but the system itself, the unfair system – and tries to undercut the criminality of our criminal justice system to make it fair and to make it just?

...

And the sad thing is, Sister Amy, that we just don't have enough free people, let alone free black people. Black people, we settled for so little, so we get a little symbolic gesture, we get a little identification, and like on MSNBC, which is part of the Obama plantation, they start break dancing again: *Oh, isn't it so wonderful? He's really one of us. We can now wave the flag again. We can now support our mindless Americanism,* in the language of my dear brother Maulana Karenga, intellectual that he is. No. We ought to be against injustice, no matter what, across the board, and be vigilant about it. I don't care what color the president or the governor or the mayor is.

Goodman: Let's talk about Stand Your Ground for a minute. You know, Stevie Wonder now says he won't play in any state that has Stand Your Ground.

West: Yeah, that's a beautiful thing, a beautiful thing.

Goodman: President Obama addressed the issue of the Stand Your Ground law in Florida, the law allowing people fearing for their lives to use deadly force without retreating from a confrontation.

...

West: Well, I certainly agree with him that we ought to fight Stand Your Ground laws, but we've got to keep in mind Stand Your Ground laws are part of the legacy of the slave patrol, which is to say it's primarily white brothers and sisters armed to keep black people under control. And I come from Sacramento, California. I remember when the Black Panther Party walked into the Capitol with their guns. Now, you noticed at that moment, all of a sudden people were very much for gun control, even the right wing. Why? Because the Panthers were saying, *Well, let's just arm all the black folk to make sure they stand their ground.* Oh, Lord. That's such a challenge. Now, see, you know, as a Christian and trying to be part of the legacy of Martin, you see, I don't want people armed across the board. I do believe in self-defense, just like I believe in self-respect and self-determination, but I don't want people armed. So it's very clear there's a class and a racial bias in these laws, and therefore we ought to fight these laws. There's no doubt about it. But we have to be very honest and candid about the hypocrisy operating when we talk about these things.

Goodman: It was rather chilling to hear both Robert Zimmerman, George Zimmerman's brother, and also Mark O'Mara, the attorney for George Zimmerman, talking about how— the fact that George Zimmerman is supposed to get his gun back, that he needs it more than ever, because he's targeted, because he's afraid. What is more frightening than a frightened George Zimmerman with a gun?

West: No, it's true. But it's— I mean, when you let criminals off, they feel, they feel as if their criminality has been affirmed, and therefore they want to be able to ... [go] back to business as usual.

Goodman: Cornel, as we wrap up this segment, ... if you were invited to speak at the 50th Anniversary celebration of the "I Have a Dream" speech, the March on Washington – August 28, 1963, is when it happened, fifty years ago – what would you say? Give us a few minutes.

West: I would say we must never tame Martin Luther King, Jr. or Fannie Lou Hamer or Ella Baker or Stokely Carmichael. They were unbossed. They were unbought. That Martin was talking about a beloved community, which meant that it subverts any plantation – Bush's plantation, Clinton's plantation, Obama's plantation – and the social forces behind those plantations, which have to do with Wall Street, have to do with multinational corporations. And we're going to focus on poor people. We're going to focus on working people across the board. We're going to talk about the connection between drones, which is a form of, a form of crimes against humanity outside the national borders. We're going to talk about Wall Street criminality. We're going to talk about how we ensure that our gay and lesbian brothers and sisters have their dignity affirmed. We're going to talk about the children.

Martin Luther King, Jr. was a free black man. He was a Jesus-loving free black man. Will the connection between drones, New Jim Crow, prison-industrial complex, attacks on the working class, escalating profits at the top, be talked about and brought together during that march? I don't hold my breath. But Brother Martin's spirit would want somebody to push it. And that's part of his connection to Malcolm X. That's part of his connection to so many of the great freedom fighters that go all the way back to the first slave who stepped on these decrepit shores.

Coda

Remembering How to Grieve

Asam Ahmad

Our President says
those responsible for the bombings
will be held accountable;
speaks of the "full weight of justice,"
dread and nausea
swells up inside me

I know
by "holding accountable"
what America really means
is visiting violence
ten
or twenty
or a hundred fold
on those America decides are
"responsible"; on those America thinks
look enough like
the ones responsible
I no longer know
how to grieve
"innocent" American victims
I can't remember how

to bear my head down low
and wring my hands and nod
in agreement yes,
this was a horrific act of violence,
yes, of course, violence is never okay

I can no longer bear the violence
of these ritualized gestures,
the violence
of this language of mourning
reserved only for the upstanding
Citizens of Empire;
lives vaunted
and cherished
infinitely more valuable
than hundreds of thousands
of brown bodies that now litter
the Middle East because America
was too hurt
or too angry
or too traumatized
to see beyond its own
misty haze of grief
There is too much pain in this world
and I'm afraid
I no longer remember

how to grieve

(April 15, 2013)

The Race Is On

Arabs, Blackness and the American Imagination

Moustafa Bayoumi

"We are so racially profiled now, as a group," the Arab-American comedian Dean Obeidallah says in his routine, "that I heard a correspondent on CNN not too long ago say the expression, 'Arabs are the new blacks.'" Obeidallah continues:

> When I heard that – I'm going to be honest – I was excited. I'm like, "Oh my God, we're cool." Before you know it, hot Asian women will stop dating black guys and start dating Arabs. White kids in the suburbs, instead of acting and dressing black to be cool, will now start pretending to be Arab.... Pimping their car to look like a taxicab. Dressing like Arabs, some old-school in traditional Arab headdress.... Tilt to the side a bit. Walkin' up to each other, goin', "What up, Moustafa?" Sayin', "Where my Arabs at?" "Arab, please!"[1]

It is a funny bit, but Obeidallah is on to something more than a joke, something about the mischievous power of race and representation in contemporary US culture both to incorporate and to reject. By taking an observation – the analogy of Arabness to blackness – to its literal extreme, Obeidallah is playing with general perceptions of blackness and whiteness along the way. And by turning a liability into an asset, he flips the script of social exclusion to one of popular inclusion. What is more American today, after all, than the African-American?

But most people mean something else when they talk about Arabs (or Muslims) becoming "the new blacks," a sentiment routinely expressed since the terrorist attacks of September 11, 2001. Perhaps most directly, the idea is meant to evoke the practice of racial profiling. "Black New Yorkers joke among themselves about their own reprieve from racial profiling," explains a *New York Times* article from October 10, 2001. "Even the language of racial grievance has shifted: Overnight, the cries about driving while black

1 Dean Obeidallah's routine is available online at: http://www.comedycentral.com/videos/index.jhtml?videoId=81074&title=arabs-are-the-new-blacks.

have become flying while brown – a phrase referring to reports of Muslim Americans being asked to get off planes." The article continues. "Ever so slightly, the attacks on the trade center have tweaked the city's traditional racial divisions." These oscillations prompted African-American novelist Ishmael Reed to write, "Within two weeks after the World Trade Center and Pentagon bombings, my youngest daughter, Tennessee, was called a dirty Arab, twice." America's racial legacy, replete with the "one-drop rule," where a single drop of African blood made a person black in the eyes of Jim Crow law, enabled Reed, after September 11, to ask the question, "Is anyone with dark skin Arab-American?"[2]

The reasons are easy to see. Racial profiling was almost universally loathed prior to 2001, so much so that candidate George W. Bush explicitly ran against it. But the practice acquired a new lease on life in 2003 when President Bush's Justice Department ordered a ban on profiling but included exceptions permitting extra scrutiny of racial and ethnic groups when officials had "trustworthy" information that members of those groups were plotting a terrorist attack or a crime.[3] While it could be said that profiling per se was officially un-American, the fine print made it clear that profiling Arabs and Muslims made good national security sense. The program of Special Registration, whereby adult males from twenty-four Muslim-majority countries had to register their whereabouts in the country, is just one example of state-mandated racial profiling. Special Registration led to approximately 14,000 deportation proceedings.[4] (The UN Committee on the Elimination of Racial Discrimination has repeatedly called on Washington to end "racial profiling against Arabs, Muslims and South Asians."[5]) After the London bombings of 2005, conservative critics like Representative Peter King, Charles Krauthammer and the Hoover Institute's Paul Sperry advocated further profiling, prompting *Washington Post* columnist Colbert King to respond with a column titled "You Can't Fight Terrorism with Racism." Echoing Reed, he wrote: "It appears not to matter to Sperry that his description also includes huge numbers of men of color, including my younger son, a brown-skinned occasional New York subway rider who shaves his head and mustache."

Prior to September 11, popular perceptions of Arabs and Muslims had no significant American component. Invisibility was the word heard most often. In *Food for Our Grandmothers*, a 1994 anthology by Arab-American

2 Ishmael Reed, "Civil Rights: Six Experts Weigh In," *Time*, December 7, 2001.
3 CBS News/Associated Press, June 18, 2003.
4 See Moustafa Bayoumi, "Racing Religion," *New Centennial Review* 6/2 (2006).
5 See UN Committee on the Elimination of Racial Discrimination, "Consideration of Reports of Submitted by States' Parties Under Article 9 of the Convention: Conclusion Observations of the Committee," UN Doc. CERD/C/USA/CO/6 (May 8, 2008). See also UN High Commissioner for Human Rights to United States, September 28, 2009. The letter can be seen at http://www.aclu.org/pdfs/humanrights/uncerdresponse_racialdiscrimination.pdf.

and Arab-Canadian feminists, the editor, Joanna Kadi, labeled Arab-Americans "the Most Invisible of the Invisibles." In "Resisting Invisibility," an essay published in a 1999 volume, Therese Saliba noted, "When Arabs are mentioned within the multicultural debate, it is often as a point of political tension between blacks and Jews, or as an afterthought, 'as the other Jewish Americans.'"[6] Through the 1980s, as Edward Said puts it in *Covering Islam*, the "ubiquitous" images of Arabs and Muslims outside the United States were "frequent caricatures of Muslims as oil suppliers, as terrorists and ... as bloodthirsty mobs." The reliance on Orientalist stereotypes was premised on the idea of an unbridgeable distance between two essentially different parts of the world, the rational Occident and unruly Orient.

'No offense, sir'

But in a present of growing immigration and international terrorism, things have changed (and, of course, also remain depressingly the same). In the domestic arrangement of race and difference, Arabs and Muslims in the United States have been pushed from the shadows into the spotlight, and the associations they carry are often ones of racial differences that can be patrolled with profiling. Such associations surface in small, curious ways. In a 2008 *New York Times* book review, for example, the Harvard sociologist Orlando Patterson, commenting on racial profiling, reaches not for the African-American example but writes that "nearly all of us have a civil liberties threshold: Imagine Pakistani madrassa graduates lining up at airport security; race matters in such cases, and need involve no animus."[7] Spike Lee's film *The Inside Man* has only one significant scene of racial conflict: a Sikh hostage in a bank heist emerges from the building hooded like the perpetrators, who have cleverly dressed in matching coveralls and forced the bank personnel and customers to do the same. The cops yank off his hood, thinking he is a bank robber, then spot his turban and lose their cool. "Oh shit, it's a fucking Arab!" one cop yells, as they back away, guns leveled. The Sikh then has his turban ripped from his head and is beaten. In the next scene, he complains to the detective, played by Denzel Washington. "I'm not saying anything until I get my turban back! I'm sick of this shit, man. Everywhere I go, my civil rights are violated. Go to the airport, and I always get pulled out. Random search, my ass!" Washington responds, "But you can always get a cab, right?" "It's one of the perks," he admits.

In John Updike's silly and thoroughly unconvincing novel *Terrorist*, there is a deep and abiding devotion to America's enduring racial hierarchies

6 Therese Saliba, "Resisting Invisibility: Arab Americans in Academia and Activism," in Michael Suleiman, ed., *Arabs in America: Building a New Future* (Philadelphia: Temple University Press, 1999)
7 Orlando Patterson, "The Big Blind," *New York Times*, February 10, 2008.

mixed with shopworn nostalgia for the WASPy simplicity that has packed up and moved away to the pages of history. Updike's story revolves around Ahmad Malloy, 18, half-Irish, half-Egyptian and totally confused. Ahmad, whose complexion Updike repeatedly describes as "dun," searches aimlessly for meaning in his failing suburb of New Prospect, New Jersey, finding solace at the feet of Sheikh Rashid, an embittered Yemeni imam who exhorts the neophyte to violence. Meanwhile, Ahmad's high school guidance counselor, Jack Levy, has an affair with his mother. Levy eventually brings the boy back from the brink, saving the nation from a senseless terrorist attack. In the meantime, he tells him that he has "fucked his mother," prompting this ridiculous exchange in the final pages of the novel:

> "No offense, sir, but do understand.... I'm not thrilled to think of my mother fornicating with a Jew." Levy laughs a coarse bark. "Hey, come on, we're all Americans here. That's the idea; didn't they tell you that at Central High? Irish-Americans, African-Americans, Jewish Americans; there are even Arab-Americans." "Name one." Levy is taken aback. "Omar Sharif," he says. He knows he could not think of others in a less stressful situation. "Not American. Try again." "Uh – what was his name? Lew Alcindor?" "Kareem Abdul-Jabbar," Ahmad corrects.

The confusion of labeling Abdul-Jabbar, who is African-American, as Arab-American is obvious, and appears to indicate Levy's own ignorance, making the character bizarrely more American in his daftness. But Levy stands for more than that. Against the foreignness of Arab-Americans, Updike uses Levy's Jewishness as a measure of successful American ethnic assimilation, as opposed to all those who now "occupy the inner city," namely those who are "brown, by and large, in its many shades."

If Arab-Americans are now frequently coded with a kind of blackness, then being Jewish today is to have earned the status of whiteness. Hindus, too, are often endowed with similar respectability. Think of Thomas Friedman's endless exultations about Indian capitalists and Silicon Valley pioneers. Or consider this paragraph from Steven Pinker's 2008 article in *The New York Times Magazine* titled "The Moral Instinct." Pinker writes about ethics and moral foundations held in common across distinct societies in the modern world. His is an effort to promote a family-of-humankind *Weltanschauung*. But in so doing, he divides the world in interesting ways.

"Many of the flabbergasting practices in faraway places become more intelligible when you recognize that the same moralizing impulse that Western elites channel toward violations of harm and fairness (our moral obsessions) is channeled elsewhere to violations in the other spheres," he writes. "Think of ... the holy ablutions and dietary restrictions of Hindus and Orthodox Jews (purity), [and] the outrage at insulting the Prophet among Muslims (authority)."

"Holy ablutions and dietary restrictions" could just as easily be attributed to Muslims (and not just the orthodox), but instead Jews and Hindus are lumped together in this benign behavioral mode. Muslims, on the other hand, are assigned rage.

What is going on here? In brief, Arabs and Muslims (who, in the real world, are two overlapping categories, but in the world of American perceptions are essentially the same thing) have entered the American imagination with full force, but their entry has been racialized. What that means in the specific inflections of the American vernacular is an association with blackness, for Arabs and Muslims in America are not a part of the immigrant fabric of the nation but a social problem. While Jews and Hindus are handed ethnicity, Arabs and Muslims are saddled with race. They have become an American dilemma.

The difference between race and ethnicity matters. To be ethnic means to have mores, habits and rites that do not interfere with being modern. In fact, the rituals often lend to bland modernity the color and richness that it so often seeks. Ethnics make tactical decisions about when and how to reveal or put away those charming, atavistic aspects of themselves when in public. They are, in other words, given agency.

Races, however, have little to no agency. Agencies, rather, formulate policies about them. Races do not make history. They are history. Social forces pulsate through them. While ethnicities are threads in the tapestry of the nation, races are the elements that make the nation's mix combustible. What James Baldwin wrote about the black man in 1955 is almost as applicable to Arab/Muslim Americans today. "The Negro in America," Baldwin writes, "is a social and not a personal or human problem. To think of him is to think of statistics, slums, rapes, injustices, remote violence."[8]

Ethnicities get their documentary histories screened during PBS pledge week. Races appear as the subjects of government and police commissions of inquiry, on episodes of PBS *Frontline* with the spooky voiceover and on the crawl on Fox News.

Political leanings matter little. Liberals view the situation of Muslims and Arabs in America as an example of the limits of the nation and its excesses in maltreating those who are irretrievably "other." Conservatives define them as a minority threat to a perceived majority. Either way, the race is on.

8 James Baldwin, *Notes From a Native Son* (Boston: Beacon, 1984 [1955])

Be all that you can be

The irony is that while Arabs and Muslims are increasingly racialized as black (in ways that approximate cold war images of African-Americans), African-Americans are featuring in popular culture as leaders of the American nation and empire. Moreover, this depiction revolves fundamentally around the idea of black friendship with Muslims and Arabs, a friendship not among equals but one that reflects a modified projection of American power. This image appears to seek to transform the image of the United States itself.

Consider two different films in this regard: *The Siege* (1998), again starring Denzel Washington, and *The Kingdom* (2007), starring Jamie Foxx. *The Siege*, having been made before 2001 and having since been lionized for its prescience in portraying a large-scale Arab terrorist attack on American soil, is essentially about how Clinton-era foreign policy failures endangered the nation's institutions. Its story centers on Special Agent Anthony Hubbard, a law degree-wielding veteran of the 82nd Airborne with a Catholic school upbringing in the Bronx. At one point, Hubbard sarcastically dubs himself "Colin Powell," and the implication is clear. Hub, as he is called, is the embodiment of African-American achievement, like the future secretary of state who was then widely thought to be Most Likely to Be Elected President While Black. Upright, industrious, serious but not dour, Hub is the film's moral center. The main spoke on his wheel is Frank Haddad (played by Tony Shalhoub), a Lebanese Shi'ite FBI agent (the only American in the film, incidentally, who speaks with a foreign accent), who serves as chauffeur and translator.

After US commandos capture a radical imam modeled after Sheikh Omar Abdul Rahman, a series of terrorist attacks plague New York City. Elise Kraft, a CIA agent of loose morals played by Annette Bening, competes with Hub in investigating the attacks. Her mole is Samir Nazhde, a Brooklyn College professor of Arab studies who appears (and later is confirmed) to be connected to the terrorists. When Hub and the FBI are unable to stop the rash of attacks, the government proclaims martial law in Brooklyn, and Bruce Willis's character, the unsubtle Gen. William Devereaux, who was responsible for the extralegal extraction of the imam, rounds up Arab-American males in ways reminiscent of Japanese-American internment during World War II. Haddad's son, 13, is jailed, leading the FBI agent to a crisis of faith in American righteousness. He rashly surrenders his badge to Hub, saying he will not be the government's "sand nigger" any longer. Hub eventually gets Haddad's son out. Hub and Haddad, meanwhile, discover that Nazhde is the final terrorist in the country, and follow him to a showdown. Nazhde is killed, Kraft is sacrificed, and Hub stands up to Devereaux's unconstitutional torture and murder of an innocent Arab-American man. Martial law is then lifted, and the Constitution saved.

With its two Arab/Muslim characters, *The Siege* operates within the logic of "good Muslim, bad Muslim" that Mahmood Mamdani has identified as central to the cultural logic of the "war on terror."

"The central message of such discourse," Mamdani explains, is that "unless proved to be 'good,' every Muslim [is] presumed to be 'bad.' All Muslims [are] now under an obligation to prove their credentials by joining in a war against 'bad Muslims.'"[9] Melani McAlister astutely describes *The Siege* as a film "incorporating the challenge of multiculturalism into the logic of the New World Order."[10] But it is also something else. *The Siege* taps into the paranoia surrounding immigration, which, together with geopolitics, has turned the streets of Brooklyn into the stereotypical "Arab street," redolent with strange smells and teetering on the edge of apocalypse. (The script identifies Brooklyn's Atlantic Avenue as "The Third World. Teeming, roiling. Kinshasa meets Beirut meets Tel Aviv meets Moscow," and Hub says, "America's the place to be if you're a terrorist.") Moreover, this frightening external world that is invading the US is suffused with an Arab and Muslim proclivity for ancestral feuds. When Nazhde is taken in, he is punched by Haddad, who apologizes to Hub saying, "Sorry, family matter." Later, Haddad is upbraided by Hub, who tells him he will "have his badge" if he "ever hit[s] a prisoner again." "Someday I'll tell you what those people did to my village in 1971," Haddad responds.

But the key message of *The Siege* is that US entanglement in these ancient hatreds has compelled the US to sell itself, body (the whorish Elise Kraft) and soul (the heartless General Devereaux). In so doing, the national security state is losing the heart of the nation. This betrayal is why Hub's character is so essential. In his enduring commitment to values, Hub is the most American of all the characters. He is uncorrupted by international politics ("I need names," he tells his agents, "I don't need a history lesson") and is willing to fight both the racist policy of internment and the brutal violence of the Arabs. Who better than Hub, after all, to show his Arab underling that the US is not, at bottom, racist, in either its foreign or domestic policy? His own story of uplift illustrates all that "America" can be. Hub is best suited to protect Arab-Americans not only from the overreach of the state but also from themselves.

9 Mahmood Mamdani, *Good Muslim, Bad Muslim* (New York: Knopf, 2004)
10 Melani McAlister, *Epic Encounters: Culture, Media and US Interests in the Middle East Since 1945* (Berkeley, CA: University of California Press, 2005)

'America's not perfect'

The Kingdom does this trope one better. Here the US empire has a Great Black Hope as well. In *The Kingdom*, terrorists attack an American compound in Riyadh. Back in Washington, the FBI itches to investigate the carnage, particularly since two of its own have been killed. Domestic politics initially holds them back. (This setting is almost certainly inspired by the FBI's inquiry into the 2000 attack on the USS Cole, where the lead investigator, John O'Neill, battled in vain with the US ambassador in Yemen, Barbara Bodine, who refused to let him interrogate Yemeni government officials he thought were in league with al-Qaeda. O'Neill later became chief of security at the World Trade Center and was killed on September 11.) The attorney general is concerned that American boots on Saudi Arabian soil will anger Muslims, but, as in *The Siege*, the FBI is independent of the dirty machinations of the political world and stands for American righteousness. "If you were running the FBI," the attorney general tells Special Agent Ronald Fleury (played by Jamie Foxx), "you might turn it into Patton's Third Army." Fleury takes the initiative by threatening the Saudi royal family, and the FBI is given immediate approval to land in Riyadh. He leads a team of four – himself, a white woman, Agent Mayes, and two men, Agent Leavitt, who is Jewish, and Agent Sykes, a good ol' boy – in the investigation.

Saudi Arabia turns out to be an odd, inverted world. The team is assigned a minder, Col. Faris al-Ghazi, a police officer who lost men at the compound but whose unit is also implicated in the attack. Just as in Washington, the FBI team must negotiate with timid politicians to gain access to the crime scene, and the agents complain constantly of their pusillanimity. More to the point, the Saudi Arabians are totally inept in their investigation. "Do you understand evidence?" Sykes asks al-Ghazi patronizingly. "Little things that are clues? Clues can be very helpful to a fellow trying to solve a crime." In this film, civilization is bestowed upon the natives through forensic science.

Initially, the Saudi Arabians are more concerned with policing morality – taking offense at swearing, uncovered women and non-Muslims touching dead Muslims – than with solving crime. But al-Ghazi slowly comes around. He is the good Muslim in this drama, a film that turns the capacious boulevards of Saudi Arabia into the dingy avenues of Baghdad. Al-Ghazi has a warm home life, as conveyed by the soft music of the soundtrack while he leads his family in prayer. Fleury and he begin a friendship.

Eventually, the FBI team commences pursuit of Abu Hamza, an Osama bin Laden wannabe who may be the mastermind of the initial attack, and the film's pace picks up as they near their quarry. After killing several junior terrorists in a firefight, the crew is congratulated for their efforts and are headed home when Leavitt is kidnapped on the road to the airport. The agents track the abductors to Suweidi, "a very bad neighborhood," which seems to be a cinematic cross between Fallujah and East LA. There, the final shootout of the film transpires. Leavitt is saved by Mayes, the female FBI agent, who stabs an Arab terrorist in the groin (and head) with her knife. Abu Hamza and his son are killed. Al-Ghazi, too, is tragically cut down, and the film ends with Fleury offering condolences to the Saudi Arabian cop's family. "Your father was a good friend of mine," he tells al-Ghazi's son.

The Kingdom only obliquely acknowledges Fleury's race. "America's not perfect," he says to a Saudi prince. "Not at all. I'll be the first to say that." It is this kind of honesty that enables Fleury to achieve a level of human communication with the Saudi Arabians that is not shared by the other characters. When he reaches out to al-Ghazi, he discovers that his Arab counterpart is thoroughly Americanized. "I spent four days in Quantico," al-Ghazi tells Fleury. "I also saw Michael Jordan play for the Washington Wizards." (It takes a real American to know that Jordan played briefly for the Wizards and not just the Chicago Bulls.) The Saudi Arabian continues that he became a police officer because he watched *The Incredible Hulk* on television as a child. And, as in *The Siege*, where one character quips of speaking to Arabs, "Ask a question, get an atlas," *The Kingdom* plays up the virtues of an anti-political position, this time attributed to the Arab character. "I find myself in a place where I no longer care why we are attacked," al-Ghazi confesses to Fleury. "I only care that 100 people woke up a few mornings ago and had no idea why it was their last. When we catch the men who murdered these people, I don't care to ask even one question. I want to kill them. Do you understand?" "Yes, I do," Fleury responds.

While *The Siege* emphasizes the Arab-ness of Haddad, *The Kingdom* highlights the American-ness of its good Arab. Why? Perhaps it is because *The Siege* is about the need for a principled national ethos for resisting the invasion of international politics (and bodies) into the domestic sphere, while *The Kingdom* is about the need for proper American tutelage in a harsh and disordered world. *The Siege*'s imagination is national. *The Kingdom*'s is more imperial.

The Siege and *The Kingdom* are two illustrations of an emerging sub-genre. Other examples include Showtime's TV series *Sleeper Cell* (2005 and 2006) and the 2008 film *Traitor*. *Sleeper Cell*'s lead character is Special Agent Darwyn Al-Sayeed, played by Michael Ealy, an African-American Muslim who is determined to save both his country and his faith from the crazy radicals (more like misfits with anthrax, really). Wearing a constipated squint throughout the series, al-Sayeed tries hard to swallow the anguish of having to pass, not as a white man but as a terrorist in the service of his beloved religion. ("Don't African-Americans have a long history of trying to pass for white?" asks al-Farik, the lead terrorist, of al-Sayeed. "I don't," responds the undercover agent.) *Traitor* replicates many of the same conventions. Don Cheadle plays the role of Samir Horn, formerly a US Special Forces man supporting the Afghan jihad against the Soviets, and currently a seller of illicit weapons to unsavory Muslims. Again, the leading man is a devout Muslim, but the film collapses the good Muslim/bad Muslim dichotomy into a single character, since the audience is left guessing for the first half of the film where his loyalties lie. Moreover, the central relationship in the film is the deepening bond between Samir and Omar, an Arab terrorist with doubts. Samir is almost able to bring him over from the dark side before Omar is killed in a climactic gun battle.

The central idea sustaining this sub-genre is the notion of African-American leadership of the Arab world, intertwined with friendship with it. Here there is a twist on a tale already told by Benjamin DeMott in *The Trouble with Friendship: Why Americans Can't Think Straight About Race*. DeMott explains how popular culture exploded in the 1980s and 1990s with images of black-and-white comity that served as a kind of "wish fulfillment" of "interracial sameness" in order to discover that people of different races "need or delight in or love each other." The black-and-white friendships of that era, symbolized by the interracial buddy movie (Eddie Murphy and Judge Reinhold, Danny Glover and Mel Gibson, Samuel L. Jackson and John Travolta, Wesley Snipes and Woody Harrelson), illustrated that

> race problems belong to the passing moment. Race problems do not involve group interests and conflicts developed over centuries. Race problems are being smoothed into nothingness, gradually, inexorably, by good will, affection, points of light.

Interracial amity popped up all over the cinematic spectrum. There was the lowbrow farce *White Men Can't Jump*, the high-minded drama *Driving Miss Daisy* and the middle-class morality play *Lethal Weapon*, where Danny Glover as the suburban black family man with a badge was a kind of precursor to the character of Hub.

Arab and African-American friendship comes similarly loaded but with an international agenda appended. Such representations suggest that African-Americans know better than whites how to talk to Arabs (Fleury learns a few Arabic words in *The Kingdom*). The semiotics of African-American leadership roles in contemporary film and popular culture suggest that racial conflict has been made residual and even overcome in the US, which is why race gets only passing mention. Moreover, African-American connections to other people of color seem based on authentic sentiment, as opposed to kneejerk reaction or bald-faced opportunism.

They are more real because of the collective past of suffering. African-American leadership of Arab characters illustrates a pilgrim's progress narrative for the twenty-first century, where the promise of America is most clearly exhibited through racial uplift. The sins of slavery, Jim Crow and Bull Connor's dogs have been redeemed by achievement. Through such representations, the US is understood as having surmounted its historic deficiencies, and the liberal (and liberating) potential of the American empire is consequently affirmed. Camaraderie, in other words, is connected to the benevolence of American imperialism, for if the face of the US belongs to an African-American, how racist could the empire be? Put another way, what is more American today than the African-American?

A lot like me at home

Such representations of blacks at the helm, speaking from the liberal heart of American empire, contradict, if not undermine, a long and powerfully expressed tradition of African-American opposition to US expansionism. That tradition connects the denial of civil rights at home with the deprivations of overseas conquest. Its history goes back at least to the US-Mexican War of 1848, which Frederick Douglass labeled "disgraceful, cruel and iniquitous." In a potent editorial opposing the war, Douglass wrote:

> Mexico seems a doomed victim to Anglo-Saxon cupidity and love of dominion.... We have no preference for parties, regarding this slaveholding crusade.... Our nation seems resolved to rush on in her wicked career.... We beseech our countrymen to leave off this horrid conflict, abandon their murderous plans and forsake the way of blood.[11]

Fifty years later, the Spanish-American War excited similar outrage among key members of the African-American leadership. Thomas Wallace Swan, editor of *Howard's American Magazine*, wrote in 1900:

> We recognize in the spirit of Imperialism, inaugurated and fostered by the administration of President McKinley, the same violation of Human Rights, which is being practiced by the Democratic Party in the recently reconstructed States, to wit, the wholesale disenfranchisement of the Negro.[12]

Even Booker T. Washington was uncomfortable with the conflict. "My opinion is that the Philippine Islands should be given an opportunity to govern themselves," he wrote. "Until our nation has settled the Negro and

11 Frederick Douglass, "The War with Mexico," in Howard Zinn and Anthony Arnove, eds., *Voices of a People's History of the United States* (New York: Seven Stories Press, 2004)
12 William B. Gatewood, Jr., *Black Americans and the White Man's Burden*, 1898-1903 (Urbana, IL: University of Illinois Press, 1975)

Indian problems I do not believe that we have a right to assume more social problems."[13]

African-Americans initially greeted the colonial war in the Philippines with mixed feelings. In an age of massive discrimination and frequent lynching, some believed military service to be a civic duty, where participation in overseas adventure would once and for all prove to the white masses that African-Americans were entitled to full citizenship rights. Others felt that the war would, as William Gatewood puts it, "divert attention from the racial crisis at home."[14] By the war's end, disillusionment had set in. Segregation had deepened, mob violence against blacks had increased, and black soldiers often felt that they were in fact exporting Jim Crow to the rest of the dark world. (Some black soldiers deserted and joined the Filipino insurgency.) Emigration schemes regained their popularity.

In the first half of the twentieth century, African-Americans spoke out against imperial aggression, linking it again to their plight at home. The Italian invasion of Ethiopia, in particular, incensed many black leaders. Paul Robeson led the effort. "The American Blacks have been yearning for freedom from an oppression which has predated fascism," he wrote:

> It dates most clearly perhaps from the fascist invasion of Ethiopia in 1935. Since then, the parallel between his own interests and those of oppressed peoples abroad has been impressed upon him daily as he struggles against the forces which bar him from full citizenship, from full participation in American life.[15]

Robeson later helped found the Council on African Affairs, and W. E. B. Du Bois would be vice chair. Du Bois, of course, was similarly driven by a principled anti-imperialism for virtually the duration of his long career as an intellectual. And both Du Bois and Robeson would pay a price for their politics, as both were investigated for subversion by the US government during the cold war.

African-American anti-colonialism ebbed during the cold war. With the rise of McCarthyism, "civil rights groups had to walk a fine line," according to Mary Dudziak, "making it clear that their reform efforts were meant to fill out the contours of American democracy, and not challenge or undermine it."[16] In this period, the American conversation on race changed from an analysis based largely on economics and politics to one oriented around sociology and psychology. According to Penny Von Eschen, "the

13 Ibid.
14 Ibid.
15 Paul Robeson, "American Negroes in the War," in Philip Sheldon Foner, ed., *Paul Robeson Speaks: Writings, Speeches and Interviews* (New York: Citadel, 1998)
16 Mary Dudziak, *Cold War Civil Rights: Race and the Image of American Democracy* (Princeton, NJ: Princeton University Press, 2000)

embrace of Cold War American foreign policy by many African-American liberals, as well as US government prosecution of Paul Robeson and the Council, fundamentally altered the terms of anti-colonialism and effectively severed the black American struggle for civil rights from the issues of anti-colonialism and racism abroad."[17] (Du Bois, never playing along with the cold war agenda, would write things like, "We want to rule Russia, and we cannot rule Alabama."[18]) By 1951, St. Clair Drake was writing, "Whether or not espousal of 'civil rights' for Negroes becomes separated, in the popular mind, from 'Communist Agitation' may be a decisive factor" in the success of the civil rights movement.[19] Cedric Robinson has described how during this period "the NAACP bent its efforts to constructing political coalitions with similarly liberal and anti-communist organizations."[20] During this period, liberal black leadership essentially accepted the cold war on Washington's terms in order to push for achievable civil rights gains.

With the rise of black militancy in the 1960s, anti-colonialism and internationalism reasserted themselves, explaining Malcolm X's desire to see the African-American struggle as one of human rights versus civil rights. "The American white man has so thoroughly brainwashed the black man to see himself as only a domestic 'civil rights' problem that it will probably take longer than I live before the Negro sees that the struggle of the American black man is international," he observed in the final chapter of his autobiography. And in 1972, James Baldwin wrote:

> Any real commitment to black freedom in this country would have the effect of reordering all our priorities, and altering all our commitments, so that, for horrendous example, we would be supporting black freedom fighters in South Africa and Angola, and would not be allied with Portugal, would be closer to Cuba than we are to Spain, would be supporting the Arab nations instead of Israel, and would never have felt compelled to follow the French into Southeast Asia.[21]

The dominant paradigm, then, for more than a century and a half, was African-American disapproval of US overseas adventurism, either because such exploits deflated the urgency of the problems at home or because they added to the problems at home and abroad. Either way, those views pointed to a change needed in the basic structure of American society.

The connection between African-American international consciousness

---

17 Penny Von Eschen, *Race Against Empire: Black Americans and Anticolonialism, 1937-1957* (Ithaca, NY: Cornell University Press, 1997)
18 W. E. B. Du Bois, "Opposition to the Military Assistance Act of 1949," in David Levering Lewis, ed., *W.E.B. Du Bois: A Reader* (New York: Henry Holt, 1995)
19 St. Clair Drake, "The International Implications of Race and Race Relations," *Journal of Negro Education* 20/3 (Summer 1951), quoted in Nikhil Pal Singh, *Black Is a Country: Race and the Unfinished Struggle for Democracy* (Cambridge, MA: Harvard University Press, 2004)
20 Cedric Robinson, *Black Movements in America* (New York: Routledge, 1997)
21 James Baldwin, *No Name in the Street* (New York: Vintage, 2007 [1972])

and the Arab and Muslim worlds is equally rich. This history, though often beset by a conservative cultural politics, is fundamentally concerned with developing alternative structures of allegiance, radical redefinitions of self and community, new universalisms through religion and a kind of critical consciousness through which to examine the structure of power and race in the US and the West. In 1887, for example, Edward Wilmot Blyden published his magnum opus, *Christianity, Islam and the Negro Race*. Blyden frequently suggested that Islam offers a better option for "the Negro, who under Protestant rule, is kept in a state of ... tutelage and irresponsibility," and wrote that African emigration to and colonization of parts of America would create a class of "redeemers" of the race from the ravages of slavery. He argued that Islam had brought dignity and advancement to Africa, while Christianity only horror: "The Mohammedan Negro is a much better Mohammedan than the Christian Negro is a Christian, because the Muslim Negro, as a learner, is a disciple, not an imitator. A disciple... may become a producer; an imitator never rises above a mere copyist."

In the early years of the twentieth century, several new urban Northern religious movements arose among African-Americans, including the Moorish Science Temple, which claimed that black people were not Negroes but "Moorish Americans." *The Divine Instructions*, the Temple's holy book, reveals that "through sin and disobedience every nation has suffered slavery, due to the fact that they honored not the creed and principles of their forefathers. That is why the nationality of the Moors was taken away from them in 1774 and the word Negro, black and colored was given to the Asiatics of America who were [of] Moorish descent, because they honored not the principles of their mother and father, and strayed after the gods of Europe whom they knew nothing of." Membership in the Temple brought one a "passport," in whose pages Drew Ali declared the holder "a Moslem under the Divine Laws of the Holy Koran of Mecca – Love, Truth, Peace, Freedom and Justice." The document ended with "I am a citizen of the USA."[22]

The creed of the Moorish Science Temple differed from that of its later competitor, the Nation of Islam, in its acknowledgement of American citizenship for blacks. The Temple opened a door of rejection for African-Americans from ascribed identities, while the Nation walked through the passage, teaching African-Americans that they must return to their original faith of "Islam." By combining nationalism and religion, the Nation sought to unite African-American aspirations for racial uplift and nationhood with promises of return to their "original

22 See C. Eric Lincoln, *The Black Muslims in America* (Grand Rapids, MI: William B. Eerdmans, 1994 [1961])

religion." Malcolm X would become the most famous member of the Nation and later of Sunni Islam in America, rivaled only by the boxer Muhammad Ali, whose Third World identifications also played into his vilification at home and heroism abroad.

But African-American affiliation with the Arab and Muslim worlds was not limited to the sacred realm. Culturally and politically, alliances have been repeatedly forged with the idea that Third World oppression and denials of domestic human rights were similar, if not identical, struggles. A 1963 novel by William Gardner Smith, *The Stone Face*, tells the story of Simeon Brown, a Philadelphia journalist and painter, who after suffering repeated racial outrages at home, packs up and moves to Paris. There he discovers the African-American expatriate community living well, but the Arabs of France surviving in conditions reminiscent of home. They wear the same "baggy pants, worn shoes and shabby shirts," and have the "sullen, unhappy, angry eyes" that Brown recognizes from the streets of Harlem. Brown is arrested one night with a bunch of Arabs, and after his release, one of the Arabs he passes in the street asks him a question that surprises him: "How does it feel to be a white man?" The novel brilliantly brings together the Holocaust, the Algerian war, racial tension in Paris and the US civil rights struggle to articulate the need for action to transform a debased and race-torn world.

And in 1976, Sam Greenlee published his little-known novel, *Baghdad Blues*. The story concerns Dave Burrell, an African-American US Information Agency man assigned to Baghdad in the 1950s, at the time that 'Abd al-Karim Qasim and his fellow officers overthrew the Iraqi monarchy. As with *The Stone Face*, this novel connects both domestic and international struggles. "More and more I began to understand the Arabs," Burrell reflects, "and not until much later did I realize that all that time I was learning more and more about myself." Later he holds a conversation with Jamil, an Iraqi intellectual and friend (unlike in *The Kingdom*, this is a friendship of equals). "We will make our own mistakes, solve our own problems, create our own nation. To hell with the Americans and the British," Jamil says. Burrell narrates:

> I loved him, envied him, identified with him. To build a nation.... "Well, man, you know I'm an American." "Oh, but you are different; you understand." "There are a lot like me at home." As I said it, I wondered if it were true.

This type of identification persisted in later decades. Andrew Young, US Ambassador to the UN, met with the PLO in the late 1970s, and lost his post as a result. June Jordan wrote powerfully about the Israeli invasion of Lebanon. "I was born a black woman / and now / I am become a Palestinian," says a stanza in her "Moving Towards Home."[23] Amiri Baraka composed

23 June Jordan, *Directed by Desire: The Collected Poems of June Jordan* (Port Townsend, WA: Copper Canyon Press,

"Somebody Blew Up America."[24]

The point is that there has been a strong and dedicated cultural politics for a very long time within the African-American tradition that seeks an alliance with the rest of the world, including its Arab and Muslim corners, and the terms of that alliance were fundamentally about transformation. Connecting with other peoples and their struggles across the planet was not about advancement of the race at home. It was about transforming the very nature of American society – and with it, global political culture – in pursuit of a world free of racist oppression and imperial aggression.

A real big promotion

But the idea of African-American global leadership as a sign of liberal success is not so novel either. It, too, has a history, dating at least to World War II. Cedric Robinson has written of how "during the 'patriotic period' of the war and for a few short years afterward, Black liberalism was on the ascendancy, achieving point of purchase among America's Black political and economic elite." (That elite would later be excoriated by E. Franklin Frazier in his 1957 book *Black Bourgeoisie.*) During this period, the image of black success, more than true integration, began to signify (white) acceptance of African-Americans in the general culture.

Black diplomacy was central to this effort. From World War II onward, African-American leaders pushed the government to employ African-Americans in the diplomatic corps. It would be seen, they argued, as a sign of racial progress, and both the Truman and Eisenhower administrations were keenly interested in counteracting Soviet propaganda exploiting American racism. A. Philip Randolph told the State Department that it should hire more black personnel for service in Asian countries, arguing, "The American race problem represents the proving ground to the colored peoples of the world as to the sincerity of the United States in the democratic cause. Jim Crow is America's national disgrace. Its existence confuses and embarrasses our foreign policy."[25]

Adam Clayton Powell, Jr. informed Eisenhower that "one dark face from the US is of as much value as millions of dollars in economic aid."[26] And the life and career of civil rights leader and diplomat Ralph Bunche assumed massive public relations proportions. Bunche, who, as the highest-ranking black OSS officer during World War II, composed psy-ops pamphlets for the

2007)

24 Amiri Baraka, *Somebody Blew Up America & Other Poems* (New York: House of Nehesi Publishers, 2003)

25 Michael L. Krenn, *Black Diplomacy: African Americans and the State Department, 1945-1969* (Armonk, NY: M. E. Sharpe, 1998)

26 Von Eschen

North and West African campaigns, stated that the key to winning over the "elite African" was the "legend of America as a liberalizing force in world affairs."[27] Sounding very much like a character out of the present, Bunche argued that "carefully chosen Negroes could prove more effective than whites [in diplomacy to the dark world], owing to their unique ability to gain more readily the confidence of the Native on the basis of their right to claim a good relationship."[28]

This line of argument accepted the terms of the cold war to push for civil rights reform at home. By doing so, the larger connections drawn between global justice and domestic oppression were severed, and black participation in various US foreign policy initiatives was understood as a way of advancing the race. (Some, like Louis Armstrong, refused to cooperate; Stokely Carmichael put it another way: "You can't have Bunche for lunch."[29])

Thus, the argument for black leadership within – rather than transformation of – the US empire reappears today, bringing with it the idea that civil rights is yesterday's news and that global leadership represents individual opportunity, the kind of "upward mobility" that, according to E. Franklin Frazier, produced "exaggerated Americans" out of the black bourgeoisie. Rihanna's video for the song "Hard" is a good example – a disturbing celebration of US military exploits somewhere in the Middle East as visual accompaniment to a song glorifying personal achievement. In *The Kingdom*, the Jamie Foxx character's friendship with al-Ghazi brings the black American to a meeting with a former al-Qaeda operative. "Does he know where bin Laden is?" Fleury asks al-Ghazi breathlessly. "Cause that'd be a real big promotion for me, if I could get that one." The East is again a career.

Race, nation and empire. Their mixing, in the end, describes a complicated, if not confused, situation. On the one hand, as they suffer social exclusion, Arabs and Muslims are increasingly racialized. But the same gesture, in a post-civil rights era, somehow manages to Americanize them. Arab and Muslim Americans signify both the incompleteness and the human triumph of the project of the American nation. African-Americans are cast at the same time in sheltering roles, protecting the nation, those vulnerable and good Arabs and Muslims and the empire. Such representations simultaneously prove that equality has been won and that there exists an enduring need for civil rights thinking in the United States. What is largely

27 See Nikhil Pal Singh, *Black Is a Country: Race and the Unfinished Struggle for Democracy* (Cambridge, MA: Harvard University Press, 2004)
28 Ibid.
29 See Charles Henry, ed., *Ralph J. Bunche: Selected Speeches and Writings* (Ann Arbor, MI: University of Michigan Press, 1995)

missing is the recognition that black heroism, for it to be truly noble, must not be staged on the backs of another people. What is required is the critical consciousness that would build an alliance between Arabs, Muslims and African-Americans against global and domestic aggression and terrorism. (To be fair, *The Kingdom* hints toward this consciousness at the end.) In the absence of that idea, such representations in fact co-opt the struggle for racial equality into the project of an unequal nation and an expanding empire.

Or do they? For is not the analysis offered here ultimately misplaced or, at the very least, out of date? Does not the election of Barack Obama lay bare the naked truth that all Americans live in a post-racial age? The country has its first African-American president, and he is an ex-community organizer, not a retired general. Does not the presidency of Obama prove – despite his expansion of drone attacks in Pakistan and Afghanistan, or his backtracking on Israeli settlements, or his failure to call for accountability for US torture, or his use of Bagram air base as a legal no-man's land – despite all of that and more, does not the presidency of Barack Obama prove that the US is prepared to engage in a dialogue with the rest of the world based not on conquest but on mutual respect, shared interests and basic human dignity? Is not a positive transformation of the US away from empire and toward the community of nations what we should expect from an African-American president who publicly cites his debt to the profound sacrifices of the long civil rights struggle and who writes intelligently and sensitively about anti-colonial struggle in his own memoir? In other words, is not Obama himself the culmination of the oppositional agitation in the face of injustice that makes up the enormous depth and richness of African-American history?

To this question, there is but one answer: "Arab, please!"

(2010)

Anxiety Is Killing Us

So What Do We Do About It?

Dani McClain

Of all the analysis offered in the days following George Zimmerman's acquittal, the most incisive and instructive came from Maya Wiley of the Center for Social Inclusion during an appearance on MSNBC. In a two-minute monologue, she unpacked something called shooter, or implicit, bias:

> The law has not kept pace with the brain science.... These things are happening at nanoseconds at subliminal levels, not at conscious levels. Civil rights laws were written at a time when, in this country, racism happened at a conscious level. We don't even understand our brains on race now.... We have not dealt with the fact that most people are still carrying unconscious bias that is racially motivated, but not at a conscious level.... Our current legal structure does not work for how we do race in America right now.

In November of 2013, as the media began to report the details of 19-year-old Renisha McBride's death at the hands of Ted Wafer, a white resident of suburban Detroit, my mind kept returning to Wiley's words. How do you hold someone accountable assuming his mind has unconsciously lead him to violence? Is there a way to anticipate these subliminal judgments, and can we retrain our responses away from the cynical, the unsubstantiated and, in some cases, the lethal?

Eleven days after Wafer killed McBride on his Dearborn Heights porch, and two days before he was charged with second-degree murder, activist and writer Dream Hampton appeared on *Democracy Now!* to draw national attention to the case. She took the bold step of naming the 54-year-old man, whose identity authorities and journalists had refused to disclose – a courtesy typically reserved for sexual assault victims and minors. Rallies were held. Online petitions were circulated. Few observers, though, amplified Wiley's point from five months earlier: in this case, whether Wafer had ever expressed a hatred of black people was irrelevant to the legal proceedings; a track record of using racial slurs or engaging in discriminatory actions would tell us less about his state of mind than his surroundings.

Dearborn Heights is 80 percent white and borders a city that, at 80 percent African-American, is the nation's blackest. "There are communities of people who have little to no interaction," Dawud Walid, executive director of the Council on American-Islamic Relations' Michigan chapter, explained on *Democracy Now!* that day. "There are basically invisible fences between communities in southeastern Michigan." Especially in such a hyper-segregated context, Wafer's unconscious bias is worth considering. It may have led to him aiming his shotgun at the teenager's face through his locked screen door and pulling the trigger.

When Wafer's trial opens this summer, the pundit class will likely try to keep us thinking about race in outdated ways. A mysterious black friend may be interviewed and given a chance to attest to Wafer's color-blindness, as Joe Oliver did for Zimmerman. Following Trayvon Martin's killing, Geraldo Rivera and the editor of The Daily Caller, a conservative website, used Martin's hoodie and tweets to sound the dog whistle, signaling that the teenager's blackness had justifiably caused the self-appointed Neighborhood Watchman to fear for his life. How will that dog whistle be sounded when national attention refocuses on McBride? The high blood-alcohol content and marijuana revealed in McBride's toxicology report will be dissected. Her school records may be combed, as Martin's were, and any infraction used to portray Wafer as understandably drawn to the use of deadly force. Wafer's attorneys have been urging the court to allow them to enter details of McBride's "lifestyle" into evidence.

Perhaps Wiley or someone just as wise will redirect us to the questions that matter most. When racial bias is unconscious but results in the death of an innocent and unarmed person, how do we hold the killer accountable? And is there a way to prevent these tragedies in the first place?

* * *

A murder trial that's risen to national prominence may be the wrong occasion to ask those questions. Emotions run high, the public's attention is narrowly focused on the killer and the dead, and urging anyone to zoom out for the long view is a hard sell. But in the fall of 2013 in Oakland a group of neighbors gathered to address this question in particular: how do we prevent tragedies caused by implicit bias?

The conversation, held one November evening at a Presbyterian church in a North Oakland community called Temescal, felt urgent. It was called in response to a series of crowd-funding campaigns to hire private security there and in nearby communities. According to organizers of the online fundraising efforts, private patrols were the best way to deal with a rash of property crimes in a city where police presence was stretched too thin to ensure public safety.

The meeting attracted people who were skeptical of that argument. No one disputed the facts around the recent spike in crime, but it was discussed alongside rapid changes brought by gentrification. Still one of the country's most racially diverse places, Oakland has seen its black population drop by a quarter in the past twenty years. Cafes and boutiques open and cater to wealthier and often white newcomers but fail to hire people born and raised in the city, especially young people of color, one person pointed out. The 100 or so people gathered to consider the effects of money and opportunity that are infusing the neighborhood but are out of reach for so many of its longtime residents.

It was there I met John and Vilma, an older black couple who had lived in the neighborhood for more than three decades. John talked about how Temescal had felt in the early 1970s, when he and his wife moved to the area from Louisiana and John began what would be his thirty-nine-year career at Chevron. You knew your neighbors; you could leave your door open, he said. These days, all the crime had him worried, but so did the thought of a trigger-happy private patrol.

"I've got a grandson that goes down the street," John told the crowd. "I don't want a repeat of the Trayvon Martin situation."

Oakland is no Sanford, Florida, but geography is not the main determinant of vulnerability. In the age of implicit bias, an anxious self-proclaimed progressive – or the poorly trained security guard he crowd-funds to hire – can cause an unjustified assault or killing. We don't have to look to the Deep South or to markers like white sheets and Confederate flags to determine who's liable to perpetrate a tragedy or create the conditions ripe for one.

Participants in that meeting shared concerns about the lack of training private security guards receive and how their inexperience could make the neighborhood less safe, even if the guards are unarmed – a condition at least one nearby neighborhood settled on before signing a four-month contract with a security company. Others expressed an apprehension that young black men would be the primary group stopped and asked what business they have on predominately white blocks.

Then came the brainstorm of other ways to increase community safety. One resident who recalled the open-air drug sales and crack houses of the 1980s suggested a tactic she'd relied on then. She described it simply as "neighbors being neighborly." That is, organizing block parties, participating in National Night Out and generally getting to know one another so they'd be more likely to communicate when something felt amiss. A man piped up to encourage others to join a monthly community walk that a North Oakland food justice project organized. That group converged at a local Baptist church and all were welcome, he said.

Someone who had recently moved to Oakland from New York suggested a model used by the Audre Lorde Project. There, organizers recruit small businesses and local organizations in Central Brooklyn to advertise that they are safe spaces and, as such, to open their doors to anyone fleeing violence. Pushing this model could force a broader discussion about safety, one in which someone who fears becoming the victim of a hate crime or police brutality is just as worthy of protection as someone who worries that her car will get broken into or his iPhone stolen. Another young man suggested crowd-funding for better lighting on the streets instead of security patrols, to which a public librarian responded, "The old-fashioned version of crowd funding is taxation." Perhaps petitioning the city for services was a better bet.

The common thread was people's willingness to look at their own role in making their neighborhoods safer, beyond opening their wallets and expecting that someone else could make the problem go away. There was also a shared awareness of whose lives and dignity are most at risk when, as Maya Wiley put it, "we don't even understand our brains on race" but act as though we do.

The people gathered in that Oakland church were searching – perhaps not decisively enough for anyone expecting a silver bullet – for new ways to talk about race and fear and safety. Their search continues, but the evening revealed that any long-lasting solution will first require people in a community to develop a willingness to trust and rely on one another. Petitions and rallies are useful tools when a Wafer of a Zimmerman tragically ends a life. But discussions like this one are a start to heading off those tragedies in the first place.

The Master's Tools

A Grassroots Fight Against Police Violence, Case Study

Jordan Flaherty

On September 17, 2013, Federal District Judge Kurt Engelhardt overturned the convictions of five New Orleans police officers who killed unarmed black civilians in the chaotic days after Hurricane Katrina, ruling that because of prosecutorial misconduct the Justice Department must either retry the officers or let them go free. Family members had fought for years for these brutal killings to be recognized, but in the end the lesson seemed to be similar to that of the George Zimmerman trial: true justice will not come from the state. Or, as Audre Lorde memorably stated, "The master's tools will not dismantle the master's house."

The story of how those convictions were won and then lost – and the more lasting victories that also came from that struggle – offers lessons on why and how the state fails to bring justice to our communities, and what activists should do about it.

The trial in what has come to be called the Danziger shootings was the most high profile of a number of prosecutions that sought to hold police accountable for post-Katrina violence. Five New Orleans police officers were convicted of federal civil rights violations and received sentences of decades in prison. Court recognition of police violence is rare in any city, and here in New Orleans it had been a long struggle to reach that point. The day of the convictions offered catharsis for many in the community.

When the sentences were overturned, the bandage ripped off, it was clear that the wounds remained. No court would bring the justice people sought.

Forgetting my usual cynicism about the US legal system, I was among those who felt relief when the officers were convicted. I had hoped the verdict would help bring a legal certainty to the counternarrative of

Hurricane Katrina. In the first draft of history, New Orleans police were heroic first responders in the aftermath of the hurricane. The Danziger trial and other investigations of the past few years brought a new narrative: the real heroes, the true first responders, were the people of New Orleans, including many of the working-class residents of black neighborhoods like the Ninth Ward and Gentilly who had been demonized as criminals. Police were, in fact, more often acting as dangers to the real rescuers: arresting and killing those who needed help.

In the days after August 29, 2005, as images of desperate survivors played on television, people around the world felt sympathy for those awaiting rescue from the post-Katrina flooding. Soon, however, images of families trapped on rooftops were replaced with stories of armed gangs and criminals roaming the streets. News reports famously described white people as "finding" food, while depicting black people as "looting." Chief of Police Eddie Compass told Oprah Winfrey that "little babies [are] getting raped" in the Superdome. Governor Kathleen Blanco announced she had sent in troops with orders to shoot to kill, and Warren Riley, second in charge of the NOPD, reportedly told officers to fire at will on looters.[1]

The NOPD acted on those instructions. On September 2, a black man named Henry Glover was shot by a police sniper as he walked through a parking lot. When a Samaritan tried to help Glover get medical attention, he was beaten by officers, who burnt Glover's body and left it behind a levee. The next day a 45-year-old named Danny Brumfield, Sr. was killed by officers in front of scores of witnesses outside the New Orleans Convention Center when he ran after a police car to demand that the officers stop and provide aid.

The following morning two families were crossing New Orleans' Danziger Bridge, which connects Gentilly and New Orleans East, two mostly middle- to upper-class African-American neighborhoods. Without warning, a Budget rental truck carrying police officers arrived, and cops jumped out. The officers did not identify themselves and began firing before their vehicle had even stopped.

James Brisette, a 17-year-old called studious and nerdy by his friends, was shot nearly a dozen times and died at the scene. Many of the bullets hit him as he lay bleeding on the ground. Four other people were wounded, including Susan Bartholomew, a 38-year-old mother who had her arm shot off, and her 17-year-old daughter, Lesha, who was shot while crawling on top of her mother, trying to shield her from bullets. Lesha's cousin Jose was shot point-blank in the stomach and nearly died. He needed a colostomy bag

1 According to testimony from a police captain, Riley directed officers to "take the city back and shoot looters," and said, "If you can sleep with it, do it."

for years afterward.

Farther up the bridge, officers chased down Ronald Madison, a mentally challenged man, who was traveling with his brother Lance. Ronald was shot in the back by one officer and then stomped and kicked to death by another. Lance was arrested and charged with the attempted murder of eight officers.

At the time, the New Orleans *Times-Picayune* reported that officers "sent up a cheer" when word came over police radios that suspects had been shot and killed. Officers had heard a radio call about shots fired in the area, and apparently were seeking "to take their city back."

A cursory investigation by the NOPD justified the shooting, and it appeared that the matter was closed. In fact, for years every check and balance in the city's criminal justice system failed to find any fault in this or any other officer-involved shooting.

The Times-Picayune, then a daily newspaper, did a miserable job. Alex Brandon, a photographer for the paper who went on to work for the Associated Press, testified years later that he knew details about the police killings that he hadn't revealed. "He saw things and heard things that proved to be useful in a criminal investigation. He didn't report them as news," wrote *Picayune* columnist Jarvis DeBerry in 2010.

Former Orleans Parish District Attorney Eddie Jordan, who led an initial investigation of the Danziger officers, agrees that an indifferent local media bears partial responsibility for the years of cover-up. "They were looking for heroes," he says:

> They had a cozy relationship with the police. They got tips from the police; they were in bed with the police. It was an atmosphere of tolerance for atrocities from the police. They abdicated their responsibility to be critical in their reporting. If a few people got killed, that was a small price to pay.

Jordan, the city's first black DA, pursued charges against officers in late 2006. When the cops went to turn themselves in, hundreds of their co-workers came out to support the officers and protest the DA. The unruly crowd cheered and called the accused killers heroes. Before the case could be tried, it was dismissed by a judge who had close ties to defense lawyers and the police union.[2] Soon after, Jordan was forced to resign. His successor, Leon Cannizzaro, has shown little interest in pursuing police officers. Jim Letten, the US Attorney at the time, was more interested in pursuing charges against black politicians than pursuing police corruption.[3]

2 Judge Raymond Bigelow, a former prosecutor, has multiple ties to Danziger defendants, including his clerk, the daughter of one of the cops' lawyers. Jordan's motion for a new judge was denied.

3 Letten, a self-styled crusader against political malfeasance, ultimately resigned in disgrace over corruption in his own office. The same corruption that ended Letten's career helped lead to the reversals in the Danziger case.

The 2006 dismissal of charges was a major defeat. Other elected officials, including the city coroner, went along with the police version of events. The coroner's office, for example, never flagged Henry Glover's body, found burned in a car and missing a head, as a potential homicide. The death certificate in 2006 called Glover's end an "accident."

But the victims' families refused to be silent. They spoke out at press conferences, rallies and directly to reporters. They worked with organizations like Safe Streets Strong Communities, which was founded by former prisoners and their allies and advocates in the days after Katrina, and Community United for Change, which was formed a few years later with some of the same members. Monique Harden, a community activist and co-director of Advocates for Environmental Human Rights, helped to bring testimony about these issues to the United Nations. Peoples Hurricane Relief Fund, an organization dedicated to justice in reconstruction, held a tribunal in 2006 that presented testimony about police violence, among other charges, to a panel of international judges, including parliamentarians from seven countries. Keith Calhoun and Chandra McCormick, two photographers based in the Lower Ninth Ward, did a post-Katrina series honoring "First Responders" that pointedly focused on community members and not police.

Activists did more than raise awareness of specific cases of police violence. "This is about an entire system that was completely broken and in crisis," said former Safe Streets co-director Rosana Cruz. "Everyone's job in the criminal justice system depends on there being a lot of crime in the city. The district attorney's office doesn't work on getting the city safer; it works on getting [civilian] convictions at any cost. As long as that's the case, we're not going to have safety."

It was not until late 2008 that a journalist for ProPublica named A.C. Thompson did what the local media had failed to do. He investigated these stories in detail, and published an expose. "It's unfortunate that it took a national publication to really dig to the root," remarked Dana Kaplan, director of the Juvenile Justice Project of Louisiana. "In New Orleans, the criminal justice system has been so corrupt for so long that things that should be shocking didn't seem to be raising the kind of broad community outrage that they should have."

As time went on, others began to tell this story. Spike Lee's post-Katrina documentaries *When the Levees Broke* (2006) and *If God Is Willing and the Creek Don't Rise* (2010) told of both police violence and white vigilante violence after the storm. Dave Eggers, in his book *Zeitoun* (2009), told of police harassing survivors and locking them up without evidence. Later, the HBO series *Treme* dramatized the investigations of the Danziger and Glover killings, and portrayed a hopelessly corrupt NOPD.

Community United for Change (CUC) asked for federal investigations of dozens of other police murders committed over the past three decades, and helped lead the struggle for federal oversight. Activists cited a wide range of cases, from the death of 25-year-old Jenard Thomas, who was shot by police in front of his father on March 24, 2005, to that of Sherry Singleton, shot by police in 1980 in front of her 4-year-old child, while Singleton was naked in a bathtub.[4]

The parents of Adolph Grimes III, who was shot fourteen times by cops on New Year's Day 2009, are among those who have spoken out. "We want those officers incarcerated so they can live with it like we live with it," Grimes's father said.

In 2009, after years of organized pressure and lobbying, the US Justice Department decided to look into the accusations of post-Katrina police violence. That decision led to one of the most wide-ranging investigations of a police department in recent US history. Federal agents interviewed witnesses who had never been talked to, reconstructed crime scenes and even confiscated NOPD computers. On those computers they found evidence that the Danziger officers had radically rewritten their version of what happened on the bridge that day. When FBI agents confronted the officers, five of those involved in the shootings and cover-up plead guilty to lesser charges and agreed to testify against the others. They revealed that officers had planted evidence, invented witnesses, arrested innocent people and held secret meetings during which they lined up their stories. Dozens of officers were fired or disciplined, and many received prison terms.

It wasn't just Danziger. From 2010 to 2011 the Justice Department also won convictions of the officers who shot Glover and burned his body, as well as of two officers who, in a pre-Katrina case, beat Raymond Robair to death and claimed (with the support of then-city coroner Frank Minyard) that he had sustained his injuries in a fall. One of the officers who had shot and killed Brumfield was also convicted, though of lesser charges of perjury and obstructing justice.

While the Justice Department pursued these cases, activists continued to press for federal oversight of the NOPD. Mayor Mitch Landrieu claimed from the beginning of his term, in 2010, that he agreed there is a need for federal supervision. In a letter to Attorney General Eric Holder, Landrieu wrote, "It is clear that nothing short of a complete transformation is necessary and essential to ensure safety for the citizens of New Orleans."

However, it appears that Mayor Landrieu spoke out in support of reform

4 This incident also led to protests and a high-profile police trial, but in the end most officers involved were not prosecuted, and those who were got light sentences.

primarily so that he could maintain a level of control over the changes dictated by the feds. After inviting the Justice Department in, and signing a consent decree, he began fighting against it in court.

Malcolm Suber, one of the founders of Community United for Change, doesn't think federal oversight is enough. "I don't think that we can call on a government that murders people all over the world every day to come and supervise a local police department," he says. For activists like Suber who view the government as racist and corrupt, federal control will not offer the wider, more systemic changes needed. While Suber wants more federal investigations of police murders, he wants those investigations to go hand in hand with community oversight and control of the department.

Organizers including Suber, victims of police violence and advocates drafted what they call a People's Consent Decree, which outlines the changes they want to see in the NOPD. They then pushed the Justice Department to adopt their language in the official federal decree. They won some important victories through this effort. For example, the Justice Department dictated major changes in the department's policy toward members of the LGBT community, a response to pressure from BreakOUT, an organization that works with LGBT youth of color. New policies on interactions with immigrants were affected by the efforts of the New Orleans Workers Center for Racial Justice, another activist group that worked in coalition with CUC and BreakOUT. The final agreement is one of the most far-reaching of its kind.

Federal oversight of the NOPD, won by organizing for systemic change, achieved more concrete success than relying on criminal prosecutions. And it empowered community members to continue to be involved. While family members could only come to court and watch the Glover and Danziger trials as silent observers, they continue to be actively involved in protesting police policies and fighting for systemic change in general. BreakOUT members and other activists continue to struggle with the police over implementation of the federal orders. Glover family members continued protests against the city coroner, who as of this writing has still not ruled Glover's death a homicide.[5] Activists also protested for change at the city jail, which has been called one of the worst in the US.

While the Justice Department has appealed the Danziger ruling, it's clear that prosecutions will not bring justice. The US court system rightly has many checks and balances, but they are much more accessible to police

5 In 2009 the coroner's office reclassified the cause of death from "accident" to "undetermined," where it remains, pending yet another review prompted by continued protest. In December of 2013, after forty years of siding with police over evidence – and generating substantial press, including an episode of *Frontline* on PBS dealing with some of his most controversial decisions – Frank Minyard, 84, finally announced his retirement. At this writing it is unclear if his successor, elected in March 2014, will be any better.

officers than they are to most defendants. In December of 2012 the Fifth Circuit Court of Appeals vacated the felony convictions against David Warren, the NOPD officer found guilty of manslaughter in 2011 for the killing of Henry Glover. The court ruled that Warren should have been tried separately from the officer who burned Glover's body. In most cases the Fifth Circuit is hostile to defendants on the issue of post-conviction relief; for police, the rules are different. The Justice Department retried Warren in December of 2013 and lost. The officer claimed self-defense, and a jury acquitted him of all charges.

Travis McCabe, another officer involved in the Glover killing, was convicted in 2010 and had his case overturned in 2011. In February of 2014, federal prosecutors announced they would not be retrying him. Norris Henderson, a former prisoner who founded Safe Streets Strong Communities as well as Voice of the Ex-Offender (VOTE), which works to build power for formerly incarcerated people, said, "When regular folks go to jail they don't get these kind of considerations and reversals. With these [police] cases, they say, *We're gonna send you to jail for five minutes*, and like a pumpkin before the clock strikes 12, you're out."

The grassroots strategy for justice is plainly not without frustrations. But these efforts, organized and led by the people who are most affected, are not demoralizing in the way that relying on criminal prosecutions is – and they have delivered real results. The popular resistance has rewritten the story of what happened after the storm. It has won important changes in the city's criminal justice system, including reform of a corrupt public defenders office[6] and the closing of a notorious youth prison.[7] It won real changes at the jail: a deep reduction in the number of people locked up and a commitment by the sheriff to refuse to comply with federal immigration holds.[8] In the end, community members found that they could not rely on the criminal justice system to police itself. They needed to organize outside the system. Or, as Adolph Grimes, Jr., father of a young man killed by police, has said, "How you gonna get the wolf to watch over the chicken coop? It's the system itself that is corrupted."

6 One of the first campaigns of Safe Streets Strong Communities was to reform the public defenders office, which (among other problems) was funded by traffic ticket receipts and allowed defense lawyers to take on paying clients (and give them much better representation) at the same time that they represented indigent clients.

7 Protests and organizing from groups including Juvenile Justice Project of Louisiana, VAYLA (Vietnamese youth activists in New Orleans) and Families and Friends of Louisiana's Incarcerated Children succeeded in mostly eliminating the Youth Studies Center, the New Orleans city jail for juveniles. A small number of youths now go to a smaller facility and for shorter sentences. A similar campaign completely closed the Tallulah youth jail in upstate Louisiana.

8 This policy of non-cooperation with federal immigration authorities may be the most far-reaching in the US, and is the only such policy of a jail in the South.

Really the Invisible Man Blues

Dave Marsh

...all unorganized violence is like a blind man with a pistol.

– Chester Himes

In his autobiography, *Really the Blues,* Mezz Mezzrow, locked up in a New York City jail on a drug charge, convinces the warden that he has a black mother and therefore must be placed in the Negro section of the prison – his life depends on it.

Mezz Mezzrow, a pot proselytizer and dealer as well as a pretty good trumpet player, was white, or at least he came from an all-white family. His is one of the few real-life stories in American history in which a white man passes for black and gets away with it. Whether John Howard Griffin, author of *Black Like Me,* in which a middle-class white writer blackens his skin in order to research what the too-much-melanin blues are like, got away with it is open to debate. He did not die, as has been widely reported, from cancer caused by Oxsoralen, the chemical he used to darken his skin, but the fact that the idea persists thirty years after his death suggests what grim desires his project may have inspired. Griffin is not by any means the only mortal casualty of the American obsession with melanin.

Give or take Mark Twain's *Pudd'nhead Wilson,* a reasonably fine novel, and Norman Mailer's essay, "The White Negro," which is a complete crock, that's about the end of the literary aspect of passing for black. In *Invisible Man,* Ralph Ellison's nameless protagonist, unquestionably a black citizen, has retreated to a clandestine life in a cellar in a whites-only building somewhere in New York. This man is invisible because other people refuse to see him. And throughout the story, whenever he is seen, disaster of one degree of another ensues.

Somewhere among these fantasies lies a truth about George Zimmerman, who, by his own account, accidentally on purpose murdered

Trayvon Martin. Somewhere in there is an authentic human being, like Mezzrow, who imagined himself a superhero. Mezz sold reefer to the stars; Louis Armstrong was his best customer. George Zimmerman stalked the streets of a podunk Florida condo community with a gun by his side, a Batman vigilante.

What fascinates me is that George Zimmerman imagined himself a *white* superhero. Well, really, it's not that so much. Name a black superhero, why don't you? Richard Pryor dressed up as one for one of his album jackets, and that just about covers the point.

Whether George Zimmerman, by the bizarre and often contradictory codes of the United States, is 'white' isn't the issue. It can't be, because the matter is not so much in the eye of the beholder as in the beholder's mind, or wherever each of our prejudices resides. There neither is nor ever will be a test of who's black and who's white based purely on skin color; thank you, Gregor Mendel. Americans appear in something more than 50,000 shades of gray and brown. Weeding us all out, separating the "Caucasian" sheep from the "Negro" goats (as Mitt Romney's tutors might have put it) is a fool's errand, a worthless quest and the core of a national argument that hasn't changed much since the Tidewater tobacco growers invented the "white race" around 1680. Whiteness as a concept – a mass illusion that really means not-blackness – guarantees a genuine enthusiasm for servile status among white working people to this day. Because, with agreed-upon whiteness comes power, including the power of life and death. It's amazing every neighborhood in the US doesn't have a yearly ritual in which people fill out their brackets for who might or might not possess the coveted lack of melanin in *their* neighborhood.

Zimmerman's mother has been described as Afro-Peruvian, and pictures alleged to be of his great-grandfather show a dark-skinned man who might well be black or brown (the photos are black and white, in a way that race in America is thought to, but never can, be). His father resembles David Brinkley, only more pallid. Zimmerman himself looks as if his ancestry might be Sicilian, or Native American, or Hispanic, or simply a polyglot genotype commonly known as American. Zimmerman's voter registration card lists him as "Hispanic."

Trayvon Martin, on the other hand, was unmistakably a black manchild, African- or Afro-American, or any of two- or three-dozen hideous epithets. That Zimmerman shot Martin because he was black may legitimately be doubted. That Zimmerman stalked Martin and put himself in the position of murdering him because Trayvon was black is beyond dispute. It's how Zimmerman's version of the events goes. Broken down between perception and reality, what the shooter tells us is as follows.

I saw a colored kid walking around where he shouldn't have been (according to Zimmerman), *dressed as a criminal* (that is to say, as one common variety of adolescent boys, many of them black), *and when I attempted to stop and frisk him* (Zimmerman doesn't cop to the frisk, but that's the general idea) *he ran, a clear* (to Zimmerman, though in reality doubtful beyond anything reasonable) *admission of guilt* (of being black where he didn't belong), *so I proceeded to accost him* (because that's what superheroes do to bad guys), *and then he tried to hurt me, so I shot him.*

It's that cold and that confused. Chester Himes couldn't have satirized it. Richard Pryor himself would have been hard-pressed to say anything sufficiently biting about it. Martin's murder was everything *but* a metaphor.

I nevertheless submit that George Zimmerman may be the Lee Harvey Oswald of this historical period. His biography is just as sordid and pathetic. In 1997, aged 14, he joined ROTC, with the stated ambition of joining the US Marine Corps. (His father, Robert, is described as "ex-military," but I've yet to find out which service.) George's post-high school jobs fulfilled no heroic fantasies: he worked for an insurance agency and a car dealership. He went back to school, to get his real estate agent's license, then to study criminal justice. He may have been in a ride-along program with the Sanford police: he claimed he witnessed "disgusting behavior" by the officers, but the local cops say they have no record of him in the program. That last role (it wasn't a job or a hobby) came to light in the context of a town meeting, which Zimmerman attended, protesting the beating of a black homeless man by white Sanford cops. He shoved a cop who was busting one of his friends for drunken behavior and was sent into an anger management program. A girlfriend accused him of domestic violence; he requested a reciprocal restraining order. He applied for a job with the local sheriff's office, and didn't get it. He took part in the Seminole College graduation program even though he was a credit shy of his degree. At his pretrial hearing in the Trayvon murder case, the prosecutors brought up all of this. The judge described George's record as "run of the mill." His father was allowed to sit in on his initial interrogations by the police about Trayvon's killing.

On the basis of all that, you'd have to say that George Zimmerman has been treated as a white man by the system, or at least a part of it. How he has been treated by classmates, teachers, administrators, recruiting sergeants and, for that matter, junk food-dispensing 7-Eleven clerks is a whole other set of issues. And we'll never know.

Maybe George Zimmerman wasn't out there stalking innocent black teenagers in pursuit of certification as an authentic European-American. You're entitled to doubt it. I don't. Maybe he had no crisis of racial identity that he was trying to work out by becoming a superhero.

On the other hand, there is that designation on his voter registration card.

So we might, if we are pondering whether George Zimmerman received anything resembling justice (let alone whether Trayvon Martin did), spare a thought for the myriad ways in which the issue of racial identity makes so many Americans crazy – the crazier, it seems, the murkier, the more borderline, their status.

The strange thing is, at trial it was the defense lawyers who kept bringing up Zimmerman's racial status (albeit outside the courtroom, but trials aren't really held in court anymore, if they ever were). It was they who allegedly provided the pictures of his mother's grandfather. It wasn't even implied; it was stated outright that if George had black blood there was no way he stalked Trayvon Martin and killed him with a pretext so thin even a blind Klansman could see through it.

And now George Zimmerman is a free man, or anyway as free as someone with an Afro-Peruvian mother can be in an America that only in its most privileged sanctuaries understands itself as "post-racial." Here is the white supremacist dilemma spelled out with remarkable clarity, by a proudly anonymous correspondent to the "conservative" blog Draw and Strike, March 29, 2012, apropos the report that Zimmerman's photograph had been craftily skin-lightened by the media (no mention of which ones, or of whether Fox had once again held the color line):

> right or wrong it's always a meme about how evil the white man is and how he be profiling everybody. But if the half jewish half peruvian Zimmerman is a white hispanic, doesn't it follow that our muti racial preznit is indeed not black but white-black-arabic, in fact?

Why do people who essentially have no quarrel with Zimmerman's vigilantism, who treat Zimmerman as if he has achieved a goal from their personal bucket lists (as indeed he has, especially the hard part, getting away with it), want him *not* to be white? Why has this question been ignored, even though it is a glaring part of the filthy residue of these crimes (the murder one, and the trial another)?

I think it's basically because George Zimmerman has a brand new double standard available to him: he is white enough to get away with the shooting and dark enough to suggest to the bigots that there is something deeply wrong. But what's wrong is *not* the shooting of Trayvon Martin, which was justified in the way that every vigilante execution has been justified since the Civil War. What we hear from the Draw and Strike crowd is a modern rendition of that tune they've danced to since Obama was elected and the chimera of post-racial society began to waver in front of blighted eyes.

In front of the cataracts of liberalism wobbles another image altogether: if this biracial society is such a swell thing, how and why did this acquittal occur? Liberals have no coherent answer, because formulating one would leave them no course except to understand the country in a way that the flag-bearers of post-racialism exist to occlude. Trayvon was shot in a mixed-race ("integrated," we would once have said) neighborhood, by a vigilante who at least part of the time identified as a member of another ethnic minority. I don't suppose this sounds like Crown Heights to you, does it?

The travesty of the trial does not stem entirely from the fact that everyone involved in the judicial system – judge, jury, prosecutors, defense counsel, cops – was non-black. Which raises another question: If we can talk about 'non-white' as a category, why *not* the more useful, because more accurate, non-black?

There's nobody raised or even living long term in the United States of America who can't answer that question accurately. There are just several hundred million Bartlebys who'd prefer not to.

Which is to say, the mystery of George Zimmerman is that there is no mystery. He did it, he got away with it without even having to deny it, and his kind will come again and again and again until we at least gain as much courage as Ishmael and crawl into bed with the truth.

> *"What started it?"*
>
> *"A blind man with a pistol."*
>
> *"What's that?"*
>
> *"You heard me, boss."*
>
> *"That don't make any sense."*
>
> *"Sure don't."*
>
> *– Chester Himes*

Anyone's Son

Tara Skurtu

– for the family of Trayvon Martin

This poem wants to write itself backwards.
Wishes it were born memory instead, skipping
time like a record needle stuck on the line
of your last second. You sit up. Brush not blood,
but dirt from your chest. You sit up. You're in bed.
Bad dream. Back to sleep. You sit up. Rise and shine.
Good morning. This is the poem of a people united
in the uniform of your last day. Pockets full
of candy, hooded sweatshirt, sweet tea. This poem
wants to stand its ground, silence force
with simple words, pray you alive, anyone's
son – tall boy, eye-smile, walk on home.

Contributors

Rodolfo Acuña is the founding chair of the country's first Chicano Studies department. A professor emeritus at California State University Northridge, he has published twenty books and more than 200 public and scholarly articles. His history book *Occupied America* was banned from Arizona schools in 2011. In solidarity with Mexican-Americans in Tucson, he organized fundraisers and support groups and wrote dozens of articles exposing efforts there to nullify the Constitution. The Tucson Unified School District un-banned the book and six others in the fall of 2013. "Sometimes You Have to Shout to Be Heard" originally appeared on CounterPunch, July 17, 2013.

Phillip Agnew is executive director of the Dream Defenders, a Florida human rights organization directed by black and brown youth confronting inequality and the criminalization of their generation with nonviolent direct action and the building of collective community power. Leah Weston (transcriber) is a soon-to-be lawyer, activist, writer and radio host based in Miami. In the summer of 2013 she was a legal intern with the Community Justice Project of Florida Legal Services, which provides legal support to grassroots community organizations in Miami's low-income communities.

Asam Ahmad is a poet, community organizer and community scholar. He is interested in translating theory outside the academy and making accessible forms of knowledge that are usually reserved for those with access to the ivory tower. His poem "Remembering How to Grieve," written in the wake of the Boston Marathon bombing, was first published on Black Girl Dangerous, on April 19, 2013.

Ajamu Baraka is a longtime human rights activist, writer and veteran of the black liberation, anti-war, anti-apartheid and Central America solidarity movements in the United States. He is currently an associate fellow at the Institute for Policy Studies in Washington, DC. "For a National Alliance for Racial Justice and Human Rights" originally appeared under the title "Trayvon Martin and the Need for an Independent Human Rights Movement" on his blog, A Voice from the Margins, on March 27, 2012.

Moustafa Bayoumi is a professor of English at Brooklyn College, City University of New York, and author of the award-winning *How Does It Feel to Be a Problem?: Being Young and Arab in America*. His latest book, forthcoming from NYU Press, is *This Muslim-American Life: Dispatches From the War on Terror*. Bayoumi edited *Midnight on the Mavi Marmara*, about the attack on the Gaza Freedom Flotilla, and, with Andrew Rubin, co-edited *The Edward Said Reader*. A slightly different version of "The Race Is On: Arabs, Blackness and the American Imagination" (with more extensive footnotes) was originally published under the title "The Race Is On: Muslims and Arabs in the American Imagination" by the Middle East Research and Information Project (MERIP), March 2010.

D. Brian Burghart is the editor/publisher of the *Reno News & Review* and the creator and administrator of fatalencounters.org, founded on the premise that Americans should have the ability to track statistics on where, how often and under what circumstances police use deadly force. He is also a dual-master's student and journalism instructor at the University of Nevada, Reno. "Fatal Encounters" is an adaptation of the project history posted on fatalencounters.org.

Yvette Carnell is a former Capitol Hill and campaign staffer turned writer. She is an editor and contributor to Yourblackworld, where "Russell Simmons Tells Black People Not to Start a Race War Over Trayvon Martin" originally appeared, on August 16, 2013.

Monica J. Casper is professor and head of Gender and Women's Studies at the University of Arizona. Her books include the award-winning The *Making of the Unborn Patient: A Social Anatomy of Fetal Surgery*. Her current research focuses on race and the biopolitics of infant mortality in the US. She's also involved in collaborative research on social and biomedical consequences of traumatic brain injury among athletes, veterans and domestic violence victims. She is editor/publisher of TRIVIA: Voices of Feminism, and a managing editor of The Feminist Wire, where a version of "White Women in the Jury Box" first appeared, on July 17, 2013.

Robert Chase is assistant professor of history at the State University of New York, Stonybrook. Yohuru Williams is chair and professor of history at Fairfield University. Their article "Gun Laws and Race in America" originally appeared on CounterPunch, July 19, 2013.

Thandisizwe Chimurenga is a Los Angeles-based freelance journalist and the author of *No Doubt: The Murder(s) of Oscar Grant* (2014). A version of "Oscar Grant, Trayvon Martin and the Protection of Police Murder" originally appeared in *San Francisco Bay View* on March 25, 2012. "'Do You Care When Blacks Kill Other Blacks?'" first appeared on The CyberGround Railroad on March 23, 2012.

Alexander Cockburn was a journalist of inestimable style and verve, and co-editor of CounterPunch from 1994 until his death, in 2012. "You Really Think the Killer of Trayvon Martin Will Ever Do Time?" originally appeared on CounterPunch, March 31, 2012.

Ibrahim Diallo is a Guinean-American living in New York City. "Face to Face With the NYPD: What They Look Like to a Guinean-American" originally appeared on the CounterPunch weekend edition, December 16-18, 2011.

Rita Dove is a former US Poet Laureate (1993-1995) and recipient of the 1987 Pulitzer Prize in poetry for her book *Thomas and Beulah*. Her most recent poetry collections are *Sonata Mulattica* and *American Smooth*, and she was sole editor of *The Penguin Anthology of Twentieth-Century American Poetry*. She is Commonwealth Professor of English at the University of Virginia. "Trayvon, Redux" originally appeared on The Root, July 16, 2013.

John Eskow is a writer and musician. He wrote or co-wrote the movies *Air America*, *The Mask of Zorro* and *Pink Cadillac*, as well as the novel *Smokestack Lightning*. "Who's Afraid of Black Men's Eyes?" originally appeared on CounterPunch, June 3, 2013.

Alan Farago, conservation chair of Friends of the Everglades, lives in south Florida. "A Senseless Shooting in a Soulless Place" first appeared on CounterPunch, May 22, 2012.

Jordan Flaherty is an award-winning journalist, producer and author (jordanflaherty.org). He has appeared as a guest on a wide range of television and radio shows, including CNN Morning, *Anderson Cooper 360*, CNN Headline News, *The Alan Colmes Show* on Fox, and *News and Notes* on NPR. Flaherty was the first journalist to bring the case of the Jena Six to a national audience, and he has so far been the only journalist identified as a subject of the New York City Police Department's spying programs. He has produced documentaries for Al Jazeera, *Democracy Now!*, PressTV and several other outlets. His most recent book is *Floodlines: Community and Resistance From Katrina to the Jena Six*. "The Master's Tools: A Grassroots Fight Against Police Violence, Case Study" is original to this anthology.

Glen Ford is executive editor of Black Agenda Report, where "Trayvon and White Madness" was first published, July 17, 2013.

Pier Gabrielle Foreman's articles, editions and books include *Activist Sentiments: Reading Black Women Writers in the Nineteenth Century*. Her article "A Riff, A Call and A Response: Renaming the Problem That Led to Our Being Tokens in Ethnic and Gender Studies" interrogates how the academic study of black subjects can thrive while black and brown people barely survive. Her forthcoming book, *The Art of DisMemory: Historicizing Slavery in Poetry, Performance and Material Culture*, examines the practices and politics of recovering buried and skeletal black pasts in relation to public history, the archive, poetry, art and performance. She is the Ned B. Allen Professor of English and Professor of Black Studies at the University of Delaware. "The Ground We Stand On: On Inaugurations, Anniversaries and the Deaths of Trayvon Martin" originated from a talk called "On Zig-Zag Switch-Back Flashbacks: African-American Historical Trauma Then as Now" for the panel Prospects for Black Literature: Recovery and Beyond at the C-19 conference in Berkeley in April of 2012. It first appeared in print as a guest blog piece at Rae Paris's Black Space: Crafting a Place for Black Women Writers, on February 27, 2013.

Kevin Alexander Gray is a civil rights/liberties activist in South Carolina, a print and radio commentator and the author of *Waiting for Lightning to Strike!: The Fundamentals of Black Politics*. A version of "'No Rights That Any White Man Is Bound to Respect': What It Feels Like to Be Black in America" first appeared on CounterPunch, July 17, 2013.

Alexis Pauline Gumbs is a queer black troublemaker, a black feminist love evangelist, a prayer poet priestess with a PhD from Duke University. She is the author of an acclaimed poetry collection, *101 Things That Are Not True About the Most Famous Black Women Alive*, and co-editor of the forthcoming volume on legacies of radical mothering, *This Bridge Called My Baby*. Alexis is the founder of Brilliance Remastered, a service to help visionary underrepresented graduate students stay connected to purpose, passion and community; co-founder of the Mobile Homecoming Project, a national experiential archive amplifying generations of black LGBTQ brilliance, and the community school Eternal Summer of the Black Feminist Mind. "cartwheel on the blacktop (Trayvon Martin 2.0)" was originally published on her blog LittleBlackBook, March 26, 2012. The title comes from a poetic response in an intergenerational workshop on June Jordan's children's literature at the 2012 Split This Rock Festival in Washington.

bell hooks is a writer, educator, feminist and social activist. She has published more than thirty books, including *Ain't I a Woman?: Black Women and Feminism*; *Yearning: Race, Gender, and Cultural Politics*; *Sisters of the Yam: Black Women and Self-recovery*; *Teaching to Transgress: Education as the Practice of Freedom* and *We Real Cool: Black Men and Masculinity*. Quassan Castro is a news and entertainment journalist. "'Just Being a Regular Teenager'" is an excerpt from an interview first published on the website of Jet, under the title "The Zimmerman Effect," July 24, 2013.

Adam Hudson is a journalist, writer and photographer. "1 Black Person Killed Every 28 Hours" is drawn from a much longer article, "1 Black Man Is Killed Every 28 Hours by Police or Vigilantes: America Is Perpetually at War with Its Own People," originally published on AlterNet, May 28, 2013.

Bruce Jackson, SUNY Distinguished Professor and James Agee Professor of American Culture at the University at Buffalo, is the author of *Law and Disorder: Criminal Justice in America*. His most recent books are *"In This Timeless Time": Living and Dying on Death Row in America* (with Diane Christian) and *Inside the Wire: Photographs from Texas and Arkansas Prisons*. "A Trial Is Never About the Truth" originally appeared on CounterPunch, July 15, 2013.

Rev. Jesse L. Jackson is the founder and president of the Rainbow/PUSH Coalition. "Investigate the Racial Context Behind Trayvon Martin's Death" first appeared on the website of *The Washington Informer*, July 15, 2013.

Tayari Jones is the author of the novels *Silver Sparrow* and *Leaving Atlanta*. She is an associate professor of English and creative writing at Rutgers-Newark University. "The Lingering Memory of Dead Boys" was originally broadcast on NPR's "All Things Considered" on March 20, 2012.

June Jordan was born in Harlem in 1936 and grew up in Bedford-Stuyvesant, Brooklyn. Poet, activist, teacher and essayist, she was a prolific, passionate voice for liberation until her death, in 2002. "Poem about Police Violence," from *Passion: New Poems 1977-1980* (1980), is also included in *Directed by Desire: The Collected Poems of June Jordan* (2005). Although written in the 1970s, it was widely pirated online following the Martin killing. It is reprinted here with permission of the June M. Jordan Literary Estate Trust, and Copper Canyon Press. Copyright 2014 June M. Jordan Literary Estate Trust. www.junejordan.com.

Robin D.G. Kelley, who teaches at UCLA, is the author of the remarkable biography *Thelonius Monk: The Life and Times of an American Original* and, most recently, *Africa Speaks, America Answers: Modern Jazz in Revolutionary Times*. "How the System Worked: The US v. Trayvon Martin" originally appeared on CounterPunch, July 15, 2013.

Margaret Kimberley lives in New York City and is an editor and senior columnist of the website Black Agenda Report. She writes a weekly column, "Freedom Rider," for BAR, where a longer version of "Obama Dog-Whistles Over Trayvon" originally appeared, July 16, 2013.

Jamilah King is a senior editor at Colorlines, a daily news site published by Race Forward, a national racial justice organization that also presents the biennial Facing Race national conference (http://colorlines.com/about). Focusing mostly on media, race and culture, her work has also appeared online for Salon, MSNBC, *The American Prospect*, Al Jazeera, *The Advocate* and in the *San Francisco Bay Guardian*. A slightly longer version of "The Deadly Legacy of Vigilantism" originally appeared under the title "Trayvon Martin and the Deadly Legacy of Vigilantism" on Colorlines, March 20, 2012.

Mike King is a PhD candidate at UC, Santa Cruz and an East Bay activist. A version of "The Cancer of Police Violence" first appeared on CounterPunch, November 22, 2012.

Chris Kromm is the editor of *Southern Exposure*. "The New Vigilantes" originally appeared on its blog, Facing South, March 21, 2012.

Yotam Marom, an activist, organizer and writer based in New York City, is the founder of The Wildfire Project, which supports grassroots groups with training, political education and group development. He has been active in various social movements, including Occupy Wall Street. His writing can be found at www.ForLouderDays.net. "A Symphony for Trayvon Martin" originally appeared on Waging Nonviolence, July 16, 2013.

Dave Marsh, rock critic, historian, anti-censorship activist, SiriusXM radio host and "Louie Louie" expert, has written more than twenty books about popular music, and has edited that many more. He co-founded *Creem*, the legendary rock-and-roll magazine, and for the past twenty-five years has edited the monthly music and politics newsletter "Rock and Rap Confidential." He is currently writing a book about why *American Idol* is evil, and completing a long-term project, *O Freedom!*, the history of music and the Southern civil rights movement. "Really the Invisible Man Blues" is original to this anthology.

Dani McClain lives in Oakland. Her writing has appeared in Colorlines, Al Jazeera America, *The Nation*, EBONY.com and other outlets. She has worked as a staff reporter for the *Milwaukee Journal Sentinel* and as a strategist with organizations including ColorOfChange.org and Drug Policy Alliance. "Anxiety Is Killing Us: So What Do We Do About It?" is original to this anthology.

Michael Meyers is the executive director of the New York Civil Rights Coalition, a past vice president of the American Civil Liberties Union and former assistant national director of the NAACP. "George Zimmerman Is Entitled to Civil Rights Protections, Too," original to this anthology, is an expansion on shorter opinion pieces he published following the Zimmerman verdict.

Chuck Modiano is an educator, facilitator and sports writer dedicated to youth development and exposing power, oppression and privilege in sport. With a focus on how sports media perpetuates broader racial and social injustice, Modiano regularly presents to staff and youth audiences at national conferences, local colleges and community-based organizations across the country. He is the co-founder of the related website POPSspot.com, where a version of "The White Right to Riot" originally appeared under the title "Right to Riot: Kentucky Fans, Trayvon Protesters, and The White Privilege Conference," on April 4, 2012.

Kyle 'Guante' Tran Myhre is a hip hop artist, two-time National Poetry Slam champion, activist and educator. Check out his music, poetry and other essays at Guante.Info. "An Open Letter to White People About Trayvon Martin" originally appeared on Opine Season, July 14, 2013.

Scot Nakagawa is senior partner and co-owner of ChangeLab, a national racial justice laboratory based in Oakland and New York. Beginning in 1980, he has worked for progressive social change, including as field director of the National Gay and Lesbian Task Force, associate director of the Western Prison Project and education co-coordinator of the Highlander Research and Education Center. "'So, I Ask You, What if Trayvon Martin Were Asian?'" first appeared on ChangeLab's blog, Race Files, on July 14, 2013.

Jill Nelson, a journalist, author and activist, edited *Police Brutality: An Anthology* and is a monthly contributor to the Op Ed page of *USA Today*. Her other books include *Volunteer Slavery: My Authentic Negro Experience* and *Straight, No Chaser: How I Became a Grown-Up Black Woman*. "The Trick Bag of the Perfect Victim" originally appeared in The Root under the title "Can Imperfect Crime Victims Get Justice?" on July 31, 2012.

Barack Obama is the 44th President of the United States.

David 'Judah 1' Oliver, known affectionately by his peers and supporters as a Renaissance Man, is a poet, author, entrepreneur, philanthropist, teacher. He is the owner and co-founder of Machine Pomona Art Gallery, which, with its Lion Like Mind State open mic every other week, serves as a nucleus for new and veteran artists in California's Inland Empire. Judah's innovative work earned him a spot on the 2005 and 2006 Los Angeles Slam Team and granted him title of coach for the 2009 and 2010 Empire Mind State Slam Team (second in the nation in 2010). He teaches as an artist in residence for the Prison Education Program at the California Rehabilitation Center for Men (Norco Prison) and Chino Men's Prison. He has toured the nation at numerous colleges and other venues, including UCLA, University of Las Vegas, UC Berkeley and the Indianapolis Black Expo. He is the author of *Child of the Sun, Man of the Moon* (2013). "Terrorist" was written following the not-guilty verdict in the Sean Bell case, in 2008.

Vijay Prashad is the Edward Said Chair at the American University of Beirut. He is the author of sixteen books, including *The Poorer Nations: A Possible History of the Global South*. "Sighs of Fire: Zimmerman as a Domestic Drone" originally appeared on CounterPunch, July 15, 2013.

Matthew Rothschild was editor-in-chief of *The Progressive* from 1994 to 2013. He has been the magazine's publisher since 2007 and is now also senior editor. His speech "In Memory of Trayvon Martin and Bo Morrison" was first published on www.progressive.org, April 7, 2012.

Jeffrey St. Clair is the editor of CounterPunch and the author of numerous books, including *Born Under a Bad Sky: Notes from the Dark Side of the Earth*. "A Very Short History of Driving While Black: Scenes From the Highway Profiling Patrol" originally appeared on CounterPunch, August 2, 2013.

Jasmine Nicole Salters (also known as j.n. salters) is a black feminist writer and PhD student at the Annenberg School for Communication at the University of Pennsylvania, where she also earned a degree in creative writing and a masters in English. Her research and teaching interests include black feminism, literary nonfiction, ethnography and the intersections of the public and private. Her website is jnsalters.com. She has written for various publications, including Huffington Post, Public Books, MadameNoire and The Feminist Wire, where a shorter version of "Am I a Race Traitor?: Trayvon Martin, Gender Talk and Invisible Black Women" originally appeared, on July 21, 2013.

Tara Skurtu, a Florida native, is a lecturer in creative writing at Boston University, a Robert Pinsky Global Fellow and a recipient of a 2013 Academy of American Poets Prize. Her poems are published internationally and have been translated into Romanian and Hindi. "Anyone's Son" was originally published by The Huffington Post, July 14, 2013.

Mychal Denzel Smith is a blogger for *The Nation* and a Knobler Fellow at The Nation Institute. His work on race, politics, social justice, pop culture, hip hop, mental health, feminism and black male identity has appeared in various publications, including *The Guardian*, *Ebony*, theGrio, The Root, Huffington Post and GOOD. 'Thank You, Rachel Jeantel' originally appeared on thenation.com, June 27, 2013.

Brenda E. Stevenson is a professor of history at UCLA. Her books include *Life in Black and White: Family and Community in the Slave South* and, most recently, *The Contested Murder of Latasha Harlans: Justice, Gender and the Origins of the L.A. Riots*. "The Critical Role of Women in the Zimmerman Decision" originally appeared on the History News Network, July 15, 2013.

Alexander Tepperman, a doctoral candidate in history at the University of Florida, studies the origins of America's penal industrial complex. He is the former co-editor-in-chief of Points: The Blog of the Alcohol and Drugs History Society, a co-author of *Deviance, Crime, and Control: Beyond the Straight and Narrow* and author of the forthcoming "Politics, Media, and the War Over the Meaning of Midnight Basketball," in *Journal of Juvenile Justice*. Lastly, he is the proud father of two rescue dogs and hopes readers will consider saving a life by visiting their local Humane Society. "Marijuana's 'Dark Side': Drugs, Race and the Criminalization of Trayvon Martin" was originally published as part of the University of Florida Center for the Study of Race Relations' 10th Annual Spring Symposium (July 2013).

Etan Thomas played nine seasons in the NBA, with the Washington Wizards, the OKC Thunder and the Atlanta Hawks. Described by Kareem Abdul-Jabbar as "the poetic voice of his generation," Thomas is the author of *More Than an Athlete* (a collection of poems, 2005) and *Fatherhood (Rising to the Ultimate Challenge)* (2012), and the editor of *Voices of the Future* (an anthology of essays and poems by young writers, 2013). He has written and spoken out on political and social issues in numerous venues, including Huffington Post, where "What I Have to Teach My Son" originally appeared under the title "Trayvon Martin Case Presents an Unfortunate Reality," on March 22, 2012.

Jesmyn Ward is the author of *Where the Line Bleeds* and *Salvage the Bones*, both novels. The latter won the National Book Award in 2011 and was a finalist for the New York Public Library Young Lions Fiction Award and the Dayton Literary Peace Prize. Her memoir, *Men We Reaped*, was a finalist for the National Book Critics' Circle Award. An associate professor of creative writing at Tulane University, Ward grew up in DeLisle, Mississippi, and lives there now. "Tried for His Own Death" first appeared on August 25, 2013, in *Printers Row Journal*, premium book section of the *Sunday Chicago Tribune*, under the title "Speaking Up for Dignity: Jesmyn Ward honors the memory of Trayvon Martin and so many other black men who die too young."

Linn Washington, Jr., is a co-founder of This Can't Be Happening and a contributor to *Hopeless: Barack Obama and the Politics of Illusion*. He lives in Philadelphia. A version of "Perversities of Justice" first appeared under the title "The Persistence of Racism in America" on CounterPunch, July 16, 2013.

Dr. Cornel West teaches at Union Theological Seminary in New York. Before that, he was a professor at Princeton University and Harvard University. He is the author of numerous books, and co-hosts a radio show with Tavis Smiley called *Smiley & West*; together they wrote *The Rich and the Rest of Us: A Poverty Manifesto*. Amy Goodman is a journalist and the host and executive producer of the daily independent news program *Democracy Now!*, where the full interview was originally broadcast, on July 22, 2013. "'President Obama Is a Global George Zimmerman'" is excerpted with permission from the transcript of that show, titled "Cornel West: Obama's Response to Trayvon Martin Case Belies Failure to Challenge 'New Jim Crow'" and appearing in full on www.democracynow.org.

Patricia Williams is a central figure in the development of critical race theory, which analyzes the fundamental relationship between race and American law and jurisprudence. She is the James L. Dohr Professor of Law at Columbia University, where she has taught since 1991. Author of numerous books, she writes a column called "Diary of a Mad Law Professor" for *The Nation*, where "The Race-Baiting of America" originally appeared, on the web on August 28, 2013, and in print on September 16, 2013.

Tim Wise is the author of *White Like Me: Reflections on Race from a Privileged Son* and *Affirmative Action: Racial Preference in Black and White*. "No Innocence Left to Kill: Explaining America to My Daughter" was originally posted on www.timwise.org on July 14, 2013, under the title "No Innocence Left to Kill: Racism, Injustice and Explaining America to My Daughter," and appeared the next day on CounterPunch.

JoAnn Wypijewski, a journalist and editor in New York, writes the column "Diamonds and Rust" for *CounterPunch* (magazine edition) and "Carnal Knowledge" for *The Nation*, among other projects. "On Queens Boulevard, the Night Sean Bell's Killers Got Off" originally appeared on CounterPunch, April 28, 2008.

Sean Yoes is an award-winning journalist, documentary filmmaker and actor. He played the role of Lt. Brent Hoskins on the HBO series *The Wire*. He was born, raised and still resides in West Baltimore, where he hosts "The WEAA/AFRO First Edition," an hour-long political talk show on WEAA-FM (88.9), which airs on Sundays at 8 p.m. He is a contributing writer for the *AFRO*, where "A Short, Racist History of Sanford, Florida" originally appeared under the title "The Racist History of Sanford, Florida," on March 28, 2012.

A Note on the Cover

The streets of downtown Oakland erupted in protest on a July evening in 2013, a revolt against the acquittal of George Zimmerman and so many similar verdicts in Oakland, a city still outraged by the 2009 New Year's killing of Oscar Grant. Cop cars were tipped over, trashcans lit on fire, storefront windows smashed, including the windows of Youth Radio. Then, as Oakland tends to do, the community coalesced. A few days later Robert Trujillo, other members of the Trust Your Struggle Art Collective and the Taller Tupac Amaru Collective came together to produce a block-long mural on the plywood sheets covering the shattered windows of the Youth Radio building. Over a weekend, the artists worked feverishly, using paint, varnish and wheat-pasted posters by Melanie Cervantes and Jesus Barraza. At the center of the dazzling work is a portrait of Trayvon Martin, a detail of which is the cover image for our book. In the mural his face radiates the golden hues of an icon, drawing in the other images: faces from the streets of Oakland, most in hoodies, parents and sisters, friends and lovers, kids from the radio project, those left behind to bear witness and fuse the resistance. Some of those images appear here in the section breaks. The mural drew people from across the Bay Area until it came down in September of 2013. Some of the panels were preserved and mounted in the performance space at the Youth Radio building at 17th and Broadway. The images in this book were photographed by the Oakland poet Tennessee Reed.

Acknowledgments

This year-long project has been a collaborative effort involving dozens of hands. We owe special debts of gratitude to Erik Clampitt for the sleek and vivid design of an unwieldy book and Tennessee Reed for her photographs of the dramatic faces on the Trayvon Martin mural at the Youth Radio building in Oakland, which are featured on the book's cover and its section breaks. The CounterPunch team of Becky Grant, Joshua Frank, Deva Wheeler and Nathaniel St. Clair kept the project rolling through some rough and foggy patches. Kimberly Willson-St. Clair lent her unique skills as a librarian in the quest to uncover hard-to-find articles and documents. We are also grateful to Ethan Schiller for his indispensable research. We want to thank Axiomamnesia.com, which has aggregated all documents from the Martin case in the public record and video of the full Zimmerman trial proceedings, from which we transcribed the testimony of Sybrina Fulton and the closing argument of Mark O'Mara. Finally, a few months ago Kevin Gray was talking over our suggestions for the book title with civil rights activists Efia Nwangaza and Marjorie Hammock. Both women responded "with all the black people killed so routinely it ought to be 'Killing Trayvons.'" Thank you ladies for stating the obvious.

17241042R00237

Made in the USA
San Bernardino, CA
05 December 2014